Development As A Battlefield

International Development Policy

Editor-in-Chief

Gilles Carbonnier (*Professor of Development Economics, The Graduate Institute, Geneva*)

Guest Editors

Irene Bono (*Assistant Professor of Political Science, University of Torino*)
Béatrice Hibou (*Senior Research Fellow at the Centre d'Études et de Recherches Internationales, Paris*)

VOLUME 8

The titles published in this series are listed at *brill.com/idp*

International Development Policy
Previous Titles
Africa: 50 Years of Independence, No. 1, Geneva: Graduate Institute Publications, 2010, ISSN print 1663–9383 | ISSN online 1663–9405 | EAN 9782940415274.
Energy and Development, No. 2, Basingstoke/Geneva: Palgrave Macmillan/Graduate Institute Publications, 2011, EAN 9780230282483.
Aid, Emerging Economies and Global Policies, No. 3, Basingstoke/Geneva: Palgrave Macmillan/Graduate Institute Publications, 2012, EAN 9781137003409.
Religion and Development, No. 4, Basingstoke/Geneva: Palgrave Macmillan/Graduate Institute Publications, 2013, EAN 9781137329370.
Education, Learning, Training: Critical Issues for Development, No. 5, Leiden|Boston/Geneva: Brill Nijhoff/Graduate Institute Publications, 2014, EAN 9789004281141.
*Large-Scale Land Acquisitions, F*ocus on South-East Asia, No. 6, Leiden|Boston/Geneva: Brill Nijhoff/Graduate Institute Publications 2015, EAN 9789004304741.
Combining Economic and Political Development, The Experience of MENA, No. 7 Leiden|Boston/Geneva: Brill Nijhoff/Graduate Institute Publications 2017, EAN 9789004336452.

THE GRADUATE INSTITUTE | GENEVA
Graduate Institute of International and Development Studies
Institut de hautes études internationales et du développement
Research Office/Publications
P.O. Box 1672
CH–1211 Geneva 1
Switzerland
publications@graduateinstitute.ch
http://www.graduateinstitute.ch/home/research/publications.html

Development As A Battlefield

Edited By

Irene Bono
Béatrice Hibou

BRILL
NIJHOFF

LEIDEN | BOSTON

Cover illustration: Street scene in the old town of Iiaret, Algeria, 18 December 2012. Photographer © Aurélie Lecarpentier [Aalek]

The Library of Congress Cataloging-in-Publication Data is available online at http://catalog.loc.gov
LC record available at http://lccn.loc.gov/2017027627

Typeface for the Latin, Greek, and Cyrillic scripts: "Brill". See and download: brill.com/brill-typeface.

ISSN 1663-9383
ISBN 978-90-04-34952-0 (paperback)
ISBN 978-90-04-34955-1 (e-book)

This book is printed on acid-free paper and produced in a sustainable manner.

Contents

PART 2
Consensus as An Expression of Conflict

PART 3
The Definition of Legitimate Conflicts

Foreword

I'm pleased to introduce *Development as a Battlefield*: an innovative exploration of the multidimensional meanings of—and interactions between—conflict and development. The two phenomena are all too often regarded as ostensibly antagonistic. This was exemplified again in the context of the Arab Spring that erupted in December 2010 and was eventually short-lived in several countries of the Middle-East and North-Africa (MENA) region. This volume—the 8th thematic issue of *International Development Policy*—is an invitation to reconsider and renew the way social scientists usually seek to make sense of socio-political and economic developments in the MENA region and beyond.

To achieve this, the guest editors bring together a set of contributions that collectively bridge anthropology, history, political sociology and political economy. The volume draws on the expertise of a dozen authors who present and discuss research carried out in countries spanning a region strictly larger than 'MENA': it includes a geographical area ranging from Afghanistan in the East to Morocco in the West, and from Turkey in the North to Sudan in the South. The multiplicity of this volume's compilation also mirrors a central premise of *International Development Policy*, which is to address critical issue domains from interdisciplinary, multi-level angles to account for the complexity of the social dynamics at work. I wish to commend the guest editors, Béatrice Hibou and Irene Bono, for bringing together such a wealth of perspectives by inviting selected scholars—all of them women—who share a deep understanding of past-present, local–global interactions that infuse power relations. Many of the authors originate from the region under study.

Overall, this special issue makes a convincing case for reconsidering widely-held assumptions about past and ongoing conflicts as well as development trajectories in 'MENA countries' and neighbouring Sudan and Afghanistan. Through an in-depth examination of the evolving social reality anchored in specific institutional and historic circumstances, the authors demonstrate the need to stay clear of homogeneous approaches that neglect the pluralistic socio-political landscapes of a region too easily subsumed under one group referred to as the Arab or MENA countries. The contributions in this volume challenge the widely-shared belief that these countries represent an exception in the developing world, a supposed space of 'ungovernability' characterised by 'extraneous' states ruling over an undisciplined population that inevitably leads to submission-revolt cycles. The chapters further challenge the assumption that Islam, or a deep sense of clan or ethnic identity, act as an obstacle to development, due to beliefs and values that prevent the advent of a techno-rational order associated with modernity. Violence associated with power asymmetries is part and parcel of political relations and could be considered analytically relevant from a development viewpoint, rather than a defining characteristic of a homogenous cultural and geopolitical 'MENA region'.

That said, the authors acknowledge that development shortfalls may partly account for the uprisings and conflicts witnessed in the countries under review. However, they question the idea of an inverse linear relationship between development and conflict. The notion of development itself, often defined as a process of profound social transformation, is contested and understood differently depending on the scale of analysis, discipline and prevailing narratives. In their introductory chapter, Irene Bono and Béatrice Hibou note that development appears not only as a practice and central paradigm in international relations, but also as a narrative and an ideology embedded in power relations. They define development as 'a set of complex social relations and a balance of power oscillating constantly between consensus and conflict'.

This compilation of chapters offers novel insights on regional, national and local dynamics involving developmental concerns such as justice, equity, governmentality and citizens' role in society. Through an in-depth examination of development cycles linked to defining historic events and by distinguishing between incremental change and disruption, the authors factor in local and global dynamics to analyse the conflicts and tensions associated with globalisation. Their insights are pertinent from both an academic and policy viewpoint. These insights on the conflict-development nexus will be of interest for all those who care about a region whose fate matters a great deal not only for the people who live there, but for all of us.

The guest editors have led this ambitious project to successful fruition, resulting in a compelling collection of articles under the title of *Development as a Battlefield*. A workshop, organized on 7–8 September 2015 in Geneva, brought together all the authors and selected experts to review each draft paper and make suggestions for improvements. I join the guest editors in thanking Jean-François Bayart, Yvan Droz and Didier Péclard for insightful remarks and suggestions at this workshop. My thanks go also to the authors, who revised their articles in two successive rounds: first after the Geneva workshop and then in response to the remarks raised by an anonymous reviewer who carefully examined the draft volume as a whole and raised critical comments on individual contributions. I wish to extend our gratitude to the anonymous reviewer. Marie Thorndahl initiated this special issue as former managing editor of our journal. Frances Rice took over by end-2015, and was supported by Emmanuel Dalle Mulle and several other colleagues. My thanks go to all of them for their efficient editorial support.

This volume is an invitation to 'think again'. It is indeed high time to reconsider the development-conflict nexus in a region whose population has been facing violence and insecurity for many decades and whose fate will determine global security, migration, development and humanitarian agendas in the years to come. This special issue makes the convincing case of dismissing sweeping statements and simple policy recipes. It calls for localising or grounding interventions in specific polities where the driving force lies above all in the citizenry—youth, women and men who wish to improve livelihoods and have a say in their own development trajectories.

Gilles Carbonnier
Editor-in-Chief

Preface

International Development Policy is a critical source of analysis of development policy and international cooperation trends and is aimed at scholars, policy-makers and development professionals. It offers a diverse range of academic views from both industrialised countries and emerging economies.

International Development Policy is edited by the Graduate Institute of International and Development Studies, an institution of research and higher education dedicated to advancing world affairs. Located in Geneva at the heart of an international centre of multilateral governance, the Graduate Institute benefits from a rich legacy linked to the founding of the international system and the League of Nations in the 1920s, and the emergence of the developing world in the 1960s.

http://graduateinstitute.ch/publications
http://devpol.org | http://debate.devpol.org

We extend our thanks to the Swiss Agency for Development and Cooperation (SDC) for its financial support.

Schweizerische Eidgenossenschaft
Confédération suisse
Confederazione Svizzera
Confederaziun svizra

List of Illustrations

Figures

Tables

List of Acronyms and Abbreviations

ADFM	Democratic Association of Women of Morocco (Association démocratique des femmes du Maroc)
AKP	Justice and Development Party (*Adalet ve Kalkinma Partisi*)
IARA	Islamic African Relief Agency
AWI	Justice and Spirituality (*Al Adl Wal Ihsane*)
BTE	Institute of Information Technologies (*Bilişim Teknolojileri Enstitüsü*)
BILGEM	Informatics and Information Security Research Center (*Bilişim ve Bilgi Güvenliği İleri Teknolojiler Araştırma Merkezi*)
BRTS	Bus Rapid Transit System
CBD	Central Business District
CDA	Community Development Association
CRI	Regional Investment Centre (Centre régional d'investissement)
DGCL	General Management of Local Groups (Direction générale des collectivités locales)
DYP	True Path Party (*Doğru Yol Partisi*)
EEC	European Economic Community
GS	Sharia Association (*Gam'iyya al-Shar'iyya*)
ILA	Israeli Land Administration
ILO	International Labour Organization
IMA	Islamic Medical Association
IMF	International Monetary Fund
INDH	National Initiative for Human Development (Initiative nationale du développement humain)
ISAF	International Security Assistance Force
MENA	Middle East and North Africa
MKEK	Mechanical and Chemical Industry Corporation (*Makina ve Kimya Endüstrisi Kurumu*)
MPDC	Constitutional Democratic Popular Movement (Mouvement populaire démocratique constitutionnel)
MUR	Movement of Unification and Reform (Mouvement de l'unification et de la réforme)
MÜSIAD	Independent Industrialists and Businessmen Association (*Müstakil Sanayici ve İşadamları Derneği*)
NATO	North Atlantic Treaty Organization
NDP	National Democratic Party
NGO	Non-Governmental Organisation
NHP	National Housing Program

NIMBY	Not in my back yard
OECD	Organisation for Economic Co-operation and Development
PDF	Popular Defence Forces
PJD	Justice and Development Party (Parti Justice et Développement)
PKK	Kurdistan Workers' Party (*Partiya Karkerên Kurdistan*)
RSF	Rapid Support Forces
SME	Small and medium-sized enterprise
SMI	Société Métallurgique d'Imider
SMNL	Sudan Movement of National Liberation
SSI	Union of Exporters of the Defence Industry and Aeronautics (*Savunma ve Havacilik Sanayi İhracatçilari Birliği*)
SWTUF	Sudan Workers' Trade Union Federation
TAI	Turkish Aerospace Industries
TOKI	Mass Housing Development Administration (*Toplu Konut İdaresi Başkanlığı*)
TÜBITAK	Scientific and Technological Research Council of Turkey (*Türkiye Bilimsel ve Teknolojik Araştırma Kurumu*)
TUC	Trades Union Congress
TÜSIAD	Turkish Industry and Business Association (*Türk Sanayicileri ve İşadamları Derneği*)
TSKGV	Foundation for Strengthening the Turkish Armed Forces (*Türk Silahlı Kuvvetlerini Güçlendirme Vakfı*)
UEKAE	National Research Institute in Electronics and Cryptology (*Ulusal Elektronik ve Kriptoloji Araştırma Enstitüsü*)
USAID	United States Agency for International Development
WAA	Workers' Affairs Association

Notes on Contributors

Fariba Adelkhah
is an anthropologist and director of research at the Fondation nationale des sciences politiques (SciencesPo-CERI) in Paris, France. She is the author of *Being Modern in Iran* (Hurst, 1999) and *Les Mille et une frontières de l'Iran. Quand les voyages forment la nation* (Karthala, 2012), and edited the special issue of the *Revue d'études du monde musulman et de la Méditerranée* on 'Guerres et terres en Afghanistan' (2013).

Yasmine Berriane
is a senior researcher and lecturer at the University of Zurich. She received her doctorate in Political Sociology from the Institute of Political Studies in Paris. Author of *Femmes, associations et politique à Casablanca* (Editions du Centre Jacques Berque, 2013), she is currently conducting research on social and political change and the commodification of land in Morocco.

Irene Bono
is Assistant Professor of Political Science at the University of Torino, Italy. She is also research associate at the Mohamed VI Polytechnic University in Rabat, Morocco. Her research interests focus on the government of inequality and the role of non-institutional actors in the formation and transformation of the state.

Ayşe Buğra
is Professor of Political Economy at the Atatürk Institute for Modern Turkish History in Istanbul, Turkey. She has written on the history and methodology of economics, development economics and comparative social policy. She is also the translator into Turkish of *The Great Transformation* by Karl Polanyi (1986).

Raphaëlle Chevrillon-Guibert
is a research fellow in political economy at the French National Institute for Sustainable Development (IRD), and at the PRODIG Joint Research Unit in Paris, France. For more than ten years, she has investigated patterns of Islamist hegemony in Sudan.

Anouck Gabriela Côrte-réal Pinto
is a post-doctoral researcher at the School for Advanced Studies in the Social Sciences (EHESS, Paris), seconded to the French Institute of Anatolian Studies (IFEA) in Istanbul, Turkey. Côrte-réal Pinto's research interests include the

sociological history of the economy, Turkish–European relations and civil–military relations.

Nadia Hachimi Alaoui
is a doctoral student at Sciences Po Aix, France, where she is completing her PhD on the *wali* and practices of government. She is affiliated to the Centre de Recherche Economie, Société, Culture (CRESC) at the Faculty of Economics and Social Sciences of the University Mohammed VI Polytechnic (Rabat, Morocco) where she is also scientific secretary to the Chair of Comparative African Studies.

Béatrice Hibou
is CNRS Senior Research Fellow at the Centre d'Études et de Recherches Internationales (CERI) in Paris, France. She is co-director of the Centre de Recherche, Économie, Société et Culture, Mohamed VI Polytechnic, University of Rabat, Morocco. Her comparative research in political economy focuses on the political significance of economic reform, state trajectories and the exercise of domination in Africa and Europe, from a Weberian perspective.

Adriana Kemp
is Associate Professor and Chair of the Department of Sociology and Anthropology at Tel Aviv University, Israel. Her areas of research are citizenship and migration, neoliberal politics and urban governance.

Nora Lafi
is a historian at the Leibniz-Zentrum Moderner Orient in Berlin, Germany. She also teaches at the Free University of Berlin (Faculty of Islamwissenschaft) and the Berlin Graduate School Muslim Cultures and Societies.

Talia Margalit
is Senior Lecturer at the Azrieli School of Architecture, Tel Aviv University, Israel. Her areas of research are urban planning and citizenship, neoliberal policies and urban development. She specialised in Israeli planning and Tel Aviv.

Marie Vannetzel
is a researcher in political sociology at the CNRS in Amiens, France (CURAPP), and a member of the European Research Council-funded programme, 'When Authoritarianism Fails in the Arab World'. She completed her PhD on the local mobilisation of the Muslim Brotherhood in Egypt and curently studies post-2011 electoral dynamics.

Elena Vezzadini
is a research fellow at the Institut des Mondes Africains (IMAF/CNRS) in Paris, France. Her research interests include the social history of the first Sudanese nationalist movement, nationalism and memory, colonialism and the abolition of slavery, and the army up to the 1920s. She is the author of *Lost Nationalism: Revolution, Memory and Anti-colonial Resistance in Sudan*, published in 2015 (James Currey).

Merieme Yafout
is a visiting professor at the University of Turin, Italy and the University of Lausanne, Switzerland. A specialist on the theme of women, religion and politics, she has conducted academic research in Morocco, Tunisia, Egypt and Italy, and has worked as a researcher for a number of international organisations.

Introduction

CHAPTER 1

Development as a Battlefield

Irene Bono and Béatrice Hibou

Abstract

Conflict and development are commonly understood as two contradictory phenomena. Some apparently self-evident ideas, such as gaps in development being a source of conflict and social and political conflict being a major obstacle to development, have been revitalised by the debate about the Arab Spring and used to orient development projects in the MENA region. This chapter aims to explore a radically different perspective: we conceive development as a complex social relationship, involving a vast constellation of actors, interests, logics, spaces, causalities and temporalities, and we consider conflict in a multidimensional sense, as an expression of struggle, competition, tension, resistance, opposition and critique. Conceived in these terms, conflict and development appear to be strictly interlinked rather than opposites. Three particular configurations characterise development as a 'battlefield': conflicts that create consensus around development; consensus as an expression of conflict; and the definition of legitimate conflicts. There is special focus on the interconnection between different temporal layers characterising the formation of the state and the transformation of capitalism, and the consequences of development for society, the assertion of sovereignty, the definition of social order and how people conduct their lives. This examination of the links between development and conflict thus sheds fresh light on injustice, inequality, modes of government and on how people interpret and live in political society far beyond the MENA region.

* Our thanks go to the members of the review team, including Gilles Carbonnier, Marie Thorndahl, Frances Rice, Emmanuel Dalle Mulle and Jean-François Bayart; to Didier Péclard and Yvan Droz, who attended the seminar we organised around this issue in September 2015 at the Graduate Institute; and to the two attentive readers of one of the first drafts of this introduction, Boris Samuel and a particularly generous anonymous reviewer.

1 Introduction

Except for studies in anthropology or in historical and political sociology that focus on highly localised processes,[1] few recent analyses have examined the process of development in what is conventionally called the 'MENA' (Middle East and North Africa) region. After the Arab Spring, the first timid approaches to the subject in the late 1990s and the decade that followed[2] gave way to an almost exclusive preoccupation with conflict. After 2011, there were very few contributions dealing with this region in major journals devoted to development issues[3] and conflicts were discussed in terms of protests and social movements, especially in Tunisia and Egypt,[4] or in terms of armed conflicts and civil wars, especially regarding Syria and Libya.[5]

This analytical turn rests on a multiplicity of causally self-evident observations underpinning a rather widespread understanding of development and conflict, in which the two terms are presented as two contradictory phenomena. However, it is still difficult to provide an overview of the different ways in which the relationship between these two phenomena has been understood over time. If we take the view that the discontent, social movements, revolts and revolutions that the MENA region has experienced are in part born of gaps in development, including the existence of pockets of poverty, the inadequate integration of the region, and difficulties in getting young people into the

1 See, e.g., Elyachar (2005) on self-entrepreneurship in Cairo, Bono (2010) on the phenomena of participation in the Moroccan town of El Hajeb, and Canesse (2014) on rural development policy in the Tunisia of Ben Ali. Implemented between 2008 and 2011, the Agence Nationale de la Recherche (French National Research Agency) programme, 'Tanmia. Le "Développement": fabrique de l'action publique dans le monde arabe?" contributed to fostering studies on development in the region. The work produced in this context includes Catusse et al. (2010), Abu-Sada and B. (2011), Ruiz de Elvira (2013) and Sbeih (2014).

2 See in particular Santucci and El Malki (1990) and Henry and Springborg (2001). Note also the launch of the *Middle East Development Journal* in 2009.

3 For example, the *Journal of Development Studies* did not refer to any country in the region between volume 46–10 (November 2010) and volume 50–9 (September 2014). By not publishing any article referring to the Arab Spring after 2011, the *Middle East Development Journal* made a significant editorial decision. In the same trend, in 2011 the *Revue Tiers Monde* devoted a special issue to the conflicts and protest movements present in the region: see Ben Néfissa (2011).

4 Camau and Vairel (2014) and Rougier and Lacroix (2015) address the cases of Tunisia and Egypt, respectively, from this point of view.

5 This view of conflict is particularly central in Burgat and Paoli (2013). It also underlies the discussion of the role of ISIS (also known as Daesh and ISIL) in the Arab world expressed in Fellous (2015).

labour market, we are implicitly drawing on the presuppositions of theories of modernisation.[6] These theories see development as essentially pacificatory, as a vector of equality and justice and as promoting inclusiveness and the dissemination of economic rationality, and thus as alleviating conflict. In this evolutionary and 'progressivist' perspective, development—it is claimed—can lead a society towards greater prosperity and, consequently, towards greater equity, peace and consensus. According to this interpretation—adopted by the majority of donors,[7] the social conflicts facing the MENA region arise from the ineffectiveness of development when viewed as a vector of equality and from its unexpected negative effects. These analyses thus bolster the classic argument that various supposedly atavistic factors are hindering the development of countries in the region. These factors include merely cosmetic reforms and the limits of economic liberalisation in the face of the interests of rentiers, clientelism, and the importance of 'clans'; the constraining influence of religion on economic behaviour, especially on the integration of women; and the way that wealth is siphoned off into security apparatuses and sociopolitical groups linked to the government.[8]

The social conflicts that have proliferated in the wake of the Arab Spring have often been seen as further evidence of the conflictual and unstable nature of the societies in the region. Echoing this, 'reverse versions' of this interpretation have developed in the form of analyses aimed at defining the negative effects of conflict on development. From this point of view, conflict is seen as the main source of underdevelopment, or as an obstacle to the pursuit of the aims of development. Violence, especially in the form of civil wars, is then perceived as one of the main causes of poor economic performance and, even more, of the growth of poverty in the world.[9] Analyses sometimes focus on issues of conflict and then show that violence feeds economic strategies that run

6 Rostow (1960) is one of the main proponents of this school of thought. Gilman (2003) provides us with material for further reflection on the relationship between conflict and development in theories of modernization.

7 Among the most recent examples of this, see in particular the World Bank (2015) and USAID (2015).

8 Analyses that consider these characteristics as typical of the countries in the region go back several years. Among the first authors to highlight them were Gellner and Waterbury (1977) and later Heydemann (2004). After the Arab Spring, these arguments were at the heart of the various studies on the 'political economy of the Arab Spring', including Springborg (2011), Malik and Bassem (2013) and Cammett et al. (2015).

9 See in particular the World Bank (2005). This argument is developed analytically in North et al. (2013).

counter to development. All analyses of the 'greed and grievance'[10] kind that flourished in the second half of the 1990s, with the end of the Cold War and the 'renewal' of armed conflict, fall within this paradigm: thus, it is claimed that resources (natural resources, financial resources from international groups or organisations such as migrants, or humanitarian aid) are turned into weapons of war, strengthening not only the parties in conflict but also the murderous competition to appropriate these resources.[11] With the same self-assurance, other analysts take the opposite view and argue for example that the fact that Tunisia was the first country to revolt is not surprising, especially because it had a higher level of development than its neighbours—witness its demographics and the level of education of its population.[12] Others highlight the negative effects of the protests, outbreaks of violence and even civil wars on the region's development.[13]

These various arguments comprise a temporal and spatial sequence of supposedly 'self-evident' relationships that are, in fact opposed, or even contradictory and incompatible—a sequence made possible by the tangled interweaving of three simplistic modes of reasoning. The first is undoubtedly the adoption of very narrow conceptions of the two phenomena studied: the notion of development is understood in a limited and economistic sense, purportedly neutral and expressed in growth rates; the notion of conflict is reduced to war, physical violence or social protest.[14] The second mode of reasoning, transposed from the economy,[15] is based on the premise that development and conflict are independent of one another. This approach transforms these complex phenomena into 'variables', which makes it possible to seek patterns, and leads to the logics of development and of conflict being separated: there cannot be any overlap between a 'period of development' (characterised by a partial or complete absence of conflict) and a 'period of conflict' (which

10 The expression comes from Collier (2000a; 2000b). These arguments have also been developed in Jean and Rufin (1996), Kaldor (1999), and Collier and Hoeffler (2002; 2004).

11 Within the community of practitioners, these arguments have in particular been raised by the Development Assistance Committee (OECD-DAC, 1997).

12 See, e.g., Todd (2011).

13 See, e.g., Amin et al. (2012). The financial press and the grey literature from donors are full of articles or reports on the subject.

14 From another very interesting point of view, albeit almost the complete opposite of our own, Cramer (2006) shows that when conflicts are examined from the angle of development, they are reduced to what becomes an oversimplified reality.

15 Marchal and Messiant (2002; 2003) pioneered this critique.

in itself can hamper the process of development).[16] Finally, the third mode of reasoning, the causal mode reduced to its simplest expression,[17] sees the relationship between development and conflict as part of the search for *one* causality, *ceteris paribus*, but also as falling within a normative analysis that claims to set out good and bad practices, define good and bad development, perceive its failure or success and highlight its positive or negative, beneficial or adverse effects.[18]

Beyond the MENA region and the Arab Spring, these modes of argument underlie and promote expertise and development projects and their bureaucratisation. Thinking, within decision-making bodies (by their 'organic' intellectuals), has indeed been heavily oriented towards the quest for strategies aimed at 'breaking the conflict trap' and creating the necessary conditions for the sole (or main) purpose of fostering the positive effects expected from development.[19] The so-called conflict-sensitive approach and its 'do-not-harm' strategies[20] are based on these assumptions. They were all responsible for the exponential growth of various schemes that claimed to provide appropriate responses to these new issues in cooperation and development policy. Manuals and training guides devoted to these approaches provide a set of standards, procedures, *dispositifs* and instruments to neutralise the conflicts arising from development projects.[21] The extremely commonplace processes that have made it possible to design these technologies, to make them operational and reproducible, to rationalise them so that they can be assessed and to standardise them to make them compatible and comparable has turned into a process that

16 This argument lies at the heart of the World Bank's *World Development Report 2011* (Word Bank, 2011).

17 For a critical view of the link between development and security, see Duffield (2007) and the debate on his book in the periodical *Politique Africaine* (Ambrosetti et al., 2012).

18 See, e.g., Thomas et al. (2000).

19 See the eloquent title of the World Bank report (World Bank, 2003).

20 For these approaches, see Leonhardt (2002) and Anderson (1999). For a critical analysis, see Schloms (2005). These arguments have been mainly developed in the grey literature. See, for example, *The Collaborative for Development Action*, http://www.cdainc.com or http://territoires.ecoledelapaix.org/mali/methode-do-no-harm (accessed on 13 July 2016).

21 For example, Conflict Sensitivity Consortium (2012) See also the 'resource pack' of PFO, CECORE, CHA, FEWER: *International Alert, Saferworld, Conflict-Sensitive Approaches to Development, Humanitarian Assistance and Peacebuilding. A Resource Pack*, http://www.saferworld.org.uk/resources/view-resource/148-conflict-sensitive-approaches-to-development-humanitarian-assistance-and-peacebuilding (accessed on 13 July 2016).

produces indifference, one that has detached them from their very meaning. Paradoxically, this process has produced other forms of coercion and domination[22] that traditional readings of the link between development and conflict neglect or completely ignore.

The limits of these perspectives become evident as soon as one engages in a rigorous exploration of the meaning of the two terms. Instead of considering development as a one-dimensional explanatory variable, we felt it would be more productive to define it as a complex social relationship involving a vast constellation of actors, interests, logics, spaces, causalities and temporalities; a social relationship that necessarily gives rise to diverse understandings. Similarly, if we do not reduce conflict to civil war, protest movements and the explicit use of violence, it can appear as an expression of struggle, forms of competition, tensions, resistance, opposition and critique. By adopting these complex and multidimensional meanings, an examination of the links between development and conflict can shed fresh light on injustice, inequality and modes of government, but also on the ways people understand and exist in political society. Then, development cannot fail to foster simultaneously a number of trends and characteristics; of different and even contradictory interpretations. It thereby becomes a more deep-rooted factor in struggle, overt competition and the asymmetry of relations rather than an element in convergence, harmony and the pacification of social relations.[23]

By observing development in all its conflictual nature, we have—in the present volume— sought to transcend the aforementioned limits by integrating the logics of action and social relationships, which are considered to be offset and out of scope by normative, mono-causal arguments. The first of these limits concerns the relationship to time. Eschewing analyses that claim that the temporality of development and the temporality of conflict succeed one another, we have sought to understand the way they are interconnected by situating the analysis of these relationships within national and global trajectories. Giving them a historical setting has led us to understand, always in a contextualised and localised way, what exactly development means, comprehending it as a multiplicity of combinations of consensus and conflict—combinations that are not necessarily tense and paradoxical. By shifting the focus to the link between development and conflict thus defined, this volume also aims to question the relevance of the MENA region as a category of

22 These processes are highlighted and analysed, in other contexts, by Hibou (2015) and Samuel (2013; 2014).

23 Bono et al. (2015) argue for this view, drawing on Weber and his confrontational conception of social relations (Weber, 1968).

analysis, to the extent that it homogenises utterly different political situations and development practices.[24]

2 Understanding How Different Temporalities are Interconnected

The sceptical gaze we are bringing to bear on this overall understanding of the region does not stop us being sensitive to the existence of several major features common to the various entities that comprise it. These extraverted societies have continually brought their own historicity, including the nineteenth century reform movement—*islah*—into dialogue with the Western matrix of development that emerged at the same time. All these societies have been integrated, in their own ways, into the grand narrative of the nation that is inseparable from the processes of globalisation, and have participated daily in the transformations of modes of government that have shaped the great paradigms of intervention with regard to development. We, as editors, felt that this return to history was required, not to illustrate the evolutionary process to which development is often reduced, but to show the diversity and originality of configurations bringing together development and conflict over the years and to help us grasp the plurality of meanings of development and its conflictual dimensions in the neo-liberal era in which we are currently living. If we are to understand the interconnections of temporalities, we must not only take into account the link between global trajectory and national or regional trajectories; we must also consider the relationship between periods of development (with their specific conception of the state and ways of governing) and periods of great events in history (such as the fall of empires, the end of colonisation, the end of separatist nationalism after decolonisation, and the end of industrial development). And we also need to take into account the link between the 'long periods' of incremental transformations and periods of contingency and abrupt change, and the connection between the 'long periods' of the intrinsic logics of development and the equally long, but more specific, span of human memory.

Understanding the link between development and conflict requires first and foremost that we situate the historicity proper to the region within the process of globalisation, particularly in the related reconfiguration of international relations. In interpreting this phenomenon without resorting to analyses focused on the clash of civilisations, on imports (of the state, modernity, or

24 In line with the ideas put forward in Bayart (2016).

the market)[25] or on dependence,[26] this reading highlights the ambiguity and complexity of interactions between two global trajectories—that of countries in the region and that which structures international relations in the context of Western hegemony. In this way, it is possible to understand the specific ways in which the great geostrategic conflicts have daily shaped the ideas, *dispositifs* and practices of development in given societies.[27]

We need to go back to the eighteenth century to understand the process by which the models of 'Western' and 'Ottoman' (or more generally Muslim) modernity grew apart and then came into conflict, ending, in the nineteenth century, with the hegemonic self-assertion of the Western model. As Nora Lafi suggests in her contribution to this volume, the practices of development in the region in the late nineteenth century were not reducible to the Ottoman configuration or to the subtle and ambiguous relations between the Sublime Porte[28] and the provinces. To understand them, our analysis needs to take account of the tensions between this Ottoman configuration and the triumph of the European world, and of the violence fomented by the colonial ambitions of the major European nations, especially on the economic level. During the colonial period, this tension was reflected in the coexistence of convergences, affinities and encounters between these two modernities, but also in the open conflicts between them, for instance in matters of education, administrative reorganisation and economic investment, as evidenced by the discussions that took place within the colonised societies.[29] As the Moroccan example paradigmatically illustrates,[30] this tension can also be seen in the processes of the 'invention of tradition' and the appropriation of tradition. The link between the temporalities of development and conflict finds one of its international expressions in the operation of the bipolar world that emerged from the Cold War. In the case analysed by Anouck Côrte-réal Pinto, the 'Turkification' of the defence industry—used both as a lever of economic development and as a symbol of technological modernity—seems inseparable from the climate of permanent conflict characteristic of the Cold War. As a full member of the North Atlantic Treaty Organization (NATO), (and thus undoubtedly belonging

25 As shown by Huntington (1996) and Badie (1992), whose ideas have caused significant reverberations in the academic and political worlds.

26 In line with the work of Frank (1968), Cardoso and Faletto (1979) and Amin (1974).

27 This approach is based mainly on Wallerstein (1979), Lonsdale (1981), Cooper (1981), Bayart (1989) and Arrighi (1994).

28 The Sublime Porte was the name of the Ottoman court at Constantinople.

29 For Tunisia, see Berque (1967), Mahjoubi (1982), Tlili (1984), Kraïem (1990), Sraïeb (1995) and Ben Achour (1996). For an overview, see Hibou (2009).

30 On this aspect, see Adam (1972), Rabinow (1995), Tozy (1999) and Hibou (2006).

to the Western Bloc), Turkey has continuously tried to assert itself as a regional player by insisting on its 'non-aligned' importance vis-à-vis its allies. In the case of Afghanistan, as analysed in this volume by Fariba Adelkhah, this interconnection is reflected in the coexistence of the time of development imposed by Western powers through the assistance they have provided for reconstruction, and the time of 'war as life' that characterises national trajectory and creates conflicts conducive to the continuation of this permanent state of war. These two experiences of the neo-liberal moment do not, of course, exhaust the possible configurations of this crossing of trajectories.

Indeed, the plural and elastic dimension of what is called 'neo-liberalism' explains how a very wide variety of forms exist behind the general principles presiding over its operation (government by norms, procedures, rules and figures; the dissolution of the specificity of the 'public' and the universalisation of the private as a benchmark of government; the imperative to create frameworks for the development of market and business logics; the replacement of general laws by pragmatism and case-by-case decisions; the replacement of collective responsibility by individual responsibility, and so on). Thus, the areas covered in this volume suggest that the neo-liberal hegemony can be understood and interpreted in an open and pluralistic manner that goes beyond the standardising paradigm of development in which guise it usually appears.[31] These areas reveal direct forms of state interventionism and strategies of delegation, the development of evergetic and charitable practices on the part of private individuals and the redeployment of social policies, the mobilisation of associations and individuals in civil society and of large administrations, and the engineering of both participation and planning. Thanks to this plasticity and the existence of a multiplicity of ways of behaving and governing 'neo-liberally', each society offers a range of behaviours and conducts that can extend to the expression of radical alternatives and oppositions. Thus, consensus and conflict can exist simultaneously. In this sense, Merieme Yafout's article on the development activities implemented by Moroccan Islamist associations that thereby seek to criticise the action of the state in this area demonstrates clearly that models of society that in principle are completely opposed—which some observers might read as 'shocks' of civilisation, rekindling the opposition between East and West—can find in the neo-liberal development paradigm both common ground and a place of conflict or even

31 On the diversity of neo-liberal principles, see Saad-Filho and Johnston (2005), Nemo and Petitot (2006), Plehwe et al. (2006), Dardot and Laval (2013) and Peck (2010). On the diversity of neo-liberal practices, there are many studies, but see especially Laurie and Bondie (2005), Ong (2006), Chang et al. (2012) and Peck and Theodore (2015).

violence. The chapter by Adriana Kemp and Talia Margalit, on urban development projects in Tel Aviv, convincingly shows that any challenge to neo-liberal practices borrows from the very repertoire of the neo-liberal paradigm—a paradigm that it also helps to renew.

The link between development and conflict must then be read as part of the historical trajectory of the formation of states. In the region as elsewhere, conflicts mark out and comprise this trajectory and mark the transition between different conceptions of the role played by state authority in development in the imperial, colonial, national and neo-liberal eras.[32]

In the Tunisian fez sector in the late nineteenth century, as studied by Nora Lafi, the strategies deployed by the workers provide us with a concrete understanding of the tensions that existed at the time between the imperial government and foreigners' ambitions. The government aimed to foster the shift in the artisanal production of the Tunis *beylik* towards proto-industrialisation through economic and administrative reforms, while foreign actors, by introducing competition, further legitimised the process of mechanisation, quickly generating conflicts within corporations and the colonial state itself (in its role as an agent both of development and of protection in the sector). The demands for the introduction of trade union rights in Sudan after the Second World War—the theme of Elena Vezzadini's contribution to this volume—take us to the heart of two other 'conflictualities'. The first conflictuality contrasts the different conceptions of development found in the metropolis and reflects the transition from a colonial state that highlights the importance of, and exploits, its colony to a colonial state that empowers its colony and places it under its tutelage. The second conflictuality contrasts nationalists with the supporters of a developmentalist colonisation likely to provide the future independent state with its guiding principles.[33] Marie Vannetzel analyses the trajectory of the Egyptian state, which is emblematic of the developmentalist and interventionist nation state that involves itself in groups and territories in the name of national interest. She focuses her initial remarks on the ways in which the conflict between the government and the Muslim Brotherhood is managed. She then examines the ways in which the different parties mobilise this developmentalist imaginary in the heart of the neo-liberal period, a period that encourages us to examine and interpret the conflicts between the multiple conceptions of the role of the state in development. The various contributions to this volume highlight the diversity of 'what development means' when the state reforms itself in the name of neo-liberalism. It probably means

32 On these aspects, see especially Bayart (2010).

33 These contrasts are highlighted in Mitchell (1991) and Berman and Lonsdale (1992).

liberalising but also nationalising; it also means intervening directly and disinvesting in the name of rationality and competitiveness in the private sector; and, yet again, it means using intermediaries and drawing on unexpected convergences but also giving free rein to market forces. Yasmine Berriane illustrates this trend with the emblematic example of collective lands in Morocco. She shows that their commercialisation lies at the crossroads of several economic and social issues linked to gender conflicts within society but also to conflicts between different social groups and territories. Raphaëlle Chevrillon-Guibert highlights the regional asymmetry characteristic of development in Islamist Sudan, an asymmetry that has widened under the impact of the neo-liberalism proper to that country—namely, the combination of institutional disinvestment and an increased reliance on the private sector in the form of incentives to resort systematically to charity.[34]

The analysis of the link between transformations in modes of government and transformations in capitalism constitutes a third approach to the link between development and conflict. Many studies have shown that, worldwide, development initiatives are indeed permeable to the major international economic paradigms, but that they do not submit passively to them: they participate in the process of the appropriation, adaptation and renewal of modes of government that are thus legitimised in the exercise of their domination.[35] Following this line of argument, the contributions in this volume highlight the innovative and inventive dimensions of this process, dimensions that are directly related to the specific characteristics of capitalism in historical configurations but also in specific national or regional forms.

In her article, Ayşe Buğra distinguishes between the development process and developmentalism defined as a strategy and as a legitimising discourse. She draws on the Turkish trajectory to uncover the process by which development becomes, in a given political situation, a knowledge of government, and shows how the shift from the paradigm of interventionist development to the paradigm of regulative development, privatised and decentralised, acquires particular and specific meaning in the capitalist configuration that characterises it. By encouraging the decentralisation of powers, favouring regulation over direct intervention and opting for the assessment of results rather than the planning of interventions, these neo-liberal modes of governing create new margins of

34 For similar analyses in other contexts, see Kuran (2003), Bonner et al. (2003), Haenni (2005) and Singer (2008).

35 On Africa, in particular see Ferguson (1990) and Hibou (1998). For a more general reflection on this aspect, see Hibou (2011).

ownership, negotiation and arrangement while renewing former practices.[36] As suggested by the example of the Casablanca Development Plan, analysed by Nadia Hachimi Alaoui, the neo-liberal revolution, especially in its managerial component, and the modes of government associated with the interests of the new players in Moroccan capitalism combine with the permanence of the imaginary but also with the Makhzen's practices of exercising power so as to create spaces for negotiation and moments conducive to action in areas that go far beyond development goals alone. By focusing on urban development in Tel Aviv, Adriana Kemp and Talia Margalit highlight another important feature of the current period. They show that those who are involved in development projects are not the only ones to provide guidance for the interpretation of government paradigms; protest and resistance also contribute to inventing, reformulating and legitimising these paradigms, partly because they are part of the same political economy and reflect the same capitalist configuration.

This extremely flexible reading of conflict defined as a social and political conflictuality, this approach sensitive to historical trajectories and their interconnections, is in the final analysis closer to studies that have addressed the history of development in terms of the singular narrative of endlessly reformulated expectations[37] than to studies on the political economy of development. The contributions in this volume may, to some degree, be read as fragments of narratives of development seen through the prism of conflictuality, allowing a very broad spectrum of social phenomena to be taken into account.

3 The Link between Development and Conflict

The contributions to this volume, then, form part of the historicity of globalisation, the formation of states, and the transformation of modes of government, and aim to grasp the links uniting these factors with periods of development and the connection between development and conflict. They capture the multiple faces of development and modes of conflict these faces convey, and they come at the problem from many different angles and scales of observation. For example, it is possible to reconstruct this variety of facets (with their different scales) by examining the vernacular terms, local translations and synonyms used in specific situations to talk about development, but also the words often associated with them, albeit in a great variety of ways. This richness better reflects the complexity of the relationship between development and conflict;

36 This aspect is also addressed by Hibou (2015) and Samuel (2013).

37 This is, in particular, the point of view of Cooper (2010) and Eckert et al. (2010).

we can move away from abstract and general analysis to observe the way development becomes an 'everyday' feature[38] through what it means in concrete terms. This volume focuses specifically on this phenomenon, examining the consequences of development for the organisation of social life, the assertion of sovereignty, the definition of social order and the shaping of how one conducts one's life.[39]

To analyse development and the conflicts that may arise from it in everyday life, it is thus appropriate firstly to analyse the reorganisation of social life in accordance with a state model favouring continuity or territorial stability, the ethnic uniformity of the population, the primacy of the individual over the group and competition between individuals. By analysing international aid as a *dispositif* and as a form of knowledge of a region (in this case Bamyan, in Afghanistan), Fariba Adelkhah shows that development can trigger a process of 'ethnicisation' and religious 'confessionalisation' among those participating in the political economy of aid, but also a process of territorialisation and therefore the affirmation of specific identities. Her contribution suggests that aid for development does not necessarily succeed conflict, even when it is intended to support the reconstruction of a region. Instead, it allows conflicts to be perpetuated beyond open warfare by supplying them with resources and providing them with a grammar. This grammar of development transforms the conflicts that had once been expressed in a warlike manner by giving them a diffuse and plural nature, albeit one that is not necessarily less cruel. This is shown by the exacerbation of violence connected with disputes over land, ethnicity and gender. The micro-social angle chosen by Yasmine Berriane allows us to observe a process of this nature embodied by the Soulaliyate movement. This movement arose in Morocco following the intensification of the commodification of collective land formerly owned by the tribes, and is led by women fighting against their exclusion from the process of the distribution of profits from the sale of these lands. Yasmine Berriane shows that the grand idea of development can also lead to the satisfaction of crassly pecuniary demands; in particular, she notes that development initiatives are likely to intensify social inequalities through an asymmetric enhancement of the territory and the 'tribalisation' of the individuals who inhabit it. Implicitly, the Soulaliyate movement reflects the fact that different land requirements may also create

38 Weber's *Veralltäglichung* is not translated here as it is usually rendered ('routinization') but as 'mode of penetration in everyday life', following Grossein's French translation (*quotidianisation*) and interpretation. See Grossein 2006: 68; 123–124.

39 This problematisation was developed by Weber: see especially Weber (1971) and Chalcraft, D.J., and A. Harrington (eds) (2001).

antagonisms between town and country, between different farming methods, and also between different social strata. Raphaëlle Chevrillon-Guibert analyses the charitable practices implemented by Darfuri traders in the Libya souk in Khartoum to benefit their region of origin. Without international aid and social policies, the traders' charitable activities have become the main pillar of territorial development and the fight against famine in Darfur, as in Khartoum. By transforming charity into the 'government of the social',[40] these initiatives undoubtedly reinforce the civilisation project fostered by the Islamist government. But they also contribute to the ethnicisation and the 'communitarisation' of solidarity—the complete opposite of Islamist rhetoric. Thus, amid the perpetuation of the war in Darfur, conflicts occur between different generations of wealthy traders, but also between antagonistic clienteles, social groups and territories that are all competing to qualify for aid.

This volume also approaches the links between development and conflict by analysing the implications that development initiatives have had for the emergence of a sovereign political authority and the sometimes conflictual modes of the assertion, exercise and legitimation of sovereignty in a given society. The spectrum and variety of viewpoints chosen by the authors highlight the characteristics of developmental conflicts in a specific period and the impact these conflicts have on how sovereignty is conceived. By studying the late Ottoman period, Nora Lafi captures the effects of development on the processes of affirmation and legitimation of political authority. The petitions denouncing the collapse of the fez industry in the Ottoman province of Tunis called into question the validity of integration into international trade as a mode of development. The protest against international competition viewed as unfair and against the deteriorating living conditions of workers following the mechanisation of the sector also denounced a new form of foreign interference and domination and criticised an Ottoman rule that, in the view of artisans, had become an agent of globalisation. Conflicts between the centre of the empire and the provinces, as well as conflicts between the various economic interests in the Tunisian province being studied, combined with conflicts with European powers to pave the way to colonisation and the loss of sovereignty.

At the other chronological extremity of the colonial experience, Elena Vezzadini's study of Sudan highlights the comparable disputes over sovereignty that can arise during national struggle. Immediately after the Second World War, the earliest legislation on employment was introduced under the leadership of the nascent Sudanese trade union movement and the developmentalist

40 For our conception of the government of the social, we refer the reader to our previous work, especially Hibou and Bono (2016).

orientation of the colonial power, influenced by the Keynesian paradigm that prevailed in England at the time. In a colonial context, the fact that the development model took into account the right to employment paved the way for an interpretation of development as a matter of citizenship, sovereignty and sociopolitical order. Thus, alongside the nationalist conflict that would give birth to a sovereign Sudanese government in 1956, there was a real proliferation of conflicts between different levels of government, different generations of employees, but also between various components of the nationalist movement, different ethnic groups and different economic interests. By reconstructing the trajectory of the Turkish defence industry during and after the Cold War, Anouck Gabriela Côrte-réal Pinto views the issue of sovereignty from a different angle. The official defence policy of the public authorities and the almost continuous (but still incomplete and perhaps impossible) promotion of the 'Turkification' of the military–industrial complex were presented at once as an example, a proof and a precondition of the country's economic, technological and political development. These investments were a pillar of the exercise of national sovereignty: lying at the heart of government legitimacy for decades, they undoubtedly supported government action aimed at defusing conflict with opposition movements. Moreover, they allowed recognition of the survival of the state and the nation, and underpinned the power and greatness of a country anxious to assert itself on the international stage in the name of a conflict forever on the verge of breaking out. The Turkish word *kalkınma* masterfully expresses this idea, since it includes the meaning of development, but also that of recovery and healing. To some extent, the graduated reading (more or less, better or worse) of development evolved into a binary reading (the life or death of the state) that forcefully enacted a consensus against a background of conflict.

Analysis of the daily implications of development also allows us to observe the characteristics of the sociopolitical order that is shaped through it.[41] At this level, conflicts of development may also set different actors, groups with conflicting interests, and conflicting world views against one another. In a Gramscian perspective, different world views, which coexist in an incoherent, disjointed and fragmentary manner, are the source of a continuous reformulation of the assumptions that discipline the way people live together through the conflicts they can trigger.[42] This third perspective in this volume is based

41 A study by Ayşe Buğra (2007), who considers this issue from the viewpoint of unequal practices of citizenship, is particularly useful for developing this perspective.

42 This is one of the central ideas in Gramsci (2011). On the concept of dislocation in Gramsci's thought, see Prestipino (2009).

on the work of Gramsci but also on other authors such as Polanyi (1944). Ayşe Buğra proposes that we must define economics as a discipline and as a form of knowledge if we are to grasp the way these different levels of conflict are interrelated in Turkey. She shows that the discourse on development fosters a socio-economic order of progress, modernisation and social cohesion and encompasses economic policies that have been created by different and sometimes opposed theories. However, as a historically and ideologically situated form of knowledge, conflict is expressed not only in its theoretical or ideological form. By analysing the economic development strategies promoted in Turkey before and after the country's integration into the world market, it is possible to understand the territorial, ethnic and class divisions within Turkish society and the mainsprings of the political order that accompanied social conflicts, especially those targeting Armenians and traditional rural society before liberalisation and, more recently, the conflicts that have set the secular urban elites against the new elites emerging from political Islam.

The development strategy in Casablanca as analysed by Nadia Hachimi Alaoui is emblematic of a sociopolitical order based on private initiative, territorial competition and the devolution of power in the name of proximity. Through various initiatives based on participation and consultation, the shapes assumed by notions of development seem so imprecise that development may act as an instrument of government and domination, despite the conflicts between different levels of political authority and between different economic interests. These conflicts, played out in non-formal areas on the edges of the development plan, have shaped the sociopolitical order that characterises Casablanca today, emphasising an apolitical vision of development, technicising it by expertise, excluding elected figures from consultations while integrating them into non-formal spaces of negotiation and giving the *wali*[43] the status of a major player in development. The city is also the level of observation chosen by Adriana Kemp and Talia Margalit to study the conflicts that development brings about in shaping modes of government and the sociopolitical order. Complementing previous analyses, Kemp and Margalit show that protests against the construction of high-rise buildings in Tel Aviv highlight issues of social cohesion and the public interest of urban development. By targeting only the partial and limited aspects of urban planning choices, these movements, often perceived as anti-neo-liberal (and viewing themselves as such), do not resist the neo-liberalism of urban space and the sociopolitical order but rather play a full part in them. Diffuse conflicts over funding for public services and the privatisation of urban space arise behind the disputes

43 A *wali* is a state representative at the territorial level. See Hachimi Alaoui (2016).

between the promoters of urban projects and their detractors, without challenging the neo-liberal order.[44]

Following Weber, the authors of the chapters in this volume also reflect the fact that development can be a vector of the expression and construction of 'the ways in which one conducts one's life' and how they characterise different 'types of person'.[45] The multiplicity of 'material and thought-based interests' that these concepts foster may result in cohabitation, confrontation or sometimes even in opposition between different ways of behaving and conceiving of the lives of individuals in society. The 'constellation' of interest, logics and behaviours that development brings together does not presuppose the existence of a spontaneous and peaceful harmony but of permanent adjustments resulting from conflicts, antagonisms, struggles, competitiveness and asymmetrical relations that lead to the emergence of different, sometimes even antagonistic worlds and world views.[46] In this fourth and final perspective, the authors have often chosen Islamist movements as a starting point for exploring the links between development and conflict. Marie Vannetzel and Merieme Yafout, respectively, study the Muslim Brotherhood in Egypt and the Wal Ihsane movement in Morocco using different scales of observation. Marie Vannetzel focuses on the continuity of the developmentalist imaginary before and after the fall of Mubarak and on the tensions between the imaginaries and the practices of development that have resulted. Merieme Yafout, meanwhile, examines a particular district in Casablanca, analysing the activities promoted by a development association whose female members are supporters of the Al Adl Wal Ihsane movement. In the case of Egypt, development is problematised through the distribution of benefits and the fostering of the spirit of service, while in the case of Morocco, it is understood as a process of emancipation and construction of 'ways in which one conducts one's life' based on positive personal social, economic and spiritual development. Going beyond the supposed existence of a conflict between a secular and an Islamic way of development (an idea systematically used in political speeches, in the community of development practitioners and in public debates), it is possible to highlight much more subtle conflicts between those two convictions, which are not rigid

44 The way in which protest movements have contributed to the consolidation of the neo-liberal order in Israel has already been stressed in connection with microfinance by Kemp and Berkovitch (2013). For a general discussion of this process in the neo-liberal era, see Hibou (2015). Theoretically, this process had already been emphasized by Weber (1978).

45 See especially Weber (1971) and Chalcraft, D. J., and A. Harrington (eds) (2001).

46 This problematic, which we adopted in order to analyse the government of the social in Morocco (Bono and Hibou 2016), is developed by Weber (1968). See Grossein (2005; 2016).

but constantly changing and evolving and continue to redeploy themselves through concrete ways of living in society.

4 Recognising the Coexistence of Consensus and Conflict on the Battlefield of Development

Development thus appears at once as a discourse, a practice, an ideology, a paradigm, a *dispositif*, a fiction and a power relationship. More importantly, the chapters of this volume point out that the meaning of development as a social action cannot fail to be historical and cultural. If they highlight national and regional differences, they also illustrate the reality of globalisation and its ideological and cultural hegemonies. Development appears as a relevant indicator of the degree of globalisation of the MENA region, where the political situation is all too often analysed as specific or exceptional. Each chapter places national experiences back in the context of a trajectory conditioned by generalising, global paradigms. Conceptions of development are not identical, and their links to conflict are not only plural but undefined and unstable. Once we abandon an abstract and general standpoint and instead observe development in its day-to-day form, the richness of this approach gives us a better understanding of the complexity of the relationship between development and conflict.

Beyond these variations, there appears one common feature: development helps build a consensus inseparable from the expression of conflicts. This becomes merely an apparent rather than a real paradox once we rid ourselves of simplistic visions of consensus. In the Weberian and Gramscian perspective adopted here, the convergence of norms, practices and interests is not the result of an intentional action or of supposed harmony, nor does it arise from a sharing of values, conceptions or meanings.[47] Instead, the multiplicity of perspectives and understandings, the differences of interests, and the plurality of logics of action feed into a continuous reformulation of the implicit factors that allow people to live together, precisely through the conflicts they are forever triggering. From this perspective, the distinction between developers and the developed—like that between rulers and those ruled and between the dominant and the dominated—is of little interest if our aim is to grasp the relationship between development and conflict: any active player is part of a

47 We develop this argument at length in Bono and Hibou (2016), drawing on Weber (1968 and 1971) and Gramsci (2011).

world view in which development is constructed as a consensual subject, while helping to preserve this conception, to modify it, and to create new ones.[48]

On the basis of shared beliefs and imaginaries, development presents itself as an indisputable fact.[49] At least two factors help explain this consensus. First, economic forms of knowledge of development tend to be considered as technical, objective and independent. This stance is based on the fiction that the economic sphere is independent of all political processes and able to regulate itself. The consensual nature of development stems partly from the way in which initiatives undertaken in its name are usually constructed and planned using tools that are intended to be technical and neutral in order to intervene on problematics themselves considered as objective. By questioning the objectivity of development, we recognise that it can be a place for the expression of subjectivity, values and ethics. Similarly, the fact that major development paradigms are legitimised internationally and that the expertise that accompanies them is often foreign—when aid itself is not directly foreign—helps give development an apparent neutrality that facilitates consensus. By questioning the neutrality of foreign intervention, we recognise that development can have different meanings in specific political situations. Second, the link forged between development and imaginaries of modernisation, progress and rationality also contributes to establishing this consensus: development is unanimously considered a desirable objective. Beyond the positive moral connotations generally associated with development, we need to carefully consider the processes of prioritisation and interests as well as the inequalities and asymmetries that any development initiative brings with it. By choosing as a case study 'development conflicts', we wanted to focus our reflection on the 'frictions'[50] that any experience of development generates. This stance has enabled us to simultaneously take into account the different conflicts and different kinds of understanding and apprehension of development and the consensus constructed around them, while defining development as a 'battlefield' on which prioritisation, discrimination and, ultimately, processes of domination are played out.[51] The situations analysed in the various chapters of this

48 On the multiple meanings of the subject in the processes of government, see also the reading of Foucault's conception of 'governmentality' in globalization proposed by Bayart (2007).

49 These issues are addressed in Rist (2002) and Cooper (2010).

50 On problematisation in terms of friction, see Tsing (2004).

51 For the same approach as applied to the government of the social, see Hibou and Bono (2016).

volume have helped to highlight three configurations that have structured this special volume.

The first part, entitled 'Conflicts that Create Consensus', brings together a series of articles that show in particular that disputes relating to the organisation of social life, the assertion of sovereignty, the definition of a social order or the construction of 'the ways in which one conducts one's life' contribute to creating a consensus on development, or at least to reinforcing it. Conflicts are necessary for a certain conception of development to become hegemonic. Hegemony, as Gramsci says, is born of conflicts and perpetuates itself through them.[52] To understand these conflicts, it is necessary to try and grasp power and domination relationships without limiting oneself to the concepts of coercion and the exercise of physical force and to give all necessary attention to the mechanisms that allow values and interests to be considered as *true and natural*, even though they are based on discriminatory and hierarchical processes. From this perspective, the point of transition between different hegemonic paradigms of development is a propitious moment at which to observe how conflicts build consensus. By studying, respectively, the assertive phase of neo-liberal developmentalism in Turkey and the role of industrialisation in the modernisation of the Ottoman province of Tunis, Ayşe Buğra and Nora Lafi show that the conflicts that accompany the shift from one consensus to another are related to the processes of 'creative destruction'[53] that punctuate the transformations of capitalism. Examining the case of Sudan as it achieved independence, Elena Vezzadini places less emphasis on the role of internal transformations within capitalism than on the paradigms that connect capitalism with the struggle for the establishment of an independent, modernising nation state. Finally, Merieme Yafout stresses the importance of laissez-faire and disengagement in the assertion of consensus with regard to a hegemonic vision of development in Morocco.

The articles in the second part—entitled 'Consensus as An Expression of Conflict'—highlight various examples of consensus with regard to development as a quintessential expression of tensions and conflicts that go well beyond such development. Indeed, development is never the work of a single group of actors who take the initiative. It should be understood as the result of a web of relationships and a constellation of social actions carried out by a variety of actors rather than as an explicit public policy that is definite, focused and unambiguous (a vision characteristic of analyses of conventional public

52 See Gramsci (2011). The analysis of Gramsci's terminology in Frosini and Liguori (2004) highlights this aspect.

53 To use the terminology proposed by Schumpeter (2010).

policies). Beyond the theme of brokers and intermediaries, it is important to consider the actors by whom development is furthered and interpreted—those who give it its colour and meaning, thanks to their style, ethos and modes of behaviour. In other words, one cannot understand the practical and conflictual dimensions of development without taking into account those people whom Weber called the 'bearers' of development.[54] By considering them in all their diversity, it is possible to observe the process by which their consensual actions vis-à-vis development can become the main field of expression for conflicts: these are embodied in the various conceptions of the common good, of the public interest and of development as well as in the many modes in which these objectives can be achieved, modes linked to different conceptions of the state and the exercise of power. Consensus about development can thus be a vector for the perpetuation and exacerbation of conflicts, as in the Afghan province of Bamyan, analysed in this volume by Fariba Adelkhah. Conversely, in their analysis of protests against urban projects in Tel Aviv, Adriana Kemp and Talia Margalit show that conflicts can paradoxically express a consensus. And consensus can also conceal conflicts of networks, power and temporality, such as those expressed in the implementation of the development plan for the city of Casablanca, studied by Nadia Hachimi Alaoui. Marie Vannetzel, finally, gives us another vision of this relationship between consensus and conflict by showing that in Egypt, for several decades, the whole machinery of development harboured conflicts of position between the nationalist elite and the Muslim Brotherhood; this machinery came to halt when conflict gave way to the triumph of one of the parties involved.

The third part, entitled 'The Definition of Legitimate Conflicts', addresses the theme of this volume from the vantage point of the contribution of development initiatives to the apprehension of questions of legitimacy. Development cannot be neutral if it is to avoid being ineffective. It does not appear here in the naive, technical, apolitical and sanitised guise that is often associated with it, but is presented as a targeted and thus inegalitarian social action (even if the targeting is extremely broad), an action that favours certain objectives and priorities over others, even if these are all numerous and contradictory. Development is by definition an action that differentiates and discriminates, often in the name of the war on inequality.[55] It is nonetheless a social action that influences processes of legitimation by modifying the representations of the state, of political space, and of social justice. The conflictual dimension of

54 Weber (1971), as highlighted by Grossein (2006).

55 Bono (2014) has analysed in these terms the construction of the 'responsible indigent' and the 'employable young person' as target categories for development aid to Morocco.

development is evident in the way its results are assessed, its inequalities are grasped, and the injustices it fosters are managed; but also in the way the violence inherent in any social action is fully taken into account. The neo-liberal consensus on development defined as a process of modernisation, reform and market expansion can then lead to the drawing of a distinction between legitimate and illegitimate conflicts, as suggested by Yasmine Berriane in her analysis of the commodification of collective lands in Morocco. In the case of Sudan, Raphaëlle Chevrillon-Guibert highlights the fact that the constitutive asymmetries of consensus regarding development can also generate conflicts. Anouck Côrte-réal Pinto, in turn, draws on the case of Turkey to remind us that it is essential to understand the means by which the national-liberal consensus underlying the developmentalist fiction makes conflicts acceptable, tolerable, marginal or even legitimate.

In our view, this threefold perspective contributes to the renewal of approaches usually adopted by studies in the social sciences to interpret the sociopolitical and economic situation in the MENA region.

First, this perspective undermines the idea that these countries are exceptions to the rule. This idea comes in different forms, including that of the ungovernability of the region's societies. The intrinsic contrast between the state and the population—related to the extraneous nature of the former and the indiscipline of the latter, or to the fact that state actors are detached from social processes—explains, it is said, the alternation of periods of submission and revolt, and makes these societies ungovernable.[56] The study by Adriana Kemp and Talia Margalit, and Ayşe Buğra's contribution to this volume, suggest that the neo-liberal moment cannot be reduced to a contrast between the state and society. Instead, they highlight a hegemony that underlies the conflicts and brings together ways of ruling and ways of opposing the rulers. In other words, neo-liberal practices form a common basis for the deployment of relations, interests and processes in which conflict and consensus, domination and resistance, inclusion and exclusion are interwoven. The idea that these countries are exceptions to the rule is also reflected in the way their markets are viewed as imperfect. This argument, often developed in terms of the economies of rent—particularly in the case of oil-producing countries and those that live by the exploitation of other natural or geopolitical resources, licit or illicit—is based on a historicist reading of the evolution of these countries and the idea that imperial and colonial experiences have imposed limits on the

56 For example, see Salamé (1994), Waterbury (1994) and Ayubi (1996). Those analyses that aim to establish the winner of the showdown between the state and civil society share this vision: see for example Fernández Molina (2011).

market economy.[57] Nora Lafi, Elena Vezzadini, Yasmine Berriane, and Anouck Gabriela Côrte-réal Pinto challenge this interpretation, and put forward three counterarguments: the inherently indigenous nature of the market, the importance of national movements in its appropriation and the ongoing process of reinvention that it is currently undergoing, for instance by the gradual placement of 'fictitious commodities' on the market.[58] Finally, the chapters in this volume offer an implicit critique of this idea of 'exceptionality' in the urban setting. With some significant exceptions, the literature on cities in the MENA region suggests that these are affected only marginally, and passively, by globalisation.[59] Nadia Hachimi Alaoui, Adriana Kemp, and Talia Margalit show instead that analyses on an urban scale allow for a detailed reading of the interrelationship between the space of the city and globalisation.

Second, this threefold perspective relativises and even undermines the idea that Islam and the strength of feeling inherent in ethnic identity act as barriers to development. In line with the theories of modernisation, it claims that Islam and ethnicity are based on values and beliefs incompatible with modernity, rationality and technical development.[60] Moreover, the low level of development supposedly fuels the rise of political Islam and the persistence of ethnicity.[61] The contributions of Merieme Yafout, Mary Vannetzel, Raphaëlle Chevrillon, and Anouck Gabriela Côrte-réal Pinto suggest the existence of different links between development and political Islam. They show that political Islam 'ordinarily' uses strategies of extraversion and fashionable international rhetoric and argue that it has thus become just as 'developmentalist' as secular political trends and plays a part in the neo-liberal paradigm as much as do other political movements. These authors also defend the view that religious reference points are an alternative source of legitimacy for new elites and enable the creation of new alliances that depoliticise inequality in the name of Muslim solidarity.[62] By exploring the reinvention of ethnicity and social and political bonds that has been produced by the processes of development, Fariba Adelkhah and

---

57 See in particular Beblawi and Luciani (1987), Richards and Waterbury (1996) and Henry and Springborg (2001).

58 This is the view of Polanyi (1944).

59 Authors who oppose this trend include Yacobi (2009) and Peraldi and Tozy (2011). For a critical analysis of this literature in the context of the Arab Spring, see Allegra et al. (2013).

60 The questioning of the relationship between Islam and modernity is a theme treated by Lewis (2003) and more recently by Masud et al. (2009).

61 Kepel's work (2003; 2006) rests on the idea that Islamism is a monolithic bloc whose birth was mainly due to an alliance between a deprived younger generation and a pious bourgeoisie.

62 Following Haenni (2005) and Tozy and Hibou (2015).

Yasmine Berriane also address the relationship between ethnicity and development in a new way. The conception of the role and place of women in Muslim or Mediterranean societies is often mentioned in this literature as another impediment to development.[63] Yasmine Berriane and Merieme Yafout address gender issues from a very different angle and show that women participate in the renewal of power relations within political movements and, moreover, that their positions as women contribute to legitimising certain struggles (and thus to delegitimising many others) and to the inclusion of certain actors (and thus to the exclusion of certain others).

Finally, looking at development via the connection between conflict and consensus allows us to see anew the issue of violence in the region.[64] These different approaches invite us to think about violence on the basis of the constitutive asymmetries of society rather than examining it frontally as a separate phenomenon; these asymmetries are considered as the normal and commonplace components of political relations and the exercise of power and not as features found only in the countries of the MENA region. Ultimately, many of our stances converge on a deconstruction of the concept of the MENA region defined as a well-delineated cultural and geopolitical area or as a homogeneous ensemble characterised by common trends in development.[65] By favouring one situated moment (the neo-liberal moment) and developing our argument on the basis of specific locations (geographic, but also sectoral, economic and cultural locations), this volume explores common conceptions of the region from a new angle so as to highlight the diversity of development patterns and thus the possible links between development and conflict. Multiplying disciplinary approaches—from history to political economy via anthropology and political sociology—we have abandoned a purely geographical or regional framework to adopt one that encompasses the relationship between global and local dimensions, including necessarily local perspectives on globalisation. Development is not analysed here as an explanatory variable or as an inevitable consequence, much less as revealing a stabilised 'culture' or the 'nature' of societies. It is defined as a set of complex social relations and a balance of power, oscillating constantly between consensus and conflict, a definition that highlights the extreme diversity of the situations observed.

---

63 This argument is omnipresent in the grey literature and in public debate. Various scholarly analyses and popular books have attempted to move beyond these stereotypes; Mernissi (1987) and Kandiyoti (1991) are among the first of these.

64 For a history of violence in the region, see Bozarslan (2008).

65 Our implicit critique of thinking in terms of 'cultural areas' draws on the analysis of this topic explicitly developed by Jean-François Bayart (2016).

This is what prompted us to put together this volume by taking the liberty of not remaining faithful to the boundaries conventionally attributed to this cultural area and not seeking regularities, convergences or divergences. Algeria, Libya, Syria, and Jordan are not among the countries studied, but we provide analyses of certain political situations often left on the margins or outside the supposed boundaries of the region, including Turkey and Afghanistan for ethnic reasons, Sudan for geographical reasons and Israel for religious and historical reasons. As the reader will have realised, the MENA region has been—for us—simply a pretext; a concrete place to think in general and generic terms of development as a 'battlefield'.[66]

References

Abu-Sada, C. and B. Challand (eds) (2011) *Le développement, une affaire d'ONG ? Associations, Etats et bailleurs dans le monde arabe* (Paris: Karthala).

Adam, A. (1972) *Casablanca, Essai sur la transformation de la société marocaine au contact de l'Occident*, Vol. 1–2 (Paris: Editions du CNRS).

Allegra, M., I. Bono, J. Rokem, A. Casaglia, R. Marzorati and H. Yacobi (2013) 'Rethinking cities in contentious times: The mobilisation of urban dissent in the "Arab Spring"', *Urban Studies*, 50(9), pp. 1675–1688, DOI: 10.1177/0042098013482841.

Ambrosetti, D., D. Chandler and V. Foucher (2012) 'Autour d'un livre: Mark Duffield, *Development, Security and Unending War*', *Politique Africaine*, 125(1), pp. 215–232, DOI: 10.3917/polaf.125.0215.

Amin, M., R. Assaad, N. al-Baharna, K. Dervis, R.M. Desai, N.S. Dhillon, A. Galal, H. Ghanem, C. Graham and D. Kaufmann (2012) *After the Spring. Economic Transitions in the Arab World* (Oxford, New York: Oxford University Press).

Amin, S. (1974) *Accumulation on a world scale: a critique of the theory of underdevelopment*, trans. Brian Pearce, 2 vols. (New York: Monthly Review Press).

Anderson, M. (1999) *Do No Harm. How Aid Can Support Peace—or War* (London: Lynne Rienner).

Arrighi, G. (1994) *The Long Twentieth Century. Money, Power, and the Origins of Our Times* (New York: Verso).

Ayubi, N. (1996) *Over-Stating the Arab State: Politics and Society in the Middle East* (London: Tauris).

66 This eloquent phrase is obviously borrowed from Enzo Traverso (2012), whose approach, combining the history of ideas, the history of practices and the history of contexts, has inspired us.

Badie, B. (1992) *L'Etat importé. Essai sur l'occidentalisation de l'ordre politique* (Paris: Fayard).

Bayart, J.-F. (2016) '"Dessine-moi un MENA!", ou l'impossible définition des "aires culturelles"', *Sociétés politiques comparées*, 38, http://www.fasopo.org/sites/default/files/varia1_n38.pdf (accessed on 13 July 2016).

Bayart, J.-F. (2010) *L'islam républicain. Ankara, Téhéran, Dakar* (Paris: Albin Michel).

Bayart, J.-F. (2007) *Global subjects: a political critique of globalization*, trans. Andrew Brown (Cambridge: Polity).

Bayart, J.-F. (1989) *L'Etat au Cameroun* (Paris: Presses de la Fondation nationale des sciences politiques).

Beblawi, H. and G. Luciani (eds) (1987) *The rentier state*, Vol. 2. (London, New York: Routledge).

Ben Achour, S. (1996) *Aux sources du droit moderne tunisien. La législation tunisienne en période coloniale*, doctoral thesis (Tunis: Faculté des sciences juridiques, politiques et sociales de Tunis).

Ben Néfissa, S. (ed.) (2011) *Protestations sociales, révolutions civiles. Transformations du politique dans la Méditerranée arabe*, Special issue of *Revue Tiers Monde*, 5, https://www.cairn.info/revue-tiers-monde-2011-5.htm (accessed on 13 July 2016).

Berman, B. and J. Lonsdale (1992) *Unhappy Valley. Conflict in Kenya and Africa*, 2 vols. (London: James Currey; Nairobi: Heinemann Kenya; Athens: Ohio University Press).

Berque, J. (1967) *French North Africa: the Maghrib between two World Wars*, trans. Jean Stewart (London: Faber).

Bonner, M., M. Ener and A. Singer (eds) (2003) *Poverty and Charity in Middle Eastern Contexts* (New York: State University of New York Press).

Bono, I. (2014) 'Indigenti responsabili e giovani occupabili. Il governo neoliberale di chi 'merita' assistenza in Marocco', *Meridiana*, 79, pp. 127–150, http://www.viella.it/rivista/9788867282814/3327 (accessed on 13 July 2016).

Bono, I. (2010) *In nome della società civile. Un caso di sviluppo partecipato in Marocco* (Milano: Guerini).

Bono, I. and B. Hibou (2016) 'Gouverner le vivre ensemble' in B. Hibou and I. Bono (eds) *Le Gouvernement du social au Maroc* (Paris: Karthala).

Bono, I., B. Hibou, H. Meddeb and M. Tozy (2015) *L'Etat d'injustice au Maghreb. Maroc et Tunisie* (Paris: Karthala).

Bozarslan, H. (2008) *Une histoire de la violence au Moyen-Orient: de la fin de l'Empire ottoman à Al-Qaida* (Paris: La Découverte).

Buğra, A. (2007) 'Poverty and Citizenship: An Overview of the Social-Policy Environment in Republican Turkey', *International Journal of Middle East Studies*, 39(01), pp. 33–52, DOI: 10.1017/S0020743807212528.

Burgat, F. and B. Paoli (2013) *Pas de printemps pour la Syrie. Les clés pour comprendre les acteurs et les défis de la crise (2011–2013)* (Paris: La Découverte).

Camau, M. and F. Vairel (2014) *Soulèvements et recompositions politiques dans le monde arabe* (Montréal: Presses universitaires de Montréal).

Cammett, M., I. Diwan, A. Richards and J. Waterbury (2015) *A Political Economy of the Middle East* (Boulder, London: Westview Press).

Canesse, A.-A. (2014) *Les politiques de développement en Tunisie: De la participation et de la gouvernance sous l'ère Ben Ali* (Paris: Archives contemporaines).

Cardoso, F-H. and E. Faletto (1979) *Dependency and development in Latin America*, trans. Marjory Mattingly Urquidi (Berkeley, London: University of California Press).

Catusse, M., B. Destremau and E. Verdier (eds) (2010) *L'Etat face aux débordements du social au Maghreb: formation, travail et protection sociale* (Paris: Karthala).

Chalcraft, D.J., and A. Harrington (eds) (2001) *The Protestant Ethic Debate. Max Weber Replies to His Critics* (Liverpool: Liverpool University Press).

Chang K.-S., B. Fine and L. Weiss (eds) (2012) *Developmental Politics in Transition. The Neoliberal Era and Beyond* (Basingstoke, New York: Palgrave Macmillan).

Collier, P. (2000a) *Economic Causes of Civil Conflict and their Implications for Policy*, (Washington D.C.: The World Bank), http://web.worldbank.org/archive/website01241/WEB/0__CO-62.HTM (accessed on 13 July 2016).

Collier, P. (2000b) 'Doing Well out of War: An Economic Perspective', in M. Berdal and D. Malone, *Greed and Grievance: Economic Agendas of Civil Wars* (Boulder: Lynne Rienner).

Collier, P. and A. Hoeffler (2004) 'Greed and Grievance in Civil War', *Oxford Economic Papers* 56(4), pp. 563–595, DOI: 10.1093/oep/gpf064.

Collier, P. and A. Hoeffler (2002) 'On the Incidence of Civil War in Africa', *Journal of Conflict Resolution*, 46(1), 13–28, DOI: 10.1177/0022002702046001002.

Conflict Sensitivity Consortium (2012) *How to Guide to Conflict Sensitivity*, http://local.conflictsensitivity.org/wp-content/uploads/2015/04/6602_HowToGuide_CSF_WEB_3.pdf (accessed on 13 July 2016).

Cooper, F. (2010) 'Writing the History of Development', *Journal of Modern European History*, 8(1), pp. 5–37.

Cooper, F. (1981) 'Africa and the world economy', *The African Studies Review*, 24 (2–3), June-September, pp. 1–86, http://www.hsozkult.de/journal/id/zeitschriftenausgaben-5504 (accessed on 13 July 2016).

Cramer, C. (2006) *Civil War is not a Stupid Thing. Accounting for Violence in Developing Countries* (London: Hurst).

Dardot, P., and C. Laval (2013) *The New Way of the World: on Neoliberal Society*, trans. Gregory Elliott (London, New York: Verso).

Duffield, M. (2007) *Development, Security and Unending War. Governing the World of Peoples* (Cambridge: Polity Press).

Eckert, A., S. Malinowski and C. Unger (eds) (2010) 'Modernizing Missions: Approaches to "Developing" the Non-Western World after 1945', special issue of the *Journal of Modern European History*, 8(1), http://www.hsozkult.de/journal/id/zeitschriftenausgaben-5504 (accessed on 13 July 2016).

Elyachar, J. (2005) *Markets of Dispossession. NGO's Economic Development and the State in Cairo* (Durham: Duke University Press).

Fellous, G. (2015) *Daech—Etat Islamique. Cancer d'un monde arabo-musulman en recomposition. Un conflit international long et incertain* (Paris: L'Harmattan).

Ferguson, J. (1990) *The Anti-Politics Machine: 'Development', Depoliticization and Bureaucratic Power in Lesotho* (Cambridge: Cambridge University Press).

Fernández Molina, I. (2011) 'The Monarchy vs. the 20 February Movement: Who Holds the Reins of Political Change in Morocco?' *Mediterranean Politics*, 16(3), pp. 435–441, DOI: 10.1080/13629395.2011.614120.

Frank, A.-G. (1968) *Capitalisme et sous-développement en Amérique latine* (Paris: Maspéro).

Frosini, F. and G. Liguori (2004) *Le parole di Gramsci: per un lessico dei Quaderni del carcere* (Roma: Carocci).

Gellner, E. and J. Waterbury (eds) (1977) *Patrons and Clients in Mediterranean societies* (London: Duckworth).

Gilman, N. (2003) *Mandarins of the Future. Modernization Theory in Cold War America* (Baltimore, London: The John Hopkins University Press).

Gramsci, A. (2011) *Prison notebooks*, trans. A. Joseph Buttigieg, 3 vols. (New York; Chichester: Columbia University Press).

Grossein, J.-P. (2016) 'Leçon de méthode wébérienne' in M. Weber, *Concepts fondamentaux de sociologie*, trans. J.-P. Grossein (Paris: Gallimard), pp. 9–90.

Grossein, J.-P. (2006) 'Présentation' in M. Weber, *Sociologie des religions* (Paris: Gallimard), pp. 51–114.

Grossein, J.-P. (2005) 'De l'interprétation de quelques concepts wébériens', *Revue française de Sociologie*, 46–4, pp. 685–721.

Hachimi Alaoui, N. (2016) 'Gouverner par moments. Le wali dans les transports urbains à Casablanca' in B. Hibou and I. Bono (eds) *Le gouvernement du social au Maroc* (Paris: Karthala), pp. 83–120.

Haenni, P. (2005) *L'Islam de marché. L'autre révolution conservatrice* (Paris: Seuil).

Henry, C.M. and R. Springborg (2001) *Globalization and the Politics of Development in the Middle East* (Cambridge: Cambridge University Press).

Heydemann, S. (2004) *Networks of Privilege in the Middle East: The Politics of Economic Reform Revisited* (Basingstoke, New York: Palgrave Macmillan).

Hibou, B. (2015) *The Bureaucratization of the World in the Neoliberal Era*, trans. Andrew Brown (New York: Palgrave Macmillan).

Hibou, B. (ed.) (2013) *La bureaucratisation néolibérale* (Paris: La Découverte).

Hibou, B. (2011) *Anatomie politique de la domination* (Paris: La Découverte) (English translation 2017 as *The Political Anatomy of Domination*, trans. Andrew Brown, London: Palgrave).

Hibou, B. (2009) 'Le réformisme, grand récit politique de la Tunisie contemporaine', *Revue d'Histoire Moderne et Contemporaine*, 5 (56–4 bis), pp. 14–39, https://www.cairn.info/revue-d-histoire-moderne-et-contemporaine-2009-5-page-14.htm (accessed on 13 July 2016).

Hibou, B. (2006) 'Maroc: d'un conservatisme à l'autre', in *Legs colonial et gouvernance contemporaine*, Les Etudes du Fasopo, pp. 154–196, http://www.fasopo.org/sites/default/files/legscolonial2_bh_1206.pdf (accessed on 27 July 2016).

Hibou, B. (1998) 'The Political Economy of the World Bank's Discourse: From Economic Catechism to Missionary Deeds (and Misdeeds)', *Les Études du CERI*, 39, http://www.sciencespo.fr/ceri/fr/papier/etude?page=11 (accessed on 30 May 2016).

Hibou, B. and I. Bono (eds) (2016) *Le gouvernement du social au Maroc* (Paris: Karthala).

Huntington, S.P. (1996) *The Clash of Civilizations and the Remaking of World Order* (New York: Simon and Schuster).

Jean, F. and J.-C. Rufin (eds) (1996) *Économie des guerres civiles* (Paris: Hachette).

Kaldor, M. (1999) *New and Old Wars. Organized Violence in a Global Era* (Stanford, CA: Stanford University Press).

Kandiyoti, D. (ed.) (1991) *Women, Islam and the State* (Philadelphia: Temple University Press).

Kemp, A. and N. Berkovitch (2013) 'Gouvernance pédagogique et financiarisation de la vie quotidienne. La fabrique de la microfinance pour les femmes marginalisées en Israël', In B. Hibou (ed.) *La bureaucratisation néolibérale* (Paris: La Découverte), pp. 23–47.

Kepel, G. (2003) *Muslim Extremism in Egypt: The Prophet and Pharaoh*, trans. Jon Rothschild (Berkeley: University of California Press).

Kepel, G. (2006) *Jihad: The Trail of Political Islam* trans. Anthony F. Roberts (London: I.B. Tauris).

Kraïem, M. (1990) *Pouvoir colonial et mouvement national. La Tunisie des années trente, tome 1: Crise et renouveau* (Tunis: Alif).

Kuran, T. (2003) 'Islamic Redistribution through Zakat: Historical Record and Modern Realities', in M. Bonner, M. Ener and A. Singer (eds) *Poverty and Charity in Middle Eastern Contexts* (New York: State University of New York Press), pp. 275–294.

Laurie, N. and L. Bondi (eds) (2005) *Working the Spaces of Neoliberalism* (Oxford: Blackwell).

Leonhardt, M. (2002) 'Providing Aid Agencies with Tools for Conflict-Sensitive Practice: Lessons Learned from Peace and Conflict Impact Assessment (PCIA)', *Journal of Peacebuilding & Development*, 1(1), pp. 39–56, DOI: 10.1080/15423166.2002.185405868970.

Lewis, B. (2003) *What Went Wrong? The Clash between Islam and Modernity in the Middle East* (New York: Harper).

Lonsdale, J. (1981) 'States and Social Processes in Africa: A Historiographical Survey', *African Studies Review*, 24 (2–3), pp. 139–225.

Mahjoubi, A. (1982) *Les origines du mouvement national en Tunisie, 1904–1934* (Tunis: Publications de l'Université de Tunis).

Malik, A. and A. Bassem (2013) 'The Economics of the Arab Spring', *World Development*, 45, pp. 296–313, DOI: 10.1016/j.worlddev.2012.12.015.

Marchal, R. and C. Messiant (2003) 'Les guerres civiles à l'ère de la globalisation. Nouvelles réalités et nouveaux paradigmes', *Critique internationale*, 18(1), pp. 91–112, DOI: 10.3917/crii.018.0091.

Marchal, R. and C. Messiant (2002) 'De l'avidité des rebelles. L'analyse économique des guerres civiles selon Paul Collier', *Critique internationale*, 16(3), pp. 58–69, DOI: 10.3917/crii.016.0058.

Masud, M.K., A. Salvatore and M. Van Bruinessen (2009) *Islam and Modernity. Key Issues and Debates* (Edinburgh: Edinburgh University Press).

Mernissi, F. (1987) *Le harem politique. Le Prophète et les femmes* (Paris: Albin Michel).

Mitchell, T. (1991) *Colonising Egypt* (Berkeley, Los Angeles: University of California Press).

Nemo, P. and J. Petitot (eds) (2006) *Histoire du libéralisme en Europe* (Paris: PUF).

North, D., J.-J. Wallis, S. Webb and B. Weingast, (2013) *In the Shadow of Violence. Politics, Economics and the Problems of Development* (Cambridge: Cambridge University Press).

OECD-DAC (Organisation for Economic Co-operation and Development—Development Assistance Committee) (1997) *Les conflits, la paix et la coopération pour le développement à l'aube du XXIe siècle* (Paris: Éditions OCDE).

Ong, A. (2006) *Neoliberalism as Exception. Mutations in Citizenship and Sovereignty* (London: Duke University Press).

Peck, J. (2010) *Constructions of Neoliberal Reason* (Oxford, New York: Oxford University Press).

Peck, J. and N. Theodore (2015) *Fast Policy. Experimental Statecraft at the Thresholds of Neoliberalism* (Minneapolis: University of Minnesota Press).

Peraldi, M. and M. Tozy (2011) *Casablanca. Figures et scènes métropolitaines* (Paris: Karthala).

Plehwe, D., B. Walpen and G. Neunhöffer (eds) (2006) *Neoliberal Hegemony. A Global Critique* (London: Routledge).

Polanyi, K. (1944) *The Great Transformation: The Political and Economic Origins of our Time* (Boston: Beacon Press).

Prestipino, G. (2009) 'Disgregato-disgregazione', in G. Liguori and P. Voza (eds), *Dizionario gramsciano* (Roma: Carocci), http://dizionario.gramsciproject.org/ (accessed on 13 July 2016).

Rabinow, P. (1995) *French Modern. Norms and Forms of the Social Environment* (Chicago, London: University of Chicago Press).

Richards A. and J. Waterbury (eds) (1996) *A Political Economy of the Middle East* (Boulder, London: Westview Press).

Rist, G. (2002) *The History of Development: From Western Origins to Global Faith* (London: Zed Books).

Rostow, W.W. (1960) *The Stages of Economic Growth. A Non-Communist Manifesto* (Cambridge: Cambridge University Press), DOI: 10.1017/CBO9780511625824.

Rougier, B. and S. Lacroix (eds) (2015) *L'Egypte en révolutions* (Paris: PUF).

Ruiz de Elvira, L. (2013) *Associations de bienfaisance et ingénieries politiques dans la Syrie de Bachar al-Assad: émergence d'une société civile autonome et retrait de l'Etat ?* PhD thesis (Madrid: Ecole des Hautes Etudes en Sciences sociales and Universidad Autonoma de Madrid).

Saad-Filho, A. and D. Johnston (eds) (2005) *Neoliberalism. A Critical Reader* (London: Pluto Press).

Salamé, G. (ed.) (1994) *Democracy without Democrats? The Renewal of Politics in the Muslim World* (London: IB Tauris).

Santucci, J.-C. and H. El Malki (eds.) (1990) *Etat et développement dans le monde arabe. Crises et mutations au Maghreb* (Aix-en-Provence: Etudes de l'annuaire de l'Afrique du Nord).

Samuel, B. (2014) 'Statistics and Political Violence: Reflections on the Social Conflict in 2009 in Guadeloupe', *Partecipazione e Conflitto*, 7(2), 238–257, DOI: 10.1285/i20356609v7i2p237.

Samuel, B. (2013) *La production macroéconomique du réel, formalités et pouvoirs au Burkina Faso, en Mauritanie et en Guadeloupe*, PhD thesis (Paris: Institut d'Etudes Politiques de Paris).

Sbeih, S. (2014) *La 'professionnalisation' des ONG en Palestine: entre pression des bailleurs de fonds et logique d'engagement*, PhD thesis (Versailles: Université de Versailles Saint-Quentin-en-Yvelines).

Schloms, M. (2005) 'Le dilemme inévitable de l'action humanitaire', *Cultures & Conflits*, 60, pp. 85–102, http://conflits.revues.org/1924.

Schumpeter, J. (2010) *Capitalism, Socialism and Democracy* (London: Routledge) (first published 1943).

Singer, A. (2008) *Charity in Islamic Societies* (Cambridge: Cambridge University Press).

Springborg, R. (2011) 'The Political Economy of the Arab Spring', *Mediterranean Politics*, 16(3), pp. 427–433, DOI: 10.1080/13629395.2011.613678.

Sraïeb, N. (1995) *Le Collège Sadiki de Tunis, 1875–1956. Enseignement et nationalisme* (Paris: Editions du CNRS).

Thomas, V., M. Dailimi, A. Dhareshwar, D. Kaufmann, N. Kishor, R. Lopez and W. Yan (2000) *The Quality of Growth* (Washington D.C.: World Bank), http://documents.worldbank.org/curated/en/2000/09/693286/quality-growth (accessed on 13 July 2016).

Tlili, B. (1984) *Nationalisme, socialisme et syndicalisme dans le Maghreb des années 1919–1934*, 2 vols. (Tunis: Publications de l'Université de Tunis).

Todd, E. (2011) *Allah n'y est pour rien ! Sur les révolutions arabes et quelques autres* (Paris: Le Publieur, Arrêt sur Images).

Tozy, M. (1999) *Monarchie et islam politique au Maroc* (Paris: Presses de Sciences Po).

Tozy, M. and B. Hibou (2015) 'L'offre islamique de justice sociale. Politique publique ou question morale?' in I. Bono, B. Hibou, H. Meddeb and M. Tozy, *L'Etat d'injustice au Maghreb. Maroc et Tunisie* (Paris: Karthala), pp. 153–207.

Tsing, A.L. (2004) *Friction: An Ethnography of Global Connection* (Princeton and Oxford: Princeton University Press).

Traverso, E. (2012) *L'histoire comme champ de bataille. Interpréter les violences du XXe siècle* (Paris: La Découverte).

USAID (2015) *Survey of USAID's Arab Spring Challenges in Egypt, Tunisia, Lybia and Yemen*, Report No. 8-000-15-001-S (Frankfurt: Office of Inspector General), https://oig.usaid.gov/sites/default/files/audit-reports/8-000-15-001-s.pdf (accessed on 13 July 2016).

Wallerstein, I. (1979) *The Capitalist World Economy* (Paris: Editions de la Maison des Sciences de l'Homme; Cambridge: Cambridge University Press).

Waterbury, J. (1994) 'Democracy without Democrats? The Potential for Political Liberalization in the Middle East', in Salamé G. (ed.) *Democracy without democrats. The renewal of politics in the Muslim World* (London: IB Tauris), pp. 23–47.

Weber, M. (1978) *Economy and Society. An Outline of Interpretive Sociology*, G. Roth and C. Wittich (eds), (Berkeley: University of California Press).

Weber, M. (1971) *Sociology of Religion*, trans. Ephraim Fischoff (London: Social Science Paperbacks).

Weber, M. (1968), *Basic Concepts in Sociology*, trans. H.P. Secher (New York: Citadel Press, 1968).

World Bank (2015) *MENA Economic Monitor. Inequality, uprisings, and conflict in the Arab World.* (Washington D.C.: World Bank) https://openknowledge.worldbank.org/bitstream/handle/10986/22711/9781464807350.pdf?sequence=4 (consulté le 11 juillet 2016).

World Bank (2011) *World Development Report 2011. Conflict, Security and Development* (Washington D.C.: World Bank), http://siteresources.worldbank.org/INTWDRS/Resources/WDR2011_Full_Text.pdf (accessed on 11 July 2016).

World Bank (2005) *Development and Aid Effectiveness: What have we learned, what are we doing, where are we going?* (Washington D.C.: World Bank), http://siteresources.worldbank.org/INTRES/Resources/469232-1127252519956/Overview_Note_Dev_and_Aid_Effect_06.23.05.pdf (accessed on 13 July 2016).

World Bank (2003) *Breaking the Conflict Trap. Civil War and Development Policy* (Washington D.C.: World Bank), DOI: 10.1596/978-0-8213-5481-0.

Yacobi, H. (2009) *The Jewish-Arab City. Spatio-politics in a Mixed Community* (London, New York: Routledge).

PART 1

Conflicts that Create Consensus

CHAPTER 2

Two Lives of Developmentalism: A Polanyian View from Turkey

Ayşe Buğra

Abstract

Developmentalism refers to a particular ideology marked by a sense of inevitability about the nature of historical change and to political interventions to implement particular strategies of development. The paradox between the ideology of development and development policy challenges the notion of market-led economic progress that proceeds without government intervention and is closely related to social conflicts engendered by economic progress. This chapter approaches capitalism as a socio-economic order where the idea of progress is central to the ideological universe. It also highlights the historically changing and societally different characteristics of capitalism that affect its ideological universe and determine the way conflicts engendered by progress are handled through political intervention. It argues that the concept of developmentalism needs to be examined with reference to the political choices that are situated in different historical varieties of capitalism and that differ in the ways in which they shape the character of economic processes and in their impact on the life and livelihood of the individual. This argument is situated in an analytical frame built by drawing on Karl Polanyi's work and by remembering the historical trends in development economics, and is developed through a case study on Turkey that shows the variations in the relationship between the economy and politics in different historical periods.

1 Introduction

Developmentalism is a term that can be defined as 'an ideological orientation characterised by the fetishisation of development, or the attribution to development of the power of a natural (or even divine) force which humans can resist or question only at the risk of being condemned to stagnation and poverty' (Dirlik, 2014). However, the term is also used in discussions of 'national developmentalism' with reference to the strategies of economic development

DOI 10.1163/9789004349551_003

promoted by international organisations and implemented by the countries of the periphery (Bresser Pereira, 2006; Kahn and Christiansen, 2011).

Developmentalism, then, refers both to a particular ideology marked by a sense of inevitability about the nature of historical change and to political interventions to implement particular strategies of development. There is, therefore, a somewhat paradoxical relationship between the ideology of developmentalism, which attributes to economic progress the characteristics of a natural force, and the very idea of development policy or strategy, which is about political action. This paradox between the ideology of development and development policy, first, challenges the notion of market-led economic progress that proceeds without government intervention. Second, it is closely related to social conflicts engendered by economic progress. The impact of the economic progress of different social classes or groups is never the same, but progress might also put social cohesion at risk in a way which might be unbearable for society at large.

Progress is central to the ideological universe of capitalism, as the following well-known passage from *The Communist Manifesto* clearly reveals:

> The bourgeoisie cannot exist without constantly revolutionising the instruments of production, and thereby the relations of production, and with them the whole relations of society. Conservation of the old modes of production in unaltered form, was, on the contrary, the first condition of existence of all earlier industrial classes. Constant revolutionizing of production, uninterrupted disturbance of all social conditions, everlasting uncertainty and agitation distinguish the bourgeois epoch from all earlier ones. All fixed, fast-frozen relations, with their train of ancient and venerable prejudices and opinions, are swept away, all new-formed ones become antiquated before they can ossify. All that is solid melts into air, all that is holy is profaned, and man is at last compelled to face with sober senses, his real conditions of life, and his relations with his kind.
>
> MARX and ENGELS, 2005 [1848], 9–10

This passage, in which we find probably the most succinct expression of what distinguishes capitalist society from all other societies, also makes us wonder whether any human society could survive without taking measures to control such a dynamic of 'creative destruction' in order to protect social cohesion. In his treatise on nineteenth century capitalism, Karl Polanyi discusses how the unleashed forces of economic progress would be inimical to the survival of society and argues that not only the form but also the pace of progress should be politically determined according to the goals of non-economic character.

However, the extent to which the forces of creative destruction are checked by political action or left to function unhampered differ in different historical periods and societal contexts.

In this chapter, I will approach capitalism as a socio-economic order with historically changing and societally different characteristics that affect its ideological universe and determine the way conflicts engendered by progress are handled through political intervention. I will argue that the concept of developmentalism needs to be examined in its relationship with the relative roles played by the market and the state in determining the character of economic processes and these roles' impact on the life and livelihood of the individual. I will try to show that the old and the new forms of national developmentalism are situated in two different historical varieties of capitalism with reference to the particular case of Turkey's economic development strategy before and after the country's insertion into the global market economy in the post-1980 period. The empirical case of Turkey also shows that the state remains an important actor in both historical contexts where development strategies are shaped within different frames of economic regulation and in both contexts state action is guided by political motives as well as economic growth related objectives. The analytical frame of the discussion is built with reference to the work of Karl Polanyi and the historical trends in development economics that closely follow the transformation of capitalism and change in nature in conformity with the characteristics of the historically different varieties of capitalism.

2 Analytical Backdrop

In Polanyi's *The Great Transformation* (1944), the word 'capitalism' appears very rarely and where it is used it is almost always preceded by a qualifying adjective—that is to say, 'early', 'industrial', 'agricultural' or 'modern'. Like capitalism itself, the existence of markets, found in all kinds of societies in all historical periods, is not the problem that is explored in this book. What Polanyi analyses is the nineteenth century market economy as a 'singular departure' from normal historical patterns where the economy remains *embedded* in society, subservient to the requirements of the norms that define the social order and assure its survival. It is only in the market society—where the totality of economic activity is guided by market exchange—that the economy constitutes an autonomous domain *disembedded* from society.

Polanyi discusses the concept of 'disembeddedness' in relation to 'the institutional separation of society into an economic and political sphere' (Polanyi

1944, 71) and the emergence of 'economic society' as distinct from the 'political state'. According to him, market society was conceived independently of law and government and its foundations were 'utterly foreign to the moral world of which body politic hitherto had formed part' (Polanyi, 1944, 116).

The separation of the political and the economic finds its expression in the principle of non-interventionism, which, in *The Great Transformation*, is explicitly discussed in relation to the problem of progress. 'Nowhere has liberal philosophy failed so conspicuously as in its understanding of the problem of change', observes Polanyi (1944, 33–35), and continues by writing that:

> Fired by an emotional faith in spontaneity, the common-sense attitude toward change was discarded in favor of a mystical readiness to accept the social consequences of economic improvement, whatever they might be. The elementary truths of political science and statecraft were first discredited, then forgotten. It should need no elaboration that a process of undirected change, the pace of which is deemed too fast, should be slowed down, if possible, so as to safeguard the welfare of the community. Such household truths of traditional statesmanship [...] were in the nineteenth century erased from the thoughts of the educated by the corrosive of a crude utilitarianism combined with an uncritical reliance on the alleged self-healing virtues of unconscious growth.

In his defence of the sixteenth century statesmen who resisted the enclosure movement only to be criticised by nineteenth century historians who qualified them as 'demagogic' or 'outright reactionary', Polanyi argues against the view that these statesmen had failed in their vain interventionist attempts and that their failure was proof of the futility of all interventionist attempts to obstruct the forces of progress by legislation. '[S]uch a view seems to miss the point altogether', Polanyi writes (1944, 36–37):

> Why should the ultimate victory of a trend be taken as a proof of the ineffectiveness of the efforts to slow down its progress? And why should the purpose of these measures not be seen precisely in that which they achieved, i.e. in slowing down the rate of change? [...] The rate of change is often of no less importance than the direction of the change itself; but while the latter frequently does not depend upon our volition, it is the rate at which we allow change to take place which well may depend upon us.

This passage clearly reveals that it is not development per se that Polanyi problematises. What is problematic, according to him, is the principle of non-interventionism informed by a blind faith in progress led by the *self-regulating market* which comprises all elements of industry including land, labour and money. As Polanyi puts it (1944, 72):

> [...] labor, land and money are obviously not commodities [...] Labor is only another name for human activity that goes with life itself [...] land is only another name for nature [...] actual money, finally, is merely a token for purchasing power which, as a rule, is not produced at all, but comes into being through the mechanism of banking or state finance. None of them is produced for sale. The commodity description of labor, land and money is entirely fictitious.

Polanyi writes that this commodity fiction is a logical absurdity, but it was according to this fiction that the nineteenth century market economy functioned and the faith in unhampered progress blocked the possibility of political intervention to prevent the inevitable human and social devastation caused by an institutional order where human beings, nature and purchasing power were treated as commodities.

While blind faith in the spontaneous forces of progress informed the liberal ideology of non-interventionism, the emergence of this strange institutional order organised according to the commodity fiction had nothing spontaneous about it: 'The road to the free market was opened and kept open by an enormous increase in continuous, centrally organized and controlled interventionism' (Polanyi, 1944, 140). Commodification of land, labour and money was realised by a series of deliberate interventionist measures and further intervention was required to make such a strange economic organisation compatible with human society.

Polanyi in fact presents detailed empirical discussion of the 'frenzy' of legislative activity as characteristic of the nineteenth century episode of capitalism, which ended after a series of disasters involving the Great Depression, the rise of fascism in Europe and the Second World War. *The Great Transformation* ends in the post-Second World War setting with Polanyi writing that 'After a century of blind "improvement", man is restoring his "habitation"' (Polanyi, 1944, 249).

Polanyi's vision of the post-war world economy was one where the diversity of instituting the economy in society was recognised. However, this diversity of choices was going to have one outcome common to all societies: 'the market system will no longer be self-regulating, even in principle, since it will not comprise labor, land and money' (Polanyi, 1944, 251).

In the period following the Second World War, in all societies grouped in the first, second and third worlds—in developed capitalist societies, centrally planned economies with communist parties in power, and (as they were then called) underdeveloped countries—the protection of the domestic economy with trade barriers and financial controls as well as a series of agricultural subsidies, wage and price controls, and different instruments of demand management precluded an economic organisation based on the commodity fiction. Labour, land and money were indeed not commodities.

The rise of development economics was situated in this international environment. As some of the pioneers of the field later observed, the global victory of Keynesian ideas over economic liberalism constituted an important source of inspiration to the daunting task they have undertaken with the optimism characteristic of the period. One of these pioneers, A.O. Hirschman (1981), later commented on this unrealistic optimism, adding that without this they would never have attempted even to understand the problems at hand. But they did attempt to understand these problems and they also understood the limitations of development economics even before the discipline had come under attack from pro-market liberals.[1]

Development economics indeed had many failings, the most important of which was probably the failure to properly address the political determinants of economic activity and society-specific policy approaches designed to shape the economy in line with the objectives of nation building and social cohesion or with the interests of ruling politicians. Such objectives often dominated the strictly economic growth oriented alternatives and seriously limited the successful application of development models.

Nevertheless, during the first phase of developmentalism these models were of a nature that provided ample room for protectionist policies, which could play a role in preventing the aforementioned kind of 'creative destruction' and its accompanying enormous human costs. This, as we know, has not been possible in the context of the market-oriented development strategies that accompanied late twentieth century globalisation.

In the early 1980s, at the end of this first phase of developmentalism, while the pioneers of development economics were engaged in thorough self-criticism,

1 See, among other essays on self-criticism by development economics, Hirschman (1981), Seers (1979), Streeten (1979), and Lewis (1984).

neo-classical economists who, until then, had been largely absent in the field, became increasingly vocal in their criticism of the sub-discipline. The demise of development economics was celebrated with the confident affirmation of the superiority of neo-classical economics and market-oriented policies. D. Lal's *Poverty of Development Economics*, which presented a particularly ferocious attack against what he called the 'dirigiste dogma' and 'the harm it had done to the vast bulk of the humanity contained in the Third World', has eventually become a very influential text, with several other editions following the first, published in 1983 (Lal 1983). This was not surprising in a period marked by statements such as Margaret Thatcher's 'There is no alternative' or Ronald Reagan's 'Government is not the solution to our problems, government *is* the problem'. The second age of global market society had begun and unbridled progress of the kind Hayek (1960, 39–40) associated with civilisation was the order of the day: 'In one sense, civilisation is progress and progress is civilisation. The preservation of the kind of civilisation that we know depends on the operation of forces which, under favourable conditions, produce progress.' It should perhaps be added that the phrase 'the kind of civilization that we know' refers to, or is even identical with, a self-regulating market society.

The global transformations of the last three decades have led to the emergence of a new capitalism with a renewed Hayekian faith in the self-regulating market mechanism strengthened by the demise of socialism. The markets, which were 'tamed' using different mechanisms in the post-Second World War period, have been freed to expand in a way that encompasses the 'fictitious commodities'. The second life of developmentalism began in the setting of this new capitalism.

As in the nineteenth century context of the self-regulating market economy discussed by Polanyi, contemporary market institutions were put in place by political intervention. In this process, international organisations such as the International Monetary Fund (IMF) and the World Bank, as well as the more recently formed World Trade Organization, have played an important role by presenting the blueprints for institution building, which have become the centrepiece of the international development policy environment. Economic stabilisation and structural adjustment were the key words and, apart from fiscal austerity, what they meant was privatisation, the liberalisation of trade and financial liberalisation, labour market de-regulation, and the elimination of agricultural subsidies.

While the previous mechanisms of protective state intervention were dismantled, the new capitalist order came with its own of mode of regulation, which is characterised less by retreat than by a thorough 'metamorphosis' of the state whereby political power becomes 'diffused' or 'de-centred' or is 'privatized'.[2] Hence, private–public partnerships of different kinds proliferate in different sectors of productive activity and in the provision of social services hitherto considered to be the realm of redistributive action by the state. At the same time, the voluntary sector is increasingly called upon to assume what were once the responsibilities of the state, and here—too—partnerships between the state and non-governmental organisations (NGOs) have become an important aspect of the models of good governance.

These models, which have been systematically discussed by the international organisations that set the present agenda for development policies considered to be viable in the context of the global market economy, are characterised by a blurring of the boundaries between the public and the private, between the governmental and non-governmental.[3] In the context of the new capitalism in which the approaches to development have been shaped, the 'network', as organisational form and analytical concept, has become an integral part of socio-economic relations and social analyses. As Manuel Castells (2000, 14) discusses in his analysis of the new network society, the state has now appeared as 'a network state made out of a complex web of power sharing and negotiated decision making between international, multinational, national, regional, local and non-governmental political institutions'.

What we observe in this context is a change from one type of developmentalism to another type where state intervention continues by taking a different form within a network society. While the nation state is limited in its capacity to interfere with the commodification of land, labour and money, intervention can still be motivated by political factors, which vary in their compatibility with the requirements of economic progress. As mainstream development theories and policies undergo an important change, they continue to be marked by the tendency to overlook the significance of those objectives of a political nature pursued by nation states. In the meantime, deviations from 'rational' policy lines continue to frustrate attempts to put national economies on the market-led path to economic progress. The case of Turkey shows how these deviations

2 The authors who use these terms do so in different paradigms of political power and state action. The terms together indicate, however, a major change from the standard forms of the modern bureaucratic state towards formations where the boundaries between the political and non-political become blurred. See, especially, Strange (1996), Chandhoke (2002), and Hibou (2004).

3 In this regard, the *1997 World Development Report* of the World Bank (1997) is particularly significant.

appear in society in specific ways that nevertheless reflect the nature of the historically prevailing variety of capitalism.

3 National Developmentalism in a Protected Economy: Turkey before the 1980s

Starting with the Union and Progress Party's rule in the early twentieth century, there have been intense debates on the development of a 'national economy' in Turkey. These debates have involved, to a significant degree the creation of an 'indigenous bourgeoisie' consisting of Muslim Turkish business people. A transfer of capital to these business people from non-Muslim minorities, who had a centrally important presence in the nineteenth century Ottoman economy, was an integral component of the new nation building project. Two historical developments have significantly contributed to an accumulation of capital in the hands of a Muslim bourgeoisie that has emerged with considerable state support: the government initiated the forced dislocation and deliberate massacre of Armenians in 1915, which reduced the Armenian population from around 1.5 million to 100,000, and the population exchange after the First World War, when 1.2 million Greeks left Anatolia. Politically supported mechanisms of capital accumulation continued to benefit Muslim entrepreneurs, at times at the expense of their remaining non-Muslim peers, as in the case of the notorious Wealth Levy of 1942.

These tragic episodes marked and tainted the twentieth century nation building experience of modern Turkey. They were obviously not in conformity with a rational economic strategy given the fact that entrepreneurship is a scarce resource and national development would necessarily be affected negatively by the elimination of the holders of that resource. Yet, even beyond the extraordinary circumstances of the war years, optimum use of entrepreneurial resources has not been the most important motive determining the state support provided to entrepreneurs. Government-business relations have continued to be influenced by political factors, and the potential to contribute to economic development has not necessarily been the main criterion guiding the choice of the beneficiaries of political support (Buğra, 1994).

Deviations from the pursuit of strictly economic goals have not been informed solely by nationalistic motives. To maintain social stability and, after the transition to multi-party rule in the post-Second World War period, to gain electoral support, Turkish governments followed a policy orientation that slowed down economic progress and prevented the commodification of land, labour and money.

The commitment to support the agricultural sector and to prevent the dismantling of the peasant economy was an important aspect of government policy from the early years of the Republic, and continued until the 1980s. In fact, one of the first economic policy decisions taken by the founders of the Republic was the abolition of the agricultural tithe—a major source of public revenue—in 1925. Agriculture was thus left out of the tax system and subsequent governments, even in the planned economy period between 1960 and 1980, have never followed a strategy of using the surplus extracted from agriculture to support industrial development.

This has been at times questioned by economic planners, among others by the important Keynesian economist Nicholas Kaldor, who was invited to advise on the tax reforms to be implemented following the establishment of the State Planning Organization by the government formed after the military intervention that had overthrown the Democratic Party's government in 1960. There are, in fact, anecdotes about Kaldor's surprise with regard to the tax statistics presented to him, which indicated that the agricultural sector, where the overwhelming majority of the workforce was employed, paid practically no taxes. According to these anecdotes, Kaldor, who could not appreciate the political significance of leaving the peasant population undisturbed, actually thought that the statistics had to be inaccurate.

Along with other forms of support provided to agriculture, the political choice that the statistics reflected was instrumental in sustaining peasant farms as the typical land tenure pattern and slowing down the pace of urbanisation. The urban population was about 25 per cent of the total population in 1945 and had only reached 44 per cent in 1980. After several decades of a first unplanned and then systematically planned policy of industrialisation, 45 per cent of total employment was still in agriculture.[4]

However, even these statistics do not give a fully adequate idea of the dynamics of rural–urban development in Turkey. The survival of family farms has defined a situation where immigration to the city has not led to a total rupture with the countryside. The remittances that immigrants sent to family members who remained in the village contributed to the survival of family farms, and these remittances—which were reciprocated by in-kind or in-cash support from the peasant economy—would constitute a mechanism of social protection for workers in urban industry or services.

4 Hobsbawm (1995, 291) observed that, in the 'neighbourhood' of Europe and the Middle East, Turkey appeared to be an exceptional case of a still remaining 'peasant stronghold' in the early 1980s.

Urban employment relations were situated in a protected economy with the risk of unemployment being much lower than that which currently prevails in open market economies. However, the integration in the urban economy did not only depend on the prevailing employment opportunities. There was another society-specific mechanism of integration, which owed its existence to the character of state–society relations. *Gecekondu*, the Turkish form of irregular housing settlements, in fact appears as a key to any analysis of the nature of the interaction between politics and the economy during the first phase of developmentalism in Turkey. The unique economic and social significance of irregular settlements in Turkey can be explained with reference to two factors. First, illegal appropriations of public land and housing developments without construction permits, which built on what were previously agricultural plots in the urban periphery, were enabled by the characteristics of urban real estate property. Hence, irregular settlements, which in another context of property relations would have met with strong opposition from the owners of private land with proper construction permits, could easily mushroom. Also significant in this development was a second factor, which was political. This pattern of irregular access to urban land was situated in a context where a proper public housing policy was absent, but electoral competition prevented political actors from being indifferent to popular demands. In this context, the habitants of *gecekondu* acquired title deeds through periodically enacted amnesty laws and the irregular settlements were regularised through the provision of municipal services, usually around election time as favours granted in exchange for votes. Hence, the *gecekondu* appeared as a society specific form of popular housing and the irregular settlements have developed to also include middle-class residences. However, it would be a mistake to regard irregular settlements solely as a response to the need for shelter. These settlements were also spaces of livelihood with a variety of both formal and informal economic activities gravitating around them. The inhabitants engaged in these activities could remain together with their family members in space and often in economic interest. Kinship ties could thus remain strong in their ability to provide support to individuals in social risk situations.[5]

This policy environment of the first phase of developmentalism in Turkey clearly reflected a disregard for the institutional norm expected to guide economic development in a market economy. Policies that were implemented checked the forces of creative destruction and slowed down the pace of economic development. Nevertheless, it would not be justified to suggest that the country's strategy of economic development was entirely unsuccessful.

5 See, on this, Buğra (1998) and Buğra and Keyder (2006).

State-owned enterprises and the modern firms in the private sector could contribute to a process of industrialisation that constituted the basis for the expansion of Turkish manufactured exports after the insertion of the country into the global market. These enterprises could also provide decent jobs—today conspicuous by their absence in Turkey, as in most other countries—at least to a limited segment of the workforce.

Nevertheless, such positive developments were overshadowed by the unstable environment created by macroeconomic mismanagement, which proved to be fatal after the oil crisis of 1973. Inflationary pressures and the growing deficit of balance of payments led the government to adopt an economic stability package imposed by the IMF in January 1980; but the package could be implemented only after the military intervention of 1980, by far the most ruthless and the most enduring of such interventions in terms of its impact on political and social relations. Turkey has thus entered the age of globalisation with a military intervention and, for those of us who were around at the time, it was quite surprising to hear the leader of the junta state, in his first public address broadcast on television, that the implementation of a market-oriented, outward-looking development strategy was among the objectives of that intervention.

4 The Second Phase of Developmentalism: Turkey in the Global Market Economy

In Turkey, the country's insertion into the global economy started with a thorough change in the foreign trade regime. Most tariff and non-tariff barriers to trade were eliminated, and the foreign direct investment regime was liberalised. Towards the end of the 1980s, capital controls, too, were eliminated with full financial liberalisation. While the barriers to agricultural imports were eliminated, agricultural subsidies, too, began to be discontinued without being fully eliminated. In the meantime, the most fertile plots of land in the western and southern regions of the country were sacrificed to tourism and real estate development, which had become the leading sectors for economic expansion in the 1980s. Thus, de-ruralisation has gained impetus; in the mid-1980s rural and urban populations reached parity and urbanisation has proceeded at an increasing rate since. Yet, the final hour of the peasant economy came only in the first decade of the new millennium, when a series of policies directed at the full commercialisation of agriculture were systematically implemented. Until then, agricultural productivity continued to decline in such a way that Turkey appeared to be one of the few countries in the world where there were no productivity improvements in agriculture between the early 1980s and the late 1990s (World Bank, 2001, 312).

At the same time, the *gecekondu* began to lose its basis of legitimacy as the indisputable need for shelter no longer seemed sufficient to morally justify irregular patterns of access to urban land. With the geographic expansion of the cities and the new popularity of suburban, middle-class residences, the inhabitants of irregular settlements and new immigrants hoping to find shelter in these areas found themselves in intense competition with real estate developers. However, the outcome of this newly competitive environment also only became clear in the first decade of the new millennium, when the urban property regime was finally established as part of a systematic strategy of urban transformation.

During the 1980s and 1990s, these trends continued without a proper regulatory framework in which a market economy could develop. Neither could the separation of the economy from politics be achieved since the political concerns of the governments in power prevented them from implementing drastic measures to eliminate all agricultural subsidies, organising the urban land market in conformity with the norms of private property relations or even refraining from attempts to control interest rates to prevent the ruin of many small and medium-sized enterprises. Ongoing state intervention in an unregulated market economy, which was nevertheless set out to function by treating labour, land and money as commodities, led to a series of crises, in 1994, 1999 and the worst in 2001. When the decision to eliminate capital controls was being debated at the end of the 1980s, Keynesian economists warned the policy makers that financial liberalisation in the absence of mechanisms to assure fiscal discipline was a recipe for disaster (Akyuz, 1990). These economists were proven right by the developments that followed.

The hold of the IMF and the World Bank on Turkey's economic development strategy became particularly strong after the crises of 1999 and 2001. In the aftermath of the devastating economic crisis of 2001, the coalition government then in power invited a high-ranking World Bank bureaucrat of Turkish origin, Kemal Derviş, to implement a series of market reforms. The main purpose of these reforms was to prevent discretionary political involvement in the economy. Hence, a series of independent regulatory agencies were put in place and existing agencies were further strengthened. The importance of the central bank's autonomy was also stressed and consolidated.

While these reforms were clearly in conformity with the logic of an efficiently functioning market economy, and could in fact play an important role in preventing serious financial crises in the following decade, the majority of the population—whose lives had already been devastated by the crisis—was not at all happy to swallow the bitter pill of economic rationality. It was thus not surprising to see the newly founded Justice and Development Party (*Adalet ve Kalkinma Partisi*, AKP)—the final reincarnation of a series of political parties that were situated in the Islamist National Outlook Movement,[6] and were closed one after the other due to their nonconformity with secularist principles—come to power in the general elections held in 2002.

The leaders of the AKP had drawn important lessons from the crisis-laden years of the 1990s. They had learned, first and foremost, the importance of the risks involved in any kind of intervention that would erode investor confidence in an open economy, given Turkey's extreme vulnerability to capital outflow. This called for respect for the regulatory framework of a market economy, but also required political stability, which any manifestation of Islamic radicalism would endanger. The rise of Islamic politics and the Islamic radicalism that marked the discourse of the Welfare Party—in which most of the leaders of the AKP, including Erdogan, had held important positions—had constituted a source of serious political tension in the 1990s. By replacing overt Islamism with references to the party's conservative liberalism and avoiding previously popular debates around Islamic economic and social institutions, the AKP, at least until quite recently, managed to keep these tensions under control by presenting its outlook as simply a culturally conservative one limited to references to the merits and potentialities of 'our culture' and the special emphasis placed on traditional family relations and philanthropy as an antidote to the social disruption caused by modernisation. But modernisation has remained an important objective and in an interview given to the *Washington Post* in 2002, Erdogan, the leader of the AKP, answered a question about his vision of a different Turkey by saying 'I will modernize Turkey' (Waymouth, 2002).

The AKP's commitment to a culturally informed process of modernisation respectful of market reforms was more than welcomed by the Western establishment especially in an international environment dominated by the fear of radical Islam. For over a decade, international media and many academic researchers presented Turkey under its 'moderately Islamic' AKP rule as a model that proved the possibility of successful economic development and a political

6 The origins of the National Outlook Movement go back to 1969 when a group of conservative members of the parliament split from the centre-right Justice Party and began to follow an independent political trajectory characterized by a religious conservatism that has taken different forms closely reflecting the political opportunity space defined by the nature of domestic and international developments. It was in the 1990s that the movement began to affirm its Islamist orientation forcefully. In this period, the Welfare Party (*Refah Partisi*, RP), situated within the movement, enjoyed significant electoral victories in municipal and national elections.

democracy in a Muslim country. 'The Turkish model' has often been discussed in terms of the extension of industrial production to some Anatolian provinces, where local business people have acquired a more important position in an economy previously dominated by big enterprises located in a few industrial centres. These new Anatolian business figures have been praised for their competitiveness and non-reliance on state support. Their Islamic mentality and outlook have been widely discussed as variables in studies on the rise of political Islam and the compatibility of Islam with capitalist development and political democracy.

While it is indeed possible to observe that religion has recently become an important element in business life in Turkey, the direction of causality between religious outlook and political developments seems to be somewhat different from the one generally emphasised in the literature. In the 1990s, the rise of political Islam with successive victories in Turkish municipal and national elections was accompanied by the emergence of voluntary business associations that used Islamic references in their organisational discourse and strategies. With close ties to Islamist politicians, these associations have played a role that is not limited to a straightforward representation of interests. They have, rather, interpreted Islamic identity in ways that are compatible with capitalist development and used this as a network resource to bind their members in coherent communities of interest and outlook situated within the constituency of political Islam. The networks thus established have been useful for small and medium-sized enterprises as channels of access to markets and as sources of input or technological know-how. They have also been beneficial with regard to relations with local government or to the formation of subcontracting relations with larger firms operating at the national level. The complex relational matrices thus formed with the active involvement of business associations could hardly be interpreted in terms of a unidirectional causality between the emergence of a provincial Muslim bourgeoisie and the ensuing political developments in the country.[7]

The extensive attention the media and academic circles have devoted to 'Anatolian Tigers' has been unable to provide a meaningful analysis of the relational matrix in question. Furthermore, it has precluded a deeper scrutiny of the nature of the country's economic development strategy and the interfaces between economic and political processes. During the AKP's first decade in power, attention was diverted from the fact that investments in infrastructure and construction had become the engines of growth and, like those in energy and mining as well as in the now commercialised health sector, these

7 For an in-depth discussion, see Buğra and Savaskan (2014, Chapter 4).

investments were carried out in a context marked by serious government intervention. The government has remained a crucial actor in investments in infrastructure and, in the construction sector, a giant of public administration—the Mass Housing Development Administration (*Toplu Konut İdaresi Başkanlığı*, TOKI)—has been able to acquire quasi-total control of developments in real estate in collaboration with private contractors. Government regulation remained important during and after the privatisations in energy and mining, which gained impetus under AKP rule. Meanwhile, the current significance of the private sector in the health care domain has not undermined the role of the government in the new system, where private provision goes together with public funding.

During the last decade, in all of these areas there has been a frenzy of legislative activity that aims to expand the scope of discretionary political intervention in these areas beyond the regulatory framework consolidated before the AKP came to power, and to limit the involvement of the judiciary in policy decisions to protect the public interest. One of the outcomes of these changes has been the limiting of the authority of independent regulatory agencies, many of which have lost their autonomous powers.[8] Higher courts still tried to intervene to protect the public interest with regards to the privatisation process, until their prerogatives in this area were largely eliminated by the constitutional amendment accepted by the referendum held in 2010.[9]

The legislative action taken to eradicate the barriers to discretionary intervention in the economy has been significantly directed at the creation of opportunities for capital accumulation in the hands of privileged business people. The spectacular rise of a group of big business figures who had no serious presence in the economy until recently has been a particularly striking development of AKP rule. Even those provincial small and medium-sized enterprises whose competitive potential has been widely praised have not been excluded from this picture of a politically shaped market economy. Although these 'Anatolian Tigers' could hardly take part in government bids related to infrastructure megaprojects or in privatisations in energy and mining, those with the right political affiliation and associational membership have been able to benefit from politically supported processes of capital accumulation as subcontractors to big business.[10]

---

8 In 2011, a government decree practically ended the autonomy of these agencies, placing them under the authority of the ministries in their respective areas of responsibility.

9 On this, see, Buğra and Savaskan (2014, Chapter 3) and Sonmez (2010).

10 In this regard, Article 15 of the Public Procurement Law, allowing the administrative unit granting the contract to demand that the contractor change the subcontractor, has been

The AKP government's cosy relations with these privileged business people have gone together with its increasingly tense relations with the established big business community, uncomfortable with deviations from the market reforms put in place after the economic crisis of 2001. Established big business figures who refused to provide their unqualified support to the AKP faced serious threats of marginalisation and, at times, punitive tax inspections. In this new setting of government–business relations, it is in fact possible to observe certain parallels with the early twentieth century history of the politically guided transfer of capital from one group of business people to another. Once again, this process is hardly in conformity with economic rationality, although it now takes place in a country that is active in the global market economy.

The policies of the AKP government have, however, conformed fully with the trend towards the commodification of life and livelihood that currently prevails in the global economy. Most of the legislative changes that have led to a complete restructuring of the agricultural system were introduced in the first decade of the new millennium. These changes include the elimination of state-supported purchases of agricultural produce; the restructuring of the tobacco, sugar and dairy product markets, which has opened them up to agribusiness; the 'seed law', which introduced intellectual property legislation that has also contributed to the increasingly important presence of agribusiness in the sector; a direct income support policy that was designed as a temporary measure to compensate farmers and support them in readjusting their crop choices during the phasing out of subsidies, but has actually led to a loss of crop diversity; and measures leading to the expansion of contract farming with the involvement of domestic and foreign companies as important actors in the trends towards the commercialisation of agriculture and the commodification of land.[11]

The dismantling of irregular settlements and the commodification of urban land has also been a particularly impressive achievement of the AKP. While the municipality laws of 2004 and 2005 have proved important in expanding the prerogatives of municipal governments in controlling urban land, the real turning point in this dismantling process came in 2007 with the Law for the Protection of Dilapidated Historical and Cultural Real Estate through Protection and Renewal. In a massive wave of demolition, eviction

useful in expanding the scope of discretionary political involvement in the business opportunities of smaller firms. For a detailed interpretation of the article, see Doganyigit (2009, 416–424).

11 For a comprehensive discussion of these transformations and their consequences for farmers, see Aydın (2010).

and reconstruction in Istanbul, Ankara and a number of other smaller cities, the inhabitants of irregular settlements were displaced. The mixed property structure of these settlements, in which owners as well as tenants lived, made the displacement process very complicated, but at times also facilitated it by allowing the authorities to benefit from the conflicts of interest existing between those entitled to different types of compensation and tenants who were often unable to secure low-cost housing elsewhere. There were episodes of resistance, supported by civil society initiatives, such as the widely known case of the gentrification project in Sulukule, the centuries-old Roma neighbourhood in Istanbul. The response of the political authorities to such resistance has involved the widespread mobilisation of the security forces, and appeals to the requirements of public morality and social order that have described the irregular settlements as hotbeds of criminality, terror and violence. As the head of the Istanbul Municipal Housing Administration succinctly put it: 'Terrorist groups and people who are involved in drug and women trafficking try to obstruct urban transformation projects, by manipulating innocent people who live in *gecekondu* settlements. Irregular urbanization breeds terrorism' (Bartu Candan and Kolluoğlu, 2008, 19).[12]

The urban transformation process was not, however, limited to the demolition of irregular settlements, neither was it only about changing forms of residential housing. In Istanbul and elsewhere, it proceeded unscrupulously at an accelerating pace through the construction of hotels, business plazas and shopping malls, and through mega investments in urban infrastructure, all proudly presented as signs of the country's impressive economic progress envied throughout the word. This 'impressive economic progress' was also related to infrastructure projects involving the construction of interurban highways, bridges and dams that extended to the country at large and contributed to the transformation of the countryside led by the previously discussed changes in the strategy of agricultural development.

While the impressive economic progress in question was not exactly blind to its impact on the process of capital accumulation, the forces of creative destruction have remained largely unchecked with regard to their impact on the socio-economic and natural environment of people. In the period following the economic crisis of 2001, Turkey's economic growth figures were quite good, although not very high compared to other Asian 'emerging countries', to emerging countries in Latin America, or even to the Organisation for Economic Co-operation and Development (OECD) average. However, unemployment

12 On popular protests against urban transformation projects, see also Deniz (2010).

remained around 10 per cent throughout the decade[13] and informal employment has continued to be important especially among female workers.[14] The failure of the prevailing economic strategy to create 'decent work' is reflected in the importance of 'vulnerable employment'—the self-employed and unpaid family workers, according to the definition of the International Labour Organization (ILO).[15] Flexible employment practices, especially the widespread practice of subcontracting, along with very repressive policies with regard to trade unions, have made it practically impossible for labour unions to be effective in their defence of workers' rights. According to OECD statistics, trade union density in Turkey fell from 20.8 per cent in 1986 to 4.5 per cent in 2012.[16] The dismantling of the peasant economy accompanied by the increasingly narrow urban opportunity space has forced people to accept extremely hard working conditions. Currently, Turkey is one of the countries where weekly working hours are the longest in the world and work accidents claim the lives of hundreds of workers annually.[17]

Under these circumstances, rural–urban migration patterns, too, have changed. As economic opportunities in the city have ceased to be attractive, people have begun to look to non-agricultural employment in rural areas where agriculture could no longer offer them a viable source of livelihood. Seasonal service work in tourism and employment in the privatised mining industry have been among the opportunities that have presented themselves.

Fatal accidents in the mining sector have recently attracted widespread attention in Turkey. Especially since a disaster in the coal mining town of Soma, which is located in a once relatively rich agricultural region in western Turkey, revealed the literally criminal neglect of basic safety measures in the mines operated by private subcontractors of public mining administrations. Unlike other mining accidents where casualties had been fewer in number, the Soma

13 World Data Bank, *World Development Indicators*: http://databank.worldbank.org/data/reports.aspx?source=2&country=&series=SL.UEM.TOTL.ZS&period (accessed on 7 October 2015).

14 Half of the country's working women are currently employed in the informal sector: TURKSTAT, *Household labour force statistics*, http://www.tuik.gov.tr/PreIstatistikTablo.do?istab_id=2258 (accessed on 17 November 2015).

15 TURKSTAT, *Basic Indicators of Workforce*, household labour force survey 2014: http://www.tuik.gov.tr/PreIstatistikTablo.do?istab_id=2257 (accessed on 8 October 2015).

16 OECD, *Trade Union Density*, https://stats.oecd.org/Index.aspx?DataSetCode=UN_DEN# (accessed on 8 October 2015).

17 ILOSTAT, Database of Labour Statistics: http://www.ilo.org/ilostat/faces/help_home/data_by_subject?_adf.ctrl-state=1au3aa3w04_321&_afrLoop=17358436464058 (accessed on 17 November 2015).

tragedy—in which over 300 miners lost their lives—received widespread media coverage that clearly showed the helplessness of a rural population that had no choice but to enter these lethal mines in the full knowledge of the threat to their lives that working there entailed. Erdogan, the then Prime Minister, reacted to the tragedy by saying 'such accidents are in the nature of mining' (Daloglu, 2014), which rightly caused outrage among a large number of people. Yet Erdogan's statement, in a way, conformed to what people were being forced to accept as natural in the context of the country's prevailing development strategy.[18]

In fact, shortly after the Soma disaster media reports emerged of a coal mine—this time in the south-eastern town of Şırnak—where the informally employed miners worked under unbelievably hazardous conditions. The mine was eventually closed by the authorities despite strong resistance from these workers, who wanted to continue risking their lives and to work in truly inhuman circumstances because they had no other source of livelihood.[19]

5 Conclusion

Protest against loss of livelihood did not always take the form it did in Şırnak. During the last two decades there have been strong popular movements against the forces of 'creative destruction' that have been unleashed in the new capitalist economy of Turkey. The massive, nation-wide demonstrations of 2013, which began in downtown Istanbul, were preceded by a series of local urban and rural protests and formed part of a wave of global anger reported by *The Economist* magazine in a cover story entitled 'The march of protest'.[20]

This march of protest was against the form developmentalism had taken within a variety of capitalism organised on the basis of what Polanyi called the 'commodity fiction', a capitalism that aimed to function by separating politics from the economy. In reality, however, government intervention continued not only to put the market economy in place but also to achieve objectives

18 For a comprehensive discussion of different aspects of the Soma mining disaster, see the report prepared by an interdisciplinary group of professors and students from Bogazici University: Bogazici Universitesi Soma Calısma Grubu (2015).

19 *Milliyet*, 7 and 8 July 2014; *Radikal*, 7 July 2014.

20 The cover of *The Economist*, dated 29 June 2013, featured four figures, representing the protests of 1848 in Europe, of 1968 in America and Europe, of 1989 in the Soviet Empire Bloc, and of 2013 everywhere. http://www.economist.com/printedition/2013-06-29 (accessed on 19 February 2017).

of a non-economic nature. In fact, in 2012 *The Economist* magazine published a special report entitled 'The rise of state capitalism: the emerging world's new model'. The report focused on the crucial role of giant national or state-controlled companies in the rapid growth and the increasing global influence of the 'emerging economies' including Russia, China, Brazil and India, as well as several others. The report's investigation of the subject was accompanied by the expressions of concerns about developments whereby 'the invisible hand of the market is giving way to the visible, and often authoritarian, hand of the state.' (*The Economist*, 2012).

The visible hand of the state in these countries was of course present also in the post-war period that preceded the globalisation of the late twentieth century. In that period, as now, economic development was an important objective pursued by policymakers and the conflicts of capitalist development were not independent of the political concerns of governments. What becomes important, then, is to see how the dynamics of conflict and conflict management articulate with the particular political economy setting proper to the existing historical variety of capitalism.

We have seen, for example, that in Turkey politically supported capital accumulation has always been important in defining the character of government intervention. Therefore, government intervention has not been neutral in its impact on different groups of people; beyond differences of class, both ethnicity and political affiliation have played a role in the way the opportunities and challenges of economic development have presented themselves to different members of society. However, during the first phase of developmentalism, the measures taken to prevent the social dislocations brought about by capitalist development from threatening social cohesion and political stability were also important. To control the dismantling of the peasant economy and to keep urban poverty under control, political authorities were willing to resist the commodification of land and labour at the expense, when necessary, of achieving a higher rate of growth.

In the current setting of the global market economy, economic-growth-oriented objectives can still be dominated by political concerns in a systematic and sustained policy orientation that serves the accumulation of capital in the hands of politically privileged business people rather than in those of other business figures who are not close to the government. However, attempts to prevent the commodification of land and labour are no longer in the picture. In other words, the forces of creative destruction are left unchecked in terms of their impact on the natural and social environment, but progress is far from blind to its impact on the business interests it serves.

The state–society relations of the past cannot provide models that can be emulated in an attempt to change the present order. What must be acknowledged is the need for a serious assessment of both the pace and the direction of progress in light of the requirements of a viable and just society. It is possible to affirm that this is the main challenge facing critical approaches to economic development in our contemporary societies—societies that increasingly appear to be neither viable nor just.

References

Akyuz, Y. (1990) 'Financial System and Policies in Turkey in the 1980s', in T. Arıcanlı and D. Rodrik (ed.) *The Political Economy of Turkey* (London: Macmillan).

Aydın, Z. (2010) 'Neo-liberal Transformation of Turkish Agriculture', *Journal of Agrarian Change*, 10 (2), pp. 149–187, DOI: 10.1111/j.1471-0366.2009.00241.x.

Bartu Candan, A. and B. Kolluoğlu (2008) 'Emerging Spaces of Neoliberalism: A Gated Town and a Public Housing Project in Istanbul', *New Perspectives on Turkey*, 39, pp. 5–46, DOI: 10.1017/S0896634600005057.

Bogazici Universitesi Soma Calısma Grubu (2015) *Geliyorum Diyen Facia* (*A Disaster Foretold*) (Istanbul: Bogazici Universitesi).

Bresser Pereira, L.C. (2006) *The New Developmentalism and Conventional Orthodoxy*, paper presented at XI Congreso Internacional del CLAD sobre la Reforma del Estado y del Administracion Publica, Ciudad de Guatemala, 7–10 November.

Buğra, A. (1998), 'The Immoral Economy of Housing in Turkey', *International Journal of Urban and Regional Research*, 22, 303–307. DOI:10.1111/1468-2427.00141.

Buğra, A. (1994) *State and Business in Modern Turkey: A Comparative Study* (Albany: State University of New York Press).

Buğra, A. and C. Keyder (2006) 'The Turkish Welfare Regime in Transformation', *Journal of European Social Policy*, 16(3), pp. 211–228, DOI: 10.1177/0958928706065593.

Buğra, A. and O. Savaskan (2014) *New Capitalism in Turkey: The Relationship between Politics, Religion and Business* (Cheltenham: Edward Elgar Publishing).

Castells, M. (2000) 'Materials for an Exploratory Theory of the Network Society', *British Journal of Sociology*, 51(1), pp. 5–24, DOI: 10.1111/j.1468-4446.2000.00005.x.

Chandhoke, N. (2002) *Governance and Pluralization of the State: Implications for Democratic Practices in Asia?* Paper presented at International Conference Governance in Asia: Culture, Ethnic, Institutional Reform, and Policy Change, City University of Hong Kong, 5–7 December.

Daloglu, T. (2014) 'Erdogan says mining accidents "nature of the business"', *Al Monitor*, http://www.al-monitor.com/pulse/originals/2014/05/turkey-soma-mine

-erdogan-accident-investigation.html#ixzz4Z7ZFyGKv (accessed on 19 February 2017).

Deniz, M.B. (2010) *Grassroots Action against Gecekondu Renewal Projects: The Case of Istanbul Basıbuyuk and Ankara Dikmen Vadi*, unpublished MA thesis (Istanbul: Atatürk Institute for Modern Turkish History, Bogazici University).

Dirlik, A. (2014) 'Developmentalism', *Interventions: International Journal of Postcolonial Studies*, 16(1), pp. 30–48, DOI: 10.1080/1369801X.2012.735807.

Doganyigit, S. (2009) *Açıklamalı, İçtihatlı, Sorun Çözümlü Kamu İhale Kanunu* (Ankara: Seçkin Yayınevi).

Hayek, F. von (1960) *The Constitution of Liberty* (London: Routledge and Kegan Paul).

Hibou, B. (2004) 'From Privatizing the Economy to Privatizing the State: An Analysis of the Continual Formation of the State', in B. Hibou (ed.) *Privatizing the State* (London: Hurst), pp. 1–47.

Hirschman, A.O. (1981) 'The Rise and Decline of Development Economics', in A.O. Hirschman (ed.) *Essays in Trespassing* (London, Cambridge: Cambridge University Press), pp. 1–24.

Hobsbawm, E. (1995) *The Age of Extremes: the Short Twentieth Century 1914–1991* (London: Abacus).

Khan, S.R and J. Chritiansen (eds.) (2011) *Towards New Developmentalism: Market as Means rather than Master* (New York: Routledge).

Lal, D. (1983) *The Poverty of Development Economics* (London: Institute of Economic Affairs).

Lewis, W.A. (1984) 'The State of Development Theory', *American Economic Review*, 74(1), pp. 1–10.

Marx, K. and F. Engels (2005 [1848]) *The Communist Manifesto* (Minneapolis: Filiquarian Publishing LLC).

Polanyi, K. (1957 [1944]) *The Great Transformation: The Political and Economic Origins of our Time* (Boston: Beacon Press).

Seers, D. (1979) 'The Birth, Life and Death of Development Economics', *Development and Change*, 10(4), pp. 707–719, DOI: 10.1111/j.1467-7660.1979.tb00063.x.

Sonmez, M. (2010) 'Anayasa'dan "Yerindenlik" Ayıklaması ve Tüpraş Örneği', *Cumhuriyet*, August10.

Strange, S. (1996) *The Retreat of the State: The Diffusion of Power in the World Economy* (London, Cambridge: Cambridge University Press).

Streeten, P. (1979) 'Development Ideas in Historical Perspective', in A.O. Hirschman (ed.), *Toward a New Strategy for Development* (New York: Pergamon Press), pp. 21–52.

The Economist (2012), 'The visible hand', 21 January 2012, http://www.economist.com/node/21542931 (accessed on 7 June 2016).

Waymouth, L. (2002) 'A Devout Muslim, Secular State', *Washington Post*, 8 November.

World Bank (2001) *World Development Report 2000/2001: Attacking Poverty* (New York: Oxford University Press), http://hdl.handle.net/10986/11856 (accessed on 7 June 2016).

World Bank (1997) *World Development Report 1997: The State in a Changing World* (New York: Oxford University Press), http://hdl.handle.net/10986/5980 (accessed on 7 June 2016).

CHAPTER 3

Workers vs Machines: Ottoman Tunis between Industrialisation and Colonisation

Nora Lafi

Abstract

The Ottoman province of Tunis between the 1850s and its integration into the French colonial sphere in the 1880s, was marked by the emergence of new issues directly arising from an international configuration undergoing profound change. This chapter aims to analyse the relationship between economic development, geopolitics and local issues in the last decades during which the province belonged to the Empire. It will home in on an emblematic conflict, one related to the fate of workers and artisans in fez factories as they protested against what they saw as unfair competition imposed by the European powers, and against the industrialisation that followed the mechanisation of production. These new operating conditions, in a market subject to the growing dominance of foreign trade and to instability in local production, gave rise to many protests. This chapter endeavours to compare and contrast the different levels and scales of this sector, to explain the impact of a new global dimension on local balances and the vectors of a new form of foreign interference. These conflicts also involved different ways of negotiating the reformed relationship between the Ottoman Empire and its province of Tunis in the face of the threat of ever-increasing foreign domination and colonisation. Focusing on the voices of the most modest local players, who spoke out to condemn the deterioration of their living conditions, and on the local and international context, the chapter aims to reveal the dynamic interrelation between different levels and issues, and individual destinies and wider perspectives, at a time of great historical change.

1 Introduction

Between 1860 and 1877, Tunis' urban society was stirred by a bitter dispute concerning not only foreign economic competition and the threat it posed to local production, but also the prospect that, in the capital of the Ottoman province, textile factories dedicated to manufacturing hats known as the fez (*shashiyya* or *chechia*) would be mechanised. Artisans and workers in the

© NORA LAFI, 2017 | DOI 10.1163/9789004349551_004

sector, threatened by this new development, protested repeatedly, addressing petitions to local authorities and the central government in Istanbul. The purpose of this chapter is to draw on these exceptional documents (the petitions themselves and the reports written in response to them) so as to interpret various issues related to the changing world of work in the context of great technological and economic change, and to the intermingling, at different levels, of local life and international realities. In Tunis, artisans and workers protested both against what they saw as the unfair competition imposed by the European powers and against the Ottoman response to this competition, which took the concrete form of a mechanisation perceived to be perverse and placed at the service of unbalanced development. They also protested against the tendency of local authorities to accept the new operating conditions of a market now dominated by foreign trade. The imposition of new conditions of production in Tunis was seen as a form of external control. This chapter will endeavour to compare and contrast the different levels and scales of this sector, in an attempt to explain not only the impact of a new global dimension on local balances, but also the vectors of a new form of foreign interference in a Tunis increasingly placed under tutelage. It also aims to decipher the different ways in which the reformed relationship existing between the Ottoman Empire and the province of Tunis was negotiated in the face of the threat of ever-increasing foreign domination and, before long, of colonisation. The development-related conflict analysed herein is read as an unfolding and deployment of broader issues that were the result not only of the economic development strategies adopted by the Ottoman Empire and the local elites of Tunis, but also of external interference exerting its influence far beyond the sphere of economic competition. A perspective 'from below' captures these issues in a way that brings out clearly the direct link between the living conditions of the population and major economic and geopolitical changes.

2 Historiographical Considerations on the Impact of the Industrial Revolution on the World of Artisans in Different Contexts

The publication in 1963 of E.P. Thompson's *The Making of the English Working Class*, a book destined to exert considerable influence, ensured that international historiography would begin to take a new look at the social consequences of the Industrial Revolution (Batzell et al., 2015). The shift from artisanal to industrial-type production began to be viewed not only in terms of economic rationality and efficiency, but also as an episode whose often traumatic social consequences needed to be studied. Thompson also stressed the need for a politicised reading of this transition, for which an analysis of the different phases of conflict can provide a crucial entry point.

The interpretation of the conflicts related to the advent and evolution of the various phases of economic transformation has since given rise to other important re-evaluations. For Europe, historians have shown that the roots of the Industrial Revolution went back to the various local forms of *ancien régime* and have stressed both the complexity of the processes of economic upswing and mechanisation (Verley, 1997) and the close link between the world of artisans and the industrial intensification of production (Guillerme, 1998 and 2007). This has led to a re-reading of mechanistic interpretations of the Industrial Revolution in which a simple technological innovation induced a paradigm shift affecting the whole economic system. Above all, we now know that the great nineteenth century economic transformation had actually started in the eighteenth century as an intensification of the artisanal economy of the *ancien régime* (Kaufhold, 1978; Cermann and Ogilvie, 1996). From arsenals to textile workshops, well before the invention of the steam engine, production had increased and the number of workers grown, fuelled by a large-scale rural exodus and sparking off rapid urbanisation. In many cities, there were real artisanal factories that employed thousands of working men and women whose work complemented that of thousands of female workers working from home. In other cities, the number of traditional shops and stalls had increased to such a degree that they changed the scale of neighbourhoods devoted to artisanal production. Hence, as recent historiography has taught us, we should move on from the outdated image of the history of artisanal production that portrays it as an activity confined to small-scale production activities. The mechanisation made possible by technical progress came to affect sectors that had not remained traditional, as might be suggested by our image of *ancien régime* artisans, since—in the eighteenth century already—workshops in such sectors had become real factories. This was especially true for Britain, France, northern Italy and Flanders. In the United States too, the link between the intensive artisanal development of the late eighteenth century and the industrial upswing of the nineteenth century has been established by economic historians (Dawley, 1976; Stott, 1996).

When mechanisation impacted on these workshops, it was not only the masters and their apprentices who were affected; thousands of workers also experienced this change at first hand. As proto-industrialisation had benefited from a large labour force, industrialisation and the mechanisation it entailed came as an even bigger shock. It was in this context that workers' protests against mechanisation developed. Logically, it was Britain, where the replacement of the working masses by new tools occurred most rapidly, that was affected first—witness what is referred to as 'Luddism', a disparate movement that was nonetheless united in seeing machines as responsible for casting workers into poverty (Randall, 1986; Thomis, 1970; Winpenny, 1990).

For regions long regarded as peripheral, it is the whole relationship to Europe that has recently been rethought in line with this questioning of the timing and the nature of the Industrial Revolution; a new critical approach to the study of the roots of domination and inequality in development has flourished. Taking into account the nuanced views developed by specialists in European economic history, and distancing themselves both from the topoi inherited from the colonial era (and even from the Enlightenment) and from those that paradoxically emerged from a critique of those former views, many historians of economic and social systems have emphasised the complexity of the phenomena of economic transformation. They have shown, for example, that the dissemination of technological changes resulting from the Industrial Revolution was not just a phenomenon that spread from North to South, losing intensity at every step due to the supposed lesser capacities of local societies to incorporate progress (Raveux and Sanchez, 2010). They have also shown that economic domination and colonisation were inextricably linked. In many cities too, from the Mediterranean to India, there had also been a phase of intensification of artisanal production in the eighteenth century. It is, of course, in the example of the Indian textile industry where historiography has made most progress in its analysis of the link between economic transition and the roots of colonial rule. In India, in fact, British colonial rule emerged in conjunction with the seizure of control over the textile sector, through predation on the markets and the clash with a competition affected by the transformation of the production system (Tirthankar, 2007). As far as Africa is concerned, recent historiography has also proposed new modes of analysis. For example, Bayart, with his concept of extraversion, is resolutely opposed to Hegelian stereotypes of an Africa rich in gold but still stuck in the early stages of exploiting its resources. Extraversion, for him, is typical of 'a systemic global economy that existed before the growth of the market and the capitalistic expansion of the West' (Bayart, 1999). Bayart disagrees with Rodney (1972) and Davidson (1969), according to whom it was changes in the European economy that led to the systems of historicity of countries that were thus relegated to the periphery. Instead, he proposes that we focus on African economies for what they were, and seek the dynamics of their evolution. He sees the formation of a rent of dependency as the historical matrix of inequality. This position is connected with the broader trend in recent historiography to adopt a critical attitude to judgments regarding what has been called 'modernism without modernity'—that is to say, technical modernisation without social reform: something of which, it is claimed, only the so-called peripheries would have been capable (Guillén, 2004). It is also connected to a critique of the narrative of economic evolution in what was seen as the peripheries, following the challenging of those ideas defended by Landes in *The Unbound Prometheus* (Landes, 1969) on the dissemination of transformations in production techniques from England to Europe and the rest of the world.

It is now accepted that ontological and civilizational types of language can no longer be used as such to explain discrepancies in development (Bryant, 2006). In many cases, local dynamics pre-existed the intrusion of Europe and its technology, and this invites further reflection on the consequences of the penetration–imposition carried out by Europe and accompanied by a destabilisation of previously existing balances. Following the lead of Latin American historiography (see for example *Dependencia y desarrollo en América Latina* by Cardoso and Faletto, 1969), a whole new vein of similar ideas has been opened up.

An attempt must also be made to write a history of colonised and colonising societies that can take into account the multiple dimensions of the relation of dominance (Conklin, 2000; Mignolo, 2001). We should also embark not only on an exercise of 'provincialising Europe', as the salutary slogan suggested by Chakrabarty (2000) has it, but also on a discussion of all of the elements underlying the narrative and analysis of the history of the aforesaid peripheries, be they southern European, African, Ottoman, or more generally colonial.

For the Mediterranean, long considered in historiography as an indolent periphery of hard-working Europe, resistant to the industrial application of technological progress for reasons often reified in a static perception of local anthropology, it has been shown that the characters of proto-industrialisation were indeed present at the turn of the eighteenth and nineteenth centuries, in the Iberian peninsula (Chastagnaret, 2000), in Italy, and even in the Balkans and on the southern coastline of the Mediterranean. The question of why industrial development over the following decades and centuries was—as has been noted—so tardy has shifted: the focus now is especially on the structures of investment and the development of logics of domination.

For the Ottoman Empire during the second half of the nineteenth century, we must also move away from the interpretive framework of the simple dichotomy between the importing and exporting of solutions based on technical rationality, and from such general ideas as 'Westernisation' and 'Europeanisation'. The reflections of Hamadeh (2004) on this subject are illuminating, as they encourage a certain scepticism towards the interpretive trend based on a skewed view of what is seen as inevitable Ottoman decline. The interpretive framework has thus been extensively revised. In contrast to inherited views stemming from the 1950s and 1960s, themselves strongly marked by a powerful colonial and culturalist heritage, a vision of industrialisation has developed, in the Ottoman context, of its origins and its dead ends, that has advanced hand in hand with the progress in analytical methods in economic history that can be observed on several different fronts. The existence of the conditions for proto-industrialisation and of strong and dynamic trading networks has been demonstrated for the main cities of the Empire, from Istanbul to Trabzon and from Thessaloniki and Alexandria to Beirut or Crete. Ottoman receptivity to technological innovation has also been highlighted, and this has demonstrated the extent to which the Empire was integrated into international circuits of technical expertise. As for the crises experienced periodically in various sectors, they have been read in the light of the link between international relations and local conditions. Stress has also been laid on the variety of local configurations and dynamics. But the Ottoman case is specific in that it presents a situation that was deteriorating as a result of European competition that was not only economic, and gradually becoming more capitalistic, but also involved an element of interference in both diplomatic and military spheres, and often led to a violent occupation of the colonial kind. Development-related conflicts arising from industrialisation in the Ottoman Empire thus need to be interpreted in a specific light, combining the rapid economic, social and technological transformations that occurred with the pressures arising from an initially ambiguous relationship and then, clearly, from aggressive hostility. Quataert (1986) illustrates this intermingling of issues and levels with regard to Anatolia. Masters (1988), meanwhile, shows how early such ambiguities arose in the Ottoman Levant. For Egypt, the pioneering work of Fahmi (1954) demonstrates the depth of the transformation of the productive apparatus in Cairo in the eighteenth century and the extent of its social consequences in the nineteenth century—a mixture of intensification, mechanisation and crisis. From the work of Faroqhi and Hanna, we also now know that the milieu of Ottoman artisans had, during the eighteenth and early nineteenth centuries, experienced profound changes characterised by huge growth in production and manpower and an upheaval in the guild-based management structures inherited from the *ancien régime* (Faroqhi, 2009; Hanna, 2011). This was followed by a real slump in economic affairs of the Ottoman Empire, as a result of both the 'Great European Depression' of the 1880s and what had by then become an asymmetrical relationship (Pamuk, 1984). European competition, the Ottoman slump, and vectors of domination were thus linked. New goods and the paths via which they were traded were often imposed by foreign consular networks in the Ottoman provinces. Patronage networks were created, that partly incorporated the economy of the *ancien régime*, with the so-called capitulations of the Ottoman Empire, while changing its nature and intensity. The structures of the local artisanal system, structures that—far from being inert—had allowed an intensification of production in the late eighteenth century were destabilised. The textile sector crisis suffered by Tunis in the second half of the nineteenth century illustrates this logic and allows us to reflect on the links between economic change, foreign domination, and Ottoman imperial destiny.

3 The Crisis Experienced by Fez Manufacturers in Tunis: A Development-Related Conflict and a Symptom of the Emergence of Colonial Issues

In Tunis during the second half of the nineteenth century, fez manufacturers, and sometimes even their workers, were repeatedly driven to protest—protests that took the form of petitions—against mechanisation, unfair competition from abroad, and the lack of protection for their products on export markets when those products were faced with the desire of other nations with ambitions to expand their own markets. The National Archives in Tunis house evidence of many such initiatives, and an analysis of these documents lies at the heart of this chapter.[1] Such an analysis enables the historian to perceive not only the actors of the conflict, their interactions and their arguments, but also the way in which they negotiated and constructed a form of consensus through conflict. These archives also help one develop a kind of micro-history of transformations that are generally interpreted only via broad globalised narratives. In these archives (where conflicts also produce further archives ...), underlying development-related conflicts are noticeable. The occurrence of such conflicts reflects the way in which the Ottoman Empire tried to implement major economic reforms in what was then—since the loss of Algeria to French colonisation between 1830 and 1850—its westernmost province, in tandem with the administrative reforms that it also promoted. In view of the involvement of foreign consulates and foreign chambers of commerce in the economic life of the province of Tunis, these conflicts also reflect the increasing influence of European powers in the Ottoman province, which in 1881 led to its military occupation and colonisation by France (Ganiage, 1959). The challenge for the entire economy of the Ottoman province of Tunis was, in fact, not only an economic modernisation linked to significant technical and capitalistic transformations, but also its relationship with the Empire and foreign domination.

1 ANT (Archives nationales de Tunisie), Series H (silsila al-tarikiyya: Historical Series), box 72, files 857 to 860.

The conflict that stirred the Tunisian textile sector in the 1860s and 1870s was indeed a development-related conflict: an entire sector revolted against the new conditions of production and integration into the international market, a major change by comparison to the previous economic situation in which the local economy had hitherto developed.

The fez had been produced in Tunis at least since the arrival of refugee artisans from Spain in the fifteenth century (Teyssier, 1962; Ferchiou, 1971; Bakalti, 1996; Ben Miled, 2010). Those refugees had fled the ethnic and religious cleansing campaigns undertaken during the different phases of the Christian reconquista as it swept through al-Andalus; they then settled in various cities of North Africa, including Tunis (Abidi, 2016). They benefited from the leniency of the various local authorities and created their guilds anew. Some historians, however, think that the fez originated in the city of Kairouan. From here, they claim, the tradition passed into Muslim Spain, and then back to Tunisia (Bachrouch, 2008). Integration into the Ottoman Empire—confirmed in 1574 but already largely effective, as regards trade, after the protection of the city against Christian attacks provided by the Ottoman corsair Barbarossa several decades earlier—comprised a favourable set of circumstances for the development of the textile industry, and particularly the production of fezzes. At the beginning of the Ottoman period, artisanal activity in Tunis was structured, to a significant extent, around this booming activity, bringing together the manpower of an entire region thanks to existence of then new outlets throughout the Ottoman world. Sheep rearing (fezzes are made of wool) also developed and provided additional prosperity to those living in the countryside. Much of the wool used was, however, still imported from Spain, as well as from Sicily and Sardinia. Urban infrastructure, including dyeing vats, was placed at the service of this sector. In Tunis, fez manufacturers were generally located in the medina, but also in the suburb of Ariana. During the sixteenth and seventeenth centuries, this activity came to represent a flagship economic sector for the Ottoman province. Each phase of production had a precise location either in town or in the surrounding area (Bachrouch, 2008). Boubaker shows that the export of fezzes to the entirety of the Ottoman Empire constituted the main manufactured item exported through the port of Tunis (Boubaker, 2003). The cities of the Levant, from Damascus to Aleppo and from Jerusalem to Beirut, were reliable markets. But the same was also true of cities such as Smyrna or Salonica. The Ottoman army was also a major customer. Fezzes were also often bought and worn throughout Mediterranean Europe, as evidenced by numerous Sardinian and Sicilian engravings and descriptions. The fez was, in short, the main example of the Imperial Ottoman dimension of *ancien régime* trade and a certain globalisation of artisanal production throughout the Mediterranean. The term 'artisanal', however, should not mislead us as to the scale and nature of production activities that, even before mechanisation, was highly intensive. It has been calculated that around 5,000 workers were employed in fez factories in the medina of Tunis and adjacent suburbs in the late eighteenth century (Spring and Hudson, 2004). The French travellers Peyssonnel and Desfontaines estimate that between 15,000 and 20,000 people were employed as manual workers, artisans, or apprentices in 1724 (Peyssonnel and Desfontaines, 1838; Bachrouch, 2008). Production in 1760 is estimated to have been 660,000 units per year, double what it was in 1740 (Boubaker, 2003). With the monopoly Tunis enjoyed in the Empire, the margins on sales of this product were, for the trading companies of Tunis, quite comfortable. Youssef Sahib al-Tabaa, active in the eighteenth century and influential in the spectacular growth of the sector at that time, is emblematic of the fortunes made by Tunisian merchants engaged in the fez trade throughout the Ottoman Empire.

The milieu of the fez manufacturers was very hierarchical, from the workers and apprentices to the big merchants. But with industrial and proto-industrial development, the pyramid of skills and symbolic hierarchies changed. A growing number of workers filled the increasingly large workshops. Along with olive oil producers, fez manufacturers (the term as used here refers to the owners of these workshops and the organisers of this trade) thus formed a well-off class that had emerged from a guild that had not originally been one of the most noble, but that was well established in the urban environment and local society, and had connections throughout the Empire (Hadi Cherif, 1970). The elite of these fez producers was made up of some 300 masters (Tunger-Zanetti, 1996).

But with the arrival of mechanisation, and new competition from Europe and other Ottoman cities engaged in an effort to modernise, the whole of the Tunis textile industry faced a major test that challenged not only the production system, but also the existence of commercial opportunities and the entire social system that depended on them, causing a significant drop in living standards for the working men and women concerned. The two phenomena were related but different: new competition emerged as new players entered the market, and as certain Tunis entrepreneurs tried to respond by mechanising their activity they came into conflict with the traditional hierarchy of the guild. But the crisis had actually begun well before mechanisation took place. So it was, first, a crisis brought about by new and aggressive competitors breaking into a traditionally exclusive market. From the 1780s onwards, trading companies in Orléans, Lyon and Marseille managed to force the whole of the Ottoman Empire to accept the textile production of their respective regions, through a mixture of commercial dynamism, (pre-)industrial espionage and diplomatic pressure exerted on the Empire.[2] From this time onwards, European consuls brought pressure to bear on local authorities and the Empire, resorting to threats of military action if necessary, to force them to agree to revise the terms of former trade agreements. The intensification of artisanal production in Europe, which foreshadowed the Industrial Revolution, also created unprecedented differences in cost prices. Even the fez sector, which had seemed to possess a cultural specificity that placed it beyond the reach of competition from another continent, was affected by this transformation (Valensi, 1969). To penetrate the Ottoman market, a veritable system of technological espionage was set up through the consular network, at a time when consuls were still generally merchants: dyes, weaving and crushing processes, trading posts, customs provisions, and transport arrangements: all were targeted for close observation by the new competitors in order to create similar products and ensure market penetration. Diplomatic efforts, requested by chambers of commerce, ensured that permission was obtained to import products into the Empire, if necessary by exerting a pressure that foreshadowed the more active interventions of the coming century. And European expansion into Tunisia, and the Ottoman Empire in general, was not unconnected to the transformations then taking place in the European textile and artisanal sector (and before long in the industrial sector too). The entire way the province of Tunis was positioned in the Ottoman market, and its relationship to the Empire, were thus rapidly undermined. This phenomenon was further complicated by the appearance of native Ottoman competition due to the development (desired by various reformers) of a fez industry in Cairo from 1825 onwards (Fahmi, 1954) and in Istanbul from 1827. Muhammad Ali's government brought in experts from the fez-makers' guild of Tunis to create a new production structure locally in Cairo. In the 1830s, fez-manufacturing workshops in Cairo employed more than 2,000 workers. The sale of fezzes, initially confined to the Egyptian army, was opened up to the general public and the export market in 1834 (Fahmi, 1954). This development symbolised Muhammad Ali's wish to see Egypt enter a phase of economic transition that would lead it towards industrialisation (Thieck, 1992). In Istanbul, to deal with the order placed by the Ottoman army for more than 50,000 fezzes, Tunisian master hosiers were asked to set up manufacturing structures (Tunger-Zanetti, 1996). These initially mimicked the guild-based structure found in Tunis, but then moved towards a less rigid, industrial-type method of organisation. The figure of 'Umar al-'Abrî, a dealer

2 See Archives of the Chambre de Commerce de Marseille, CCC, LIII, 360: Correspondants à l'étranger: Barbarie.

in fezzes who was close to the government in both Istanbul and Tunis, embodied this transfer between 1829 and the 1860s. His networks in the imperial capital and the way he drew upon them to further his business interests naturally led to arguments with the artisans of Tunis (Tunger-Zanetti, 1996). The conflicts discussed below also stemmed in part from a rivalry between, on the one hand, people from Tunis living both there and in Istanbul, who were keen on industrial modernisation (these included 'Umar al-'Abrî and Yahyâ Arway, who were close to the reformer Khayr al-Dîn), and, on the other, the profession's guild base.

Thus, in the mid-nineteenth century, the position of Tunis exporters had already become difficult due to the shrinking of the Ottoman market and the advent of European competition—but also because of emerging tensions in Tunis itself. The artisanal sector in general was facing an almost existential crisis (Penec, 1964). And it was here where the first popular Maghrebi opposition to mechanisation occurred. Even if we cannot quite use the term 'Luddism', as the archives for Tunis do not directly record any acts of sabotage targeting the machines being introduced into the artisanal sector as it transformed into an industry, the rhetoric of protest against the replacement of the labour force by machines was clearly in evidence. First and foremost, the various players in the industry resorted to petitions in an attempt to express their grievances both to the provincial authorities and to those in Istanbul. In the Ottoman administrative system of the *ancien régime*, the petition lay at the heart of the processes of mediation and of consensus building during phases of conflict (Lafi, 2012).[3] It also lay at the core of decision-making procedures: any petition entailed, both in Istanbul and in the province concerned, the opening of an official file, and the response to each petition involved an investigation, interviews, and a rescript—that is to say, the formalisation of the decision taken (Lafi, 2011). A summary of each petition was placed by the administration at the beginning of the file. Local chronicles—true civic annals—recorded the submission of petitions and provide evidence of their existence and kind.[4] For fez makers, the submission of these numerous petitions points to a shared economic, social, civic and political awareness of the group as an urban and professional milieu faced by the economic adversity occasioned both by foreign competitors and by Ottoman modernisers close to the Tunisian local government. These petitions are evidence of a collective mobilisation that aimed not only

3 It also needs to be said that, in terms of mentality, this feature largely survived the modernising reforms of the era of the *Tanzimat* (Reforms), which—between the 1830s and the 1870s, and throughout the whole Empire—promoted a new bureaucratic rationality.

4 See the accounts in Bayram al-Khâmis (2000) and Ben Diaf (2004).

to draw attention to a particular problem, but also to force the political system to respond and recreate the conditions necessary for a local consensus. They also reflected the way in which—at every level—local, imperial and geopolitical issues were interrelated.

The Ottomans and the Tunisian local government—in an effort to develop the province and the Empire and to ward off the new competition—decided, in the late 1850s, to mechanise the manufacture of fezzes. To do so, they called on various foreign experts, who offered to supply steam engines. The Ottomans also modernised the infrastructural framework by building dams to improve the supply of water to fez factories. The souks themselves were modernised in a similar way. All this took place in the context of the Tunisian province following the enactment of the Fundamental Pact in 1857, and the negotiations between the government, reforming ministers and foreign consuls that led, in 1861, to the adoption of the constitution. Khayr al-Dîn played a decisive role in this movement (Van Krieken, 1976). The negotiations were largely concerned with determining the extent to which foreigners would be allowed to wield economic influence over the province. Reformers such as Khayr al-Dîn were proponents of economic modernisation aiming for industrial development that alone could free the province from foreign domination; they were also, in this modernisation process, the ambiguous partners of consuls, bankers and foreign investors. The rejection of mechanisation by the guild base, whose organisation was itself challenged by the reforms, was therefore both a rejection of the reformers (and the imperial and local Tunis-based economic circles close to them) and a rejection of foreign influence, already perceived as a vehicle for domination, in the economy. The guild base had already, in support of its leadership, mobilised en masse a few decades earlier to prevent fezzes produced in Europe being sold in the Tunis souk: 'In the past, Christians introduced fezzes they had produced at home. They were forbidden to approach the Tunis souk as it would harm our industry' (Bachrouch, 2008, 800). Several petitions submitted at the time had led to the banning of these imports and protected Tunisian production throughout the Empire. In 1860, in a context that had itself evolved due to the opening of the Tunisian market to foreigners following the Fundamental Pact and its various accompanying measures, protests against the import of European fezzes resumed, led by Hassûna al-Wazîr, the *amîn* (representative of the guild) of fez traders and producers: 'Today we are seeing them launch a new offensive. If this goes on, we will completely lose our profession' (Bachrouch, 2008, 802–803). The petition was ignored by the authorities. Hassûna al-Wazîr was not allowed to present his case to the ministry. None of the negotiating procedures normally instigated in response to a petition was opened. The following year, faced with the worsening of the sector's economic situation, and also with the prospect of modernisation leading to increasing mechanisation—modernisation supported by the authorities themselves—the case took a new turn.

The main petition considered here was part of this context in which the leaders of the profession, and its base, mobilised against the local government of the province and against the entrepreneurs who, in their view, were siding with both modernisers and foreigners.[5] The petition resides in an archive file that includes several petitions regarding the sector.[6] It was probably addressed to the prime minister of the local Tunisian government (*Sayyidnâ al-wazîr al-akbar Adam Allah*) in 1861.[7] It was signed by 77 individuals who describe themselves, in the text, as members of the guild (*arbâb al-sinâ'*) and as poor workers in the fez manufacturing sector (*min al-fuqarâ' al-mushtaghalîn bi sinâ'a al-shâshiyya*). The main demand of the petitioners was that measures be taken to ban the import of machinery for the manufacture of fezzes. For them, these machines were literally killing thousands of fez makers in Tunis (*al-hâdira*) and the rest of the country (*al-watan*). They pointed out—and this indicates how grave the crisis really was—that the situation no longer allowed the children of the capital and of the nation, men (*zukûr*), women (*anâth*), widows (*arâmal*) and even orphans (*aytâm*), all working day and night (*yachtaghilûna bihâ bil-layl wa al-nahâr*), to survive. The use of these strong words, which connoted a koranic religious ethic that protected widows and orphans—an ethic to which sura 4 (*al-Nisa'*) of the Koran gives the most powerful expression, indicated a desire to force the administration addressed by the petition to face up to its social and moral responsibility:

> If our Sayyid allows the import of machinery by foreigners (*ajânib*), he will be causing the abandonment (*ihmâl al-ahâli*) of all those people who have only their craft skills and their hands to work with, and of all those who depend on this work [...] We weak people (*nahnu al-du'afâ'*), through our voices and by submitting this petition (*bi saddad baththal-chikâyya*), remind our Sayyid that his duty is to protect us and ensure that he does not open doors that will never close again.

---

5 ANT, Series H, box 72, file 859, document 6.

6 ANT, Series H, box 72, files 857 to 860.

7 The document bears no date. Its date can be deduced from a reading of the context and the other documents in the same file.

The petition is written in the urban dialect typical of Tunis at the time, substantially different from the one we find in petitions submitted by notables from the civic councils, who were more familiar with this exercise (Lafi, 2005). These notables wrote in classical Arabic and deployed a finely honed administrative and legal rhetoric. Artisans and workers could quote the Koran in moral support of their demands, but they were obviously less familiar with the imperial style of communication embodied by the petition. Still, they were proficient in the essentials. Their insistence that they were ordinary working people could even be seen as a deliberate choice made to reinforce the impact of their petition. The petition does not directly include any large-scale economic argument: the emphasis is solely on the social consequences, at the local level, of decisions over which the petitioners have no control. The archive file shows that, before addressing the highest authorities, they had gone through the whole gamut of protest and mediation within the guild hierarchy, itself in the process of being reformed. But in the face of a stalemate, the artisans and workers exercised their right of petition to address the higher authorities directly. They were expressing the distress of a social group united in adversity. Because of their decision to focus on social issues, some of the main issues were not addressed in the petition: international competition, import taxes, measures to support artisans, general points about the industrialisation of the province. But in other petitions, and investigative files of the local and imperial administration, these themes were sometimes addressed. Some petitions protested directly against mechanisation.[8] Others were submitted by trades that represented the different phases of fez production, such as pressing.[9] In fact, in those years—the 1860s—the whole artisanal sector was affected by this manner of threat and by the economic slump it induced, as illustrated by protests in the leather and dyeing sectors (*Amîn al-dabâgha wa mâ yata ʾallaq bil-sinâʿa*), whose petitions are to be found next to those of the fez producers in the archives.[10] Throughout the 1860s, this type of agitation left its mark on the Tunisian social landscape and on the political debate concerning the opening up of the economy; this was when Khayr al-Dîn and the reformers were attempting to modernise the province, attempts that were riddled with ambiguity. The influence of European penetration was also starting to be perceptible: this involved competition and exemptions, and undermined Tunis' market

8 ANT, Series H, box 72, file 860.

9 ANT, Series H, box 72, file 857, 19 petitions and documents.

10 ANT, Series H, box 59, file 658 (dyeing). Box 59, file 659 (tanners). See also Sebag (1959).

share and the local and imperial responses to this new context. The reform of guilds, in the Empire in general and in Tunis in particular, was part and parcel of such reactions.[11] It triggered a number of political and institutional debates that lasted for several years (Quéméneur, 1942; Louis, 1973).

These episodes show that the European influence in the Ottoman province of Tunis was fundamentally ambiguous from the outset and that Ottoman efforts to bring about economic modernisation were already trammelled by an increasingly colonial situation. Faced with the industrialisation of Europe, the Ottoman Empire tried, in various contexts including that of fez production, to promote a transition to a mechanised, industrial-type economy. But during this transformation, which included multiple development-related conflicts over several decades, several elements merely intensified ambiguities and a growing dependency: the importation of technology, investment mechanisms, the redefinition of marketing channels, relationships with foreigners, and changes in social relations at the local level. Regarding this last dimension, the shock of the disappearance of guilds as such was a powerful blow in the Ottoman context of the *Tanzimat* and their local variations in Tunis, from modernising economic reforms to the destabilising effects on the cohesion of the social milieu of production. These facts, if interpreted in the context of reflections on the overall history of development-related conflicts discussed here, suggest that we go along with the suggestions of Kenneth Pomeranz (2000) on the high degree of pre-industrial productive development in certain areas, including—in this case—Ottoman Tunis, which historiography has tended to consider right from the outset as peripheral. But we should also see these suggestions as an invitation to compare and contrast different levels, from the local and social micro-level to the geopolitical level, to understand the mechanisms that led to the gradual surrender to what was becoming a colonial order: the pressure to open up markets, the ambiguities of mechanisation, and the debates in local societies regarding how modernisation should proceed and the role of the state. In the context of Ottoman Tunis, the affirmation of modernity as a hegemonic paradigm was thus enacted through a seizing of power of the mechanisms of economic decision-making by circles situated outside the guild heritage, and resulted in an abrupt transition, the increasingly colonial nature of which only served to increase its gravity. The social body of

11 See ANT, Series H, box 59, files 644–669, on the end of the corporations in the medina (dyers, tanners, potters, burnous makers, butchers, blacksmiths, etc.). Here too, the petition turned out to be a fundamental vector of mediation.

the former productive milieus was dismantled in the process—as the petition studied here demonstrates.

4 Conclusion

With French colonisation, which was formalised in Tunisia in 1881 after two decades of progressive losses of Ottoman imperial sovereignty, a paradoxical swing occurred: it was now the colonial authorities who were responsible for defending Tunisian artisanal production on the international market. While, for several decades, it had been partly against the French that Tunis had had to defend its production and marketing conditions, French colonial administrators were now asked to intervene with regard to the issues affecting the sector—requests submitted in the form of petitions, from 1882 onwards. This is the context in which, twenty years later, the archive file on which the research for this chapter has drawn was created: a French colonial official apparently asked, at the beginning of the twentieth century, for a file to be opened so that the issue could be studied, and we see, here and there, his comments added in pencil to the original documents. Papers dating back several decades were collected, taken out of their original archival context and compiled in a newly opened file.

From the mid-1880s, the situation continued to worsen for Tunis fez manufacturers. German and Austrian competitors entered the market, challenging the position of the Tunis manufacturers even more severely, and the situation became completely untenable. In 1895, *Le Jacquard*, a French journal of the wool industry, waged a negative campaign aimed—this time—at protecting Tunisia (now a French colony) from European competition, indicating that Austrian fezzes were available in Tunis for 'even less than the cost of the actual amount of wool needed to make a fez [...] Germany and Austria have managed to monopolise the exclusive sale of this item of clothing' (*Le Jacquard*, 1895, 345, our transl.). Tunisia was pushed right out of the international market. Fez production in Tunisia reverted to an artisanal stage that it had already outgrown back in the eighteenth and nineteenth centuries, and became almost irrelevant. Despite efforts by the Tunisian nationalists of the 1940s and 1950s, followers of Habib Bourguiba, to assert that the wearing of the fez was a form of cultural distinction and a political sign of support for independence, production continued to decline. Cultural debates about the symbolism of the fez between the Tunisia of Destour and the Turkey of M. Kemal Atatürk (Doğaner, 2009), regardless of how the hat itself developed, did not alter the economic reality of the sector and the social situation of those who had dedicated their skills and labour to it. Over the following decades, the fez gradually became less central to the culture of Tunis, and was finally confined to the folklore of the souks in the context of tourist development. In terms of economic history, it became the symbol of a failed attempt to boost artisanal production in the industrial age.

References

Abidi, B. (2016) *Refugees from Al-Andalus and the Urban Evolution of the Lower Medjerda Valley*, paper presented at the Urban Studies Seminar, ZMO, Berlin, 7 March.

Bachrouch, T. (2008) *La médina de Tunis avant le Protectorat*, Cahier de CERES, Série Histoire, 17 (Tunis: CERES).

Bakalti, S. (1996) *La femme tunisienne au temps de la colonisation* (Paris: Harmattan).

Batzell, R., S. Beckert, A. Gordon and G. Winant (2015) 'Writing Social History 50 years after the Making of the English Working Class', *Journal of Social History*, 48(4), pp. 753–758, DOI: 10.1093/jsh/shv036.

Bayart, J.-F. (1999) 'L'Afrique dans le monde: une histoire d'extraversion', *Critique Internationale*, 5, pp. 97–120, DOI: 10.3406/criti.1999.1505.

Bayram al-Khâmis, M. (2000) 'Safwa al-i'tiba', 5 vol., (Tunis: Ministry of Culture).

Ben Diaf, A. (2004) 'Ithâf al-zamân bi-akhbâr mulûk tûnis wa 'ahd al-amân, Dâr al-', 5 vol. (Tunis: arabiyya lil-kitâb).

Ben Miled, M. (2010) *Chéchia: le bonnet de feutre méditerranéen* (Carthage: Editions Carthaginoiseries).

Boubaker, S. (2003) 'Négoce et enrichissement individuel à Tunis du XVIIe siècle au début du XIXe siècle', *Revue d'histoire moderne et contemporaine*, 50(4), 29–62, https://www.cairn.info/revue-d-histoire-moderne-et-contemporaine-2003-4-page-29.htm (accessed on 26 May 2016).

Bryant, J. (2006) 'The West and the Rest Revisited: Debating Capitalist Origins, European Colonialism and the Advent of Modernity', *Canadian Journal of Sociology*, 31(4), pp. 403–444.

Cardoso, F.H. and E. Faletto (1969) *Dependencia y Desarrollo en América Latina* (Buenos Aires: Siglo Veintiuno).

Cermann, M. and S. Ogilvie (1996) *European Proto-industrialization* (Cambridge: Cambridge University Press).

Chakrabarty, D. (2000) *Provincializing Europe. Postcolonial Thought and Historical Difference* (Princeton: Princeton University Press).

Chastagnaret, G. (2000) *L'Espagne, une puissance minière au XIXème siècle* (Madrid: Casa de Velazquez).

Conklin, A. (2000) 'Boundaries Unbound: Teaching French History as Colonial History and Colonial History as French History', *French Historical Studies*, 23(2), DOI: 10.1215/00161071-23-2-215.

Davidson, B. (1969) *The African Genius: an Introduction to African Cultural and Social History* (Boston: Little Brown and Company).

Dawley, A. (1976) *Class and Community: the Industrial Revolution in Lynn* (Cambridge: Harvard University Press).

Doğaner, Y. (2009) 'The Law on Headdress and Regulation on Dressing in the Turkish Modernization', *Bilig*, 51, pp. 65–86, http://bilig.yesevi.edu.tr/yonetim/kcfinder/upload/files/bilig-51-guz-2009.pdf (accessed on 26 May 2016).

Fahmi, M. (1954) *La révolution de l'industrie en Egypte et ses conséquences sociales au XIXème siècle (1800–1850)* (Leiden: Brill).

Faroqhi, S. (2009) *Artisans of Empire. Crafts and Craftspeople under the Ottomans* (London: Tauris).

Ferchiou, S. (1971) *Technique et société: l'exemple de la fabrication des chéchias en Tunisie* (Paris: Institut d'ethnologie).

Ganiage, J. (1959) *Les origines du Protectorat français en Tunisie (1861–1881)* (Paris: PUF).

Guillén, M. (2004) 'Modernism without Modernity? The Rise of Modernist Architecture in Mexico, Brazil and Argentina, 1890–1940', *Latin American Research Review*, 39(2), DOI: 10.1353/lar.2004.0032.

Guillerme, A. (2007) *La naissance de l'industrie à Paris: entre sueurs et vapeurs (1780–1830)* (Seyssel: Champ Vallon).

Guillerme, A. (1998) *Révolution artisanale, révolution industrielle: la technique face aux métiers* (Paris: CNAM).

Hadi Chérif, M. (1970) 'Expansion européenne et difficultés tunisiennes de 1815 à 1830', *Revue de l'Occident musulman et de la Méditerranée*, 8, 111–114, DOI: 10.3406/remmm.1970.1035.

Hamadeh, S. (2004) 'Ottoman Expressions of Early Modernity and the "Inevitable" Question of Westernization', *The Journal of the Society of Architectural Historians*, 63(1), pp. 32–51, DOI: 10.2307/4127991.

Hanna, N. (2011) *Artisan Entrepreneurs in Cairo and Early Modern Capitalism* (Syracuse: Syracuse University Press).

Kaufhold, K.H. (1978) *Das Gewerbe in Preussen um 1800* (Berlin: Schwartz).

Lafi, N. (2012) 'La gouvernance ottomane des équilibres locaux: le rôle du bureau central des pétitions et l'usage de ses archives', *Cahiers du Ceres*, 21, pp. 261–274.

Lafi, N. (2011) 'Petitions and Accomodating Urban Change in the Ottoman Empire', in E. Özdalga, S. Özervarlı and F. Tansuğ. (eds.) *Istanbul as seen from a distance. Centre and Provinces in the Ottoman Empire* (Istanbul: Swedish Research Institute), pp. 73–82.

Lafi, N. (2005) 'Les pouvoirs urbains à Tunis à la fin de l'époque ottomane: la persistance de l'ancien régime', in N. Lafi (ed.) *Municipalités méditerranéennes* (Berlin: K. Schwarz), pp. 223–244.

Landes, D. (1969) *The Unbound Prometheus: Technological Change and Industrial Development in Western Europe from 1750 to the Present* (Cambridge: Cambridge University Press).

Le Jacquard (1895) *Le Journal de l'industrie lainière* (Paris: H. Saint-Denis).

Louis, A. (1973) 'Les industries du cuir à Tunis hier et aujourd'hui: éléments bibliographiques', *Revue de l'occident musulman et de la Méditerranée*, 15, pp. 145–151, http://www.persee.fr/doc/remmm_0035-1474_1973_num_15_1_1234 (accessed on 26 May 2016).

Masters, B. (1988) *The Origins of Western Economic Dominance in the Middle East. Mercantilism and the Islamic Economy in Aleppo, 1600–1750* (New York, London: New York University Press).

Mignolo, W. (2001) 'Coloniality at Large. The Western Hemisphere in the Colonial Horizon of Modernity', *The New Centennial Review*, 1(2), pp. 19–54.

Pamuk, S. (1984) 'The Ottoman Empire and the Great Depression of 1873–1896', *The Journal of Economic History*, 44(1), pp. 107–118, DOI: 10.1017/S0022050700031399.

Penec, P. (1964) *Les transformations des corps de métiers de Tunis sous l'influence d'une économie externe de type capitaliste* (Tunis: ISEAAN).

Peyssonnel, A. and R.L. Desfontaines (1838) *Voyage dans les Régences de Tunis et d'Alger* (Paris: Gide), http://catalogue.bnf.fr/ark:/12148/cb30330700f (accessed on 26 May 2016).

Pomeranz, K. (2000) *The Great Divergence: China, Europe, and the Making of the Modern World Economy* (Princeton: Princeton University Press).

Quataert, D. (1986) 'Machine Breaking and the Changing Carpet Industry of Western Anatolia, 1860–1908', *Journal of Social History*, 19(3), pp. 473–489, DOI: 10.1353/jsh/19.3.473.

Quéméneur, J. (1942), 'Contribution à l'étude des corporations tunisiennes: Les Belghajia de Tunis', *IBLA*, 5, pp. 26–51.

Randall, A. (1986) 'The Philosophy of Luddism: The Case of the West of England Woolen Workers, ca. 1790–1809', *Technology and Culture*, 27(1), pp. 1–17.

Raveux, O. and A. Sanchez (2010) 'La adaptación tecnológica como factor de localización industrial. Una revisión de las investigaciones sobre la industria de hilados de algodón en Cataluña (1772–1885)', *Investigaciones de Historia Economica*, 17(6), pp. 65–94.

Rodney, W. (1972) *How Europe underdeveloped Africa* (London: Bogle-L'Ouverture Publications).

Sebag, P. (1959) 'L'industrialisation de la Tunisie: une expérience dans l'industrie de la chaussure', *Cahiers de Tunisie*, 7, pp. 147–173.

Spring, C. and J. Hudson (2004) 'Urban Textile Traditions of Tunisia', *African Arts*, 37(3), pp. 24–41, DOI: 10.1162/afar.2004.37.3.24.

Stott, R. (1996) 'Artisans and Capitalist Development', *Journal of the Early Republic*, 16(2), pp. 257–271.

Teyssier, P. (1962) 'Le vocabulaire d'origine espagnole dans l'industrie tunisienne de la chéchia', *Mélanges offerts à Marcel Bataillon*, Bordeaux, 1962, pp. 732–740.

Thieck, J.-P. (1992) *Passion d'Orient* (Paris: Karthala).

Thomis, M. (1970) *The Luddites: Machine-Breaking in Regency England* (Hamden: Archon Books).

Thompson, E.P. (1963) *The Making of the English Working Class* (London: Victor Gollancz).

Tirthankar, R. (2007) 'Out of Tradition: Master Artisans and Economic Change in Colonial India', *The Journal of Asian Studies*, 66(4), pp. 963–991, DOI: 10.1017/S002191180700126X.

Tunger-Zanetti, A. (1996) *La communication entre Tunis et Istanbul 1860–1913: Province et métropole* (Paris: L'Harmattan).

Valensi, L. (1969) 'Islam et capitalisme: production et commerce des chéchias en Tunisie et en France aux XVIIIe et XIXe siècles', *Revue d'histoire moderne et contemporaine*, 16(3), pp. 376–400.

Van Krieken, G.S. (1976) *Khayr al-Dîn et la Tunisie (1850–1881)* (Leiden: Brill).

Verley, P. (1997) *L'échelle du monde. Essai sur l'industrialisation de l'Occident* (Paris: Gallimard).

Winpenny, T.R. (1990) *Bending Is Not Breaking: Adaptation and Persistence Among 19th Century Lancaster Artisans* (Lanham: University Press of America).

CHAPTER 4

'An Uphill Job Demanding Limitless Patience'. The Establishment of Trade Unions and the Conflicts of Development in Sudan, 1946–1952

Elena Vezzadini

Abstract

This chapter focuses on conflicts of development from the point of view of the entanglement between development, labour legislation, and labour conflicts during the time of decolonisation. It describes the origins of the trade union movement in Sudan, created after the Second World War, and covers the history of that movement up until 1952, the year in which its curve of radicalisation was stopped and it turned towards more conciliatory labour relations. Dwelling on internal sources emanating from the colonial government and the various labour attachés sent to Khartoum, the chapter aims to shed light on the reciprocal influences and feedback effect between the three main actors of these conflicts: the British government, whose agenda set colonial labour welfare as a top priority; a reluctant Sudanese government accustomed to decades of laissez-faire in matters of labour; and the workers, who quite suddenly discovered that they had the power to compel the government to listen to their demands.

1 Introduction

> It is not enough to say that the Sudan is not capable of modern industrial development and should therefore be left alone. [...] It is certain that neither the world opinion nor a growing political consciousness in the Sudan itself will tolerate stagnation...; there must be, in the Sudan as elsewhere in the world, progress in standards of living, security, health,

* I wish to express my gratitude to Irene Bono and Béatrice Hibou for letting me embark on this project. I am grateful for their comments, and for those of Didier Peclard, Nadia Hachimi and the other participants of the workshop in Geneva on the 7–8 September 2015.

> education and generally in those humane practices which go by the name of civilisation.[1]

> Trades Unions would have been premature [in Sudan, that is] predominantly an agricultural country … Trade unions will not change the traditional 'Arab' contempt for manual labour; shop stewards and workers' committees will not make sense in the conditions which are permitted and encouraged by popular opinion and the teachings of Islam.[2]

These two quotes, the first taken from the report of a Foreign Office resident minister in Cairo on the labour situation in Sudan, dated 1944, and the second from notes written in 1946 by the Civil Secretary of Sudan, Robertson (the highest colonial authority after the Governor General), in response to London's recommendations to begin to form trade unions in Sudan, are fascinating glimpses into the conflict of visions as to which role to assign to the colonial state. The first maintained that the state had to provide for welfare and development for all. The second—in line with indirect rule—considered that state intervention had to be minimal because people were better governed by their own 'traditions', and thus that exogenous institutions such as trade unions should not be introduced. And yet, at the end of 1952, six years after Robertson had expressed such an opinion, there were as many as 99 registered trade unions in Sudan, representing an estimated 100,000 members.

This chapter will focus on the uncertainties, ambiguities and unpredictable outcomes spawned by conflicting visions of which role the state had to play in the lives of the colonised people, by studying one case in point—namely, the conflicts triggered by the new labour legislation of the late 1940s in Sudan. By choosing the theme of labour and development in the context of decolonisation, the author is aware that she is on a well-trodden path, in two ways. First, the connection between development and the elaboration of a system of workers' welfare (Cowen and Shenton, 1991 and 1996; Butler, 1999; Lewis, 2000; Havinden and Meredith, 2002; Burton, 2003; Constantine, 2005; Duffield and Hewitt, 2009; Seekings, 2011) and the political implications of labour conflicts in the era of decolonisation have received much scholarly attention (see for example Berman and Lonsdale, 1980; Freund, 1988; Shane 1989; Howe, 1993; Maul, 2012; Tijani, 2012; Teelucksingh, 2015); and all the more so following the

1 The National Archives of the UK (TNA): R. Peers, *Labour in the Middle East: Sudan*, Undated, 1944. Enclosed in Peers to Robertson, 22.7.1944, FO 921/305, p. 10.

2 The National Archives of the UK (TNA): Comments on Mr. Audsley's Notes on His Recent Visit to the Sudan, JW Robertson, Civil Secretary, undated, included in Robertson to Speight, Khartoum, 4.6.1946, LAB 13/479.

influential studies of Frederick Cooper (to cite just a few: Cooper, 1992, 1996; Cooper and Packard, 1997). However, because of its atypical status as an Anglo-Egyptian condominium, Sudan is usually left out of such scholarship.

Yet, in spite of the lack of dialogue with the rest of the continent, there exists solid scholarship on labour in Sudan. Authors such as Fawzi, Sikainga, Cross and many others have explored in great detail several aspects of labour conflicts that occurred on the eve of independence (Fawzi, 1957; Sikainga, 1996 and 2002; Ali Taha, 1970; Cross, 1997; Curless, 2013). Such scholarship bears many resemblances to the angle of analysis chosen here: first because it focuses on the relations between labour, politics and the colonial state, and second because it mostly relies on the colonial archive. The primacy of colonial sources is not due to a lack of alternatives—such alternatives abound. Not only are many witnesses still alive, newspapers such as *al-Saraha* (Frankness in Arabic) and *al-Shaab* (the People), strongly sympathetic to the labour movement, reported on labour-related news for decades.[3]

Nevertheless, my choice here has been to mobilise colonial sources, because it is from these that the historian can perceive best the uncertainties, entanglements, and unintended feedback effects generated by the interaction between three main actors: London's Labour government, the Sudan colonial government and the workers' movement. In this way, this contribution aims to echo the main preoccupations of this special issue: the imbrication of development policies with stories of globalisation and market extension; the transformations of typologies of governmentality; the centrality of development in the formation of states, in particular in the context of decolonisation; and finally the fragmentizing impact of development plans, first as enacted by, and impressed upon, a multiplicity of actors with different aims, and second as entangled with social hierarchies and visions that the state had. Finally, the case of the conflicts triggered by the introduction of labour legislation in Sudan reveals how development plans were ridden with contradictions, between the universalism of their intentions, the implications of their norms—which carried a political, moral and emotional message about who were the 'right' actors, their 'right' attitudes and the modalities of the realisation of labour negotiations—and the discriminatory way in which these plans were eventually implemented on the ground.

Because Sudan studies have long suffered from insularity (Sharkey et al., 2015), I shall begin this chapter by inscribing development conflicts related to labour in Sudan into two entangled international stories, although narrated very sketchily: first, that of how British imperial development policy fostered

3 These newspapers can be found at the National Records Office, Khartoum.

the creation of trade unions in the colonies; second, the story of circulation and mutual learning among radical labour movements, and in particular between those in Egypt and those in Sudan.

2 Labour in Sudan, from Indirect Rule to the 1940 Colonial Welfare and Development Act

The most important event of the political history of Britain in the first half of the twentieth century was probably the coming to power of the Labour Party. This happened following a century-long process of sharp societal conflicts around questions of labour. From the end of the nineteenth century, heterogeneous radical groups and militant workers that had been, until then, hostile to the formal political arena finally agreed to participate in institutional politics and came to be absorbed into a labour coalition that coalesced into the Labour Party, officially founded in 1900. The party grew in strength and prestige, and became the main opponent of the Conservative Party, finally coming to power for the first time in 1924, and again in 1929–1931 (Howell, 1983). It was under the Labour party that the first act was passed concerning the duty of a government to develop its colonies not only economically, but also socially and politically—the British Colonial Development Act of 1929. The crisis of 1929 left this act a dead letter for a decade (Constantine, 2005, 141–166).

In 1935, severe labour agitations were carried out by the miners of the Copperbelt of northern Rhodesia, and between 1934 and 1939 the planters of the British West Indies went on strike. In the 1930s, while these mass strikes were occurring, the Labour Party remained in opposition. However, each of these episodes fed the party's struggle against the Tory government, providing them with arguments to use in harsh attacks on their Conservative adversaries (Thorpe, 1997). As a consequence, systematic denunciations in political debates of cases of exploitative colonialism kept the issue of colonial workers' welfare in the spotlight (Vickers, 2004; Worley, 2005; Corthorn and Davis, 2008).

Amid the struggles between the Conservatives and Labour was a third important actor—the Communist Party. The Labour Party was soon confronted with the problem of how to avoid the defection of its more radical wings to communism, especially in light of the fascination that Soviet Russia held among leftist circles (Lilleker, 2004). When the Labour Party eventually returned to power in 1946 (remaining in government until 1951), it adopted a policy of pulling out all the stops on welfare and of co-opting the larger trade unions, notably through the Trades Union Congress (TUC) (Orr, 1966; Hobsbawn, 1967; Ravier, 1981; Thorpe, 1998, 2000), also explicitly to counter communism.

In the colonies too, trade unions and workers' welfare ordinances were introduced also to defuse the drive towards communism and radical anti-colonialism. The administrators repeatedly noted the anti-colonial leanings of the strikers and the proximity between labour grievances and political radicalism. As Cooper and others have demonstrated in detail, it was in this context that the 1940 Colonial Development and Welfare Act was approved (Cooper, 1996). Development and the amelioration of the living conditions of workers, but also a solid labour legislation were meant to stop the drift towards anti-colonial radicalism. Thus, one of the clauses of the Act stated that: 'no territory might receive aid under [the Act's] provision unless it had in force legislation protecting the rights of trade unions, and unless the works for which the aid was to be used were carried out under a contract that embodied a fair wages clause…' (Zeilig, 2009, 72). The Colonial and Foreign Offices were duly instructed to supervise its implementation in the colonies.

In Sudan, the government adopted the new directives with a certain delay. In 1946 a five-year development plan was launched, followed in 1951 by a second one, larger and more ambitious.[4] The wording of the 1946 plan followed closely the guidelines of the colonial Act: to provide 'the raising of the standard of living of the population by increasing the national income and by the provision of additional social services, education particularly.'[5] In order to fully capture the novelty of this paradigm, it must be compared with native Sudanese policy prior to the 1940s. The country, an Anglo-Egyptian condominium from 1899 on, was governed by a hybrid rule of two countries with the majority of powers held by the British. After a short failed essay at integrating the educated elites into the government, and as a backlash against the nationalist uprising of 1924, the administration had turned wholeheartedly to indirect rule. Its core principles had clear economic implications, at least in theory: according to indirect rule, economic needs were shaped by local culture and traditions and thus were very limited, as Sudanese were not accustomed to global economy. In reality, the opposite was true: Gezira, an irrigated territory as large as Great Britain between the Blue and White Niles, was devoted to the growth of cotton for export, in a highly organised scheme run by the Gezira Plantation Syndicate (Gaitskell, 1959; Bernal, 1991). The government supervised closely the

4 The National Archives of the UK (TNA): *Sudan Five-Years Development Plan*, enclosed in Huddleston, Khartoum, to British Ambassador, Cairo, 17.2.1947, FO 371/63063. Sudan Government, Development Budget Estimates, 1951/56 Programme, 1st July 1951 to 30th June 1952, Sudan Pamphlet 10, Sudan Library, University of Khartoum.

5 The National Archives of the UK (TNA): Notes on the Expansion of Colonial Production, Memo No. 17, enclosure in Butters to Riches, Dover House, Whitehall, 25.8.1947, FO 371/63064.

marketing of this commodity, and the same happened to other export products such as gum arabic, sesame and millet.[6]

The majority of state revenues were generated by agricultural exports, and depended on the mobilisation of a substantial labour force. Most salaried workers were employed either as farmhands, or in domains connected to trade, such as ports and railways. However, the scarcity of wage workers fostered high salaries (in comparison to living costs) during most of Sudan's colonial history. This made workers quite an assertive group, perhaps the best evidence of this being the frequency of strikes. From the beginning of the condominium, workers went on strike confidently, and often.[7] It was common for employees to walk away from their employers in order to exert pressure for better conditions (be they salaries, food, lodging, or other improvements). On average, colonial administrators signalled a strike at least once per year. The strikes involved different categories of workers and geographical sites: for instance, employees of a ginnery at Sinkat, dockers at Port Sudan, tram drivers in Khartoum, Gezira cotton pickers, and so on. However, such strikes were dealt with locally and never generated country-wide debates. The local administration considered them to be spontaneous phenomena generated by the invisible hand of the market and by the 'laziness' of the Sudanese. More generally, the administration attempted to force certain specific categories of Sudanese into work (former slaves in particular (see Sikainga, 1996; Cross, 1997; Vezzadini, 2010), but with only limited success.

What is important to emphasise for the purpose of this chapter is that before the 1940s workers were invisible to the eyes of the state, both as economic

6 How to control agricultural produce was vividly debated, as evidenced in the agenda and papers of the Board of Economic and Trade; see the following files: Civsec 1/53/144, Civsec 1/53/145, Civsec 1/53/146, and Civsec 1/54/147 (Khartoum: National Records Office).

7 A few examples will suffice: in 1908, government workers went on strike seeking better pay; in 1909, the government noted the occurrence of a strike in the Kamlin estate and another in the Fadlab agricultural scheme; in 1910 labourers supplied by the Central Labour Bureau refused to work at the wage offered; in 1912, a wave of strikes aimed at securing better working conditions involved dockers in Port Sudan. It is probable that further industrial action went unrecorded. Other strikes were overtly political: in 1919, a large strike involving railway employees (at the time they were mostly Egyptians, enrolled in a corps—supervised by the military—known as the Railways Battalion) occurred in Atbara in support of the Egyptian Revolution (Vezzadini, 2015). Similarly, during the 1924 revolution several strikes took place in Atbara, Khartoum and Port Sudan in protest against the arrest of the leaders of the revolt. As for the 1930s, after a period of economic depression the number of strikes rose again. Their pace is described by Cross (1997, 236); see also Sikainga (1996, 90–91) and Perkins (1993, 70–71).

and as political actors. For instance, during the 1924 revolution the British believed that workers attended demonstrations because they were paid or manipulated to do so, and not because they had decided to attend (Vezzadini, 2015, 234–254). All this was to change drastically after the Second World War.

Against this backdrop of indirect rule and of the lack of concern for waged workers, the disposition to simultaneously introduce general development plans and a labour legislation—both steered from London—were truly a sign of a new era for Sudan. In 1946, the Labour Board (renamed the Labour Branch in 1949) was duly instructed to begin to work under the aegis of the Civil Secretary. That year, Edward H. Macintosh, a former Sudan Political Service employee, was appointed Labour Officer. In addition, in 1947 the Foreign Office sent—from London—a labour expert, R. Brown, seconded directly from the Ministry of Labour, chosen because of his experience of the West Indian strikes; the same was the case for his successor, M.T. Cowan, who replaced Brown in April 1948, and who had been a labour advisor in Jamaica from 1945 to 1948 (Cross, 1997, 248). In 1949 the Foreign Office changed strategies and sent an independent syndicalist from the TUC, D. Newman, in harmony with the new line of involving the TUC in settling colonial labour disputes (Weiler, 1984; Cross, 1997, 248–249). In addition, the Sudanese government received at least three visits from Cairo from M.T. Audsley, a key figure of these years who was employed as labour counsellor at the British Embassy in Cairo and as Labour Adviser to the Middle East Office. His notes and reports include essential information on trade unions in Sudan.[8]

The number of envoys sent to advise the Sudanese government should not be missed, as it reveals the determination of London to supervise closely the labour question in the country. This level of involvement from the part of London on internal Sudanese affairs was a radical change for Sudan's government, which until then had enjoyed total freedom on matters relating to domestic policy.

The second story of entanglement I shall briefly discuss here is that of the labour movement in Sudan and the international workers' struggles in the

8 According to Beinin and Lockman (1998, 304), 'Audsley was the chief architect of postwar British labour policy in Egypt', who struggled 'to promote a non-political trade union movement.' His reports are: Note on Visit to the Sudan, 25th February to 15th March 1946; Note on Visit to the Sudan from 10th to 20th March 1947 inclusive, FO 371/63088; Notes concerning the Sudan Railway Strike, M. Audsley, Cairo, 26.4.1948, FO 371/69235; Report on visit to the Sudan from 1st to 20th February 1951 inclusive, FO 371/90299; all in the The National Archives of the UK (TNA). On the subject of Audsley, see also Labour Attache, Cairo, House of Commons Debate, 15 May 1950, vol. 475 (863–864), http://hansard.millbanksystems.com/commons/1950/may/15/labour-attache-cairo (accessed on 21 August 2015).

empires, beginning with the influence of the Egyptian labour movement. British officials noticed such connections early. The commission on living standards of 1948 maintained, for instance, that: 'The whole trend of world opinion is towards raising the wages and standard of living of the worker and the Sudanese worker does not intend to be left behind in this movement…'.[9] While the Second World War was raging in North Africa, information on trade unionism came to Sudan through various channels. There was, of course, British propaganda: as the historian Fawzi recounts, people came to know about trade unionism 'in response… to the British Ministry of Information war pamphlets about the British way of life, one of which, on trade unionism, had been the subject of study by a discussion circle in the Atbara Technical school Old Boys Club' (Fawzi, 1957, 38). As mentioned previously, from 1950 on, dedicated newspapers such as *al-Saraha* and *al-Shaab* carried news about international labour developments. In this sense they filled a gap, as the main Sudanese newspapers, such as *al-Ray al-'Amm* or *al-Nil* usually did not cover such news. However, Sudanese most probably read about labour struggles even earlier through the Egyptian press.

Al-Saraha and *al-Shaab* watched the workers' movement in Egypt very closely and exposed their readers to its communist, anti-imperialist language. Labour conflicts shook Egypt from the late 1930s through the 1940s (Vatikiotis, 1969, 337–342; Beinin and Lockman, 1998). The scope of this chapter only permits me to highlight the most salient of these events here. In 1932, a mission from the International Labour Organization exposed the scandal of the labour situation in Egypt, where most industries imposed fourteen to sixteen daily working hours, employed children, and ignored the most elementary forms of worker protection (Beinin and Lockman, 1998, 204–205). The introduction of worker protection measures advanced sluggishly, and strikes took place incessantly amidst difficult economic conditions connected to the 1929 crisis, with a government in constant oscillation between labour reforms and repression. For instance, in 1938 a general strike at one of the largest textile factories in Egypt, al-Mahalla al-Kubra, was violently repressed. In 1939, the leaders of the General Federation of Labour Unions staged a three-day hunger strike, highly popular and widely covered by the press. When martial law was imposed on the country because of the war, tramway workers challenged the decision, launching a strike in March 1940. In 1942, finally, the government officially recognised the syndicates and passed trade union legislation. More strikes were to follow after the war. In 1946 for instance, Egyptian industrial workers of the

9 The National Archives of the UK (TNA): Report of the Independent Committee of Enquiry, Khartoum, 14.4.1948, FO 371/69235, p. 13.

major textile industries walked out en masse, followed again by the tramway workers. Even the police, in Cairo and Alexandria, went on strike in 1948.

The political impact of Egyptian labour struggles on Sudan should not be overlooked. As with many other junctures in Sudanese colonial history, Egyptian anti-colonial nationalism was a powerful inspiration for the Sudanese. In Sudan, Egypt had historically played the role of a counterweight to British colonisation (Abdel-Rahim, 1969; Beshir, 1974; Warburg, 1978; al-Safi, 1989). For the Ashiqqa, the most important pro-Egyptian party in Sudan (yet connected to the largest Sudanese Sufi brotherhood, the Khatmiyya), unity with Egypt was a synonym of liberation from colonialism. But for Sudanese workers there was another reason for their closeness to Egypt: Egyptian workers were struggling against the dominant classes as much as against British economic colonisation. Like them, the Sudanese were waging a double war against the British: first as their colonisers, and second as their managers. In fact, the colonial government was the country's largest employer and manager of the economic system.

3 The Workers Affairs Association and the Beginning of Trade Unionism

As already mentioned, in June 1946 Civil Secretary Robertson stated that there was no scope for creating trade unions in Sudan. And yet, in July 1946, some Sudan Railways craftsmen founded the Workers Affairs Association (WAA) in the city of Atbara—home to the headquarters of the Sudan Railways Department. The association was headed by Sulayman Musa, and al-Tayyib Hassan al-Tayyib. The two were no hotheads: quite the contrary, they were two artisans with long careers behind them as permanent employees of Sudan Railways (Curless, 2013, 806).[10] The association was founded at the beginning to provide for social support (Fawzi, 1957, 38–39). As Cross notes, its statute made no reference to the strike as a weapon, excluded any political aims, and reassured the reader that the WAA would take 'meticulous care to avoid any action likely to cause the management any inconvenience or trouble' (quoted in Cross, 1997, 241).

Simultaneously, the colonial Sudan Labour Board attempted to form Works Committees. These were to function as a link between employers and employees. In the words of the Civil Secretary, they represented a way for 'the artisan

10 The first was a supervisor, employed since 1926, and the second a pattern maker, employed since 1928 (Sikainga, 2002, 105).

and labouring classes' to 'take an intelligent and constructive interest in the internal running of their business or department' (Fawzi 1957, 26–27).[11] However, the committees had no power to advise on matters directly connected to industrial relations, such as salaries and terms of service, matters that instead the WAA wanted to debate. In August 1946, the WAA asked to be recognised. The government refused on the grounds that the association was not adapted to such a role; but the WAA did not let the issue rest. Following one entire year of fruitless talks, the WAA decided to instruct all railway employees to stop work. The extent of the strike and its success made it an immensely popular event. From 17 to 23 July, the railway system was paralyzed.[12] People throughout the country supported the activists in many ways, including by sending food (Sikainga, 2002, 107–108). Eventually, the WAA succeeded in being recognised as the representative voice of railways workers.

Following on from this victory, the association confidently began to work on labour conditions. In October, it formulated demands that included an increase in salaries, annual leave for all workers, and the reduction of working hours.[13] These demands were sent to railways management, but with the request that they be forwarded to Khartoum, thus expressing the idea that labour negotiations were a governmental responsibility. The Sudanese government gave a cold welcome to the demands, considering as 'extravagant claims' the WAA proposal for a pay increase of between 25 and 40 per cent.[14] However, it responded by raising the minimum basic wage and promised the establishment of an independent committee of British and Sudanese experts to enquire into the situation of the railway workers. In January 1948, the commission had not yet begun its work, but by now the WAA had understood the power of the strike as a weapon. A second general strike of railway workers was launched for 26–28 January, and a third, 'indefinite' strike on 16 March.[15] On 4 April, Sulayman Musa was arrested and charged with having given a 'highly seditious

11 Civil Secretary's Circular No. CS/37, 19.8.1946, quoted in Fawzi (1957, 26–27).

12 The National Archives of the UK (TNA): Correspondence about the strike is included in FO 371/63088. For a detailed account, see Sikainga (2002, 105–107).

13 The National Archives of the UK (TNA): Strikes of Railway Workers in the Sudan, FO Minute, 23.3.1948, FO 371/69235.

14 The National Archives of the UK (TNA): Governor General of the Sudan, Khartoum to Foreign Office, London, 29.1.1948 (repeated for information to Cairo), FO 371/69235.

15 The National Archives of the UK (TNA): The third strike was launched because the deadline announced by the government to publish the findings of the independent committee had not been respected. Sudan Government, Sudan Railways' Employees, Report of the Independent Committee of Enquiry, Establishment Branch, Khartoum, 14.4.1948, FO 371/69235.

speech' at the Atbara mosque.[16] The sentence pushed the workers to extend the strike to include the first two weeks of April. Finally, Musa was given a fine, and was released on April 17. The strike ended on the following day, on his instructions.

It is worth pausing a moment to reflect on why the government gave up its plans so quickly and recognised the WAA. It is possible to identify two main reasons: first, the dire conditions of salaried workers; second, London's injunction to develop labour regulation.

Indeed, from the beginning of the Second World War on, Sudan had been experiencing an economic boom. With the outbreak of the Korean War removing Korean cotton from the market, the price of Sudanese cotton soared. Government revenues multiplied spectacularly, tenfold from 1939 to 1951, and the country was awash with cash. So much cash, however, triggered unprecedented inflation.[17] The evolution of the cost of living index is eloquent: considering 1938 as 100, the index soared to 170 in 1945, 229 in 1947, and 307 in 1949 (Fawzi, 1957, 22; Daly, 2002, 312–313).[18] The redistribution of such cash was uneven: after the war, a drought that hit the north provoked famine conditions in some rural areas, and grain had to be imported from abroad. Against this backdrop of extreme inflation, the independent committee of 1948, enquiring into the plight of the railways workers, did not note any severe signs of malnutrition or illness.[19] It did, however, underline that the workers' conditions were as bad as anywhere else in Sudan, and had never been good.[20] Everywhere, in urban, working-class areas sanitary conditions were dire, lacking even the most basic

16 The National Archives of the UK (TNA): Telegram from Dakhlia, Khartoum, to Sudanology, London, 4.4.1948, FO 371/69235.

17 To counter inflation, the government tried to protect at least its own employees by issuing special bonuses, called Cost of Living Allowances. These were increased every year and could be quite sizeable. In 1947 for example, they stood at 70 per cent of a salary. The WAA still considered such bonuses to be inadequately matched to the cost of living.

18 Daly reports that at the end of 1948, *dhurra* (millet), the cereal used as a staple food by Sudanese families had risen to a price 736 per cent higher than its price in 1938 (Daly, 2003, 302–303).

19 'Statistics provided by the Medical Authorities for hospital admissions do not reveal that there exist in Atbara any industrial diseases directly due to conditions of work or to bad housing or sanitation… The Medical Authorities have no evidence to show that railway workers are suffering from malnutrition or an inadequate diet'. The National Archives of the UK (TNA): Report of the Independent Committee of Enquiry, Khartoum, 14.4.1948, FO 371/69235, p. 11.

20 The National Archives of the UK (TNA): Report of the Independent Committee of Enquiry, Khartoum, 14.4.1948, FO 371/69235, p. 14.

services (Fawzi, 1955; Lewis, 1962; Perkins, 1993, 99–122; Sikainga, 1996, 73–95 and 149–183). From the government's perspective, any refusal to improve such a debasing environment was deemed impossible in the framework of the London directives, which—as we have seen—had made improvements in working conditions a precondition of development funding. Thus, Khartoum had no choice but to listen carefully to the demands for reform put forward by the workers.

But the divergence of opinion between London and Khartoum was only barely concealed. Bevin, Secretary of State at the Foreign Office, accused the Sudanese government of not keeping up with the new ideas about development and labour, while others in London considered the government as outright reactionary.[21] Thus, it fell to the labour officers, people like Audsley and Brown, to mediate between these two visions and find a consensual narrative that would work on the ground. So, for example, in April 1948 Audsley provided the Sudanese Government with a functional way of interpreting the WAA strike. He blamed the association, but with certain reservations:

> [The leaders of the WAA] ... have had no experience of collective bargaining and negotiation and there is an absence of tact, calmness in debate and discretion in argument; their oriental political mindedness and practice weight against them regarding, to us, normal Trade Union behaviour.[22]

Therefore—Audsley went on—the duty of the government was not only to elaborate legislation, but also to teach its counterparts how to negotiate: 'A heavy responsibility rests upon these officials to prepare the Sudanese for industrial self-government…'. Meanwhile, he was also suggesting how British officers should set their own emotional tone: trade unionists had to be treated 'with patience and helpful encouragement by the British officials.'[23] This discursive repertoire is widely present in the sources. Another report on trade unions admonished British officers to attend to 'the tender plant of mutual

---

21 The National Archives of the UK (TNA): Minute to Atlee, 7.7.1947, FO 371/62557, NA, quoted in Cross (1997, 246); Notes concerning the Sudan Railway Strike, M. Audsley, Cairo, 26.4.1948, FO 371/69235.

22 The National Archives of the UK (TNA): Notes concerning the Sudan Railway Strike, M. Audsley, Cairo, 26.4.1948, FO 371/69235, p. 3.

23 Ibid.

confidence'.[24] Cowan, the labour officer that followed Brown, expressed this concept eloquently: 'It is going to be an uphill job demanding limitless patience on the part of all British officials, who are being constantly reminded that they are the representatives of an alien Government.'[25]

A tangible example of how labour attachés managed to reconcile Sudan's administrators hostile to the new labour directives is the framing of the new Trade Union Ordinance in 1948 by R. Brown. A civil servant with extensive experience in labour conflicts, Brown perceptively understood that the Sudanese government had to be given some safeguards. While being almost a word-for-word copy of the nineteenth century British Trade Union Act, the ordinance contained one fundamental difference: in order to be recognised, trade unions had to register, and to do so, they had to draft their statutes and submit them to a Registrar of Trade Unions, which would examine them, and approve—or not—the union. Despite this, Brown was more sympathetic than others to Sudanese labour, and worked hard to convince the government to adopt a conciliatory approach.[26]

Nevertheless, if one compares government statements with regard to labour and these statements' concretisation on the ground, a great discrepancy clearly emerges. When disincarnated and disembodied, the demands of the workers were deemed to be just and reasonable. Documents show, unmistakeably, a consensus among government officials that the situation of Sudanese workers had to be improved. And yet, the incarnations of the labour movement—including Sulayman Musa and, later, two other famous trade unionists, al-Shafi Ahmad al-Shaykh and Muhammad al-Sayyid Sallam—were systematically harassed and their statements criminalised. All spent quite some time in prison, and all were portrayed as opportunists pursuing personal gain. When the new Trade Union Ordinance was issued in late 1948,[27] for example, the WAA bitterly

24 The National Archives of the UK (TNA): Development of Trade Unions in Sudan, undated, unsigned, included in Robertson to Allen, 1.11.1950, LAB 13/480.

25 The National Archives of the UK (TNA): Cowan to Gee, Civil Secretary Office, Khartoum, 15.2.1949, LAB 13/480.

26 The National Archives of the UK (TNA): '[we must] avoid giving any impression that Government is out either to break up the WAA or 'victimise' its leaders... so that there can be no question of allegations that Government is using its powers as such, in furtherance of its interests as the employer.' The Threatened 'Indefinite' Strike of the Railways, R. Brown, 4.3.1948, FO 371/69235.

27 The National Archives of the UK (TNA): The ordinance was issued together with a set of new labour laws: the Employers and Employed Persons (Amendment) Ordinance, the Workman's Compensation Ordinance, the Regulation of Trade Disputes Ordinance,

criticised it.[28] In the opinion of Cowan, this criticism was driven by the personal agendas of WAA leaders:

> When all is said and done, the WAA have two objections to the Ordinance, unexpressed, but none the less real. These are -
> 1- It gives freedom to all to organise and WAA 'leadership' will in due course be challenged.
> 2- They will have to account for their funds by responsible audit, whereas last year a substantial balance of some thousands of pounds sent down from Cairo quietly disappeared.[29]

In other words, for Cowan, the WAA leadership opposed the ordinance because they were corrupt and power-hungry. But there was more: they had been 'inoculated' by communism, a fact that—for Cowan—was 'amply confirmed by our meeting with them, and by the propaganda they issue'.[30]

Demonstrators suffered similar harassment. Demonstrations would typically take place after a strike, or in protest against the arrest of a union leader, and often ended with injuries to the participants. For example, during the strike of July 1947 a crowd of around 1,000 people marched to the office of the General Manager of the Railways;[31] riots followed and dozens were hurt during clashes with the police. The army was sent in and 57 participants were arrested. During the strike of March–April 1948, when news of the arrest of Sulayman Musa spread, a series of demonstrations took place in Khartoum, Port Sudan and Atbara. Khartoum was the largest of these, attracting between five and six thousand people. Here too, the police was sent in, tear gas used, and people wounded, 59 being arrested.[32] Such episodes were frequent.

What were the results of this ambiguity between disembodied government fantasies regarding the patient taming of childlike labour militants, the

---

and the Workshop and Factories Ordinance. Most of this legislation can be found at FO 371/69235.

28 The National Archives of the UK (TNA): Cowan to Gee, Civil Secretary Office, Khartoum, 15.2.1949, LAB 13/480.

29 The National Archives of the UK (TNA): Cowan to Gee, Civil Secretary Office, Khartoum, 15.2.1949, LAB 13/480.

30 The National Archives of the UK (TNA): Cowan to Gee, Civil Secretary Office, Khartoum, 15.2.1949, LAB 13/480.

31 Sikainga (2002, 106) gives a figure of 5,000 demonstrators.

32 The National Archives of the UK (TNA): Telegram from Dakhlia, Khartoum, to Sudanology, London, 15.4.1948, FO 371/69235, NA. Telegram from Khartoum, unsigned, to Sudanology, London, 14.4.1948, FO 371/69235.

physical repression of the workers—and, in particular, their leaders—and the important concessions made to the labour movement? This oscillatory pattern shaped the peculiar form of the labour struggles of the time. First, the workers' movement began to make systematic use of strikes, because it had learnt that strikes worked. The WAA went on strike in order to be recognised in the first place, and then to increase wages and to protest against the existing trade union regulations; they got it all, even if with certain reservations. Indeed, when in 1952 the workers' movement broke down, it was not because strikes had lost their effect, but because the workers refused to go on strike. Second, the violent oppression of the government against the workers' leaders generated a strong wave of popular sympathy, a wave which transcended social strata. For the workers' movement, this lent strength and legitimacy to its strategy of confrontation. For the colonial administration, such punctual violence neutralised and defused the image that the government was patiently trying to build for itself—as a development provider and benefactor of all workers.

4 'No bargaining with Employer, no Exemptions from Strikes'[33]

Even if, by 1949, the WAA had learnt of the power of the strike and spoke a language that was more confrontational than that of 1946, its leaders limited themselves to discussions about labour and kept politics out. And it was from 1949 that trade unions spread like wildfire among wage workers, for reasons that still remain unclear. The numbers are eloquent. After the promulgation of the Trade Union Ordinance at the end of 1948, the registration of new unions began. Their numbers rose from five in 1949, to 42 at the end of September 1950, and to 99 in 1952.[34] In March 1949, the WAA broke into two different organisations: the Sudan Railways Trade Union, which—by 1951—had 19,000 members and was by far the most powerful union in Sudan, and the Workers' Congress, an umbrella organisation federating all unions, even if the government never recognised it officially.[35]

The British viewed the Workers' Congress as a more moderate organ than the WAA. The government found it easier to negotiate with it, and at the end

33 The National Archives of the UK (TNA): Sudan Political Intelligence Summary, December 1951, FO 371/96846.

34 The National Archives of the UK (TNA): Development of Trade Unions in Sudan, undated, unsigned, included in Robertson to Allen, 1.11.1950, LAB 13/480, and Fawzi (1957, 92).

35 Ibid.: 'There is no special provision in the Trade Union Ordinance for the registration of federations of unions.'

of 1950 its assessment was that it 'had on several occasion exercised a wise and restraining influence.'[36] Indeed, when the congress's first elections were held, neither Sulayman Musa nor al-Tayyib Hassan al-Tayyib presented themselves as candidates (they were also close to pensionable age), and only four out of the 15 original leaders of the WAA were re-elected. The role of the congress as an umbrella organisation whose leaders were trained to defend small unions was essential to the spread of unionism. Indeed, the number of unionised Sudanese in relation to the overall number of waged workers—in spite of the uncertainties inherent in such a calculation—is spectacular. In 1951, the number of union members was estimated to be between 70,000 and 120,000, set against a total number of salaried, urban workers estimated to be between 150,000 and 200,000.[37] By comparison, in Egypt in 1944 there were 350 registered unions with an estimated total membership of 120,000 (Beining and Lockman, 1998, 293), but Egypt had twice the number of inhabitants and was much more industrialised.[38] A list of registered Sudanese trade unions compiled in 1951 included workers from the private and public sectors, and more specifically elementary school teachers, employees of the Sudan Post and Telegraph, bakers, tailors and domestic servants, and the staff of private companies such as the Gellatly and Hankey (the main shipping company of Port Sudan) or Shell.[39]

In spite of the higher opinion that those in colonial ranks had of the Workers' Congress, the number of strikes and workdays lost increased. In January 1950, the Workers' Congress asked for a 75 per cent increase in basic salaries, a request defined by Robertson as 'quite fantastic'.[40] As their demands were not met, the Sudan Railways Trade Union took the initiative and organised a three-day strike (5–7 March). In some places, including Khartoum, the call to strike was supported by 100 per cent of the workforce.[41] Smaller unions launched numerous other strikes. On 23 April, the workers of the Medical Dressers Union went on strike—to secure their demands for eight-hour shifts—and so did,

36 The National Archives of the UK (TNA): Development of Trade Unions in Sudan, undated, unsigned, in Robertson to Allen, 1.11.1950, LAB 13/480.

37 Ibid. Note, however, that the census of 1956 estimates the number of urban, waged workers to be 350,000; quoted in Cross (1997, 245).

38 The National Archives of the UK (TNA): See also—FO 371/41380: Labour and trade unions in Egypt, and FO 371/41379, Labour and the Trade Union Question.

39 The National Archives of the UK (TNA): Note on Trade Unionism in Sudan, D.H.J. Newman, Trade Union Adviser, Khartoum, 26.4.1951, LAB 13/480.

40 The National Archives of the UK (TNA): Mayall to Allen, African Department, FO, London, 3.3.1950, FO 371/80607.

41 The National Archives of the UK (TNA): Telegram from Dakhlia, Khartoum, to Sudanology, London, 6.3.1950, FO 371/80607.

on the same day, the Workers Union of the Sudan Light and Power Company. In October the medical dressers went on strike again. It is to be noted that in all such cases the unions opted for strike even before attempting to negotiate.[42] Another general strike, from 5 to 8 August 1950, was organised in protest against a resolution passed in May by the Legislative Assembly—a Sudanese institutional organ set up to frame the steps that would take Sudan towards self-determination—for an increase in salaries and cost of living allowances that was judged inadequate. And yet, in November, Robertson still could assess the situation as 'not wholly unsatisfactory.'[43] He, like many others, was convinced that such strikes were a necessary step along the way of learning how to conduct 'right' labour negotiations.

New elections at the Workers' Congress consigned such hopes to bitter disappointment. Between 15 and 21 November, 160 delegates of 48 unions elected two individuals considered to have radical leanings—namely, Muhammad al-Sayyid Sallam as president and al-Shafi Ahmad al-Shaykh as secretary. They were described as 'extremists using the Communist jargon'.[44] Al-Shaykh had been a member of the WAA steering committee, and he was the general secretary of the Sudan Railways Trade Union.[45] The Workers' Congress moved its headquarters from Atbara to Khartoum and changed its name to the Sudan Workers Trade Union Federation (SWTUF) (Fawzi, 1957, 103; Daly, 2002, 323).

With the SWTUF, the language of labour rights merged, to an unprecedented degree, with anti-colonial, communist and pro-Egyptian discourses. Even for the labour advisor Audsley, who had several times defended the labour movement, the turn taken by the SWTUF represented 'an ominous development,' due to both the communist leanings of its leaders and the dictatorial tendencies of the federation, the leaders of which were ready to use their 'power as they thought it fit.'[46] The actions of the SWTUF matched its radicalisation. While limits to the scope of this chapter make it impossible to describe here all the events of the period, outlining just a few should clearly illustrate this transformation. The new leadership immediately passed a resolution in

42 The National Archives of the UK (TNA): Telegram from Governor of Khartoum to all Heads of Department, Sudan Agent in London, Sudan Agent in Cairo, 22.4.1950, FO 371/80607.

43 The National Archives of the UK (TNA): Robertson to Allen, Khartoum, 1.11.1950, FO 371/80607.

44 The National Archives of the UK (TNA): Development of Trade Unions in Sudan, undated, unsigned, in Robertson to Allen, 1.11.1950, LAB 13/480.

45 Al-Shafi Ahmad al-Shaykh would be hanged by the Nimeiri regime in 1971 along with two other communist leaders of the SWTUF, Abd al-Khaliq Mahjoub and Joseph Garang.

46 The National Archives of the UK (TNA): Audsley, Report on visit to the Sudan from 1st to 20th February 1951 inclusive, FO 371/90299.

which they threatened a general strike unless the government revoked both an anti-communist decree (the Defence of the Sudan Ordinance) that appeared to be tailored against trade unions, and the expulsion of the students of Khor Taggat—a secondary school near El Obeid.[47] The students had been expelled en bloc because they had gone on strike to protest against the bad conditions at the school, but in reality the government suspected that they were being 'infected' by communist teachers.[48] The link between Khor Taggat, the SWTUF and the former's communist sympathies was disturbing for the government. While negotiations continued back and forth between the government and the SWTUF, at the end of 1950 railway firemen[49] went on indefinite strike in protest against their working conditions.[50] The 'limitless patience' of colonial officers had, by then, almost been used up. Audsley, who at the beginning of 1951 travelled to Khartoum once more, stated: 'Government continued its patient attitude but dealt firmly with the threats ... [These threats] were withdrawn but veiled warnings ... [were given] ... as to what the Government could expect if the demands of the workers ... were not conceded.'[51] Dealing 'firmly with the threats' meant once again arresting the leaders: at the end of December, the Railways Management charged five railways union members and al-Shafi Ahmad al-Shaykh with 'defamation'. They were tried and found guilty, and on the day of the sentence, railway workers called a sudden three-day general strike (27 to 30 December), although the call was not backed by the federation as it did not respect the 15 days of notice required.[52] In total, 52 railway workers were arrested, even if they were quickly released.

---

47 The National Archives of the UK (TNA): The protest of the students of Khor Taggat was fully covered by the press (see, for instance, the following issues of *al-Shaab*: 12, 20 and 27 January 1951). In English: Political Intelligence Summary, January-February 1951, FO 371/90108. Secondary literature on the strike is scarce, but see Daly (2002, 346). In total, 76 of the 119 boys expelled were later readmitted to the school.

48 The National Archives of the UK (TNA): The strike was covered by the leftist newspaper *al-Saraha*, issues of 3, 8, and 14 December 1951. It was also described in the Sudan Political Intelligence Summary, November-December 1950, FO 371/90108, and covered generally in FO 317/90229.

49 Stokers tending the fireboxes of locomotives.

50 The strike was fully covered in the Weekly Press Reviews of December 1950 (Khartoum: National Records Office).

51 The National Archives of the UK (TNA): Audsley, Report on visit to the Sudan from 1st to 20th February 1951 inclusive, FO 371/90299.

52 The National Archives of the UK (TNA): Sudan Political Intelligence Summary, January-February 1951, FO 371/90108.

And yet, it was exactly at this moment that several unions under the umbrella of the SWTUF began feeling uncomfortable with the federation's strategy. Two general strikes were called in three months—the first on 17 February and the second on 23 April 1951—both demanding that the government deliver the usual 75 per cent increase in salaries. However, the first strike was described by the British as 'unpopular'[53] creating severe tensions within the federation as many unions were against it,[54] while with regards to the second, 20 unions out of 43 bluntly refused to participate in the proposed industrial action.[55] This gave the government hope that the obdurate strategy pursued by the SWTUF was losing ground and that finally moderate forces were raising their heads.

In the following months, the same pattern repeated itself: the government exerted force not on trade unions as a whole, but on specific individuals; it was 'firm' with the heads and 'patient' with the members. Yet, this attitude led only to further mass protests. And the popular support generated for the federation as a reaction to government harassment further fuelled the SWTUF's drive to radicalism, without the federation realising that its members were apparently not ready to follow it in its politicisation.

In June 1951, the police went on strike (usually referred to as mutiny). The strike has been discussed in detail elsewhere (Berridge, 2011), and here it suffices to mention that it became, for the government, a pretext for arresting the 'communist' leaders of the SWTUF—Muhammad al-Sayyid Sallam and al-Shafi Ahmad al-Shaykh—despite the fact that they had not been involved in the decision to strike or its implementation. Their imprisonment on dubious charges triggered a new wave of popular protests. The SWTUF organised a general strike from August 26 to 29, supported by two-thirds of the unions. In Khartoum the workers staged a silent protest, holding 'placards carrying "Long live the struggle of the workers"'.[56] This demonstration was momentous also for its female participation, even a British telegram noting 'Nurses at Khartoum

53 The National Archives of the UK (TNA): Trade Union in the Sudan, Allegations by the World Federation of Trade Union (Draft), included in Secretariat, Khartoum to African Department, London, 26.10.1951, FO 371/90230.

54 The National Archives of the UK (TNA): Audsley, Report on visit to the Sudan from 1st to 20th February 1951 inclusive, FO 371/90299.

55 The National Archives of the UK (TNA): According to an intelligence report, the Executive Committee of the SWTUF tried several times in May to pass resolutions regarding strikes, but these resolutions were defeated. Sudan Political Intelligence Summary, May June 1951, FO 371/90109.

56 The National Archives of the UK (TNA): Sudan Political Intelligence Summary, July–August 1951, FO 371/90109.

hospitals took part in the demonstrations. This is the first time in the history of the Sudan that women have taken part in public demonstrations.'[57]

By December 1951, the political radicalisation of the SWTUF was complete. At the elections held between 16 and 21 December, the two arrested leaders were reappointed in absentia, and the federation adopted a new constitution—voted on by its members—the summary of which is worth quoting at some length:

> Conference amended the constitution of the federation to permit political activities and announced its programme as immediate termination of all forms of imperialism in Sudan and reservation of right of self-determination. The means of achievement were to be non-cooperation with any form of imperialism and formation of a common front with political organisations having similar objects … The demand for a general 75% increase in all wages was reiterated and it was decided to stage a series of general strikes, one three-day, one four-day, one five-days, each separated by a fifteen day interval.[58]

Such statues explicitly contravened the Trade Union Ordinance—notably the clause on political activities. They convey the message that the scope of the federation was now the struggle against 'imperialism', a struggle to be pursued by means of strikes. This attitude was best expressed by the new motto of the federation: 'No negotiation and the strike the only weapon.'[59] At this juncture, the federation was incarnating possibly the worst-case scenario for the British, and indeed had become the opposite of what they had intended it to be: rather than being instruments of development, created to ensure the general betterment of society by teaching workers how to defend their interests and be good producers, unions had become political organs in the hands of a virulent, communist-inspired anti-colonial crew, who moreover saw development as a imperialistic ruse.

In early 1952, the federation began to apply its strategy of head-on confrontation by calling repeated, short general strikes. The first was called from 20 to 23 January, and was fully observed by all the unions. The second was called on

57 The National Archives of the UK (TNA): For details of the female nurses' demonstration—ciphered message entitled: First Women Demonstrators, FO 371/90230.

58 The National Archives of the UK (TNA): From Governor General, Khartoum, to Foreign Office, London, 20.12.1951, FO 371/90230.

59 The National Archives of the UK (TNA): Sudan Political Intelligence Summary, September 1951, FO 371/90109.

23 March, and again was 'observed by nearly all government employees', even if it was noted that it enjoyed less public sympathy.[60] But when it came to the third strike things went wrong. Muhammad Sayyid Sallam was finally released from prison on 3 April, only to be arrested again on the charge of giving an inflammatory anti-colonial speech. Immediately the SWTUF called for a general strike of an unlimited duration, to begin on 28 April. However, the Railways Union flatly refused to participate since the 15-day notice period had not been respected. The federation considered that there was no need to comply with the requirements of an imperialist ordinance, but not all the unions shared this position. That the SWTUF seemed to have lost contact with the workers was also confirmed by further evidence: first, the strike had been called just before payday, meaning that the workers did not have the funds necessary to sustain an indefinite strike; second, the federation's leaders had not consulted anyone before calling the strike—a fact that was deeply resented. Grudges with regard to the undemocratic tendencies of the federation had been around for a while, and the government had been careful to nurture them. Also, since the radicalisation of the federation had begun, the government had shrewdly courted a potential opposition element. For example, the arrest of Muhammad Sayyid Sallam, who was also the head of the Railways Union, opened the way for the election of 'Abdallah Bashir, who was known both for his anticommunism and for his mild sympathies for the federation'.[61]

The strike of 28 April went ahead nevertheless. In retaliation, the police immediately arrested 12 members of the federation and carried out house-to-house searches during which communist literature was allegedly found. This time, the colonial government did not hesitate to apply a heavy hand, broadcasting a message in which it threatened that anyone who was not at work on the symbolic date of 1 May would be fired. By 30 April, the strike was over. On 11 May, a further 17 members of the federation were arrested, of which 11 were sentenced to one-year jail terms. The failure of the strike coincided with the rise of moderate forces among the unions, and the re-centring of the discussion on labour negotiations.[62] More importantly, following Najib's coup d'état in Egypt in 1952, it became clear that Sudan would imminently gain its freedom. The politicians preparing the government of national liberation asked

60 The National Archives of the UK (TNA): Sudan Political Intelligence Summary, March-April 1952, FO 371/96846.

61 See, for instance, The National Archives of the UK (TNA): Political Intelligence Summary, September 1951, FO 371/90109.

62 The National Archives of the UK (TNA): Sudan Political Intelligence Summary, May-June 1952, FO 371/102701.

the workers to collaborate and to suspend industrial action, and so they did, remaining mostly silent during the process of self-determination between 1953 and 1956.

The last point I wish to analyse here, by way of a conclusion, is a sketchy close-up of the SWTUF's communism. It is important to note that while there is a tendency in the literature to conflate workers' movements and communism, their stories do not coincide. The historian Nuri El-Amin (1986, 1987, 1989, 1996a, 1996b, 1996c, 1997) has demonstrated at great length the influence of communism on intellectuals and secondary school students. However, this section of the population was quite different to that of salaried manual workers. The difference was not necessarily based on literacy—highly skilled artisans were literate—but rather on corporate identities and socio-professional categories. The founders and leaders of Sudan's first communist organisations (such as the Sudan Movement of National Liberation, or SMNL) were from the educated elite and not from the rank and file of the SWTUF.[63] In the first trial in Sudan of individuals accused of communism under the Defence of the Sudan Ordinance, in April 1951, 21 people faced charges; six were acquitted. One of those released was Muhammad al-Sayyid Sallam, president of the SWTUF—as it was impossible to prove that he belonged to the Communist party.[64] Other union leaders, instead, such as al-Shafi Ahmad al-Shaykh and Qasim Amin were, admittedly, communists. They had turned to communism, however, more because they were militant anti-colonialists than for a close adherence to a Marxist ideology. In the communist-inspired party they found a framework sufficiently radical and uncompromising to fit their views (Cross, 1997).

A remark of 1951 by Robertson is helpful to understand the sense in which the federation's leaders were communists:

> We seem to be in some anger of confusing the meaning of 'Communism'. We have in the Sudan two types of Communism: the strictly theoretical and ideological types emanating from the higher schools and the ignorant inferiority complex type emanating from the 'hates and fears fast over taking Africa'. I prefer to call the latter 'revolutionaries'. The former

63 The National Archives of the UK (TNA): Note on Communist Activities in the Sudan, Security, Civil Secretary's office, Khartoum, 4.6.1951, FO 371/90125: 'There is abundant evidence that the communist movement is led by teachers, and in particular those of them in National Schools who have less attractive careers and prospects than their contemporaries in Government service'. See also: Daly (2002, 280) and El-Amin (1996a, 1996b, 1997).

64 The National Archives of the UK (TNA): Extracts from Sudan Weekly Newsletters (Published by Public Relation Branch, Civil Secretary Office, Khartoum, 21.4.1951, FO 371/90125.

> are the real 'Communists'. We have them of course in various walks of life, but particularly as teachers in our schools... The latter type, the 'revolutionaries', are persistently called 'Communists'. I do not think them such unless a definite link is established either in funds or in statements with the former...'[65]

It was of course easy to mistake one communism for the other, and the above remark is one of the rare occasions on which such a distinction was made. The mistake was made easier by the fact that the language of the federation—as expressed, for example, in its statutes—with its strong anti-imperialist tone, appeared to be very radical, and thus similar to, and certainly inspired by, that employed by communists. However, the actual bridge between communist elite politicians and waged workers was an uneasy one, at least in the early 1950s. In 1952, the federation's leaders sought to connect politically with the SMNL. However, the literature reveals that this was a strategic mistake, since union rank and file had little sympathy for the party. Even if more research is needed to understand why workers employed a radical language in labour negotiations, but when it came to vote they supported traditional parties, some hypotheses can be forwarded. The communist-inspired language was listened to very carefully when issues were connected to work. Many workers were employed by British or Europeans; they were experiencing hardship because of an international economy dominated by colonial powers; and they were living their lives in shanty towns where all services were lacking. But, perhaps, when these real-life concerns were expressed by an educated elite that had little or no connection with the life of the workers, it was harder for the workers to trust that elite.

5 Conclusion

This chapter has sought to paint a picture of the steps that led to the birth of the workers' movement in Sudan. The re-conceptualisation of the role of the state in development entailed a real redefinition of the negotiating power of the workforce. Using a strategy of confrontation, the latter realised that it could force the state to listen to its demands. In this sense, the development paradigm had an enormous influence on transforming workers into legitimate political actors, for the first time in Sudan's twentieth century history.

---

65 The National Archives of the UK (TNA): J.W. Robertson to Allen, Khartoum, 15.7.1951, FO 371/90125.

However, the focus here has been less on who the actors of the movement were and how it worked, than on the relationships and feedback effect between three actors: the Sudanese government, the Labour Party in power in London, and the workers' movement. Because of the centrality of colonial labour debates to the identity and history of the Labour Party, London was determined to introduce labour legislation in Sudan, and subordinated the granting of development funding to the introduction of measures aimed at labour protection. The Sudanese government was very sceptical of this, but was convinced by labour advisors sent from London that it was impossible to stop the march of development. But as events got out of hand, the workers' movement transformed into the worst thing the state had feared it could become—a radicalised movement that struggled to secure the quickest possible end to colonialism.

The curve of the radicalisation of the workers' movement described in this article must not be seen as something inevitable, but as the outcome of a volatile situation. The richness of colonial sources consists precisely in their ability to show how this story was ridden with accidents and evolved in a manner unexpected by all its actors. Such uncertainties, which were kept confidential for fear of losing face with actors that the colonial British officers had no experience of dealing with, emerge clearly from the dense internal correspondence deposited mostly in the National Archives at Kew, London. The Sudanese labour movement was founded by a moderate group whose only previous organisational experience had been to arrange cultural activities in an old boys' club. It is true that the international situation, and in particular the Egyptian example, favoured confrontational attitudes, but as seen, by vocation and ideology the WAA was essentially moderate. And yet its interaction with the state generated a rapid and unplanned transformation, as a consequence of its leaders feeling harassed, maltreated and not taken seriously by the government, and experiencing the state's actions as incomprehensible and unjust.

And in a mirror-like manner, the government hardened its response because it saw the workers' reactions as equally inexplicable: they were ungrateful and unmoved by the government's 'limitless patience' in teaching them how to run good trade unions. Colonial officers that perceived themselves to be merciful and forgiving, patient and pedagogical, watched with stupor as each of their initiatives triggered more protests. And this in turn provoked self-defeating strategies such as the persecution of trade union leaders, which contributed to a great extent to the success of the movement beyond the wage workers.

Finally, the third unexpected development was the exhaustion of the workers' bellicose strategy. A series of blunders revealed that labour had ceased to be at the centre of the preoccupations of union leaders, and that those leaders had lost sight of workers' basic needs. Eventually, a form of consensus emerged through these conflicts, with the elaboration of a status quo that lasted until the end of the 1950s.

References

Abdel-Rahim, M. (1969) *Imperialism and Nationalism in the Sudan: A Study in Constitutional and Political Development, 1899–1956* (Oxford: Clarendon P).

Ali Taha, A.R.E. (1970) 'The Sudanese Labor Movement: A Study of Labor Unionism in a Developing Society', PhD Thesis (Berkeley: University of California).

Beinin, J.Z., and Z. Lockman (1998) *Workers on the Nile: Nationalism, Communism, Islam, and the Egyptian Working Class, 1882–1954* (Cairo: American University in Cairo Press).

Berman, B.J. and J.M. Lonsdale (1980) 'Crises of Accumulation, Coercion and the Colonial State: The Development of the Labor Control System in Kenya, 1919–1929', *Canadian Journal of African Studies / Revue canadienne des études africaines*, 14(1), pp. 37–54, DOI: 10.1080/00083968.1980.10803948.

Bernal, V. (1991) *Cultivating Workers: Peasants and Capitalism in a Sudanese Village* (New York: Columbia University Press).

Berridge, W.J. (2011) '"What the Men Are Crying Out for Is Leadership": The Khartoum Police Strike of 1951 and the Battle for Administrative Control', *The Journal of Imperial and Commonwealth History*, 39(1), pp. 121–142, DOI: 10.1080/03086534.2011.543797.

Beshir, M.O. (1974) *Revolution and Nationalism in the Sudan* (New York: Barnes & Noble Books).

Burton, A. (2003) 'Townsmen in the Making: Social Engineering and Citizenship in Dar Es Salaam, c.1945–1960', *The International Journal of African Historical Studies*, 36(2), pp. 331–365, http://www.jstor.org/stable/3559387.

Butler, L.J. (1999) 'Reconstruction, Development and the Entrepreneurial State: The British Colonial Model, 1939–51', *Contemporary British History*, 13(4), pp. 29–55, DOI: 10.1080/13619469908581559.

Constantine, S. (2005) *The Making of British Colonial Development Policy 1914–1940* (London: Frank Cass).

Cooper, F. (1996) *Decolonization and African Society: The Labor Question in French and British Africa* (Cambridge, New York: Cambridge University Press).

Cooper, F. (1992) 'The Dialectics of Decolonization: Nationalism and Labor Movements in Postwar Africa', CRSO Working Paper n. 480, https://deepblue.lib.umich.edu/bitstream/handle/2027.42/51246/480.pdf?sequence=1 (accessed on 20 May 2016).

Cooper, F. and R.M. Packard (1997) *International Development and the Social Sciences Essays on the History and Politics of Knowledge* (Berkeley: University of California Press).

Corthorn, P. and J.S. Davis (2008) *The British Labour Party and the Wider World Domestic Politics, Internationalism and Foreign Policy* (London, New York: Tauris Academic Studies).

Cowen, M. and R.W. Shenton (1996) *Doctrines of Development* (London, New York: Routledge).

Cowen, M. and R.W. Shenton (1991) 'The Origin and Course of Fabian Colonialism in Africa', *Journal of Historical Sociology*, 4(2), pp. 143–174, DOI: 10.1111/j.1467-6443.1991.tb00101.x.

Cross, P. (1997) 'British Attitudes to Sudanese Labour: The Foreign Office Records as Sources for Social History', *British Journal of Middle Eastern Studies*, 24(2), pp. 217–260, DOI: 10.1080/13530199708705647.

Curless, G. (2013) 'The Sudan Is "Not Yet Ready for Trade Unions": The Railway Strikes of 1947–1948', *The Journal of Imperial and Commonwealth History*, 41(5), pp. 804–822, DOI: 10.1080/03086534.2013.790226.

Daly, M.W. (2003) *Empire on the Nile: The Anglo-Egyptian Sudan, 1898–1934* (Cambridge, New York: Cambridge University Press).

Daly, M.W. (2002) *Imperial Sudan: The Anglo-Egyptian Condominium, 1934–1956* (Cambridge, New York: Cambridge University Press).

Duffield, M.R. and Hewitt V.M. (eds.) (2009) *Empire, Development & Colonialism: The Past in the Present* (Woodbridge, Rochester: James Currey).

El-Amin, M.N. (1997) 'The Sudanese Communist Movement, the First Five Years—III', *Middle Eastern Studies*, 33(1), pp. 128–151, DOI: 10.1080/00263209708701146.

El-Amin, M.N. (1996a) 'The Sudanese Communist Movement, the First Five Years—I', *Middle Eastern Studies*, 32(3), pp. 22–40, DOI: 10.1080/00263209608701117.

El-Amin, M.N. (1996b) 'The Sudanese Communist Movement; The First Five Years—II', *Middle Eastern Studies*, 32(4), pp. 251–263, DOI: 10.1080/00263209608701128.

El-Amin, M.N. (1996c) 'The Role of International Communism in the Muslim World and in Egypt and the Sudan', *British Journal of Middle Eastern Studies*, 23(1), pp. 29–53, DOI: 10.1080/13530199608705621.

El-Amin, M.N. (1989) 'International Communism, the Egyptian Wafd Party and the Sudan', *British Journal of Middle Eastern Studies*, 16(1), pp. 27–48, DOI: 10.1080/13530198908705484.

El-Amin, M.N. (1987) 'The Role of the Egyptian Communists in Introducing the Sudanese to Communism in the 1940s', *International Journal of Middle East Studies*, 19(4), pp. 433–454.

El-Amin, M.N. (1986) 'The Impact of the Sudanese Unionists on Sudanese Communism', *Middle Eastern Studies*, 22(3), pp. 418–434, DOI: 10.1080/00263208608700673.

Fawzi, S. Ed Din (1957) *The Labour Movement in the Sudan, 1946–1955* (London, New York: Oxford University Press).

Fawzi, S. Ed Din (1955) 'The Wage Structure and Wage Policy in the Sudan', *Sudan Notes and Records*, 36(2), pp. 159–175, http://www.jstor.org/stable/41716694.

Freund, B. (1988) *The African Worker* (Cambridge, New York: Cambridge University Press).

Gaitskell, A. (1959) *Gezira; a Story of Development in the Sudan* (London: Faber and Faber).

Havinden, M.A. and D. Meredith (2002) *Colonialism and Development Britain and Its Tropical Colonies, 1850–1960* (London, New York: Routledge).

Hobsbawm, E.J. (1967) 'Trade Union History', *The Economic History Review*, 20(2), pp. 358–364, DOI: 10.1111/j.1468-0289.1967.tb00142.x.

Howe, S. (1993) *Anticolonialism in British Politics: The Left and the End of Empire, 1918–1964* (Oxford, New York: Clarendon Press, Oxford University Press).

Howell, D. (1983) *British Workers and the Independent Labour Party, 1888–1906* (Manchester, New York: Manchester University Press; St. Martin's Press).

Lewis, B.A. (1962) 'Deim El Arab and the Beja Stevedores of Port Sudan', *Sudan Notes and Records*, 43, pp. 16–49, http://www.jstor.org/stable/41716823.

Lewis, J. (2000) *Empire State-Building: War & Welfare in Kenya, 1925–52* (Oxford, Nairobi, Athens, Ohio: James Currey, E.A.E.P., Ohio University Press).

Lilleker, D.G. (2004) *Against the Cold War the History and Political Traditions of pro-Sovietism in the British Labour Party 1945–89* (London, New York: I.B. Tauris).

Maul, D. (2012) *Human Rights, Development and Decolonization the International Labour Organization, 1940–70* (New York: Palgrave Macmillan).

Orr, C.A. (1966) 'Trade Unionism in Colonial Africa', *The Journal of Modern African Studies*, 4(1), pp. 65–81, http://www.jstor.org/stable/159416.

Perkins, K.J. (1993) *Port Sudan: The Evolution of a Colonial City* (Boulder: Westview Press).

Ravier, J.-P. (1981) *Les syndicats britanniques sous les gouvernements travaillistes: 1945–1970* (Lyon: Presses universitaires de Lyon).

al-Safi, Mahasin A. (ed.) (1989) *The Nationalist Movement in the Sudan* (Khartoum: Institute of African and Asian Studies, University of Khartoum).

Seekings, J. (2011) 'British Colonial Policy, Local Politics, and the Origins of the Mauritian Welfare State, 1936–50', *The Journal of African History*, 52(02), pp. 157–177, DOI: 10.1017/S0021853711000247.

Shane, S. (1989) *Trade Union Development in Sub-Saharan Africa* (Pretoria: Human Sciences Research Council).

Sharkey, H.J., E. Vezzadini and I. Seri-Hersch (2015) 'Rethinking Sudan Studies: A Post-2011 Manifesto', *Canadian Journal of African Studies / Revue canadienne des études africaines*, 49(1), pp. 1–18, DOI: 10.1080/00083968.2015.1046256.

Sikainga A.A. (2002) *City of Steel and Fire: A Social History of Atbara, Sudan's Railway Town, 1906–1984* (Portsmouth: Heinemann).

Sikainga A.A. (1996) *Slaves into Workers: Emancipation and Labor in Colonial Sudan* (Austin: University of Texas Press).

Teelucksingh, J. (2015) *Labour and the Decolonization Struggle in Trinidad and Tobago* (Basingstoke, New York: Palgrave Macmillan)

Thorpe, A. (2000) 'The Membership of the Communist Party of Great Britain, 1920–1945', *The Historical Journal*, 43(03), pp. 777–800, http://journals.cambridge.org/article_S0018246X99001181 (accessed on 20 May 2016).

Thorpe, A. (1998) 'Comintern "Control" of the Communist Party of Great Britain, 1920–43' *English Historical Review*, 113(482), pp. 637–662, DOI: 10.1093/ehr/CXIII.452.637.

Thorpe, A. (1997) *A History of the British Labour Party* (New York: St. Martin's Press).

Tijani, H.I. (2012) *Union Education in Nigeria: Labor, Empire, and Decolonization since 1945* (Basingstoke: Palgrave Macmillan).

Vatikiotis, P.J. (1969) *The Modern History of Egypt* (New York: Praeger).

Vezzadini, E. (2015) *Lost Nationalism: Revolution, Memory and Anti-Colonial Resistance in Sudan* (Woodbridge, Rochester: James Currey).

Vezzadini, E. (2010) 'Making the Sudanese: Slavery Policies and Hegemony Construction in Early Colonial Sudan' in J. Spaulding, S. Beswick, C. Fluehr-Lobban and R. Lobban (eds.) *Sudan's Wars and Peace Agreements* (Newcastle upon Tyne: Cambridge Scholars Publishing), pp. 71–101.

Vickers, R. (2004) *The Labour Party and the World* (Manchester, New York: Manchester University Press).

Warburg, G.R. (1978) *Islam, Nationalism and Communism in a Traditional Society: The Case of Sudan* (London: F. Cass).

Weiler, P. (1984) 'Forming Responsible Trade Unions: The Colonial Office, Colonial Labor, and the Trades Union Congress', *Radical History Review*, (28–30), pp. 367–392, DOI: 10.1215/01636545-1984-28-30-367.

Worley, M. (2005) *Labour inside the Gate: a History of the British Labour Party between the Wars* (London, New York: I.B. Tauris).

Zeilig, L. (2009) *Class Struggle and Resistance in Africa* (Chicago: Haymarket Books).

CHAPTER 5

The Activities of Adl Wal Ihsane in the Neighbourhoods. How to Build a 'Non-Legal' Consensus from a 'Tolerated' Conflict

Merieme Yafout

Abstract

Based on observation of the activities of the female members of the Moroccan Islamist movement Justice and Spirituality (*Al Adl Wal Ihsane*, AWI) at neighbourhood level, this chapter analyses the conception of development fostered by this movement and tries to answer the following questions: how do conflicting visions of development (those of AWI, the authorities and other associations) live together in the same neighbourhood, and what do the interactions between these different active participants tell us about modes of government on the local scale? If we view Islamists as agents of human development, and religious education and spirituality as important elements in this development, we see how complex the social and political relations are that the Islamist movement has with power and with society as a whole. The interactions of Islamist movements with various local players highlight a dialectic between conflict and consensus based on a 'Western' hegemonic model of development. This dialectic allows other strategies to find expression—strategies that flourish in daily activities—and other conceptions of what is seen as a 'good' way of conducting one's life. Intentional or not, strategies of discharge, differentiation, discretion, competition or compliance, and the alternative modes of governance and conduct of life that this article highlights, show that the relationships between different players cannot be reduced just to conflict or consensus, and that their behaviour cannot be explained solely as a form of rejection or acceptance. The neo-liberal paradigm of development can comprise both a common ground and a place of conflict between quite different models of society.

1 Introduction

Assoc[1] is a women's association founded in 2006 that works in a poor neighbourhood of Casablanca. The association operates an economic micro-project

1 This is one of the women's associations that I observed during field research I conducted as part of my doctoral thesis on the status of women in Islamist movements in Morocco (Yafout,

© MERIEME YAFOUT, 2017 | DOI 10.1163/9789004349551_006

for local women who also benefit from literacy courses, awareness campaigns, and workshops that provide training in manual work. In addition to these activities, Assoc provides extra classes for students of different ages and conducts other long-term activities such as health campaigns, legal awareness classes and lectures on women's issues. According to one official from Assoc, all of these activities are meant to 'help women evolve from their status as mere consumers and gain financial independence and participate fully in development. Through these activities, we motivate women to emerge from their cocoons and attend various training courses that educate them to adopt a spirit of production and productivity and, above all, a critical mind, which will prevent them from falling into the trap of Wahhabism.'[2]

In principle, these activities are no different from those of the majority of active women's groups in poor neighbourhoods and rural areas. Literacy programmes, awareness campaigns, workshops giving training in manual work, and cooperatives are all part of the current hegemonic model of development consisting in particular of assistance to micro-projects, micro-credit, income-generating activities, literacy, etc. Similarly, the vocabulary and lexicon used by Assoc are those of the dominant dogma with its references to economic efficiency, participation and individual responsibility. However, these activities can be seen in a quite different light if we take into account the fact that Assoc is forced to deploy an arsenal of precautions simply in order to exist, and in particular to conduct its activities in such a way that they are not prohibited. Indeed, two members of its governing bodies belong to the Islamist movement Justice and Spirituality (*Al Adl Wal Ihsane*, AWI);[3] a movement considered as

2012). The research was conducted between 2008 and 2012. The data analysed in this chapter are mainly the result of participant observation of the activities of the women studied and of semi-structured interviews I conducted with them. To ensure the anonymity of the association, neither its name nor the name of the neighbourhood will be cited. [The author's pseudonymous name for this association is 'Ass', which I have replaced, passim, by the less equivocal name 'Assoc'—translator's note.].

2 Interview with one of Assoc's officials; Casablanca, 23 January 2009.

3 The history of this movement is linked to that of its founder, Abdessalam Yassine, who in 1974 sent a letter of advice to King Hassan II. Following this act, he suffered a series of acts of repression. In 1982 he created the Islamic charitable association that in 1987 adopted the slogan Al Adl Wal Ihsane (Justice and Spirituality), and, until his death in 2012, led radical opposition to the Moroccan political regime. The position taken by this movement led to the imprisonment and repression of its leaders and many of its members. During the 1990s, the movement expanded dramatically in universities and then became the largest Moroccan Islamist movement. Until now, AWI has refused to engage itself in institutional political life

'not legal but tolerated'.[4] This proximity shifts the focus of the analysis from 'development' to 'development conflicts', highlighting the competition, differences and alternative modes of government at the local level.

The history of the AWI movement has been marked by its conflict with the monarchy. Indeed, since its birth in 1974 it has opposed the very bases of the latter: its hereditary character and its religious legitimacy.[5] This is what explains its ambiguous status, reflected in the journalistic description of the movement as 'semi-tolerated'. Having failed to establish a change from above by persuading the head of the regime to reform the country,[6] this movement is in favour of a change of society from the bottom up and places the concept of *tarbiya* (education) at the centre of its programmes. In AWI's theory, this concept derives its meaning from emphasising the importance of the human being and his or her happiness in earthly life and in the hereafter, thus establishing the link between a spiritual dimension that aims to change individuals from within and the values of social justice and dignity. The primary purpose of education, it claims, is to help make the human being 'free and independent', living 'with dignity'—and this objective can be achieved only if human beings suffer neither poverty nor injustice (Yassine, 1998). It is on the basis of this logic that the movement campaigns for social justice and is critical of the neo-liberal policies adopted by the state, which in its view ignore the facts and are ineffective, alienating, elitist, and produce injustice. AWI criticises the fact that the state accepts the 'ready-made recipes' imposed by hegemonic forces that consider the human being as a resource, as a 'consumer' and as a 'market' (Yassine, 1994, 189). However, this does not prevent the movement

---

but advocates non-violence and gradual change through education. It was one of the key players of the 20 February movement, which was initiated in 2011 as part of the 'Arab Spring'.

4 This expression is frequently used by the media to describe the legal status of AWI. See, for example, the article in *TelQuel* (2015).

5 The monarchy in Morocco bases its religious legitimacy on the principle of the 'Commander of the Faithful'—a traditional title reinvented during the reign of Hassan II granting the King a double 'mission': the safeguarding of religion and the management of public affairs. See Tozy (1999).

6 Abdessalam Yassine, at the time a senior figure in education and training, a former follower of the Boutchichiya *zawiya* (a Sufi brotherhood), sent a letter to King Hassan II requesting that he seeks redemption (*attawba*) and calling on him to 'take the initiative in the authentic rebirth of Islam'. The King's reaction was to intern Yassine in a hospital wing for tuberculosis patients, and then in a mental asylum for a total of three and a half years. Yassine is considered to have been one of the leading ideologues of Islamism (Tozy, 2009, 72) from 1973 to his death in December 2012; he wrote dozens of books setting out his project and his vision of Muslim history, of modern society and the state.

from using the data produced by this dominant dogma. So it draws on international statistics and reports, including those that rank countries according to human development indices, to show the negative impact of these policies on the daily lives of Moroccans. The sectors of education and health, it claims, have been continually at risk since the adoption of structural adjustment programmes. Through the privatisation of several sectors, the opening up of the economy to international markets, internal economic liberalisation, and the increasing financial dependency of Morocco on investors and foreign lenders, these policies have, it is claimed, caused widening inequalities.

These critiques bring out the very different conception of development promoted by AWI: it views the state as a central agent of development and therefore establishes an ideal-typical construction of the role of a 'good government' whose priority is to deconstruct dependency on the West and to adopt a strategy that takes into account local contexts, with their own norms, values and structures. As Abdessalam Yassine noted, a 'good government' should adopt an education policy that 'frees us from alienation' (Yassine, 1994, 120), producing, in different areas including industry, skills that are essential for liberating Muslims from their status as 'consumers, importers and debtors' (Yassine, 1994, 182). So it is a reading of development focused simultaneously on Third World and nationalist values that emerges from these criticisms; a relatively interventionist conception of the state, different from the one developed by liberal Islamists of the Justice and Development Party (Parti de la justice et du développement, PJD).[7] Thus, to a concept of development considered as superficial and alienating, the AWI movement prefers a concept of education that puts human beings at the centre of all 'real' development by focusing on their spiritual, social and economic fulfilment.

However, the critical vision of state development policies adopted by the AWI movement contradicts its earlier assessment of the Assoc association, even though Assoc is close to AWI. Assoc pursues activities that are 'mundane' and 'ordinary' compared to what other associations do, and undoubtedly fits into the development policies and liberalisation reforms introduced by the

7 The PJD is an Islamist party and has been in government since 2011, following the early elections held as part of the 'Arab Spring'. It was created in 1996 following the integration of a group of members of the Islamist Movement of Unification and Reform (Mouvement de l'unification et de la réforme: MUR) into the party of the Constitutional Democratic Popular Movement (Mouvement populaire démocratique constitutionnel: MPDC) created in 1967 by Abdelkrim Al Khatib. Under the colours of this party, members of the MUR participated in elections for the first time in 1997, before the party changed its name, in 1998, to the Justice and Development Party (Parti de la justice et du développement: PJD) and continued to prepare for its gradual entry into institutional politics.

government at the local level. This assessment lies at the origin of this chapter. Based on observation of the activities of the women members of AWI at neighbourhood level, this chapter tries to show how the different view of development fostered by AWI is realised, how conflicting visions of development (those of AWI, the authorities and other associations) live together in the same neighbourhood, and what the interactions between these different active participants tell us about modes of government on the local scale. The neighbourhood will thus be considered as a place where the conceptions, activities, convergences, divergences and strategies of different active participants all fit together.

Thanks to its existence as 'tolerated' despite being 'non-legal', the AWI movement has, since the late 1990s, proceeded to create neighbourhood associations. These provide it with a legal framework in which residents can approach it without fear. However, the creation of an association by AWI members must be achieved without the knowledge of the authorities and, for the association to exist and carry out its activities, a number of precautions and adaptations are necessary, as explained below. It is also important to note that community action is only complementary to other AWI activities in the neighbourhood. Despite its status, the presence of AWI in the neighbourhood is still based on the educational activities it carries out as an Islamist movement that sees itself as legal.[8] Thus, the women members of AWI studied in this paper act in the neighbourhood primarily as a branch of the national women's section that conducts spiritual education work and 'consciousness raising'. Then, depending on how closely they are controlled by the authorities, they act through one or more associations that provide development activities 'like all the other associations'.

2 A Women's Association Like All Others

While observing the various actions performed by women members of AWI in the neighbourhood under consideration, I paid particular attention to the Assoc women's association for social development. Of the seven members who form its executive office, two are members of AWI while the five others are sympathisers. Aged between 25 and 35, they are conducting an economic micro-project that benefits almost forty residents in the neighbourhood. Early in the morning, certain women come into the association's premises to bake

8 AWI members state that several verdicts pronounced by Moroccan law courts confirm that the movement is indeed legal.

their own bread, while others prefer to do so at home and bring it to the association. At 11:30 a.m., they begin to sell these products in a small shop belonging to the local association. 'All the women who live in the surrounding streets buy our products; they know that it's clean and it's properly made', says a young woman responsible for sales in the shop.[9] Afternoons are devoted to the different workshops open to women of the neighbourhood. Thus, one of the four little rooms on the premises is used by women of various ages taking literacy classes provided by two young women, each of them supervising one group. Thirty-eight women benefit from these courses and, as only one room is available for education, the supervisors are forced to divide them into two groups: the first group is taught between 2 p.m. and 4 p.m.; the second from 4 p.m. to 6 p.m. Soumaya, one of the supervisors, tells us that 'the number of women who want to get involved in reading and writing keeps increasing but, unfortunately, we have only one room. To solve this problem, the board members have managed to establish a partnership with a nearby school that opens its rooms from 6 p.m. onwards so as to cater for other women.'[10]

The second room on the premises is reserved for learning crafts. Three workshops are held jointly: a sewing workshop set up in a corner equipped with sewing machines; a glass painting workshop in another corner; and a ceramic workshop in a third corner. The third room, meanwhile, opening onto the kitchen and equipped with a large oven, is intended for learning the culinary arts: women come here to swap and prepare different recipes, and their products are also sold in the aforementioned shop: Moroccan-style pancakes (*msemen, baghrir*), rolls, cakes, etc. At night, from 7 p.m. onwards, extra lessons for children and teenagers are provided. Direct support from AWI members is more important here: 'The teaching "sisters" or "brothers"[11] of the youth section have access to the free extra lessons, while the parents of recipients pay a nominal fee to the association', says the association's president.[12]

In addition to these daily activities, the board of the association organises weekly or monthly activities: health campaigns, legal awareness classes, lectures on women's issues, etc. Moreover, the treasurer of Assoc says that the association supports several women economically: in addition to the aforementioned forty women, there are also those who, thanks to various workshops, have set up small-scale sewing projects or bake cakes to order, for

9 Interview; 23 January 2009.

10 Interview with an Assoc literacy teacher; Casablanca, 23 January 2013.

11 The terms 'sister' and 'brother' are part of the lexicon usually employed by the militants of the Islamist movement to refer to one another.

12 Interview with the president of Assoc; Casablanca, 23 January 2009.

example. With the exception of the secretary, who is paid a small sum, the work of the board members and workshop supervisors is voluntary. Thus, the treasurer of the association explains that 'the association earns ten *santimat* for each product sold in the store. This provides us with just enough to pay the rent for the premises and the local store and the various expenses: water, electricity [...] As for equipment, such as ovens, tables, sewing machines, kitchen utensils and so on, they are usually donations.'[13] In addition to the activities held within the association, others are organised from time to time in penitentiaries or orphanages, and the board of the association partners with colleges and high schools to sensitise teenagers to the dangers of drugs and alcohol and prevent all forms of juvenile delinquency.

Volunteers are motivated by a wide range of 'moral sentiments': commitment, altruism, self-sacrifice. But not these alone. Some are also driven by a love of community work or by the desire to occupy their free time, to communicate with others, to find work opportunities, and to feel useful. The association represents a friendly and feminine space where everyone knows everyone else, including the beneficiaries. In addition, mothers like it there because the activities they carry out in this space do not conflict with their roles as mothers. On the contrary, their maternal role is facilitated. In addition, various financial resources ensure the survival of the association: the income from the sale of products covers the major expenses (rent, water, electricity) while donations from benefactors and partnerships provide free premises for literacy classes.

To complement these resources, the association's board has prepared an application for financial aid from USAID[14] and other international organisations, as well as from the National Initiative for Human Development (Initiative nationale du développement humain, INDH). The latter is part of a social and solidarity policy that Morocco adopted in the late 1990s and is one of those projects that are given priority treatment and media coverage as they are associated with the King (Bono, 2009; Catusse, 2011). Launched in 2005, this initiative funds local development micro-projects in order to fight against poverty by providing the poor with the means of breaking out of poverty by themselves (Bono, 2010 and 2013). It likewise encourages charitable activity. If the activities carried out by Assoc are no different from those performed by other neighbourhood associations, applying for funding from the INDH and international

13 Interview with the treasurer of Assoc; Casablanca, 23 January 2009.

14 The US Agency for International Development (USAID) says it supports projects in Morocco in the fields of economy and employment, for participation in governance, education and social reforms as well as for gender equality. See https://www.usaid.gov/morocco (accessed on 1 June 2016).

agencies constitutes a tactic for obtaining additional resources and a legitimation that does not necessarily amount to an endorsement of reigning dogmas. The fact remains that this strategy, which validates the compliance of Assoc's activities with the hegemonic model so heavily criticised elsewhere by AWI, constitutes an active participation in this model and, more generally, is a way of spreading this dominant paradigm.[15]

3 Strategies of Differentiation, Compliance and Restriction in the Community Field

While these programmes seem to converge with those of other associations active in the same neighbourhood, and with development policies more generally undertaken by public authorities and international organisations, interviewees try to assign to them a different meaning, which in fact confirms the ideological link between members of the executive office of Assoc and the AWI movement. Take literacy, for example; for these people, it assumes the following meaning: 'For us, literacy is not limited to learning how to read and write. Indeed, through this operation, we transmit a body of knowledge whose primary aim is to know God [...] This is for us a community framework that combines traditional programmes with an awakening of consciences and a spiritual education.'[16]

Literacy, then, becomes a means of inculcating a system of values in its beneficiaries. One interviewee reveals that, at first, some women resort to the association 'out of curiosity' but that subsequently they may break off their activity with it because of family commitments or a certain fatigue, or simply due to a lack of motivation. To avoid this type of failure, the leaders of Assoc motivate participants by highlighting the Islamic model: 'We motivate women to play a positive role in their circle by drawing on the historical models of the female companions of the Prophet, the Hadith [the words and deeds of the Prophet], and koranic verses: this makes them more easily convinced of the virtues of community action.'[17]

---

15 This constrained participation, which stems from opportunism, a tactic of recognition, or a strategy aiming at efficiency and a very specific goal, was already highlighted by Weber (2006) and is very common in the world of development, given its bureaucratisation (Hibou, 2012; Kemp and Berkovitch, 2013).

16 Interview with an Assoc literacy teacher; Casablanca, 23 January 2013.

17 Interview with an Assoc official; Casablanca, 23 January 2009.

The awakening of consciences and the spiritual education mentioned by the interviewees recall the educational project sponsored by AWI since the 1980s. According to this project, the individual must change from within to realise his or her spiritual journey to God. But change from within can only be achieved if the individual has not suffered from injustice. Thus, education is presented as a multidimensional process of change that acts first on the individual, presented as the main agent in the change, then spreads throughout society and reduces injustice. One of the basic mechanisms is coaching people with the aim of 'awakening their consciences.' This education 'from below' requires an AWI member to 'be ubiquitous among the people, in addition to being really close to all the social, economic and political difficulties the people are forced to suffer',[18] and 'the awakening of consciences' is achieved by coaching, spreading the ideas of the movement, and acting as a role model. It is in this context that we must understand the community action and all the activities carried out by AWI members in the neighbourhood, as well as the implications of their 'coaching' the people.

For AWI members, this difference in the meaning attributed to community activities marks a move away from the hegemonic meaning imposed by Western players, which in their view is 'superficial'.[19] In the case of literacy, for example, while the hegemonic sense is limited to learning how to read and write, the implementation of a 'broader' meaning—insofar as it includes the behavioural and spiritual dimensions attributed to it by AWI—sets it apart from other players in this sector. AWI is, however, not the only body that works towards the education of women. In highly concrete terms, the movement faces two types of competition that help to distinguish it. First, the state has taken a firm grip on this activity following the reform of its religious policy based on a bureaucratisation of the religious bodies managing mosques:[20] in 2005, the Ministry of *Habous* and Islamic Affairs began the feminisation of the religious bodies in charge of managing mosques. It proceeded to train *Murshidat* (female preachers)[21] and female trainers who provide literacy classes for women in mosques. These trainers have the status of civil servants. Literacy classes

18 These are the words of an interviewee; I spoke to her, together with a female AWI member, in Casablanca on 28 May 2009 for my doctoral research.

19 In the words of the previous interviewee.

20 Tozy notes that this religious policy, based—inter alia—on the management and supervision of the use of mosques and the training of the technicians of worship, dates from the early 1980s (Tozy, 2009, 66), but that it has gained momentum since the terrorist attacks of 16 May 2003 in Casablanca (Tozy, 2013).

21 On *Murshidat*, see Yafout (2012).

and sermons result in the creation of paid jobs. While these public policies undoubtedly increase the provision of literacy and thereby form part of a practice of development, they take on a particular meaning in the Moroccan political context: they express a desire to compete with Islamist movements, starting with AWI, on their own ground; a strategy designed to restrict the audience for these movements by limiting the scope of their actions in this area.

At the same time, the community field is also a field of competition between different types of associations, whether they are affiliated with other Islamist movements or secular movements or are 'independent'. For all these associations, including those that serve as local conduits between the people and the public authorities (Berriane, 2009, 183), literacy classes are a privileged way of winning women's sympathies, creating propaganda for a local councillor (Berriane, 2009, 173), or encouraging women to participate in demonstrations. Again, this competition points to the very different nature of associations linked to AWI, which—while developing similar or even identical programmes—aim to instil in their offerings a different direction and occupy the 'other' dimension of development that they integrate into education programmes.

4 Between Compliance and Discharge: Strategies of Discretion and the Price to be Paid for Existing

For the interviewees, Assoc is an example of a 'successful' association. For not all associations manage to obtain authorisation or to carry out their activities, due to their proximity to AWI and the fact that AWI members belong to their governing bodies. The creation of associations is subject to control, and sometimes repression: an association receives its authorisation only once an investigation has been carried out into each member of its executive; and the experiences of the women members of AWI that I interviewed suggest that if that investigation reveals that one or more members of an association have any connection with the movement, the association is not authorised. Interviewees say they face many challenges on this point: 'We prepare our files properly and with respect for the law, and we deliver them to the authorities, yet they still don't grant us authorisation. They don't openly refuse; they keep telling us to come back some other time, until we finally understand that the authorities are indirectly refusing to grant us our authorisation…'[22]

When the authorities discover, only after granting authorisation, that a member of an association's board is connected to AWI, either they apply the

22 Interview with an Assoc official; Casablanca, 23 January 2013.

procedure of 'arbitrary closure' of the association, or they bring a set of pressures to bear on that association's activities. Interviewees refer to 'the cancellation without notice of our activities' and 'the categorical and unexplained refusal to let us use public places for our activities'.[23] Faced with such repression and surveillance, AWI members deploy what I call 'strategies of discretion'. The process of creation of Assoc reveals what this discretion consists of and the precautions that are taken. For example, AWI members must convince both the neutral and its supporters that community action is important, so it is they, and not the AWI itself, who approach the authorities to file the application for authorisation. In addition, only one or two members of the movement—who should not be known to the authorities—join the executive board. The necessity of these precautions shows that the community field continues to be largely controlled by government bodies that are trying to limit the development of the network of community activities set up by their opponents. Yasmine Berriane notes that control relies on a set of processes: a preliminary inquiry is held into potential executive board members prior to the authorisation being issued; each new activity and each demonstration is the subject of a report that must be submitted to the general affairs division of the prefecture; and the presence of a representative of the local authorities is mandatory at all general assemblies (Berriane, 2009, 165). And in the case of associations linked to Islamism, Mohamed Tozy emphasises that 'the state responds to the very dense community fabric created by the Islamists by restricting public freedoms' (Tozy, 1999, 180). So these control measures also explain the above-mentioned strategies, both of adherence to dominant norms and, specifically, of compliance with hegemonic paradigms. Arguably, in the case of associations related to AWI, the at least apparent compliance of their activities and their adherence to the orthodoxy of development is a 'strategy of discretion' that makes them seem perfectly ordinary, allowing them to blend into a dense fabric of activities that do not distinguish them from other associations, do not make them particularly visible, and do not expose them to prohibition or pressure. This compliance is in large part forced, for financial reasons among others, since obtaining financial resources from the INDH and international organisations requires compliance with formal rules, but also adherence to institutional structures that embody the great ideologies of the moment. The chairs of the local committees of the INDH (often chairs of the local arrondissement) play an essential role in defining local needs and screening projects for funding (Berriane, 2009, 178). This means that any active participant who aspires to have his or her project funded must comply with the

23 Interview with an Assoc official; Casablanca, 24 January 2013.

definitions of needs established by these local committees (Bono, 2009). Thus, the INDH works 'as an instrument for domesticating a micro-community field that is rapidly growing and difficult to control' (Berriane, 2009, 187).

But this strategy of discretion only works because public authorities are willing to let it. And they 'are willing' partly because these associations fulfil certain duties and responsibilities of the state. This is the strategy of 'turning a blind eye' or 'laissez-faire', which is a classic example of indirect government: as in other types of developmental intervention, this strategy of letting social dynamics flourish, so long as they do not fundamentally interfere with the policies or visions defended by public institutions, is commonplace and easily accepted, as it allows the state to 'discharge'[24] its responsibilities onto others so as to achieve its goals.[25] In fact, women's associations have a dual function: by increasing the funding opportunities for development micro-projects at the local level, the various community players contribute to providing a sense of socio-economic security; by providing an association member with status and a more or less extensive network of connections, community action contributes to 'hiding' the problem of unemployment. What applies to associations in general also applies to those associations related to AWI. This is true of Assoc: five out of the seven members of its board have university degrees (biology, English literature, Arabic literature and Islamic studies) and two hold technical diplomas. Only three have jobs—as teachers in primary or secondary schools. The other four, including the chair of the association, are unemployed. For these women, working for the association helps mitigate the impression of having nothing to do or of being useless.[26] 'Here, I can meet up with people, I can pursue different activities that give me a sense of relief even if I do them for free, and I feel useful.'[27] The chair of the association says: 'When I'm seeking aid for the association or seeking to form partnerships, I go out to people; I meet important individuals (head teachers in schools, benefactors) and this gives me the opportunity to introduce myself and to demonstrate my skills, and it can also open up work opportunities.'[28] So community action can be a gateway to the labour market thanks to the networks of relationships that it enables community workers to develop. Irene Bono calls community activity 'a

24 In Weber's sense, as developed by Béatrice Hibou (Hibou 1999a and 1999b).

25 This idea, inspired by the work of Michel Foucault, is highlighted by Béatrice Hibou (Hibou, 2011). See also Pereira (2009) and Meddeb (2015).

26 Many studies of community action agree that it helps to conceal the problem of unemployment (Bono, 2010; Berriane, 2009).

27 Interview with a member of the executive board of Assoc; Casablanca, 23 January 2009.

28 Interview with the chair of Assoc; Casablanca, 23 January 2009.

business card' (Bono, 2010, 41). Be that as it may, this finding suggests strategies of 'discharge' since the Islamists of AWI (though the same can be said of those of the Movement of Unification and Reform (Mouvement de l'unification et de la réforme, MUR)) reject violence and support the sensitisation of young people to the virtues of non-violence through spiritual education,[29] to the great benefit of both social order and the public authorities.

The charitable and benevolent activities carried out by AWI as an Islamist movement make another form of 'discharge' possible. Competition brought about by government intervention has not succeeded in excluding Islamists from the neighbourhoods, where they continue to have a presence and to influence everyday life.

Thus, the media report on the various charitable actions carried out and the assistance provided by AWI in neighbourhoods and towns where the government has clearly failed in its duty. This is the case, for example, with regard to the aid provided to those populations that, in February 2009, suffered from floods in the Gharb[30] region and to the victims of a factory fire in a working-class district in Casablanca, ignored by the authorities.[31] These examples can be seen as reflecting a desire on the part of AWI to embarrass the government by forcing it to face up to its shortcomings; but we can also see them as an opportunity seized by the authorities to discharge some of its responsibilities onto AWI, even though the movement is opposed to the Moroccan regime. It is thus clear that not all outcomes are intentional, either on the government side (which in spite of itself legitimises AWI), or on the side of AWI (which unwittingly contributes to a political order that it condemns).

5 Change the Individual to Change Society: The Different Senses Given to Education and the Conduct of Life

In the neighbourhood under study, women members of AWI also perform activities of 'spiritual education' and 'education of consciences', acting as the

29 On spiritual education, see the following section on changing the individual. On non-violence, see Cavatorta (2006, 214).

30 The flooding occurred in the regions of Sidi Yahya, Sidi Kacem and Sidi Slimane. News organisations even revealed that the local authorities sought help from AWI to rescue and support the people affected. See http://www.hespress.com/faits-divers/11125.html (accessed on 1 June 2016).

31 According to a community activist close to AWI, interviewed in Casablanca on 13 April 2009, AWI came to the aid of the families of fire victims who had been abandoned both by the authorities and by the officials of the factory in question.

female section of the movement. Unlike those activities promoted by associations open to all women in the neighbourhood, these activities primarily target members of AWI.

These members follow an intense programme of spiritual activities: 'sittings', good advice and spiritual retreats. 'Sitting' is the translation of the Arabic term *jalassates*, commonly used by Islamists to refer to weekly religious education meetings that assemble a very limited number of members (not exceeding ten). The programme includes *dhikr* (litany); learning the Koran; and lessons that exhort participants to practise *dhikr*, citing its importance and benefits; as well as learning the basic practices of religion (ablutions, prayer). As for *majlis annassiha* (good advice), these are meetings that are held monthly and whose programmes are essentially based on *dhikr* and learning the 'moral behaviour' recommended by Islam, including 'good behaviour' such as kindness towards parents, neighbours, friends and people in general. Spiritual retreats are part of a journey towards God and are based primarily on *dhikr*, optional prayers, evening prayers, and so on. These programmes are part of a spiritual dimension of education that recalls the movement's adherence to Sufism.[32] Focused on concern for the evolution of mankind and on mankind's ultimate destiny, spiritual education consists of programmes that constantly remind the individual that there is a hereafter and that his or her earthly life is a continuous preparation for this. Thus, through this intense spiritual programme, members are supposed to change from within and acquire strength and inner peace that will affect their daily behaviour and contribute to positive change around them, in accordance with the AWI motto: 'Change the individual to change society.'

Education is thus endowed with a specific meaning that derives directly from the connection it is supposed to have with the spiritual values present and put into practice in everyday life with the aim of changing behaviour and, thereby, of changing the ways we understand the social aspects of people's lives. In other words, following the Weberian analysis, education is understood by AWI members as a social action meant to help guide how people conduct their lives through the values it conveys, and to shape 'types of men' or, in this case, types of women.[33] We can now understand the conflicts concealed behind the consensual perspective that views education as the engine

32 François Burgat believes that the personal route followed by Abdessalam Yassine illustrates both the Sufi contribution to the Islamist outlook and the urgent need to move beyond the narrow paths of the *tariqua* (Sufi Muslim Brotherhood) if one is to gain access to that contribution (Burgat, 1995, 20).

33 On the importance of the notions of life conduct and 'types', see Weber (2006) and Grossein (2006).

of development: the very special way in which AWI activists conduct their lives reveal interpretations of the world, and especially practices based on these interpretations, that are very different from those produced by associations of a secular persuasion, but also different from those of other Islamic associations and, of course, the government.

The spiritual education project promoted by AWI does indeed strive to be different from the religious education offered by others; its difference resides in its multidimensional aspects. To begin with, its Sufi dimension promotes another facet of development—namely, the 'change from within' realised by the above programmes (*dhikr* and spiritual retreats) prescribed by a spiritual guide. Yet while AWI adopts this Sufi-style approach, it differs from the latter by its ambition to supplement that approach with a struggle against injustice, which—the movement claims—can be successful only if the movement has a permanent presence among the people and provides them with support on a daily basis. It is in this sense, too, that AWI's specific character can be seen as regards development; 'conflicts' (or at least differences) with other social actors and groups on the Moroccan scene emerge: religious beliefs are made more 'everyday' and routine, and need to be placed at the service of economic and social practice and thus be more deeply embodied in the way one conducts one's life. It thus becomes easier to understand the place of 'mentoring', which involves another dimension of the educational project fostered by AWI and combines good behaviour and activism in pursuit of sociopolitical rights. Education in virtue and morality must make the AWI member into the very model of a good Muslim, who distinguishes him- or herself by good conduct; being constantly ready to help others, to defend their rights and to assist them on every level—economic, social and moral.

6 Meetings of the 'Sisters for Eternity': Islamist Feminism, Empowerment and Increased Conflict

At the neighbourhood level, women from AWI also organise monthly meetings open to all women. Meetings of the 'Sisters for Eternity' make concrete the project begun by women from AWI in 2000 to train women *'alimates* (theologians). Although they adopt the view that Muslim women are compelled to occupy a degrading position and forced to remain marginal, AWI women believe that it is not Islam as a religion that is responsible for this situation but rather the restrictive readings of its texts, for many centuries, by an *ulama*, more influenced by the cultural context in which its individual members lived than by the liberating spirit of Islam. For the women of AWI, the discriminatory nature of classical jurisprudence vis-à-vis women is due in part to the male domination that has prevailed in the field of interpretation of sacred texts throughout the history of Islam: female scrutiny, which they consider necessary if the reading of sacred texts is to emancipate women, having been almost completely absent. It is on this basis that AWI women claim to take up the challenge of *ijtihad* (the effort to reinterpret and re-contextualise the sacred texts), seeking to master the necessary knowledge and to develop the tools needed to accomplish this task of reinterpretation (Yafout, 2012). This project was directly encouraged by the thought of Abdessalam Yassine and his promotion of multidimensional renewal, especially his call for the emancipation of women and their mastery of the tools of *ijtihad*. Thus, the *'alimates* of AWI organise monthly meetings of the 'Sisters for Eternity' in certain cities and neighbourhoods in order to study Koranic verses, the Hadith, and historical facts that have often been interpreted by classical jurisprudence in a way that marginalises women.

So here we find another point of convergence, at least apparent, with neoliberal hegemony: the ability to empower the suppressed (and especially women) and allow them to take control; something that echoes the notion of 'empowerment' at the heart of the current dogma of international donors, but also of most development programmes in Morocco and elsewhere. Obviously, this ability is, in the case of Western developmentalist hegemony, linked to economic empowerment, while the empowerment referred to by the women of AWI results from an intellectual and spiritual effort. It is in this latter sense that certain studies describe these meetings as spaces of 'collective empowerment' (Salime, 2005, 153). But in either case, we find the same emphasis on individual action in support of women to change the way in which they are integrated into society and the world. Indeed, AWI women members reconsider the sacred texts in the light of the life of the Prophet (*Sira*) and the lives of his companions (men and women), but also in the light of the context in which these texts were revealed. They adopt a method that takes into account the circumstances of revelation (*asbab annouzoul*), the historical and social context of the text and the spirit of gradual change (*attadaruj*) conveyed by the koranic message. The objective of this work is to question any restrictive interpretation associating Islam with the subordination of women and to move away from any form of discriminatory theory. Thus, in the context of these meetings, controversial jurisprudential concepts are challenged, including those that refer to the superiority of men over women, or others prohibiting co-education or permitting polygamy. The *'alimate*s of AWI deconstruct these concepts in order to develop new ideas based on the sacred texts and historical facts. In short, the meetings of the 'Sisters for Eternity' are spaces for reflection, meant to give women back their confidence and strengthen their self-esteem by presenting them with the model of the emancipation of the women companions of the Prophet (*sahabiyates*). These companions, thanks to the place they occupied in original Islam, contributed to the construction of Muslim society through their commitment, alongside men, to supporting the Prophet and to building a new society.

Meetings of the 'Sisters for Eternity' are part of the political 'education of consciences' and 'awakening of consciences' discussed above in the context of a particular neighbourhood. The 'women' question thus involves religious, historical, and political dimensions: for the movement, the degradation of a woman's condition is linked to the monopoly of political power over the interpretation of religious texts. So we can glimpse a development conflict that opposes the movement to feminist groups and public authorities; a conflict that is hidden by the discursive consensus on the need to improve the position of women in Moroccan society.

In fact, these attempts at reinterpretation made by AWI women represent a challenge to the rule established by official Islam in Morocco, which states that the rulings of the official *ulama* are the benchmark for *ijtihad*. Many interviewees interpret the initiative of the Ministry of Habous and Islamic Affairs to train *mourchidates* (female preachers) as a reaction to their own plan to train *'alimates*. Moreover, when it was launched, the *mourchidates* project was widely publicised and presented by the media—both Moroccan and international—as a revolution in the religious field and a great innovation in the Muslim world.[34] Yet female preachers have played a real role, as volunteers, in Moroccan mosques since the 1970s (Yafout, 2012). The Ministry's project has merely reorganised this role in a formal setting by offering *mourchidates* formal training and granting them the status of paid officials. These *mourchidates* deal with the religious orientation of women in one or more mosques in every neighbourhood. However, *mourchidates* do not have the right to produce a religious interpretation or issue legal opinions, as this is the 'exclusive role of the *Majlis Al 'Ilmi* (scholarly council of the *ulama*)', according to one *mourchida* interviewed.[35] When they explain the differences between their project and the Ministry's, AWI women members specifically mention the practice of interpretation. For them, *'alima* and *mourchida* differ mainly on two levels: training, and the knowledge transmitted (Yafout, 2012). The *'alimates* have, in their view, reached an advanced level of knowledge through specialised and extensive training, while official *mourchidates* have attended only short courses. Moreover, the *'alimates* are able to produce scholarly knowledge, reinterpreting and

34 See, for example *La Tribune* (2014).

35 Interview with a *mourchida* for my doctoral research; 9 May 2009.

comparing religious texts, while the role of the *mourchidates* is limited to giving *dourous* (lessons/sermons). The latter therefore are confined to passing on a less sophisticated form of religious knowledge.

Conflict with the public authorities is not always hidden. While before 2005 the meetings of the 'Sisters for Eternity' were 'tolerated', they were directly repressed from that date onwards, and opposed by the religious policy of the Ministry of *Habous*. The interviewees report that, before 2005, the 'Sisters for Eternity' meetings attracted many women: AWI members, sympathisers or those wishing to explore the movement's ideas or to learn religious teachings from it; their number could reach up to a thousand in certain cities or neighbourhoods. However, from May 2005 onwards, these meetings became the target of strong pressure from the authorities. They were interrupted by the police several times and the women running them were taken to the police station, questioned, and released late into the night. Faced with this situation, women members of AWI have limited the extent of their meetings and reduced the number of beneficiaries, in a strategy meant to bypass constraints by taking more precautions and adapting their activities to the new security conditions prevailing.

Between AWI and feminist movements too, the apparent consensus conceals conflicts over the values promoted by those of one or the other orientation. In fact, like secular feminists, AWI's women members aspire to women's empowerment; but, like Islamic feminists, they use the tools provided by the Islamic tradition. But they defend a 'different feminism', which advocates an analysis of the feminine condition combining historical, religious and political elements. Their reading of Muslim history links the degradation of the feminine condition in Islam to the birth of despotism and defines the enemies of women's emancipation as machismo and authoritarianism. However, AWI women members do not define themselves as feminists. On the contrary, they differentiate themselves from this movement, which they believe is part of a story quite different from that of the marginalisation of Muslim women. In their view, while religion has been a factor of discrimination against women in the West, it is—on the contrary—a factor of emancipation in the Muslim world.

Moreover, the appropriation by AWI's women members of *ijtihad*, conceived as a field reserved for the official *ulama*, partly explains the pressure exerted on them; but it also explains the conflicts within the movement. Indeed, meetings of the 'Sisters for Eternity' ceased in 2012 due to the resignation of most of the women who ran them, following differences with certain of the movement's leaders. These leaders were often hostile to the autonomy enjoyed by the women in the movement, both in the conception and the execution of their projects. Also, the male leaders of the movement view the interpretation of sacred texts as an exclusively male field, despite the personal position of the founder of AWI, who always, in both his theory and his practice, encouraged the female dynamic by supporting the militancy of his daughter, Nadia Yassine. The gradual withdrawal, due to illness, of the founder of the movement from 2007 onwards allowed the male leaders to begin the process of marginalising women within the movement; a process that led to these women's resignation in early 2012, a few months before the AWI founder's death. Here, development conflicts are directly related to the gender positions and stratifications that shape power relations in Moroccan society.

7 Conclusion

The example of the practice of 'development' proposed and implemented by AWI and its female institutions allows us to glimpse the great number of processes that are at work. Through this prism, the presence of AWI in the neighbourhoods is first manifested in community work, in spiritual education and the education of consciences, which results in the transmission of a vision of women's emancipation based on Islamic tradition.

The first point that emerges from this analysis is that we can only understand the ideas and actions of AWI if we take into account the complex encounter between two historically constituted matrices: firstly, the Muslim matrix, which understands development in terms of reforms (*islah*), but also of interpretation and contextualisation (*ijtihad*); and secondly, the Western matrix in the neo-liberal mode that characterises it today. Only thus can we understand that there are both formal similarities with development projects inspired by the prevailing doxa and implemented by the public authorities and other local players, and divergences in the meaning given to these same actions; a meaning which, for AWI, resides in an 'added spiritual value' combined with a quest for social justice. Which brings us to a second point: behind the consensus on the importance of development, especially education, and behind the apparent consensus on the very aims of educational action (to foster development, progress and well-being), and behind the consensus on the techniques, institutional structures, and even practices of development—a consensus partly constrained by the rules governing the funding of projects—many conflicts lie concealed; conflicts in which some strive to establish themselves in the terrain that is society in the face of competition from state actors as well as other types of actors, both Islamist and secular. There are also internal conflicts within AWI over the place of women in society. And, above all, conflicts over values, which reflect differences in the ways of living in society, as well as in the world and in the Hereafter, are envisaged; and related conflicts over lifestyles and how one should conduct one's life.

Education enables one to gain a deep understanding of a society, in this case Moroccan society, and to question the most widespread vision—one that sets system against anti-system. This is the third point one can make on the basis of an observation of AWI's efforts in the sphere of women's education: the complexity of relations rules out binary visions such as alignment/repression, convergence/divergence, and competition/cooperation, although Abdessalam Yassine's movement is considered the fiercest opponent of the 'system' and sees itself as such. Thus, religious education is also fostered by other participants of society. Islamists from MUR, the PJD's religious wing, also organises religious sittings, including programmes ranging from those urging morality, to learning the Koran and the Hadith, to an introduction to Islamic jurisprudence (*fiqh*). They even carry out ad hoc ethics campaigns, employing caravans that visit cities denouncing moral depravity and calling for religious teachings to be respected.[36] In mosques managed by the Ministry of Habous and Islamic Affairs, the *mourchidates* also teach women about their religious obligations and how to organise their daily conduct in accordance with religious principles. Since the 1980s, religious education has been a field in which the various Islamist movements compete against the official religious authorities. The latter, especially since the 2005 reform, intervene in mosques via imams and preachers and exclude any imam propagating views opposed to their own,[37] starting with the imams and *mourchidates* close to AWI. But this strategy of control and repression, implemented by enforcing competition in projects for development and education (both religious and non-religious education), is combined with a laissez-faire approach that allows the public authorities to discharge some of their responsibilities, voluntarily or not, and shapes existing collaborations even when the active participants themselves are unaware of this. As we can see, AWI's radical political position triggers the bans imposed by the authorities and a range of competitive strategies meant to curb the movement's influence; but at the same time, the laissez-faire attitude of the authorities allows the movement to make an undeniable contribution to solving problems at the micro-local level. Similarly, AWI continues to refuse to nominate candidates for election and will not support established policy—but it is nonetheless an important political player because of the activities of

36 On the MUR's and PJD's campaigns to improve public and private morality, see Zeghal (2005, 235).

37 In this respect, Tozy mentions the dissident imams of the 1980s and contemporary imams such as Sheikh Nhari (Tozy, 2013, 148).

proximity in which it engages. According to AWI, these activities carry a different meaning and make real the way in which Islamism is viewed as a form of daily presence among the population.

Thus the sphere in which AWI conducts its community and activist work highlights the complexity of the relationship between development and conflicts, and thus of 'development conflicts'. This is the fourth and final conclusion of this chapter. Far from conflict and pacification being seen as opposites, they are interwoven in everyday practices. The commitment of AWI members to education also explains their ability to organise demonstrations and to mobilise (Cavatorta, 2006), as was seen in the 20 February movement (Bennani-Chraïbi and Jeghllaly, 2012). This ability—which also brings with it a significant potential for conflict—fosters the pacification of social relations and enables some support to be given to the moral and political order. The uses of the term 'education', in its behavioural dimension, make this explicit: the word is often mentioned by AWI supporters, who say, 'they are well-educated people' (*hadouk nas mrabyine*). In its behavioural dimension, the term is central to the daily lives of Moroccans and is far from being typical of the movement's supporters alone. To describe the conduct of persons, use is often made of expressions such as *mrabbi* (well educated), *ma mrabbiche* (not well educated) or *naques trabi* (he lacks education). This ambivalent use of the term is also evident in the relations between AWI members and those around them, again highlighting the fuzziness of the meanings involved. If supporters use it in a positive way, attributing a great capacity for mobilisation to AWI members, it becomes, in other cases, a barometer to judge their conduct. 'Is that education?' (*hadi hiya tarbiya?*) is an expression used by individuals and groups when they encounter what they believe to be an inappropriate attitude in an AWI member; as if to judge such people by turning their own terminological corpus against them.

These four points converge to illustrate the importance of the idea of development in certain movements of contemporary Islamism. The local approach used in this chapter brings out an element too often overlooked. In fact, by focusing almost exclusively, in the case of the urban environment, on economic players and on political and community players linked to the secular world (Catusse, 2011), and, in the case of rural areas, on village development associations and migrants' associations (Lacroix, 2005), and by endeavouring to apprehend the reality (or not) of the 'social state' through its public policies, development studies in Morocco do not take Islamism into account.[38] As a result, religious education and spirituality are simply not seen as playing any part

38 One exception are Tozy and Hibou (2015); however, these authors focus on the relative influence of the intellectual matrix of political Islam on daily economic practices when this

in development, because development is linked to a form of economic rationality, including when it takes the form of 'human development'. This chapter has tried, instead, to show the richness of these dimensions and the important role they are granted both by Islamists and by the powers that be; a role that thus affords them an important role in development.

These four observations suggest another point of convergence: considering AWI as an active local participant in development, the analysis presented here has shown the complexity of the social and political relations that the Islamist movement has with power and with society as a whole. Taking into account its interaction not only with the authorities but also with the populace in general and with other local players in particular, what we see is a dialectic between conflict and consensus based on a hegemonic 'Western' model of development. This dialectic gives expression to other strategies that flourish in daily activities and other conceptions of a 'good' way of conducting one's life. Intentional or not, the strategies of discharge, differentiation, discretion, competition, or compliance, and the alternative modes of government and life conduct that this chapter has highlighted, show that relationships between the various active participants cannot be reduced to conflict or consensus, and these participants' behaviour cannot be explained solely as a form of rejection or acceptance. As Irene Bono and Béatrice Hibou show in their introduction to this volume, the neo-liberal paradigm of development can be both a common ground and a place of conflict between quite different models of society. Conflicts relating to the concept of development (economic development versus human and spiritual development) can generate consensuses that force each other to coexist in the same space, to use the same institutional structures and resort to the same models and even the same donors, and to achieve some of their goals while sacrificing others. An approach that focuses only on AWI's oppositional and political dimensions, where AWI's positions are seen as totally antithetical to those of the government and anti-hegemonic vis-à-vis the West, can shed light only on the movement's oppositional dynamics. Such is the case with those elements of the literature that analyse only the vertical relationship between AWI and power, or with those that see the horizontal relationship with other political movements, particularly with secular movements, as solely and necessarily conflictual and polarising. This perspective leads analysts to study only the repression suffered by this movement or the attempts to co-opt it made by a government obsessed with its desire to maintain control over a rapidly growing and oppositional Islamism (Burgat, 2008, 310–311). Much of the literature focuses on AWI's dissident character and

tendency is in power, and not, properly speaking, on their conceptions of 'development'. However, they do point to the importance of the 'relation to values' (Weber, 2006).

particularly its challenge to the religious legitimacy of power: the relationship between AWI and the latter is then analysed as a struggle between counter-projects and control (Burgat, 2008; Zeghal, 2005; Tozy, 1999, 2009). Other analyses, or sometimes the same ones, also show the relationship between AWI and social movements (whether secular or inspired otherwise by Islam) as arising from conflict; whether this concerns a monopoly of political protest, strategies of appropriation of the discourse of social justice, or the control of campuses (Burgat, 2008; Zeghal, 2005; Cavatorta, 2006). AWI is not the only association to be studied in such Manichaean terms. It is clear that Islamist movements in the MENA region are most often presented as domesticated and co-opted movements (Zeghal, 2005, 193), as victims of the powers that be (Burgat, 2008), or—conversely—as a threat to the powers that be and the West (Kepel, 2000). This chapter has tried to show that beyond this threefold interpretation, while movements such as AWI—presented and presenting themselves as radicals in their position vis-à-vis power—continue to enjoy a strong following and a great capacity for mobilisation, this is partly because of the leeway that exists concretely, in everyday life, between conflict and consensus. This leeway allows each of the protagonists to achieve some of their objectives without having to yield to a domesticating consensus or a violent conflict.

References

Bennani-Chraïbi, M. and M. Jeghllaly (2012) 'La dynamique protestataire du Mouvement du 20 février à Casablanca', *Revue française de science politique*, 62(5), pp. 867–894, DOI: 10.3917/rfsp.625.867.

Berriane, Y. (2009) 'Intermédiations stratégiques: l'engagement de militantes associatives locales dans la campagne pour les législatives marocaines de 2007', in L. Zaki (ed.), *Terrains de campagne: Les législatives de septembre 2007 au Maroc* (Paris: Karthala/IRMC), pp. 161–191.

Bono, I. (2013) 'Comment devenir employable?', in B. Hibou (ed.) *La bureaucratisation néolibérale* (Paris: La Découverte), pp. 49–75.

Bono, I. (2010) 'L'activisme associatif comme marché du travail: normalisation sociale et politique par les "activités génératrices de revenus" à El Hajeb', *Politique africaine*, 120(4), pp. 25–44, DOI: 10.3917/polaf.120.0025.

Bono, I. (2009) *Cantiere del Regno. Associazioni, Sviluppo e Stili di Governo dans Morocco*, doctoral thesis in political science (Turin: University of Turin).

Burgat, F. (2008) *L'islamisme au Maghreb* (Paris: Payot et Rivages).

Burgat, F. (1995) *L'islamisme en face* (Paris: La Découverte).

Catusse, M. (2011) 'Le "social": une affaire d'Etat dans le Maroc de Mohammed VI', *Confluences Méditerranée*, 78(3), pp. 63–76, DOI: 10.3917/come.078.0063.

Cavatorta, F. (2006) 'Civil Society, Islamism and Democratisation. The Case of Morocco', *Journal of Modern African Studies*, 44(2), pp. 203–222, DOI: 10.1017/S0022278X06001601.

Charrad, W. (2015) 'Al Adl Wal Ihsane appelle à un discours "humaniste" pour contrer le terrorisme', *TelQuel*, http://telquel.ma/2015/12/14/al-adl-wal-ihsane-appelle-discours-humaniste-contrer-terrorisme_1474173 (accessed on 1 June 2016).

Grossein, J.-P. (2006) 'Présentation', in M. Weber, *Sociologie des religions* (Paris: Gallimard-Tel), pp. 51–114.

Hibou, B. (2012) *La bureaucratisation du monde à l'ère néolibérale* (Paris: La Découverte). English translation: *The Bureaucratization of the World in the Neoliberal Era*, translated by Andrew Brown (New York: Palgrave Macmillan, 2015).

Hibou, B. (2011) *Anatomie politique de la domination* (Paris: La Découverte).

Hibou, B. (1999a) 'La décharge, nouvel interventionnisme', *Politique africaine*, 73(3), DOI: 10.3917/polaf.073.0006.

Hibou, B. (ed.) (1999b) *La Privatisation des États* (Paris: Karthala).

Kemp, A. and N. Berkovitch (2013) 'Gouvernance pédagogique et financiarisation de la vie quotidienne. La fabrique de la microfinance pour les femmes marginalisées en Israël', in B. Hibou (ed.) *La bureaucratisation néolibérale* (Paris: La Découverte), pp. 23–47.

Kepel, G. (2000) *Jihad, expansion et déclin de l'islamisme* (Paris: Seuil).

Lacroix, T. (2005) *Les réseaux marocains du développement* (Paris: Presses de Sciences Po).

Meddeb, H. (2015) 'Rente frontalière et injustice sociale en Tunisie' in I. Bono, B. Hibou, H. Meddeb and M. Tozy (eds.) *L'Etat d'injustice au Maghreb. Maroc et Tunisie* (Paris: Karthala).

Pereira, V. (2009) 'L'émigration clandestine portugaise vers la France et les paradoxes de l'intégration européenne', *Sociétés politiques comparées*, 19 November, http://fasopo.org/sites/default/files/article_n19.pdf (accessed on 31 May 2016).

Salime, Z. (2005) *Between Islam and Feminism: New Political Transformations and Movements in Morocco*, PhD Thesis, (Urbana and Champaign: University of Illinois).

TelQuel (2015) 'Al Adl Wal Ihsane appelle à un discours "humaniste" pour contrer le terrorisme', http://telquel.ma/2015/12/14/al-adl-wal-ihsane-appelle-discours-humaniste-contrer-terrorisme_1474173 (accessed on 1 June 2016).

Tozy, M. (2013) 'Des oulémas frondeurs à la bureaucratie du "croire"', in B. Hibou (ed.) *La bureaucratisation néolibérale* (Paris: La Découverte), pp. 129–154.

Tozy, M. (2009) 'L'évolution du champ religieux marocain au défi de la mondialisation', *Revue internationale de politique comparée*, 16 (1), pp. 63–81, DOI: 10.3917/ripc.161.0063.

Tozy, M. (1999) *Monarchie et islam politique au Maroc* (Paris: Presses de Sciences Po).

Tozy, M. and B. Hibou (2015) 'L'offre islamiste de justice sociale: politique publique ou question morale?' in I. Bono, B. Hibou, H. Meddeb and M. Tozy (eds.) *L'Etat d'injustice au Maghreb. Maroc et Tunisie* (Paris, Karthala).

La Tribune (2014) 'L'expérience des Mourchidates "séduit" l'Oncle Sam !' http://lnt.ma/lexperience-mourchidates-seduit-loncle-sam/ (accessed on 1 December 2014).

Weber, M. (2006) *Sociologie des religions*, edited and translated by J.-P. Grossein (Paris: Gallimard-Tel).

Yafout, M. (2012) *Le statut des femmes au sein des mouvements islamistes marocains: entre exégèse au féminin et participation politique*, Thèse de doctorat (Casablanca: Université Hassan II).

Yassine, A. (1998) *Islamiser la modernité* (Casablanca: Al Ofok).

Yassine, A. (1994) *Dialogue avec les honorables démocrates* (Casablanca: Al Ofok).

Zeghal, M. (2005) *Les islamistes marocains, Le défi à la monarchie* (Casablanca: Le Fennec).

PART 2

Consensus as An Expression of Conflict

CHAPTER 6

War and State (Re)Construction in Afghanistan: Conflicts of Tradition or Conflicts of Development?

Fariba Adelkhah

Abstract

Foreign aid provided for the (re)construction of the Afghan state since 2001 has, paradoxically, intensified the 'ethnicisation' and sectarianisation of economic and political relations, contradicting the criteria of good governance advocated by donors. Conflicts apparently related to tradition and identity have become more common and indeed point to more fundamental contradictions between the culturalist representation of Afghan society and the effects of the country's integration into the world capitalist economy. Thus, viewing Islamic radicalisation, ethnic polarisation or tribal atavism as responsible for the social and political violence in Afghanistan gives an incomplete picture of the situation as it ignores transformations in society and the new challenges of this supposedly traditional conflict.

1 Introduction

On 20 January 2014, a fight broke out between three people in the main thoroughfare of the bazaar of Bamyan, near the Azizi Bank. Before long, a hundred men had become involved in this altercation: they included inhabitants of the city but there were also men from surrounding areas—Asiyab, Shahidan, and Jagrakhil—and Fatmasti, the home town of the three protagonists located ten minutes' drive away on the road to Shashpul. What were they quarrelling about? Presumably a bag of money that one of them was taking to deposit at a bank. But as the subject of the dispute has vanished, and no one seems to want to talk about it today, it would be better to ask why the conflict intensified in

* My thanks to Mahdi Mehraeen (journalist and consultant) and Ibrahim Tavalla (editor of the weekly *Sada-I Shahrvand-i Bamayn*) for their help throughout this research project. I have simplified the transcription and accentuation of Dari for easier reading.

the days that followed, when ever more men gradually arrived, spoiling for a fight, from Yakawalang, Kabul, Baghlan, and Mazar-i Sharif. To restore calm, at least momentarily, the prefecture (*wilayat*), the Council for Peace (*Shora-i Solh*) and the High Council of Ulamas (*Shora-i Ulama*) had to intervene jointly to impose, on the party held responsible for the renewal of violence, relatively high financial damages. It was stipulated that if any family took the initiative in reviving hostilities, it would be definitively deprived of any political and administrative positions it held. Although this agreement was based on the Koran, few residents of Bamyan thought that the case had been settled once and for all. Indeed, it was only the latest episode in a 30-year conflict that had cost the lives of 74 people. 'The same grandfather (*padar kalan*), the same mosque, the same religious membership, the same cemetery—except for five of the victims who were interred in another town in an attempt to heal the wounds', as I was told. Despite this, the dispute could still at any moment lead to a massacre.

The small town of Fatmasti is home to some 300 families. Since the 1970s, it has been the scene of 74 tragic deaths—martyrs for some, victims of murders for others—often within the same family, involving a series of vendettas. The residents of Fatmasti sometimes call themselves Hazara and sometimes Parsiwan, and claim they are Sabzevari from Iran. Their story is mentioned in the mausoleums of Mir Hashem Agha and Seyed Ali Yakhsuz Bamyan, the two main pilgrimage sites in the city. 'The Hazaras are descendants of Genghis Khan the Mughal, but our origins date back to the dynasty of Key, a dynasty of *aria* (Aryans),' says Khalifa Aziz,[1] the *babeh kalan* (the grandfather of the place), who no longer lives in Fatmasti and has lost most of his family in conflicts between cousins (*mama* and *khala*). Most of these violent deaths occurred during the jihad against the Soviets and the 'war of the commanders' (1992–96), during which his family split between supporters of Hizb-i Nasr—later absorbed by the Hizb-i Wahdat of Mohammad Ali Mazari—and the Hizb-i Harakat-i islami of Ayatollah Asef Mohseni. But the intra-family conflict was rooted in land demarcation (*polvan*), a process that has usually involved placing brothers-in-law (*baja* in Dari or *yazna* in Pashto) in competition with one another. The general opinion was that it was intensified by two factors specific to this time of war: the flow of arms and the political exile or economic emigration that were forced upon the men. So this was a war between cousins, fuelled by marital disputes. Tellingly, the men were the protagonists of the violence, but women cast an ubiquitous shadow. They contributed, indirectly, to the production of the society and its conflicts.

1 Personal observations, 2014 and 2015.

Be that as it may, the division of Fatmasti between the two main Shi'ite political forces involved in the jihad was grafted onto older rifts. According to the young men in the village, who now longed to flee from it, residents had not been able to enjoy 'a single quiet night' since the mid-1980s. Fatmasti provided the jihad with its share of *qumandan*, but after 2001 it also provided the administration of the Karzai government with many of its local officials, whose decisions in turn fuelled resentment and vendetta. This war in Fatmasti was a small-scale replica of political life in Bamyan. In June 2015, the tumultuous appointment of the new prefect was a reminder of the persistent disputes between the Hazaras and among the Shi'ites, divisions inherited from jihad and a more ancient local history. This event also reawakened another dimension of the social history of Afghanistan: that of the *arbaki*. These 'protectors', who often created the need for the very protection they were supposed to provide, re-emerged in the form of proxy militias of the North Atlantic Treaty Organization (NATO), which Fatmasti supplied in great number.[2]

The village of Fatmasti, then, is a compendium of the complex social affiliations and political issues in contemporary Afghanistan, especially the central region of the Hazarajat on which we will be focussing. We will see that foreign aid provided since 2001 for the (re)construction of the Afghan state has paradoxically intensified the 'ethnicisation' and sectarianisation of economic and political relations, in total contradiction with the criteria of good governance advocated by the donors. Conflicts apparently related to tradition and identity have become more common, and indeed point to more fundamental contradictions between the culturalist representation of Afghan society and the effects of the country's integration into the world capitalist economy. Thus, viewing Islamic radicalisation, ethnic polarisation or tribal atavism as responsible for the social and political violence in Afghanistan gives an incomplete picture of the situation, as it ignores transformations in society and the new challenges of this supposedly traditional conflict. In addition, donors often use a naive language, trapped within general models and paradigms disconnected from the reality of the country whose problems they are attempting to solve.

2 The Primordial Experience of War

History, then, is essential if you want to understand Afghanistan. Ethnicity, language, tradition and even Islam cannot be considered as explanatory categories in themselves. We will start from the premise that the problems of

2 Personal observations, 2014 and 2015.

Afghanistan's post-conflict reconstruction are part of the old, if constantly updated logics of which they are echoes, and into which they largely merge. And this is true even if the fight against the Taliban, the neo-liberal zeitgeist, and globalisation have given the military actors, non-governmental organisations (NGOs) and the diaspora an important role, in addition to or instead of governments and their public agencies of cooperation.

Before getting to the heart of the matter, it is worth mentioning the historical context in which foreign intervention in Afghanistan, one of the least developed countries in the world, has occurred. In 1978, the People's Democratic Party of Afghanistan fomented a coup that helped overthrow the government of President Dawood Khan and triggered a Soviet occupation that lasted until 1989 (Andishmand, 2009; Roy, 1985). Since then the country has been shaken by a civil war (1989–96)—including the Battle of Jalabad in 1989 and the successive battles of Kabul (*jangha-ye kabol*) between 1992 and 1996 (Qhodus, 2009; Azimi, 2012–2013; Dorronsoro, 2000)—and by foreign interventions. Afghanistan holds a sad record: in the 1990s, the country produced the highest number of refugees in the world.

On Afghan soil, poverty and the presence of weapons have combined to exacerbate land issues, intensify urbanisation and swell migration. Since 2002, the problems arising from this conjunction, far from being resolved, have worsened, especially when it comes to property (Adelkhah, 2013). The Karzai Administration has merely endorsed the overlapping and layering of laws and regulations handed down from prior periods, pragmatically using, to its advantage, the local balance of power between institutions, between social and ethnic groups, and between commanders. In reality, over and above the make-believe discourse presented to foreign donors, this policy has led to a centralisation of the land allocation process and then to land-grabbing on the part of those in power and their clientele, in their own names (or those of their families) and in the name of the state. From this point of view, the general relations maintained by both the dominant political class and the state with the mass of the population—especially with residents in rural, sedentary or nomad zones—is probably more important than the extent of interethnic or religious relationships, although they are often two sides of the same coin. The only major legislative reform in this area was passed in 2008 and aimed at the opening of the land market to foreign investors. Even if its application is still limited, this reform has created more problems than it has solved. It has absolutely not broken with the logics of accumulation of the national ruling class that controls the granting of agricultural and mining concessions, since this class still holds the keys to the market and the signing of contracts. If these foreign investments are indeed made, they will trigger the alienation of considerable amounts of land, to the detriment of small farmers and shepherds. Similarly, after the trauma of the destruction of the Bamyan Buddhas in 2001, 'cultural heritage' has been turned into a matter of creating sanctuaries: this measure, however laudable, was imposed by the government on powerless populations. Among its side effects, we can mention the fact that the Tajik lands in Bamyan can, because of this 'sanctuarisation', no longer be cultivated or built on even though the mountainous nature of the region does not make it possible for this land to be exchanged for other arable plots.[3]

Despite the superposition of texts, the heterogeneity of proofs of ownership, the coexistence of often contradictory legal legitimacies, the fragmentation of the land, the tangle of ethnic identifications, and the extreme diversity of agricultural situations, this development has now been well documented, both by academic research and by experts (Adelkhah, 2013; Alden Wily, 2013a).[4] But it is largely seen as a failure in 'post-conflict' management or as the result of the evanescence of a state that, in the absence of any 'national sentiment', is now 'bankrupt', succumbing to the dual pressures of a 'corrupt' political class and 'tradition'. Certainly, the responsibilities of Afghan actors are substantial. However, had not the rot already set in because of the inconsistencies of foreign intervention? The basic problem lies, perhaps, in the idea or in the very principle of the aid in the name of which Afghan actors interact. The legacy of the violence of the years 1979 to 2001 and the painful memory they left did not miraculously disappear thereafter. The war is still very present in the minds of Afghans. It continues to provide the grammar and even the lexicon of day-to-day social life. In fact, it has formed the matrix of present-day Afghanistan, as a result of the population movements and the destruction and transfer of property that it caused. In addition, it has shaped the social consciousness of Afghans, who continue to zigzag between past and present in their daily conversations, if only because of the still visible traces of the battles of the 1980s and 1990s or the transformations of the landscape—especially in terms of urbanisation—that the conflict caused. The landscape has a mnemonic function and the war remains the great founding narrative of contemporary Afghanistan. It is all the more an active presence in that the belligerents were not abstract geopolitical entities such as communism, Islam, or the nation, but flesh-and-blood actors bound by close, and even intimate relations arising

3 Personal observations, 2014 and 2015.

4 See also the publications of Integrity Watch Afghanistan (http://iwaweb.org, accessed on 16 June 2016), the Afghanistan Public Policy Research Organization (http://appro.org.af, accessed on 16 June 2016) and the Afghanistan Research and Evaluation Unit (http://www.areu.org.af, accessed on 16 June 2016).

from neighbourhood (*shafa'a*) or kinship (*owdourzadegi*), either politically or economically constructed (*qawm*) (Roy, 1985; Alden Wily, 2004, 27). Of course, war brings violence, destruction and death. But the experiences of Afghans cannot be reduced to this tragic dimension. From the political and social point of view, war is also an existential experience. The Islamic intellectual Azizullah Royesh[5] admirably sums up this idea in his book *bogzar nafas bekasham* (*Let Me Breathe*). In particular, he says that it is through war that we learn about life: 'War is everything, it is life, work is war, home is war, thought is born of war, relationships proceed from war. Feelings, the understanding of conviction and religion, all this is war. Men breathe for war, work for it, think for it, pray for it and… they die for it' (Royesh, 2013, 130, our transl.).

3 The Invention of Ethnicity in the Hazarajat

This chapter is based essentially on two field surveys conducted in 2014 and 2015 in the central region of the Hazarajat. To the extent that the name of this region refers to the idea of the Hazara ethnic group, it should be noted at the outset that ethnicity refers less to objective groups of belonging, with an origin and a clearly defined territory, than to categories by which actors define themselves (or are defined).[6] According to Olivier Roy (1985), the war was a crucial vector of ethnic consciousness in Afghanistan. It endorsed our major groups that cannot be defined according to objective and unambiguous criteria: Pashtuns, Tajiks, Hazaras and Uzbeks. By definition, these categories are historically situated. They are contextual, relational and relative: you are a Hazara in relation to the Pashtuns, the Tajiks, and the Sayyids, at a given historical moment that refers to a more or less distant and more or less traumatic past as well as to completely contemporary issues interpreted using the yardstick of this memory. Following Richard Tapper (1983), and in agreement with Olivier Roy (1985) and Alessandro Monsutti (2004 and 2005), we therefore disclaim any primordialist definition of ethnicity. Today, this definition stems in particular

5 Azizullah Royesh is a Shi'ite and Hazara reformer who has been greatly influenced by the Iranian philosopher Ali Shariati. As the founder and director of the pioneering Marefat school in Kabul, he was ranked—in the context of its Global Teacher Prize—by the Varkey Foundation among the top ten teachers in the world in 2015.

6 Afghanistan has been a hotspot of the problematisation of ethnicity inspired by the founding work of Fredrik Barth (see especially Tapper, 1983, and Digard, 1988). This approach has been adopted by Adlparvar (2015). For a scholarly overview of ethnicity in Afghanistan, see Centlivres (1991).

from the relation to the state, via war and also via political parties. The *Hizb-i Wahdat*, more especially, had a decisive role in the ethnicisation of the social consciousness of the Hazara, while this despised minority group saw itself forced to face the challenge of life after the Soviet departure in 1989. However, though we will be paying attention to the political economy of this form of social consciousness in a context of civil war, this should not lead us to reduce it to a purely material struggle, a contest fuelled by greed and grievances between rational actors eager to maximise their profits, in accordance with a rightly criticised paradigm (Marchal and Messiant, 2002; 2003). Nor should it lead us to forget the extreme fluidity of feelings of belonging and thus solidarity in everyday life, on both collective and individual levels. The lines of identification are manifold and subject to negotiation. And it is not uncommon for different parties or factions to come together in the same *qawm*. In this regard, Alessandro Monsutti (2005, 99) mentions in particular the existence of 'a veritable strategy to diversify affiliations as a way of providing some assurance in the event of unfavourable political and military developments'.

Important as it is, the ethnic dimension should not be exaggerated. It is significant only through its inclusion in the political dimension, whether or not this is militarised. It is also mixed with the linguistic dimension that in many ways relativises it and opens new fields of conflict, especially between Dari speakers and Pashtun speakers. But the language dispute at least has the advantage of blurring or even diluting the binary inter-sectarian antagonism between Sunnis and Shi'ites, as well as interethnic oppositions.

From the nineteenth century onwards, the modern Afghan state was formed on the basis of an Anglo–Russian agreement creating a buffer state between the two empires, on a vector of Hanafi rite Pashtun and Sunni elements to which the other ethnic groups and Islamic legal schools (Nizari and Jafari) were subordinated, not to mention the Hindus and Sikhs, who were completely marginalised or expelled after the breakup of the British Raj in 1947. The Hazaras, Shi'ites of the Jafari rite, were the big losers in this process until 1979, and the Hazarajat became the cursed land of their subjection in the 1891–93 war—even though Kafiristan (now Nuristan), in the east, and Turkestan, in the north and north-east, were also conquered by force and colonised by the new Pashtun dynasty (Ghobar, 2011, 483ff. and 490ff.).

The Hazarajat is a historical area that has never been an administrative unit.[7] Until the constitutional revision of 1964, it was essentially divided between

7 I have used the following translations of Afghan administrative terms: prefecture (*wilayat*) and prefect (*wali*); sub-prefecture (*woluswali*) and sub-prefect (*woluswal*); district (*ghariya*). The term *manteqa* (literally *region, locality*) has no official administrative significance, but

four of the five *wilayat* of the country: Herat, Turkestan, and—especially—Kabul and Kandahar. Today, it covers ten or so territorial entities that are home to the Hazaras (Arez, 2003). The city of Bamyan is the historic heart of the Hazarajat, though it was never exclusively Hazara and Shi'ite. Today the *wilayat* of Bamyan and Daikundi are the two parts of the country in which Hazara Shi'ite populations predominate, although since 2003, the addition to the Bamyan prefecture of the sub-prefectures of Saighan and Kahrmard of the *wilayat* of Baqlan—with Sunni Tajik populations of, respectively, 63 per cent and 82 per cent—has relativised the demographic and religious domination of Hazara Twelver Shi'ites. In addition, the Hazarajat is home to most of the Ismailis of Afghanistan and a minority of Sayyid Twelver Shi'ites. The title Sayyid refers to a lineage indicating descent from the Prophet's family, but some of them are of course Sunni Sayyids. Alessandro Monsutti (2005, 91) calls this a 'religious aristocracy.' The Qizilbash group is distinguished by its Turkish origins and its claim to descend from the entourage of the Persian ruler Nadir Shah, who invaded Afghanistan in 1738. In 2010, it was estimated that the population of the sub-prefecture of Bamyan comprised 75 per cent Hazara, 15 per cent Sayyid, 10 per cent Tajiks and 0.5 per cent Qizilbash. Furthermore, out of a population of 86,550 inhabitants, the *woluswali* today numbers 8,345 people who settled there between 2002 and 2012, having returned from exile or from other parts of the country; this is a little less than 10 per cent of the total population.

Before the 'iron rule' of Abdurrahman (1880–1901), the founder of modern Afghanistan, the Hazarajat had never been politically unified and was ruled by tribal leaders (*amir*). From the reign of Sher Ali Khan (1863–79) onwards, the so-called Kuchi Pashtun nomads raided the region to lead their flocks in transhumance to the high mountain pastures. Under the pretext of fighting the 'heresy' that existed in this region, Abdurrahman decided to conquer it, after driving its population to revolt in 1891 by subjecting it to an intolerable tax burden and plundering its land and herds, carrying out many arrests and deporting part of its population to Kabul. This military campaign of 1891–93 resulted in massacres, but it also had serious consequences for the future of this region, colonised through the almost total deportation of the Pashtun Kuchi Ghilzai. The Hazaras who survived and remained in the Hazarajat—many of them took refuge in the Iranian city of Mashhad, in the city of Quetta in the British Raj, and in Russia—were enslaved and stripped of their land, including pastures.

indicates the basic unit of territorial consciousness, which encompasses several villages in a clearly identified area of land, below the *ghariya*. This level of territorial belonging played a decisive role in the war and constitutes a factor of solidarity just as important as the principle of lineage and community associated with the principle of *qawm*.

They have therefore been forced, until today, to farm in a mountainous country with long winters where arable land is sorely lacking. Abdurrahman's successors—Amir Habibullah Khan (1901–19) and Amanullah (1919–29)—brought the reign of terror in the Hazarajat to an end. They abolished slavery, withdrew some of the measures discriminating against Hazaras, and restored to them some of their rights by granting titles to their leaders (*amir*), though this exacerbated the rivalries between these leaders and involved additional exploitation of the peasantry (Ghobar, 2011, 484). Later, the reigns of Nadir Shah (1929–33) and Zahir Shah (1933–73) put the seal on the Pashtun and Sunni domination of Afghanistan and the relegation of Hazara Shi'ites to the position second-class subjects. The great famine of 1971–72, with its accompanying drought, was terrible. During the tenure of President Dawood (1973–78), the subjugation of the Hazaras was intensified; land-grabbing by the Kuchis was encouraged under cover of the 1970 law on pastures, a law that recognised the state ownership of all land suitable for forage production—not just high mountain pastures—and prohibited the conversion of pasture land to cropland. But the Kuchis' interests were not limited to their pastoral activities. Over these decades during which the Hazaras were excessively exploited, they developed shops and transport companies, which guaranteed their economic stranglehold on the region, especially as usurers. In the wake of the great disaster of 1891–93, the Kuchis therefore seized the few land rights that had been preserved by the vulnerable Hazara peasantry, using debt as a means. (De Weijer, 2007; Alden Wily 2013b; Tapper, 2008; Mousavi, 1998; Monsutti, 2004 and 2005).

Only after the Soviet invasion—which, despite the presence of a small garrison in the town of Bamyan, left the Hazarajat virtually unaffected, as this deprived region offered little of interest and the resistance there was strong and immediate (Mohaghegh, 1984)—could the Hazaras begin to free themselves from the Pashtun, Tajik and Sunni yoke. First, they were able to interact with the central government thanks to the appointment as Chairman of the Council of Ministers of Babrak Karmal (1981–88), Mohammad Najibullah (1989–91) and finally Soltanali Keshtmand, a Hazara from Fouladi, a *woluswali* from the *wilayat* of Bamyan, whose parents had been deported to Kabul by Abdurrahman (Keshtmand, 2009). In 1987, under the influence of Tehran, armed groups claiming to be acting more or less for the Islamic Republic of Iran—the Sazman i-Nasr group, close to Ayatollah Montazeri, and the Sapah-i Pasdaran group, close to the Revolutionary Guards—united as a Council for the Alliance (*Shura-i ittifaq*), based in the district of Yakawlang, and this eventually gave birth to a political party. The Hizb-i Wahdat was created in Bamyan in 1989 and its presidency was entrusted to the charismatic Abdul Ali Mazari (Dorronsoro, 2000, 158ff. and 240ff.; Monsutti, 2005: 92ff.; Roy, 1985; Mo'aseseye farhangi

Saghalain, 1999). Most Tajiks and almost all Pashtuns then left the area, leaving the Hazaras in a position to recover their land and property. They took control of the new bazaar of Bamyan, though the Tajiks remained commercially active there through land and property leased to the Hazaras and the excellence of their connections with Kabul, Mazar-i Sharif and Baghlan. They also speculated on land by selling, as plots of *sharak* (residential area), properties belonging to Pashtuns from the village of Dasht-i Issa Khan on whose territory the airport was built. Upon the fall of the communist regime in 1992, Hizb-i Wahdat became the champion of the Hazara Shi'ite cause in Kabul. But during the battle that devastated the capital in 1993, it failed to prevent the massacre of Afshar, perpetrated in the western districts. During this episode, hundreds of Hazaras were killed, officially by the Tajik and Pashtun troops of Commander Ahmed Shah Massoud and President Burhanuddin Rabbani but the complicity or betrayal of Hazara elements could not be excluded.[8] Having retreated to the Hazarajat, the forces of Hizb-i Wahdat nevertheless succeeded, after hard fighting, opposing in 1995 attempts made by Ahmad Shah Massoud's movement to conquer it (Dorronsoro, 2000, Chapter 7).

After the assassination of Abdul Ali Mazari by the Taliban in 1995, Hizb-i Wahdat split into two factions. One, led by Abdul Karim Khalili from Behsud (Wardak), joined the Northern Alliance of Commander Dostom; the other, led by Mohammed Akbari from Waras (Bamyan), allied with the Taliban but also with the Islamic Republic of Iran. The two sides confronted one another until 1998, when the Taliban conquered the Hazarajat after subjecting it to a harsh economic blockade. They quickly entrusted the administration of the region to the supporters of Mohammed Akbari. But Abdul Karim Khalili's men continued to resist, launching an unsuccessful offensive on Bamyan in May 1999. The fighting claimed many lives and led to the destruction of almost one-fifth of the city's buildings, including the bazaar. Almost all of the population, some 13,000 families, fled, and Tajik traders took over the bazaar. Building on the victory of the Taliban, the Kuchis returned to the region to try to recover their property and land rights. In January 2001, fighting duly resumed in the district of Yakawlang, causing a new exodus of the Hazaras under the pressure of Taliban reprisals—a mass killing (*qatl-i 'am*) that remains intensely present in regional memory.

In November 2001, the Hazarajat moved on to a new stage in its history. The Taliban left the area following the US intervention, giving the Hazaras

8 This version of events is disputed by the Hazaras themselves, who place the blame on factional rivalries between Hazara commanders and even on the Sayyids (interviews in Bamyan and Kabul, 2014). See also Royesh (2013, 139 ff.).

the opportunity to gain access to the Kabul government through Abdul Karim Khalili, who had become the second vice-president alongside Hamid Karzai in 2004. They also challenged the interests (including property interests) of the Kuchis and Tajiks who had taken advantage of the Taliban regime while not being marginalised by the coalition that emerged from the Bonn agreement, signed in 2001. This new context, though more favourable to their interests, did not allow the Hazaras to unite politically. We can at present identify four trends within the Hizb-i Wahdat: that of Abdul Karim Khalili and his Hizb-i wahdat-i islami; that of Mohammad Akbari and his Hizb-i wahdat-i islami-i Afghanistan; that of Mohammad Mohaghegh and his Hizb-i wahdat-i islami-i mardom-i Afghanistan; and that of Erfani Yakawalangi and his Hizb-i wahdat-i islami-i mellat-i Afghanistan. In 2015, the tumultuous appointment of Tahar Zohair to the post of prefect by President Ashraf Ghani, with the support of Abdul Karim Khalili, showed that the antagonisms were still intense. Four Hazara MPs, including Mohammad Akbari, opposed the appointment by organising a sit-in outside the prefecture lasting sixteen days (7 to 22 June). On 19 June, young academics organised a counterdemonstration. The arrival of Tahar Zohair on 1 July did not calm matters as the protesters locked the premises of the prefecture while the supporters of the new prefect marched by holding bouquets of flowers.[9]

Within a century, the formation of the state and the social phenomena that came with it—such as urbanisation, emigration, and the confiscation or redistribution of land—had resulted in the sorrowful construction of a Hazara identity seen as an ethnic, even racial fact. Since the late nineteenth century, the Hazaras had indeed been considered Mongols by Tajik, Pashtun and Sayyid elites, and some of their physical characteristics, such as their flat noses, had been the subject of daily jokes. Various factors contributed to this 'invention of ethnicity'. First, the Shi'ite religious awakening of the 1960s, related to the Iraqi and Iranian holy places and under the influence of Ayatollah Mir Ali Ahmad Hojjat[10] and Sayed Esmael Balkhi.[11] Second, the flowering in Iran of a Hazara literature of resistance (Olszewska, 2009). Third, a musical renaissance, promoted by Radio Hazarahgi in Quetta from 1975 onwards. And lastly, the fact that in 2002 the US military intervention paradoxically allowed the celebration

9 Personal observation, 2015.

10 Mir Ali Ahmad Hojjat was the main Afghan Shi'ite authority and founder of the first religious school of this branch of Islam in Kabul, in the district of Chandawul. He died in 1974.

11 Sayed Esmael Balkhi was the founder of the modern Shi'ite Islamic movement, and is known as the father of the Hazara movement for political autonomy. He died in 1968.

of Nowruz and the public commemoration (publicised in the media) of Ashura to be resumed in Afghanistan—these rituals had been perpetuated by Hazaras living in Quetta or in Iran (Monsutti, 2007).

De facto, the formation of the state also turned the Shi'ite branch into the subordinate religion in an Afghanistan that was presumed to be Sunni, although the constitution did not mention any religious distinction and confined itself to making Hanafi Islam the state religion. Since 2008 and under the new 2004 constitution, the law on personal status—*ahwal-i shakhsiya*—has allowed Hazaras to resort to *fiqh jafari* when both parties are Shi'ites.[12] Nevertheless, the ethnicisation of the Hazaras is now undergoing an interesting development that tends to separate it from Shi'a Islam. Indeed, some Sunni Hazaras, assembled in council, demand this dual ethnic and religious affiliation and are now—surprisingly—well received by Shi'ite Hazaras pleased to see their ranks being swelled in anticipation of an ethnically connoted electoral competition and to have one foot in the camp of the majority religious affiliation, which allows them to interact with other identity groups on equal terms (Bouda, 2015). Ethnicisation is therefore a process whose outcome is less a well-defined Hazara than a 'Hazarification' of heterogeneous or hybrid populations such as the Hazaras of Pashtun culture or the 'mixed' or 'mixed race' (*doraga*) Hazaras.[13] In all ethnic groups, then, a distinction is drawn between original Hazaras (*asli*) and those to whom Hazara identity is ascribed (*wasli*), which makes it possible for the 'authenticity' and 'native status' of families to be claimed or contested.

Hazaras and Shi'ites do not constitute a homogeneous group. Beyond their different backgrounds and inequalities in terms of education, wealth, and gender, they have been divided politically since the 1978 coup. As we have said, some joined the Sazman-i Nasr of Mohammad Abdul Ali Mazari while others supported the Hizb-i harakat of Ayatollah Mohseni (Mohaghegh, 1984), thus leading to the break-up of the Hizb-e Wahdat a few years after its establishment. After the split, some made their peace with the Taliban or even joined them (Alden Wily, 2004, 23), while others supported the Hizb-i harakat, including many Sayyids, Qizilbash or Ismailis (Mo'aseseye farhangi Saghalain 1999, 190ff.). These internal political differences which have led to military confrontation for three decades, to conflicts over land and real estate, and to commercial and financial quarrels, fuel distrust and animosity between Shi'ites,

12 This is the law relating to marriage, divorce and inheritance, http://www.bsharat.com/id/16-f-h/01.html (accessed on 16 June 2016).

13 See Yazdani (2011, 267 ff.). The author is convinced of the existence of 'true' Hazaras, while stating that matrimonial alliances may have altered their physical characteristics and that there are 'Pashtunized' or 'mixed' (*dorageh*) Hazaras.

especially between Hazaras and Sayyids, the latter often accused of taking advantage of Taliban domination (or, under the monarchy, of having compromised with the Pashtun ruling class). In some ways, the war gave the Hazaras an opportunity to emancipate themselves socially from the domination of the Sayyids, as well as from the Pashtuns and the Tajiks. This process followed a pattern partly comparable to that observed in Lebanon, in that Abdolali Mazari, its ideologue, was close to Chamran, the Hizbollah leader, and absorbed this experience alongside other Iranian or Palestinian anti-imperialist fighters.[14] Since 2002, reconstruction has followed the lines laid out by this emancipation, but it is complicated by rivalries between the Hazaras who remained in the provinces during the war (*watani*), those who chose exile, especially in Iran (*zawari*), and returned fortified by their diasporic experience, and those who had come from other parts of the country[15] to settle in the Hazarajat, now perceived as the land of the Hazaras by definition.[16]

4 Reconstruction of the State, Development Aid and the Invention of Ethnicity

The Western military intervention of 2001, and the 'reconstruction' of the state that ensued, reproduced and extended the process of the invention of a Hazara Hazarajat and the ethnicisation of the Hazaras. The foreign presence, the financial flows it generated, the economic opportunities it opened up, and the institutional patterns that it established intensified the ethnicisation and/or sectarianisation of Afghan society, as well as the return of refugees and migrants, investments from the diaspora, and urbanisation. And this happened even though, politically and ideologically, aid for reconstruction was meant to transcend these divisions inherited from the past, these incarnations of 'tradition' allegedly behind the political crisis into which the country had sunk since the 1970s. Inspired by the experts of the International Security Assistance Force (ISAF), the 2004 constitution also drew on a primordialist vision of ethnicity and sectarianism to explicitly recognise the rights of ethnic groups, who found themselves reified as a result. The fact that the theory of nationalities (*mellat*) proposed by the People's Democratic Party of Afghanistan (1978–79)

14 Interviews with Saleh Aliyar, Chairman of the Peace Council, and Mostafa Makarem, director of the television channel Rahe-e-Farda (Kabul, 2014 and 2015).

15 These Hazaras came in particular from Ghazni, the historic stronghold of intellectual elites thanks to its links with Pakistan.

16 Personal observation (2014–15); Adlparvar (2015, 152 ff.).

and the Soviets (1979–89) has re-emerged under the 'umbrella' of NATO is an irony of history. 'Reconstruction' was conceptualised in an ethnic and sectarian fashion, and on that basis laws were enacted, funding awarded, ministerial and administrative posts allocated, voters mobilised and property or matrimonial disputes voiced. Given their historical subordination, the Hazaras, now for the first time the objects of affirmative action rather than of discrimination, were the major beneficiaries of this policy of allocating public resources on an ethno-sectarian basis, while continuing to experience this policy in a sorrowful way. As we know, they achieved the legitimisation of the Jafari legal school through the 2004 constitution and the *ahwal-i shakhsiya* law passed in 2008. But their age-old rivals, the Kuchis, were also given the status of an ethnic group in their own right; a group whose living conditions and education the constitution seeks to improve (Tapper, 2008). The double reification of these 'complementary enemies' is of course fraught with potential dangers, as has already been shown by the bloody clashes between Hazaras and Kuchis in Wardak in 2010, and in Nahoor, in Ghazni, between 2010 and 2012, and the subsequent ethnopolitical activism of Hazara and Pashtun MPs defending their respective clienteles as the general elections approached.[17] The fact that the post of prefect (*wali*) of the *wilayat* of Bamyan was given to a Hazara for the first time in history is one of the most eloquent illustrations of the ethnicisation of the reconstruction of Afghanistan under the aegis of foreign aid. This position was successively occupied by Mohammad Rahim Aliyar in 2003, Habiba Sarabi in 2005—the first woman to hold a position of this significance in the country, Gholamali Vahdat in 2014, and finally, not without difficulties, Tahar Zohair in July 2015. Similarly, and by way of example, a dozen low-ranking officials of the sub-prefecture of Shibar, in the *wilayat* of Bamyan, are Hazara Twelver Shi'ites, while the administrative district includes 30 per cent Sunni Tajiks and many Ismailis (almost half of the population in Shibar are Shi'ites).

These appointments were followed by the recruitment of Hazara officials and administrative officers, chosen in accordance with the ethnic logic of the spoils system—or even in accordance with party or faction, as the above-named prefects are all close to the Hizb-i Wahdat, of the Khalili/Mohaghegh tendency. These appointments have therefore had an immediate impact on the policy of land allocation, the recognition of land rights and the allocation of state resources in favour of Hazaras and to the detriment of Tajiks and Sayyids (Adlparvar, 2015, Chapter 5). Beyond politics and administration, ethnicisation

17 See the relevant press articles (in Persian), including: http://kabulpress.org/my/spip.php?article10066 (accessed on 16 June 2016) and http://urozgan.org/Clear/fa-AF/print/article/print/1604/ (accessed on 16 June 2016).

has thus been extended more clearly to encompass the economic sphere, including the issue of land and the control of the bazaar of Bamyan, which now counts only a small minority of Tajik traders instead of the 2,500 or so who ran the old bazaar at the foot of the Buddhas in the 1970s and 1980s. Moreover, Hazara consumers buy only from Hazara traders. 'The Hazara does not eat the bread of the Tajik' is an oft-heard remark.

The political economy of 'reconstruction' has inevitably grafted itself into the ethnopolitical memory of the war and prior periods, in a country where the traceability of property is a highly contradictory matter, depending on the nature of the evidence adduced (political, legal, customary, scriptural or oral), thus giving a contemporary, conflictual character to any reference to the past (Alden Wily, 2004; Monsutti, 2008). When elections take place, Afghans can immediately identify among the candidates the fighters who resisted the Soviet occupation—those who, in Afghanistan, are referred to as jihadis—and the migrants who have returned home (*mohajer*). Similarly, they distinguish economic actors depending on the origin of their fortunes and their projects. Everyone is familiar with the career of a given hotel owner, residential development promoter (*sharak*) or bazaar trader.

The ethnic and religious identity of entrepreneurs and recipients of development aid is thus self-evident and foreign actors adapt to it when not exploiting it. For example, the influx of NGOs with Western and Japanese financial support in the prefecture of Bamyan, anxious to meet the needs of one of the poorest regions of the country and to rescue its women, was immediately configured in accordance with interethnic and inter-religious relations as the war had redefined them (Anjoman-i nevisandegan-i Bamyan, 2011). The armed resistance of Abdul Karim Khalili to the Taliban offensive from 1996 to 1998, and his political rise under President Hamid Karzai, consummated the process of the 'Hazarification' of a province previously dominated by Tajiks and Sayyids (though the former continued to exert economic and financial control from Kabul, Baghlan, Mazar-i Sharif and Kunduz), and of a population that previously perceived itself as Shi'ite rather than the ethnic mode favoured by the structure of military resistance in political parties—in this case by the Hizb-i Wahdat, or rather by its four branches. In return, most foreign aid actors have taken for granted the essentially Hazara nature (the 'Hazarity') of the Hazarajat. And after 2004, the Hazara themselves came in great numbers from Ghazni, Balkh, Herat and other locations favoured by the diaspora, hoping to profit from the windfall of aid, claiming they were 'returning to their roots'. Abdul Karim Khalili encouraged this movement in order to strengthen his electoral base as the 2003 presidential election approached—an election in which he supported the candidature of Hamid Karzai—which involved mobilising women's suffrage, to the great satisfaction of the NGOs of international civil society. So, the ethnicisation and sectarianisation of a region can sit comfortably alongside the priorities of development aid and the 'reconstruction of the state'. Similarly, by seizing on 'runaway marriages' (*izdiwaj farari*) between, for example, a young Hazara man and a young Sayyid woman according to a bureaucratised and judicialised logic of identity that is completely different from the former procedures for conflict resolution between families or *qawm*, the Independent Commission for Human Rights in Afghanistan, the UN Assistance Mission in Afghanistan and women's rights NGOs reify matrimonial relationships by combining them within ethnic categories (Adlparvar, 2015, 138; weekly *Sada-I Shahrvand-i Bamayn,* 1, jawza 1393/2014, 1). Conversely, international aid sometimes produces 'negative' ethnic identities, especially when it abandons its attempt put down roots in radical or conservative areas deemed too dangerous, including the Tajik-dominated provinces of Sayghan and Kahmard, Shibar, or the south of the country, which is in the hands of the Taliban.

But these processes cover more complex lines of division. As we have seen, the Hazaras in Bamyan are divided. Indigenous Hazaras (*watani*) now live together, in a state of some tension, with Hazaras who came from Ghazni, Herat and Mazar-i Sharif after the fall of the Taliban to enjoy the windfall of the Hazarajat, as well as with the *zawari* Hazaras back from Iran. Like other ethnic groups in the country, the Hazaras as a whole are ultimately driven by progressive internal divisions that are less part of identity in the abstract sense than of social inequalities, starting with inequalities in gender and education. As shown by the case of the village of Fatmasti, the situation is even more complex on the micro-local level of historical lands. In this fragmented social landscape, generally governed by the twin principle of lineage (*qawm*) and locality (*manteqa*), Olivier Roy (1985) was among the first to demonstrate the need to keep in mind that the ethnicisation of Afghan society is a fluid process, situated historically and politically constructed, at least since the centralising reign of Abdurrahman. The nature of this process has been confirmed by Alessandro Monsutti's research on the Hazaras (2004 and 2005). This ethnicisation is not based on a territorialisation of tribal membership which might be explained by one of those notorious (and improbable) 'ethnic cards'. It rests instead on population movements that are either voluntary and motivated by economic interest, or constrained by central government initiatives—as we saw in connection with the Hazarajat, by the convulsions of land reform (1976–79) or by war (1979–2001).

It is thus necessary to combine the issue of the local and segmental with that of population mobility in the context of transhumance—but also of seasonal migration, emigration, and membership of the diaspora—and with that of the fluidity and fungibility of ethno-sectarian identifications. It is also essential to give a central place to a third principle, that of neighbourhood (*shafa'a*) between residents and between ethnic groups; a principle that is the source of conflict and compromise, of competition and solidarity (Mumtaz, 2013; Monsutti, 2008).

5 The Political and Moral Economy of Ethnicity

'Reconstruction' is only one moment among many in this long history, an episode that is changing its direction thanks to the extent of the resources pumped into the country and the introduction of representative institutions conducive to the ethnicisation of political life through elections. From this point of view, foreign intervention has, since 2001, deemed it politically correct to promote the integration of the 'minority' par excellence—that is to say, the Hazaras—into the Afghan political system, at the cost of the ethnic reification of their identity but without bringing them out of their socio-economic subordination, including in the Hazarajat, a particularly deprived area for mainly geographical reasons. In the regions, the bulk of land speculation focuses on plots that would have little market value outside this mountainous country, as they are located on steep terrain, are hard to sustain and are exposed to rainwater run-off, erosion and landslides.

Favoured by the securitisation of land ownership, the territorialisation of ethnicity strengthens the community bias of development aid. Sometimes donors exploit this for strategic, religious or cultural reasons of their own, as is the case with Iran (which promotes the Hazaras), Pakistan (the Pashtuns), Turkey (the Uzbeks) and the Aga Khan Foundation (the Ismailis). But beyond these political approaches, the operational requirements of the land are self-evident. While most foreign actors endeavour to remain politically correct by recruiting several Hazaras, they must in all cases rely on Pashtuns to work in the south, or Tajiks or Uzbeks in the north. Of course, the same reasoning applies to the Hazarajat, where it is essential to use Hazaras. Despite this, the NGO labour market initially benefited the Sunnis, if only because they form the majority and are often better trained and more commonly English-speaking.

Ethnic networks, meanwhile, are endeavouring to tap into the flow of development aid and the foreign presence. Thus, the Hazaras benefit from institutions or projects connected with human rights, and the Tajiks from scientific and cultural cooperation: the former focus on commissions for women's rights, the latter on think tanks and the media. As for Pashtuns, they are irreplaceable in the crucial area of telecommunications, for obvious reasons of security—only they can travel confidently in Pashtun areas—and because they trained in Pakistan while in exile during the 1980s and 1990s.

Since 2002, the diaspora, development aid and the foreign troops and NGOs in the territory have pumped substantial funds into Afghan society. These funds have caused a sharp increase in prices in certain sectors, including real estate, hotels and restaurants, airlines, car rental companies, and the consumption of international products and certain local services, such as the provision of must-have items for wedding venues. But this influx of money was grafted onto existing social relations, especially in families, and transformed their balance and even their very nature. This resulted in a complex mixture of traditionalisation and monetisation of one's kin. In all social circles, as the dollar is king, the father does not so much give his daughters away in marriage as trade them, sometimes at a very high rate, and sometimes right from the cradle.[18] If an interesting offer comes along, a farmer may for example be compelled to give away his child. But the head of a good family whose reputation triggers tantalising financial proposals from suitors who wish to climb up the social ladder can proceed in just the same way. At this point, complex social strategies intervene and usually contribute to dowry inflation. For instance, a father wanting to reserve his daughter for one of her cousins can try to turn away, without offending him, an inopportune suitor by demanding a very high dowry (or 'milk price', *pul-i shir*). But if the ploy fails, as often happens, the increase is considered effective. The marriage market has thus become judicialised as a result of its monetisation and the intervention of the Independent Commission for Human Rights in Afghanistan, the United Nations Assistance Mission in Afghanistan and NGOs concerned to defend the condition of women and the cause of rights. In return, this judicialisation has led to an acceleration of the monetisation of this market in a context where the courts, which not only need payment but are also, it is said, lured by the smell of money, continue to promulgate financial decisions relative to the amount of the dowry or to blood, which follow the exponential curve of the cost of living. The combination of money, legal system and custom tends to extend, reify and dramatise the practical exercise of the last of these, for example in the shape of marriage exchanges of the compensatory type intended to avert or stop the 'evil' (*bad* or *badal*)—that is to say, violence between families, clans and ethnic groups. Some might even seek, these days, to trigger a family or marital conflict, hoping to reach an agreement of this type. The idea of antagonism is immediately associated with that of the profit that might be drawn from it, which induces a form of intentionality: thus, the complainant will be suspected of having

18 This is called *gahvara bakhshi* (making a gift from the cradle); see Ghazali (2013).

provoked a dispute so as to avoid having to pay a dowry (similar practices make it possible to consolidate the legal status and securitisation of land).

The distortions introduced within Afghan society by the foreign presence—and by the influx of money, the land speculation, and the ideological dissonance it generates—come with a high human cost. First and foremost, they lead to a split or even a generational divide. The youngest people are often better educated and more familiar with international practices, and their command of English allows them to benefit from professional and economic opportunities that are more or less beyond the reach of their elders. This imbalance has led to the widespread destabilisation of social status: the young suffer from not holding decision-making power that is proportional to their skills in what is still a patriarchal and tribal society; older people believe that the success of their juniors is a challenge to their authority. Added to this is a destabilisation of conjugal roles, evident for example when a woman has her own income, for example because she works for an NGO, while her husband is unemployed or has to settle for the meagre rewards of the normal Afghan economy. In addition, women are beginning to express their demands with regard to inheritance rights: this is an explosive development from the point of view of customary law and Islamic law. Moreover, development aid and its collateral effects are intensifying intra-generational and intra-family rivalries, fanning 'competition among peers, or even between cousins' (*sayal dari* or *sayal shiriki*) or even rivalry between the descendants of brothers (*owdourzadegi*). So a woman may have to pay a significant amount of rent to her husband in order to turn a room in the family home into a nursery. A young man who organises a too lavish wedding can create a bad precedent for his brothers, cousins or friends, who may not have the same financial means as he does and will see their reputations suffer accordingly. Women working for NGOs should be careful not to tarnish the honour of their colleagues. If they were to separate from their husbands, they would not only lose their social status but also their jobs, and find the chances of them being elected significantly limited, if they are thinking of getting involved in this sphere. Should they be obliged to go to court to see their rights enforced, or simply see their demands recognised, the process will cost them around USD 8,000.

Generally, the multiple lines of division and conflict running through Afghan society are amplified by its extremely fragmented character and the tangle of landholdings, ethnic and religious memberships, and clan and family allegiances. Any allocation of resources, especially investment, involves a choice in favour of one locality and therefore at the expense of others. This phenomenon is evident in the field of rural engineering: water supplies, the charges that determine their use, the waiting time required to obtain access to them, and their sometimes unwanted consequences on the natural environment all create a new field of conflict in which the violence between villages or towns (*ghariya*) finds expression. The financial and consumerist bubble that has been constantly swelling since 2002 is causing devastating social disruption. Those in power give free rein to their sexual predation, exerted at gunpoint or with the aid of great sheaves of money and of college qualifications. The individuality of women who have returned from abroad—from the West, or from Iran or Pakistan—and the independent spirit of those who have been educated triggers the brutality of husbands, fathers or brothers who refuse to accept that these women might be any different from others. Marital jealousy can also play a part—a feeling all the more dangerous as it is supposed to express family honour. The human toll of these tensions is appalling. Many women even commit suicide by atrocious means (self-immolation or swallowing pesticide or rat poison), or suffer senseless corporal punishment, such as having their nose, ears or lips cut off; the press has described these abuses extensively as occurring in Bamyan, Daikundi and Hera. If we stick to these sources, the cases seem, curiously, to be less numerous in the Pashtun, Tajik and Uzbek areas, even though these are reputedly more conservative.[19] As shown by the murder of the young woman poet Nadia Anjoman, 26 years old, in November 2005, the physical elimination of women deemed to have made a nuisance of themselves has become commonplace. But deadly violence is also the rule when it comes to settling land disputes and quarrels of a romantic, inter-familial, ethnic or sectarian nature. The overt militarisation of this sphere, on the initiative of the commanders, is only the most extreme example of the use of force as a mode of social regulation.

Rightly or wrongly, the population holds the providers of aid responsible for the uncontrolled circulation of firearms: Provincial Reconstruction Teams sent out to rebuild the provinces are left without means of defence, and are therefore unable to sell weapons on to Afghans, especially as the searches carried out by US troops in private homes have prompted many households to provide themselves with the tools necessary to protect their privacy and safeguard their honour. The massive recruitment of local police (*polis-i mahalli*)—some 30,000 of them—plays a part in the militarisation of Afghan society, as these security forces are readily viewed by the population as *arbaki*, those swashbuckling figures who controlled the neighbourhoods and played a central role in social violence and civil war (Dorronsoro, 2000, 127). In other words, aid and

19 See in particular these articles (in Persian): http://www.afghanirca.com/newsIn.php?id=22126 and http://www.afghanpaper.com/nbody.php?id=68734 (accessed on June 16, 2016).

widespread armed violence feed on one another and are part of a spectrum that extends from private confrontation to civil war—the very same civil war that the foreign presence is supposed to avert.

One final factor needs to be considered. The self-proclaimed return to peace following the US intervention in 2001 and the formation of an elected government has delegitimised Afghan emigration in the eyes of foreign countries, particularly Western states and Iran, which are now trying to hamper such emigration since it no longer seems to involve refugees and asylum-seekers in the strict sense of these terms. Nevertheless, the work of Alessandro Monsutti has long since dismantled any excess rigidity in the classification of the mobility of Afghans, including Hazaras. Hazaras do indeed live as 'travellers' (*mosâfir*), as members of an age-old diaspora that has always circulated according to cycles and migration patterns that stem successively or simultaneously from political exile, from flight in order to survive, from professional expatriation, from study abroad or time spent abroad for religious reasons, and from seasonal migration. Travel is a means of protection as well as a means of livelihood or enrichment, but it is also a way of confirming one's maturity, and a veritable lifestyle in itself. In addition, the remittances of migrants are essential to the development of this country, under considerable pressure as it is from demographics and land-related issues (Monsutti, 2004 and 2009; Gehrig and Monsutti, 2003). The Hazarajat alone apparently receives approximately USD 200 million per annum from Afghans working in Iran (Monsutti, 2009, 102, note 37). There is a glaring contradiction between the display of good intentions and the real effectiveness of the policies implemented. Afghan teenagers who slip across the borders of Iran, Turkey, the Balkans and EU countries only to see their hopes stagnate, or who try and make a new life for themselves by hanging around the Gare du Nord in Paris or the approach roads of the Channel Tunnel in Calais, are the pathetic illustration of the side-effects of the territorial approach to reconstruction when applied to mobile populations.

6 Conclusion

The sometimes dramatic distortions introduced into Afghan society by Western intervention stem from a scissor effect. First, donors, foreign institutions, and NGOs remain prisoners of a cultural, if not an orientalist approach to the country; a country that they are helping to traditionalise and particularly to ethnicise. They will, for example, be the first to invoke 'custom' (*rawaj*) and to seek the opinion of the 'elders' in order to implement their projects. They set aside the fact that the advice they are given is sometimes motivated by material interests or factional alignments and is likely to exacerbate social conflicts, in particular over land, in which they play a part, and neglect the contradictions between 'customs' that favour men over women, brothers over sons, the elderly over the young, and the rifle over mere paper documents and their own empowerment objectives with regard to subordinate social groups, especially women, and the construction of a rule of law that would be legal-rational—that is, bureaucratic in nature. Similarly, foreigners take for granted the Islamic nature of Afghan society and its local law, whereas this society is not systematically Islamic, especially in terms of land and inheritance, which are not governed by *fiqh* (Islamic jurisprudence).

Second, development aid is just as likely to destabilise this so-called traditional society by ignoring its mysteries, dreaming of forgetting the past, accelerating its monetisation and commercialisation, encouraging a securitisation of property that undermines the rights of joint ownership and the historical compromise of neighbourhood (*shafa'a*), creating new minorities while being unable to guarantee their safety, providing education and employment to a tiny fraction of women and young men, thereby giving them the resources to challenge their social subordination and, finally, by bringing in or consolidating new repertoires of political or professional legitimacy, most often at the expense of the authorities of 'custom'.

This series of contradictions inherent in development aid brings social, political and even military conflicts in its wake. However, the complex logic behind these conflicts is rooted in the mysteries of the locality (*manteqa*) and 'segmentarity' (*qawm*) that are closed books to foreign governments and donors as well as NGOs, readable only through the distorting, outrageously reductive prism of the culturalist construction of Afghan society. By simplifying and reifying this society, disguising it in the deceptive features of tradition and ethnicity, this prism totally neglects the radical transformation that Afghan society has experienced as a result of war and emigration.

The foreign providers of development in Afghanistan, pressurised by the calendar of the civil year, which controls their budgets, and dependent on intermediaries chosen for their ease of access, command of English, and interpersonal and managerial skills, move like bulls in a china shop. Even worse, they burden society with unprecedented conflicts over land issues, trade, banking, wages and education. The three pillars on which Afghan society still rests—*zan* (woman), *zar* (money) and *zamin* (land)—are, more than ever, factors of competition and confrontation. Development, economic growth and the internationalisation of trade conflicts stoke conflict as a result of the resources they generate and the desires they arouse. At the same time, the rational-legal, bureaucratic rule of law, if indeed it has the political and financial resources necessary to emerge, does not appear to be best placed to peacefully resolve social disputes, particularly over land. Informal arbitration procedures between protagonists, at which the Taliban excel, are probably better suited to the concrete conditions of the country, at least in the countryside, even though they tend to reproduce social domination (Sadeghi, 2013; Baczko, 2013; De Lauri, 2013). In addition, 'capitalism' will not easily resolve the crucial issue of coexistence between shepherds and farmers, and any exclusive securitisation process of arable land or commercialisation of pastures will have devastating consequences (Alden Wily, 2013b). On the ground, those involved are demanding property deeds, which alone, in their eyes, can guarantee any protection (even illusory) for their property, while demanding respect for customary law, particularly that of the neighbourhood (shafa'a), as these laws convey an ethic of collective responsibility.

Furthermore, such a mountainous and arid country as Afghanistan cannot expect an endogenous socio-economic take-off in a context where the scarcity of arable land adds to the demographic pressure. For decades, the mobility of populations has been the primary means of their survival, and sometimes their relative enrichment. For thirty years, remittances from emigrants have constituted a real lever for the transformation of society. Conversely, any obstruction to this movement of human beings aggravates internal tensions. In the late 1940s, the independence of Pakistan, for example, hindered the cross-border transhumance of the Kuchis, bringing extra pressure to bear on the pastures of the Hazarajat. There will be no development in Afghanistan without international mobility for Afghans. Funding and policies that fail to reflect this reality will bring neither social change nor economic growth, and will not even manage to 'fix' populations in their place, as Western states and Iran hope.

For fifteen years, the world has been scared of the extremism of the Taliban and the threat it poses to the international system, and has seen Afghanistan only through the reductive prism of jihadi threat. At the same time, the country has tried to send a different message to Europe, one that Europe has refused to hear—a message whose urgency and complexity are currently being revealed through the influx of refugees: how can one shape a state that follows the rule of law and is consistent with international standards while generating a basic minimum of economic growth and social justice, and take into account people's imperative need to be mobile and interact with the several million-strong diaspora? It would be unreasonable to deny all merit to the foreign intervention of 2001. The new regime has undoubtedly created a political space in which all the so-called ethnic groups in the country can discuss sharing the external financial windfall, if not on an equal footing at least in an atmosphere conducive to effective competition and compromise (in this specific case, the influx of resources plays a role comparable to that of tax in Western states). Given the history of Afghanistan over the last two centuries, such an evolution is a real breakthrough. But this mode of development is still hampered by imbalances and uncertainties.

References

Adelkhah, F. (ed.) (2013) 'Guerre et terre en Afghanistan', *Revue des mondes musulmans et de la Méditerranée*, 133, https://remmm.revues.org/7936 (accessed on 16 June 2016).

Adlparvar, N. (2015) *'When Glass Breaks, It Becomes Sharper': de-constructing ethnicity in the Bamyan Valley, Afghanistan*, PhD thesis, (Brighton: University of Sussex), http://sro.sussex.ac.uk/56083/ (accessed 16 June 2016).

Alden Wily, L. (2013a) *Land, People, and the State in Afghanistan: 2002–2012* (Kabul: Afghanistan Research and Evaluation Unit), http://www.areu.org.af/EditionDetails.aspx?EditionId=622&ContentId=7&ParentId=7 (accessed on 16 June 2016).

Alden Wily, L. (2013b) 'The Battle for Pastures: The Hidden War in Afghanistan', *Revue des mondes musulmans et de la Méditerranée*, 133, pp. 95–113, http://remmm.revues.org/8021 (accessed on 16 June 2016).

Alden Wily, L. (2004) Land Relations in Bamyan Province. Findings from a 15 Village Case Study (Kabul: Afghanistan Research and Evaluation Unit), http://www.areu.org.af/EditionDetails.aspx?EditionId=179&ContentId=7&ParentId=7 (accessed on 16 June 2016).

Andishmand, M.E. (2009) *Hizb-i democratik-i khalq-i afghanistan. Koudata, hakemiyat va foroupashi* (*Le parti démocratique du peuple d'Afghanistan. Le coup d'Etat, la souveraineté et l'effondrement* [*The People's Democratic Party of Afghanistan. The coup, the regime and the collapse*] Translated by the author) (Kabul: Mayvand, 1388/2009).

Anjoman-i nevisandegan-i Bamyan (2011), *Shanasnamah nahadha-i madani va ahzab-i siyasi-i welayat-i Bamyan va Daikundi* [*The booklet of institutions of civil society and political parties in the regions of Bamyan and Daikundi*], (Bamyan, 1390/2011).

Arez, G.J. (2003) *Sarhadat va taghsimat-i idari-i afghanistan dar toul-i tarikh* [*The borders and administrative divisions of Afghanistan in history*], (Peshawar: Kor, 1382/2003).

Azimi, M.N. (2012–2013) *Yadmandehai az jang-i Jalalabad* [*What is left of memories of the Battle of Jalalabad*] (Kabul: Vatan, 1391/2012–2013).

Baczko, A. (2013) 'Les conflits fonciers comme analyseurs des guerres civiles: chefs de guerre, militaires américains et juges Taliban dans la Kunar', *Revue des mondes musulmans et de la Méditerranée*, 133, pp. 115–132, http://remmm.revues.org/8034 (accessed on 16 June 2016).

Bouda, A. (2015) *Barnahadehai bar bab-e 'shora-i hazaraha-i ahl-i sonnat dar afghanistan'*, 26 Sowr 1394/2015, http://urozgan.org/fa-AF/article/9024/ (accessed on 16 June 2016).

Centlivres, P. (1991) 'Exil, relations interethniques et identité dans la crise afghane', *Revue du monde musulman et de la Méditerranée*, 59(1), pp. 70–82, http://www.persee.fr/doc/remmm_0997-1327_1991_num_59_1_1492 (accessed on 16 June 2016).

De Lauri, A. (2013) 'Terre, normes de propriété et litiges à Kaboul', *Revue du monde musulman et de la Méditerranée*, 133, pp. 133–149, http://remmm.revues.org/8051 (accessed on 16 June 2016).

De Weijer, F. (2007) 'Afghanistan's Kuchi pastoralists: change and adaptation', *Nomadic Peoples*, 11(1), pp. 9–37, DOI: 10.3167/np.2007.110102.

Digard, J.-P. (ed.) (1988) *Le Fait ethnique en Iran et en Afghanistan* (Paris: Editions du CNRS).

Dorronsoro, G. (2000) *La Révolution afghane. Des communistes aux talibans* (Paris: Karthala).

Gehrig, T. and A. Monsutti (2003) 'Territoires, flux et représentations de l'exil afghan: le cas des Hazaras et des Kaboulis', *A contrario*, 1, pp. 61–78, http://www.cairn.info/revue-a-contrario-2003-1-page-61.htm (accessed on 16 June 2016).

Ghazali, B.A. (2013) 'Gahvara bakhshha bayad az zananeshan ham bogzarand', *Killid*, 585, 21 September, p. 23.

Ghobar, M.G.M. (2011) *Afghanistan dar masir-i tarikh* [*Afghanistan and its historical trajectory*] (Téhéran: Erfan) 1390/2011.

Keshtmand, S. (2009) *Danishnameh Aryana* (*Encyclopédie Aryana*), 23 farvardin 1388, http://database-aryana-encyclopaedia.blogspot.fr/2009/04/blog-post_12.html (accessed on 16 June 2016).

Marchal, R. and C. Messiant (2003) 'Les guerres civiles à l'ère de la globalisation. Nouvelles réalités et nouveaux paradigmes', *Critique internationale*, 1(18), pp. 91–112, DOI: 10.3917/crii.018.0091.

Marchal, R. and C. Messiant (2002) 'De l'avidité des rebelles. L'analyse économique des conflits par Paul Collier', *Critique internationale*, 3(16), pp. 58–69, DOI: 10.3917/crii.016.0058.

Mo'aseseye farhangi Saghalain (1999) *Shorayi etelaf, zamineh saz-i ettehad-i shi'ayan*, Tehran, Mo'aseseye farhangi Saghalain, 1378/1999.

Mohaghegh, Mohammad (1984) Khaterat-i yek sangar neshin. Goushei az jenayat-i khawanin dar enghelab-i eslami-i afghanestan [*Memories of a man of the trench*, Vol. 1, *Some of the crimes of landowners in the Islamic revolution of Afghanistan*], n.p., Sayed Habibollah Shafagh, 1363/1984.

Monsutti, A. (2009) 'Itinérances transnationales: un éclairage sur les réseaux migratoires afghans', *Critique internationale*, 44(3), pp. 83–104, DOI: 10.3917/crii.044.0083.

Monsutti, A. (2008) 'The impact of war on social, political and economic organization in Southern Hazarajat', in M.-R. Djalili, A. Monsutti and A. Neubauer (eds.) *Le Monde turco-iranien en question* (Paris: Karthala), pp. 195–209.

Monsutti, A. (2007) 'Image of the Self, image of the Other: social organization and the role of "Ashura" among the Hazaras of Quetta (Pakistan)', in Monsutti, A., S. Naef and F. Sabahi, (eds.) *The Other Shiites: From the Mediterranean to Central Asia* (Berlin: Peter Lang), pp. 173–191.

Monsutti, A. (2005) *War and Migration. Social Networks and Economic Strategies of the Hazaras of Afghanistan*, translated by Patrick Camiller (New York: Routledge).

Monsutti, A. (2004) *Guerres et migrations. Réseaux sociaux et stratégies économiques des Hazaras d'Afghanistan* (Paris: Editions de la Maison des Sciences de l'Homme).

Mousavi, S.A. (1998) *The Hazaras of Afghanistan. An Historical, Cultural, Economic and Political History* (Surrey: Curzon Press).

Mumtaz, W. (2013) 'Three Faces of Shafa'a. Land Ownership on Trial in Ningarhar', *Revue des mondes musulmans et de la Méditerranée*, 133, pp. 169–185, http://remmm.revues.org/8071 (accessed on 16 June 2016).

Olszewska, S. (2009) *Poetry and its Social Contexts among Afghan Refugees in Iran*, DPhil thesis (Oxford: Wolfson College, Oxford University).

Qhodus, S.A. (2009) *Jangha-i Kabol 1371–1375* [*The Battles of Kabul 1992–1996*] (Bochum: Nashr-i Ida), 1387/2009.

Roy, O. (1985) *L'Afghanistan. Islam et modernité politique* (Paris: Seuil).

Royesh, A. (2013) *Bogzar nafas bakasham* [*Let me breathe*] (Kabul: entesharat-e tak), 1391/2013.

Sadeghi, A.R. (2013) 'La protection de la propriété terrienne entre loi et arbitrages', *Revue des mondes musulmans et de la Méditerranée*, 133, pp. 83–91, http://remmm.revues.org/8004 (accessed on 16 June 2016).

Tapper, R. (2008) 'Who are the Kuchi? Nomad self-identities in Afghanistan', *Journal of the Royal Anthropological Institute*, 14 (1), pp. 97–116, DOI: 10.1111/j.1467-9655.2007.00480.x.

Tapper, R. (ed.) (1983) *The Conflict of Tribe and State in Iran and Afghanistan* (New York: St Martin's Press).

Yazdani, H.A. (Haj Kazem) (2011) *Pajouheshi dar tarikh-i hazaraha*, [*A study of the history of the Hazaras*] (Tehran: Erfan) 1390/2011.

Chronology

1880–1901: 'Reign of Iron' of Abdurrahman, the founder of modern Afghanistan, under British tutelage

1891–93: 'Three-year War' in the Hazarajat

1928: Major reforms of the constitutional King Amanullah (1919–29)
1933–73: Reign of Zaher Shah
1973: Coup of Mohammad Dawood Khan, the King's cousin and former Prime Minister (1953–63), and proclamation of the Republic
1978: Coup of the People's Democratic Party
1979–89: Soviet occupation
1992: Fall of the pro-Soviet regime
1992–96: Coming to power of the Mujahideen, who resisted the Soviet occupation, and the 'War of the Commanders'
1996–2001: Taliban regime, overthrown by US military intervention
2001–14: Karzai Administration
Since 2014: Coalition government of Abdullah Abdullah–Ashraf Ghani

CHAPTER 7

Resisting Neo-Liberal Skylines: Social Mobilisations and Entrepreneurial Urban Development in Tel Aviv

Adriana Kemp and Talia Margalit

Abstract

The article examines recent social mobilisations against the planning and building of towers in Tel Aviv to address ongoing debates over the impact of social activism on the neo-liberalisation of urban development in times of neoliberalism's 'legitimation crisis.' Contrary to binary views of 'neoliberalism vs. resistance' prevalent in scholarly debates, we look into the uneven ways in which urban mobilisations are conditioned by local configurations of neo-liberalisation, and how, in their turn, they affect neo-liberal practices as they oscillate between resistance and integration. Based on empirical analysis, we argue that while recent mobilisations introduced novel claims and tactics against the institutional methods and decisions that produce urban space, and succeeded in politicizing towers as the flagship of neoliberal urban development, their actions have been reinserted in the deepening neo-liberalisation of the city. Our findings raise broader insights about the ways in which neo-liberalisation processes sit *inside* society and not above it, as they shape the actors concerned, their positions, and their visions of development.

1 Introduction

In summer 2011 expensive residential towers in Tel Aviv became visibly synonymous with social injustice when thousands of demonstrators waved mocks-ups of the flashy towers that were sprawling across the city, while marching to protest against the high cost of food, housing, health and education. This massive protest was the first to highlight the popular local struggle against the changing skyline of Tel Aviv as a symptom of broader social discontent with the 'trickle-down' promises of neo-liberal development.

The young leaders of the protest, and the thousands that joined them in numerous tent cities, identified the sharp escalation of urban accommodation costs as the main social crisis of their generation: since the late 1970s, the government had stopped building affordable housing and the reservoir of public housing had dried up. No laws protect tenants, and many fear of being pushed out of the city's apartments, and of jobs, and of society itself (Alfasi and Fenster, 2014; Margalit, 2014; Marom, 2014). Like in other contemporary 'Occupy' campaigns worldwide, protesters denounced the symbolic and material links between the building of elitist towers and the ongoing political agendas that, in recent decades, have forcefully promoted the narrow set of interests of a small elite (see Peck et al., 2013; Aalbers, 2013; Sklair and Gherardi, 2012) while neglecting other groups' pressing needs (Schipffer, 2015).

Inspired by the 2011 'social justice' protests, and leveraging the momentum that those protests created towards bolder and more politicised forms of activism, several groups of residents, activists and planning professionals organised opposition to the planning and building of towers as the flagship of urban development in Tel Aviv. In this paper, we analyse two of these mobilisations as a starting point for addressing ongoing debates on the impact of social activism on the neo-liberalisation of urban space in the current moment of neo-liberalism's 'legitimation crisis'.

Broadly speaking, critical scholarship on urban development and the 'right to the city' (Purcell, 2003) underscores how the subordination of urban space to speculative profit making at the expense of use values, social needs, and public goods has resulted in a rise in the regularity with which the political legitimacy of neo-liberal policies is challenged (see Burningham and Thrush, 2001; Ellis, 2004; Dixon 2010). Central to these approaches is an emphasis on the counter-hegemonic power of urban mobilisations against corporate market rule, especially since the Occupy and 15-M movements diffused into many of the urban strongholds of neo-liberalism. However, much of this scholarship also tends to overlook how social movements' struggles may actually advance neo-liberalisation or remain trapped in its sweeping logic (for such a critique, see Blokland et al., 2015). Conversely, political economy approaches highlight the structural market forces underlying the neo-liberal towering skylines, but largely disregard the significance of social protest and how it is being transformed (Fuller, 2012).

Contrary to celebratory portrayals of current mobilisations claiming rights to and through the city (Nicholls and Vermeulen, 2012), but also to agonistic diagnoses of the overriding power of neo-liberalism as a coherent project, we suggest going beyond binary views of 'neo-liberalism vs. resistance.' Following Margit Mayer (2013), we offer a more nuanced and contextualised analysis of the mutually constitutive relations between actual existing mobilisations and urban neo-liberalisation as a starting point for rethinking the dialectics between development (as an ideological project, a form of governance, and a form of social action) and conflict. According to Mayer (2013), the unfolding of the financial and political crisis in the Global North and South has created new tactics, broader redistributive claims, and more heterogeneous coalitions between the 'discontented' urbanite middle classes and 'dispossessed' social groups (Marcuse quoted in Mayer, 2013, 4) than the 'new social movements' and professionalised mobilisations of preceding decades. Yet, as she points out, despite general trends, we are yet to uncover the uneven ways in which these mobilisations are conditioned by local configurations of neo-liberalisation and ensuing visions of what is possible or even desirable, and how, in their turn, social mobilisations affect neo-liberal practices as they oscillate between resistance and integration (Künkel and Mayer, 2012, 3).

Drawing on the understanding that neither neo-liberalisation nor its challenges are uniform or external to each other (Peck et al., 2009), this chapter compares two types of mobilisation that emerged with respect to towers in Tel Aviv amid the context of broader social protest: the first concerns two towers that were planned close to a gentrified, upscale neighbourhood (Yitzhak Elhanan Projects);[1] the second concerns the privately-owned public spaces (POPS) built around towers throughout the city. We chose these mobilisations because, unlike previous NIMBY- and aesthetics-related objections, they posed principled challenges to core dimensions of entrepreneurial urban development policies: the financing of public services through the exaction of side benefits, case-deal negotiations with private developers and the privatisation of public spaces.

To examine the types of challenges to urban development that are emerging, we ask the following questions: Who are the challengers in terms of their social positions? Which policies are they challenging and by what means? How do they frame the conflictual aspects of urban development? And what counterclaims do they raise? Finally, to understand the type of 'crisis' they are alluding to, we analyse current social mobilisations in the context of the longer history of socio-economic restructuring in which they are embedded. Therefore, we examine current forms of resistance as building upon, reiterating, or

1 Empirical data on both cases are based on personal interviews with key activists and on the systematic tracking and analysis of a variety of documentary sources: newspapers' publications, court petitions and court verdicts, planning authorities' protocols, personal e-mail correspondence between the activists (in the case of Yitzhak Elhanan), and activists' Facebook pages and blogs (in the case of POPS). The empirical analysis is part of wider joint research into objections to, and justifications of, planning decisions, and social stratification in eight different cities situated across the socio-economic and ethno-national spectrum of Israeli society—research funded by the Israel Science Foundation (ISF 1080/13).

challenging those previous repertoires of mobilisation that evolved during recent decades in the wake of new forms of deep neo-liberalisation of urban development.

Based on our analysis, we suggest that while recent mobilisations have introduced novel claims and tactics against the institutional methods and decisions 'that produce urban space' and have succeeded in politicising towers as the flagship of neo-liberal urban development, their actions have remained trapped in the fragmented dynamics of neo-liberalisation. By failing to connect discursively and strategically the conflicts created by entrepreneurial development, we argue, current mobilisations tell more about the particular crises of the social groups that they represent than they do about the systemic crisis of neo-liberalism itself. In that sense, our findings raise broader insights into the ways in which neo-liberalisation processes sit *inside* society and not *above* or *against* it, as they shape the actors concerned, their positions, and the ways in which they imagine what development is or can be.

The chapter is organised as follows: first, we introduce a critical analysis of urban entrepreneurial development, the institutional justifications of towers, and their critiques; the second section examines the path-dependent course of urban neo-liberalisation and tower planning and building in Tel Aviv; the third section analyses our case studies of counter-mobilisation. In the final section, we discuss the implications of our study for current debates on conflicts in and about urban development.

2 Neo-Liberal Urban Development, Institutional Justifications of Towers, and Their Critiques

Neo-liberalisation is a shorthand description of processes that deepen market-oriented behaviours, institutions and regulations (Brenner et al., 2010). At the urban level, neo-liberal or 'entrepreneurial' development represents a mode of socio-economic regulation that incentivises market agents to invest, develop, and create workplaces, infrastructure, and social and spatial amenities (Harvey, 1989; Swyngedouw et al., 2002; Enright, 2014). The preliminary push to urban entrepreneurialism came in the 1970s, as municipalities in the US and UK faced bankruptcy due to the severe cutbacks of federal aid (Tasan-Kok, 2008; Theodore et al., 2011). To support public budgets and encourage private investment, municipalities both privatised centrally located public land and advanced megaprojects (Fainstein, 2008; Sagalyn, 2007). In the following decades, the linkage between privatisation, flexible planning, expensive development and urban finances became common to many cities, together with the 'trickle-down' promise that liberation from state interference would lead to optimal economic operation and benefit all parts of society (Harvey, 2005). In this context, a family of planning methods gained importance. It included flexible, local spot-zoning amendments to statutory planning schemes, made with the purpose of advancing site-specific projects and public–private (PP) ventures. To this end, authorities strike specific planning 'deals' with private actors that allow the exchange of public goods and tasks—'side benefits'—for extra floor rights (Fainstein, 2008; Tasan-Kok, 2008; Alfasi, 2006; Sagalyn, 2007; Margalit, 2014; Fox-Rogers and Murphy, 2015).

The increase of high-rise ventures designed for local and international elites (Sklair and Gherardi, 2012) was intimately linked to entrepreneurial paradigms of urban growth and development. Famously defined as 'a machine that makes the land pay more' (the architect Cass Gilbert, 1901, in Willis, 1995, 19), more tall towers have been planned in recent years than at any time previously in Asia, the America and Europe (Leiper and Park, 2010). The systemic preference for high towers has been legitimised by an array of ideological and practical justifications that invoke the master frame of 'the public interest' (Alexander, 2002). Advocating the belief that 'market and business rationality can be made to operate as effectively in the public interest as it does in securing private interests' (Sager, 2011, 153), planning and municipal authorities offer spatial and economic incentives for building expensive projects as a means of urban revival and beautification. As new hubs 'of a radiating renaissance', these projects are said to facilitate increases in land values to adjacent areas (Loftman and Nevin, 1995, 300) and the 'trickle down' of prosperity to the local economy (Fox Gotham, 2001, 14). Entrepreneurial practices are further legitimised as a social must in an era of global intercity competition, with the argument that 'corporations today have the economic and political power to take their investments elsewhere should local officials not prove compliant' (Fox Gotham, 2001, 16).

The 'flexibilisation' of planning and its subjection to market rule is also justified by public officials' need 'to get things done', thereby signalling economic success and political efficiency to different constituencies (Stone, 1993). This agenda is vindicated in terms of past failures, mostly related to the failed outcomes of 'rigid' Keynesian direct public spending on urban redevelopment and housing programmes (Aalbers, 2013). In this way, municipal authorities extend generous building rights to private developers in exchange for the financing of public tasks such as affordable housing, open spaces, heritage preservation, infrastructure and the like (Sagalyn, 2007; Tasan-Kok, 2008). This semi-opaque practice of striking deals with private developers is justified by the need to compensate communities for the disruptions incurred by the building of megaprojects and the need to cover the costly infrastructure required while keeping back public funds for other, less profitable areas and tasks (Alterman, 1990). Thus, urban communities are said to enjoy, in practical terms, side benefits channelled through budgetary and spatial reallocation, even if their involvement in the details of the negotiations is mostly minimal (Tasan-Kok, 2008).

Entrepreneurial policies have sparked several academic critiques for deepening uneven spatiality and socio-economic inequality. Urban theorists have criticised PP ventures for 'reclaiming' public spaces only for groups who possess economic value (Heeg and Rosol, 2007; Sager, 2011), and distancing themselves from areas where needs are great but the probability of value extraction is slight (Weber, 2002). Instead of activating other plans and redistributing investment, this project-based growth strategy extends the easing of regulation to attract more massive and expensive projects. According to Fainstein (2008), as such projects are the only ones that can generate the profits needed to finance complex municipal demands, smaller, less expensive or long-term programmes are postponed. One of the results of this is the creation of 'prosperity clusters', socially and economically segregated from nearby neighbourhoods and from wider urban society (Graham and Marvin, 2001, 222).

Another line of critique goes against the claim that flexible planning methods accelerate the bureaucratic process and avoid political favouritism. Scholars note that far from the illusion of free market competition, entrepreneurial ventures intensify political intervention and arbitrariness (Aalbers, 2013), as governments often facilitate one set of agents in market transactions, identifying them as the sole engine of urban growth and wealth (MacLeod, 2002; Brenner and Theodore, 2002). Likewise, spot-zoning techniques informed by individual decisions (Booth, 1995) benefit mainly large investors and large projects by singling them out 'for preferential treatment' (Cullingworth, 1993, 49).

Finally, critics also point to the power differentials that shape the negotiations between the developer and the 'public'. These negotiations are managed by local government, which plays the double role of regulator and economic stakeholder (Sagalyn, 2007; Gielent and Tasan-Kok, 2010), and is often eager to maintain a 'good business' atmosphere by making compromises that work mostly for the benefit of private developers (Margalit, 2013 and 2014; Fox-Rogers and Murphy, 2015). Negotiating public goods is even harder when flexible planning and 'deal-making' are used as commercial assets for municipal governments' global competitive agendas (Tasan-Kok, 2008).

With no alternatives offered, the business logic of neo-liberalisation has become 'doxic "commonsense"' that utilises flexible development to foster its own institutionalisation (Keil, 2009; Peck et al., 2013, 1094). Yet, the entrepreneurial city and its growing vertical architecture have ignited broadening waves of urban social protest across the globe. Scholarship on social mobilisations in urban settings stretching from Saint Petersburg (Dixon, 2010), through Buenos Aires (Crot, 2006) and Tokyo (Saito, 2003), to cities on the Pacific Rim (Marshall, 2003), demonstrate that towers are increasingly interpreted as a spatial signifier of corporate power, gentrification and inequality (see Burningham and Thrush, 2001; Grubbauer, 2014). The case of Tel Aviv-Jaffa exemplifies these dynamics of deepening neo-liberalisation and mounting discontent. Yet as we will now show, the local case has some particularities, as both the development of 'entrepreneurial' towers and the critiques against it have followed their own path dependency, pointing towards the hybrid nature of neo-liberal urban development but also towards the contextual nature of counter-mobilisations as part of a longer history of neo-liberalisation.

3 'Entrepreneurial Centralism' and the Politics of Towers in Tel Aviv-Jaffa

Contemporary Tel Aviv-Jaffa with its 400,000 residents is the centre of a 'metro region' inhabited by three million people. The city is historically divided along clear socio-economic and ethno-national lines, with most of the affluent quarters located to the north and settled by mainly European Jews, while the poor quarters remain the southern quarters and in those in Jaffa where Arabs and Jews originating from the Middle East and North African countries live (Marom, 2014). The vertical socio-spatial divisions have evolved since the 1950s and have gradually magnified the uneven local socio-economic cartography. Today, mid-height constructions (three–six floors) compose most of the urban built fabric, with dotted enclaves of higher constructions (eight–14 floors) and taller towers (15–50 floors) mainly located in the affluent northern quarters, and some 'high-end' central locations (Margalit, 2013, 377).

Although projects are spread out across the urban layout and appear to be isolated, they are the result of a complex structure of entrepreneurial methods and policies that have been layered through dozens of spot-planning deals struck by consecutive urban regimes. Indeed, since the establishment of the state of Israel and the creation of the national Israeli Land Administration (ILA), a foremost particularity of the urban development scene in Tel Aviv (and more broadly in Israel) has been its 'entrepreneurial centralism'. While in the US and Western European countries, post-Keynesian restructuring resulted in a significant decrease in central land management and centralistic–hierarchic planning, the Israeli land and planning regimes combine a high degree of spatial management centralisation and market entrepreneurialism. 'City Hall' and the national bureaucracy continue to play a leading role in the development regime as, simultaneously as landowners, entrepreneurs and regulators, while at the same time adapting state-of-the-art tactics of extraversion such as PP ventures, case-and-deal making, and private financing of public tasks. The map of high-rises in Tel Aviv reflects this particularity. An examination of their development in the city shows that, with almost 70 per cent of the urban land assets in Tel Aviv–Jaffa centrally managed and owned, the seeds of entrepreneurial planning were planted in the 1950s, when the socialist Labour Party led both the national government and the city (Margalit, 2013). Until the 1990s, plans for high-rises were mainly issued for plots owned, managed and planned by either the ILA or the Tel Aviv Municipality and then assigned by the city and/or the government to private entrepreneurs through a combination of 'flexible' practices (Margalit, 2013). These practices are still dominant in the planning of towers today, along with the encouragement for large private landowners to build high-rise towers, mainly for affluent citizens or large companies, or as hotels.

Throughout the 1990s, as several flashy projects of historic preservation and the urban renewal of the old Central Business District (CBD) were advanced by city planners, the methods for achieving side benefits and the obligations to finance and develop public spaces were extended (Margalit, 2014). Since 1998 to date, Mayor Ron Huldai's administration has solidified these practices albeit in many more and much higher tower schemes, and presented preservation, open spaces, and infrastructure improvements as the leading elements of towers developers' obligations. The side benefits are channelled mainly to urban beautification, and tower ventures have been justified as beneficial to the public in terms of 'the actual design and the supply of public spaces for the neighbourhood residents.'[2] In this manner, dozens of site-specific schemes were negotiated as specific planning deals, where planners obligated developers to finance and execute spatial improvements in exchange for extended heights and building rights in prime locations.[3]

2 Tel Aviv Regional Planning Committee, decision protocols for schemes no. 3753 and 3853; http://mavat.moin.gov.il/MavatPS/Forms/SV3.aspx?tid=3 (accessed on 28 July 2016).

3 See for example scheme no. 2650a. Following the nomination of the White City of central Tel Aviv as a World Heritage site in 2003, the scheme encouraged the owners of historical buildings to sell air rights to developers. Such transactions were explained in the statutory documents by 'the need to preserve this building and assure its usage for tourism.' http://gisn.tel-aviv.gov.il/iview2/ (accessed on 28 July 2016).

Currently, the planning and construction of towers in Tel Aviv dramatically exceeds earlier cycles in terms of the number of buildings, their height and their price. With an average of 30 stories per tower, this new cycle has changed the residential landscape and the levels of real estate prices, and has surpassed the previous scale of high-rise construction.[4] At the same time, a strip of only 500 metres separates the most fashionable tall hubs of the city from the southern neighbourhoods that most locals see as the city's backyard (Kemp and Raijman, 2004), and only a ten-minute drive separates them from the poor Arab and Jewish neighbourhoods in Jaffa. There, despite sprawling gentrification and beautification efforts (mainly along the beachfront areas) (Marom, 2014; Monterescu, 2009), most residents still rank lower on all socio-economic and environmental indicators, and planning projects hardly materialise in this area (Marom, 2014; Margalit and Vertes, 2015).[5]

The local situation thus echoes the conflictual side of towers and other neo-liberal megaprojects in other contexts where towers are seen as transforming space into prestige sites that generate both financial and cultural capital (Vicario and Monje, 2003), erasing urban diversity through the creation of homogeneous spaces that serve a limited area and the particular interests and visions of elite groups (Saito, 2003; Crot, 2006), marginalising alternative uses of space closer to the needs of everyday existence (Dirlik, 2005), triggering identity struggles (Dixon, 2010), and non-democratic megalomania (McNeill, 2002). Moreover, we find that as the scope of entrepreneurial practices in Tel Aviv expanded, the semantic field of 'public interest' considerably narrowed to align itself with the particular aesthetics and needs of affluent and cosmopolitan city dwellers, tourists, and *wannabe* Tel Avivians. What has nonetheless changed in the current phase of neo-liberal development is the emergence of broader social protest denouncing the ways of 'getting-things-done' through tower construction. In the following, we analyse these contestations.

4 The Huldai Administration has so far issued 53 site-specific spatial schemes for 118 high-standard residential towers, of which 50 have already been completed or are under construction. For comparison, between the mid-1960s and 2002, only 46 high-standard residential towers of 15 floors or more were built in the entire city, 18 of which were built in the centre, with the luxury facilities now common (Margalit, 2013). In addition, many proposed office towers and hotels received permits and were built, and a large new northern suburb was built with mid-height, upscale residences along the seashore.

5 The southern quarters rank lower on all socio-economic and environmental indicators than the rest of the city (Margalit and Vertes, 2015).

4 Two Types of Mobilisation, Two Legitimation Crises?

The planning and building of towers in Tel Aviv have been the objects of criticism and objections throughout the years.[6] When the municipality tailored its policies with regards to tower construction to the historic CBD and the beach strip in the late 1990s, criticism escalated but those policies typically focused on specific locations and schemes that aimed to utterly alter the old CBD area (Hatuka and Forsyth, 2005). Although some journalists criticised the elitist inclinations of municipal politicians, in the following decade local communities mostly proceeded by objecting to particular planning schemes in their areas. For years, the limited scope of objections and the ways in which they were framed mirrored the entrepreneurial method of development: based on 'not in my back yard' (NIMBY) and heritage preservation arguments concerning specific ventures, these protests reflected the fragmented nature of spot-zoning and case-deals policies, while leaving intact institutional convictions about the virtues of entrepreneurial development for the 'public interest'. It was not until the upsurge of the massive social protest in 2011 that urban mobilisations began to address the systemic elements of tower planning and to demand alternatives.

According to Mayer (2013), one of the legacies of the period following the 2008 financial crisis has been that demands with regards to 'the right to the city' in the global North, have refocused from professionalised and consumer-based claims into counter-hegemonic forms of resistance against the institutional methods and decisions 'that produce urban space' (Purcell, 2003, 577). This qualitative shift was enabled by the fact that austerity policies and deepening socio-spatial polarisation within cities are affecting not only the marginalised urban 'outcasts' but also societies' youth, students and the middle classes (Mayer, 2013, 10–11). These groups have created the possibility of new coalitions, bolder mobilisation strategies, and a reframing of the apolitical rhetoric of the consumer and professional citizen into broader claims for social redistribution (see also Bodnar, 2015). Nowadays, Mayer observes, 'urban activism on both sides of the Atlantic finds itself surrounded, in some places inspired, periodically swept up in and often supported by movements like the *Indignados* or Occupy. These groups pose new practical and political challenges as well as opportunities' (Mayer, 2013, 6).

6 For examples of critiques published in local newspapers (in Hebrew), see A. Ayalon, Ha'aretz, February 23, 1962; I. Vinkler, Ha'aretz, April 11, 1971; A. Erlik, Ha'aretz, September 9, 1975; E. Dotan, Ha'ir, March 7, 1997.

We take Mayer's observations as a starting point from which to examine what dimensions of urban development are challenged nowadays in Tel Aviv, by whom, and how. How do they relate to the local version of 'centralised entrepreneurialism' and to previous repertoires of resistance? Which types of justification are mobilised and to what extent do they depart from the institutional justifications? Finally, what type of 'crisis' are they alluding to, and to what effect?

4.1 *The Yizhak Elhanan Towers: Old Strategies, New Claims, Gentrifiers' Crisis*

Scholars of social mobilisations argue that the 'judicialisation' of social protest during the 1990s has resulted in it becoming increasingly disciplined and depoliticised (Scheingold and Sarat, 2004). Our first case study shows, however, that the law—as an institutional mechanism and type of discourse—can be also mobilised in ways that challenge the core of the local neo-liberal development project where other mobilisation channels and strategies have failed.

This case concerns the high-rise ventures built around the historic neighbourhood of Neve Tzedek. Ever since these ventures had been planned, the neighbourhood's residents consistently objected to the towers, claiming that they would disregard the historic cityscape, create environmental hazards, and overload the already poor public facilities and infrastructure of the area. These claims were repeatedly rejected by municipal and regional planning committees, which maintained that the ventures advanced the positive urban regeneration dynamic.[7] However, as we will show next, it was the official rejection of this NIMBY type of claim that led the residents to reframe their grievances and challenge the legitimacy of spot-zoning policies and the PP transactions that would lead to the building of the towers, through the courts.

These citizens were a mixed group: upper middle class and professionals of the creative class who organised themselves into the 'Neve Tzedek Association' and the neighbourhood's 'Parents' Group' but also residents from adjacent districts inhabited historically by lower-class Oriental Jews. Equipped with know-how regarding planning practice and with legal representatives, the first group played a leading role in the mobilisation. The driver for the residents' discontent relates to a major shift in the planning of the area and concomitantly in the privileged position that they had enjoyed until then in the socio-spatial regime. In the 1980s, the municipality encouraged the preservation and

7 The head of the regional planning committee, in a letter to the Neve Tzedek residents' association, 18.11.2010; Regional Planning Committee decision regarding objections to planning scheme 2615 (Yizhak Elhanan) b and c 13.7.2011, 14.7.2011.

renovation of historical districts with small, old, family houses. These efforts gave rise to a bold gentrification process in Neve Tzedek. The neighbourhood became one of the upscale areas of the city, but still suffered from a lack of public and education facilities because the district's schools had been transformed into cultural and artistic centres that aligned with the boho rebranding of the area. The well off newcomers demanded time and again that a school be built and infrastructure improved, but to no avail.

In 2006, the struggle against the encroaching wave of luxury towers planned for the area escalated. These towers constituted a new wave of 'plutocratic' gentrification that threatened to displace the upper middle classes' rights to and privileges in the city. The first tower built in the area—the 'Nechushtan' tower—was completed in 2007, boasting 44 floors. The residents' environmental and aesthetic objections to it were rejected and their demands for infrastructure went unanswered. As the head of the municipal planning team for the central area explained to a real estate journalist in June 2009: 'In reality, the city does not have the money to buy lands for public uses. These parcels are occupied and the purpose of towers' planning is to create public spaces.' (Margalit, 2014, 79).

This tower became emblematic of future struggles as the construction of several other high-rises in the area was approved or planned in the following years. In May 2009, the local planning committee approved the construction of a high-rise on the site of a former chocolate factory south of Neve Tzedek (Shiloh, 2011). Residents objected and though a judge's decision supported their arguments, he noted that the court cannot rule in planning matters. In 2011, plans for the Yitzhak Elhanan Projects pushed the conflict surrounding towers in the area one step further, tying them more clearly to the entrepreneurial deals made by the municipality. These projects were advanced through a series of complementary schemes. The A Plan (2615a) was intended to 'strengthen the residential area' between Neve Tzedek and adjacent historic neighbourhoods (Tel Aviv Regional Committee, 2006, plans objectives, 1), and to transform Yitzhak Elhanan Street into the main commercial thoroughfare between the CBD and the beach. The plan included a 29-floor tower with spacious apartments and private leisure facilities. In exchange, the developers were to create spaces for a kindergarten, a small synagogue and a small public garden.

In the same period, the spot-zoning plan Yitzhak Elhanan B (2615b) was drafted 'to encourage CBD use and urban renewal' in the area located between the Yitzhak Elhanan A tower and the CBD (Tel Aviv Regional Committee, 2006, 2). The scheme included a 28-floor tower, half of which was designated for luxury apartments. Public side benefits included the partial widening of the street and the preservation of one historic building. One of the architects that planned these projects explained that, as Tel Aviv is becoming denser, Neve Tzedek is becoming a low-density 'island in an urban ocean', adding 'Residents of Neve Tzedek enjoy low-rise construction, but they cannot force themselves on the entire city. To preserve spaces and nature around the city, one has to create density and therefore turn the relatively low-rise construction of the past into taller building' (Shiloh, 2011).

Following the 'deal logic' of entrepreneurial centralism, planners drafted two additional schemes that designated additional floors to towers 'A' and 'B'. In exchange for 11 more floors for the latter, they demanded from the developer the evacuation of a public lot in order to build the public school that the neighbourhood residents had been demanding for so many years (Tel Aviv Regional Committee, 2015). At this point, the neighbourhood committee submitted its objections to the regional planning committee arguing against the spot zoning and the deals that the municipality strikes with developers. 'The city approves high-rise after high-rise due to pressure from developers and the improvement taxes the projects generate,' argued one of the organisers of the Neve Tzedek residents' association, 'It's already been decided that the Neve Tzedek Tower was a horrible mistake, yet they're continuing to plan additional towers' (Shiloh, 2011). In response, the district planner said that those who were objecting, who were generally well off and had the means to fight developers, must understand they are just one of a number of legitimate interest groups (Shiloh, 2011). Finally, the planning committee gave in to the appeal and 'recalculated' the developers' costs and benefits, lowering the height of the tower by three floors. It was at this point that the residents' committee decided to go to court, this time enlarging both the scope and framing of their claims.

In claims submitted to the regional court in September 2011, the committee argued that measuring public benefits against floor ratios was illegitimate and that it was the state's obligation, and not the private developer's, to provide public goods. In its response, the municipality argued that such transactions are indispensable for effective urban regeneration.[8] In 2013, the regional court accepted the residents' claim arguing that according to the Israeli Planning and Building Law, the creation of financial engines for public tasks is not under planning institutions' jurisdiction and that municipal tasks are mandatory and their provision should not be conditioned on being subsidized by the taxes exacted from developers.

8 All claims are elaborated in the verdict regarding petition no. 47348-09-11, signed January 15, 2013.

The legitimation issues raised in this case were thus novel in that they brought into a court, for the first time, what had been the cornerstone of local planning's doxic common sense—namely, developments' side benefits and the exactions made to 'compensate' the public for the erection of massive and expensive new towers. However, *long durée* entrepreneurial 'habits' and power relations cannot be easily undone. The municipality appealed to the Supreme Court of Justice arguing that all spatial development is based on the principle of exactions from PP ventures, that PP planning as a method for increasing municipal revenues is a just means to an end, and that they can grant the extra floor permits and decide what would be the side benefits.[9] Finally, the court declined to discuss the appeal; the Elhanan Projects have been built to their full height, and are showcased as part of the municipality's efforts to offer housing solutions.[10] Neve Tzedek's affluent residents did not get their school. However, their appeal against 'the way of getting things done' set a court precedent and pioneered a debate on the (legal) legitimacy of PP practices—and on the jurisdictions, criteria, and duties of planning in the city—that has wider repercussions.

4.2 *POPS Group: New Strategies, Old Claims, Professional Crisis*

The second case relates to a group of young architects and planners who focused their activism on POPS. POPS are one of the oxymoronic recipes advanced as side benefits of PP ventures for public space 'regeneration' and 'securitisation' (Bodnar 2015, 2096). The group crystallised in 2014 when architect and web journalist Naama Riva published a survey showing the low usage levels and pedestrian traffic in local POPS, and then invited her Facebook followers to join her in picnics in the sanitised and unwelcoming POPS located next to luxurious towers (Riba, 2013). The aim of the group was to mobilise public awareness against the poor service these spaces offer the public and, in the spirit of the 2011 nationwide 'social protest' that inspired the group, to raise the question 'who is getting what and why' in the city.

'These ventures [the towers] gain extended building rights. To 'compensate' the public for this, the developers are obligated to give presents […] The local planning milieu let entrepreneurs shape it, in manners that only serve their clientele in expensive towers.' With their picnics they thus aimed 'first, to make the public realize that these spaces are theirs by law. Second, to advance the understanding of bureaucrats, planners and the wider public that open

---

9 Municipality's appeal, no. 1366/11, submitted to the Supreme Court on February 19, 2013.

10 Kerem Israel, In the heart of Tel Aviv, http://www.kerem-israel.info/new_projects/white-city (accessed on 2 December 2016).

spaces are significant for the city, and that they are threatened by this practice' (Naama Riva interviewed by Noifeld (2014a), our transl.).[11]

Therefore, alongside the picnic events, the group also launched a public campaign via the conventional media and several blogs, to explain the obscure technical language used by planners and expose how planning decisions that produce unfair spaces are made. The name of the group, *Hana'a B'zika*, was a successful gimmick that simultaneously hinted at the members' professional expertise and criticised the incomprehensible professional jargon that replaced traditional land expropriation through the usage of new 'public–private' terminology. In Hebrew, the name means literally 'joy in a POPS', and also—with its elements transposed—*Zikat Hana'a*, the legal term for that part of a private plot designated for public passage and usage.

Social activism among young planners and architects like those who created the POPS group is relatively new in Israel. Throughout the first decade of the twenty-first century, professionals created several non-governmental organisations (NGOs) that contested development and environmental policies through advocacy, litigation, and consultation activities (Yacobi, 2007; Alfasi and Fenster, 2014). These organisations opened the way for a discourse with regard to planning that challenged the self-assured language of 'professional knowledge' used by planning authorities (see Margalit and Kemp, 2015) and their constant reference to a 'phantom public interest' (Bodnar, 2015, 2098). Likewise, the POPS activists viewed the planning establishment as submissive to the restraints imposed on it by market-led governments, and at the same time patronising. In Riva's terms, the local municipal planning discourse is 'almost confidential, with very little public exposure', while 'they actually function as interior designers or rubber stamps' to market demands (Noifeld, 2014a). However, in contrast to the NGOs that preceded them, which introduced new critiques but also 'NGOised' the field of activism with regards to planning (Yacobi, 2007), POPS activists aimed at reaching broader publics, by using bolder strategies of direct action and social media.

The POPS group's critique of the planning establishment and its search for new forms of activism expressed its members' sense of personal and professional crisis as young planners trying to make an impact on the public space and, simultaneously, to afford to remain in the expensive city. Inspired by the Occupy and *Indignados* movements in Tel Aviv and elsewhere, the activists focused on 'hacking' the urban space, reclaiming it for uses that defy its underlying, dominant entrepreneurial logic (Bodnar, 2015, 2100). The actual picnics

11 See also Noifeld (2014b) about a picnic in the front yard of Shari Arison, the owner of the largest Israeli bank.

took place over six consecutive weekends during the winter of 2014–15 and created the atmosphere of an 'urban guerrilla' happening (see Lugosi et al., 2010). The organisers asked participants to 'bring tables and folding chairs and also a smoking barbecue' to disrupt the complacent calmness of the POPS.[12] Activists made frequent allusions to the 'cold' sterility of the towers, emphasising their estrangement from the humming streets of the surroundings: 'We considered setting on fire the wooden benches', one of the organisers wrote jokingly, 'I fully understand young kids that vandalize the benches in public gardens and set them on fire. The planning of the public space in (most) Israel is meant to repress the soul of human beings. We've been doing this only for two weeks and we feel already like burning something.'[13]

The picnics were held in central locations where they could attract crowds and media exposure. The first and second events took place near busy commercial areas, where the mere gathering of participants demonstrated how deserted the POPS usually were. The third event was much bigger, and the police intervened. The site, near the Neve Tzedek Tower, had bred much local resentment throughout the planning process concerned (see above). The picnic clearly surprised the tower's residents, who called the police, earning the group widespread media coverage. When the organisers explained the POPS designation of the site—with the help of Knesset member (and former city council member) Tamar Zandberg, who attended the event—the officers promptly left. On a later prime-time TV show, Zandberg praised the picnickers' efforts, explaining that while the government is supposedly working to solve the housing crisis, many more plans for isolated towers and POPS are actually shaping the urban future.[14]

Up until this point, the organisers had intentionally focused on issues related to the design of POPS rather than on wider problems of neo-liberal development. They claimed that, unlike well-designed POPS elsewhere, the local designs minimise public use and create empty areas in the middle of dense neighbourhoods. As Riva explained: 'Instead of making a nice garden or pleasant piazza, they use uncomfortable materials and unwelcoming outlines' (Noifeld, 2014a). Yoav Lerman, another organiser, attributed the poor function of POPS to the lack of public political representation: 'The city council

12 Naama Riba, https://www.facebook.com/naama.riba?fref=ufi (accessed on 2 December 2016).

13 Yoav Lerman, https://www.facebook.com/yoav.lerman?fref=uf. (accessed on 2 December 2016).

14 MAKO,http://www.mako.co.il/news-channel2/Economy-Newcast/Article-4e1fb3584e7144 1004.htm. (accessed on 2 December.2016).

members [...] are also responsible for these failures [...] Reading the councils' protocols teaches us that they only consider POPS sizes, asking developers, 'Please give me 600 square meters of empty concrete, or 800 square meters.'[15]

Nevertheless, following criticism from participants, the locations of the subsequent picnics were chosen to somehow expand the original mission of the group. The last picnic was in Jaffa, near the Andromeda Cluster, a mid-sized gated community built in the 1990s as a Jewish gentrified enclave in the heart of the local Arab community (Monterescu, 2009). By this time, several individuals had invited the picnic group to mobilise in their neighbourhoods and cities, but the group was running out of steam. It was partly rejuvenated a year later through an online community named tlvPOPS, via which Riva and a computer expert, collect and share POPS information.

5 Concluding Discussion

In this chapter, we set out to examine the ways in which the legitimation crisis of neo-liberalism and its deal logic of the city and its people affect current contestations regarding one of the boldest spatial symbols of entrepreneurial development. The reconfigured urban settings in which neo-liberal ideas and policies have been the subject of experiment and practice worldwide have been crucial to the successful adaptation and reproduction of neo-liberalism (Kunkel and Mayer, 2012, 3). In this context, politicians and pundits promote luxurious towers and megaprojects as a major driver for urban economic development and regeneration (Grubbauer, 2014), a precondition for global entrepreneurial competition (Sklair and Gherardi, 2012), and a means of making private money 'work' in the public interest (Enright, 2014). However, as we have shown, these towers have become both a site and a medium of social contention. Conflict around towers has accentuated in the current phase of neo-liberalisation, shaking the apolitical apathy of consumer- and professional-based urban claims characteristic of previous phases. As Mayer (2013) observes, movements like the *Indignados* and Occupy have created a window of opportunity for the politicisation of current forms of urban activism

15 Yoav Lerman (2014) 'Another Blog from Tel Aviv', 5 February, http://tlv1.co.il/2014/02/05/%D7%90%D7%95%D7%9B%D7%9C%D7%99%D7%9D-%D7%90%D7%95%D7%AA%D7%94-%D7%91%D7%96%D7%99%D7%A7%D7%95%D7%AA-%D7%94%D7%94%D7%95%D7%A0%D7%90%D7%94-%D7%91%D7%99%D7%95%D7%9D-%D7%A9%D7%A9%D7%99-%D7%91%D7%A6%D7%94/ (accessed on 28 July 2016).

in many of the affluent urban nodes, by introducing new strategies, claims and coalitions.

Our case studies largely confirm that the 'spectre' of crisis hovers over current mobilisations in Tel Aviv; it does so, however, following the particular assemblages of local neo-liberalisation. The local version of urban entrepreneurialism in Tel Aviv involves a strong centralism that is supported by institutionalised power settings and justified by the side benefits of PP ventures for urban regeneration and beautification. Side benefits and PP negotiations have thus become the main object of current local contestations. Yet, as we have shown, contestations have also been shaped by the actors concerned, their positions, and the ways in which they imagine what development is or can be.

Regarding the actors, their modes of mobilisation and positions, we found that, equipped with financial and social capital, the Neve Tzedek residents used conservative means of judicial mobilisation while radicalising previous NIMBY claims against towers. Their struggle was conducted from the position of upscale gentrifiers who, in the past, had benefited from the privileges of urban development but had now lost faith in the system and its distributive politics. The POPS youngsters resorted to creative means of mobilisation by physically reclaiming public space across the city. Occupying space and explaining how it is produced, they aimed to distinguish their professional selves from generations of older planners working for the establishment and private firms. In the activists' view, these older professionals have betrayed their mission by becoming mere 'interior designers' or 'rubber stamps', submissive to market-rule and governance.

The language of current contestations also showed continuity with the 'social justice' protest of 2011. The grievances in Neve Tzedek began way before the social protest; nevertheless, the neighbourhood committee's appeal on the Yitzhak Elhanan Projects aligned with the broader redistributive claims raised by the popular protest. Thus, they reframed their claims in universalising terms of urban citizenship, arguing that the law mandates 'City Hall' to provide public services and infrastructure directly to citizens and not through conditional 'side benefits' issuing from PP negotiations. The POPS group was created a couple of years after the local tent camp protest had been dismantled. Nevertheless, the POPS activists presented their mobilisation as part of the wider struggle for the right to urban spaces and for more equitable planning. In that sense, both mobilisations addressed the same crucial questions—who gets what, and why, and how public decisions are made—seeking to disclose the systematic ways in which uneven and non-democratic development is created.

Nevertheless, our case studies also showed the fragmented and limiting dynamics that struggles for rights to the city and against market rule often display.

As Blokland et al. argue, 'whereas the organising of citizens for their right to the city constitutes a counterforce against corporate and ethnonationalistic influences on urban policies, such claims [...] are often strikingly specific regarding their thematic focus and the groups they speak for' (2015, 656–657). Our case studies show that raising overall claims to public space and denouncing the corrupting market logic of urban policies often obscure rather than overcome the multilayered conflicts of urban development and inequality. Gentrifiers in Neve Tzedek reclaimed their 'republican' rights to public services as discontented urban citizens endowed with a clear sense of deservedness (Marcuse, 2009). Yet they limited their claims to the methods of producing 'side benefits' through towers, without touching upon the harsh dividing impacts neo-liberal development has on the undeservedly dispossessed in the city (Marcuse, 2009). Their appeal did indeed produce a meaningful judicial precedent, but its impact on later schemes has so far been minimal, as policymakers continue promoting the competitive agenda with promises of future 'trickle-down' impacts for other 'legitimate' interest groups.

Similarly, when the POPS organisers strategically chose to focus their message on the 'design' of the POPS, they actually set the parameters of their protest: 'It seems impossible to fight the major economic forces now working in Israel's urban centres, especially in Tel Aviv,' explained Riva, 'It is possible, though, to reject the destruction of the street level' (Noifeld, 2014a). When participants challenged them to address broader issues of segregation and argued that on-site actions cannot ignore the history of a place and its former residents, these challenges were disregarded. 'Perhaps in the war on tycoons, Huldai and luxury towers, we should cooperate with Palestinians [...] and Mizrachim (Oriental Jews),' stated one of the participants in the picnic held in an exclusive enclave of towers built on the remains of a Jewish slum and a former Palestinian village, 'after all, their slums are also in danger of takeover.'[16] But the idea of creating broader coalitions was rejected on the grounds that 'there is no difference between former Jewish, German, or Arab lands, what drives the building of towers in Tel Aviv and Israel, is only one thing. Money.' In this manner, their critique of the 'power of money' as erasing the public space was based on the erasure of the many class, ethnic, and national divisions that make up the public and that public's different demands and needs in Tel Aviv-Jaffa (see Marom, 2014).

A similar dynamic of universalised claims to rights to the city that misrecognise the particularities of the activists involved (Harvey, 2005) was manifest

16 Asaf Even-Chen, 14 December 2014, comment, facebook event page Hannaa Bazika no. 4, https://www.facebook.com/events/746169022067573/?active_tab=discussion.

in the group invocation of a binary image of the 'rich' tower dwellers and the general and largely indifferent 'public', waiting to be enlightened: 'People have little interest in planning matters, which they also hardly understand, we need to explain and focus their attention' (Noifeld, 2014a). In that sense, the POPS discourse remained closer to the planning milieu's discourse—on a 'general public interest'—that it set out to challenge, and it thus undercut the activists' radical potential and actual impact.

Moreover, similar to the self-limited critique of their Neve Tzedek counterparts, the POPS group avoided dealing with the deeper troubles of local neo-liberalisation. While they exposed the methods that privatise the right to urban space, the alternatives they proposed relied on the 'new urbanism' idea that 'good' urban design is the best means of achieving social mixture and social justice (Alfasi and Fenster, 2014). In this manner, both groups clearly challenged the ethos and modus operandi of entrepreneurial development as a form of socio-economic redistribution, yet to a large degree their critique remained trapped in the fragmenting dynamics that feeds neo-liberalisation as an ongoing form of 'dividing and ruling' society while re-engineering its multilayered social divisions.

Looking at urban development through the prism of its challengers thus brings insight into the non-binary articulations between conflict and development. A close-up look into the politics of contention regarding urban development—the mobilisation strategies of challengers, the ways in which they frame what are the wrongs of development and what ought to be done about them, and the social position from which they articulate their discontent—reveals that contestations can actually highlight the deeper layers of consensus that make neo-liberalisation processes so resilient, even when the latter are allegedly experiencing a 'legitimation crisis'.

References

Aalbers, M.B. (2013) 'Neoliberalism is Dead … Long Live Neoliberalism!' *International Journal of Urban and Regional Research*, 37(3), pp. 1083–1090, DOI: 10.1111/1468-2427.12065.

Alexander, E.R. (2002) 'The Public Interest in Planning: From Legitimation to Substantive Plan Evaluation', *Planning Theory*, 1(3), pp. 226–249, DOI: 10.1177/147309520200100303.

Alfasi N. (2006) 'Planning Policy? Between Long-term Planning and Zoning Amendments in the Israeli Planning System', *Environment and Planning A*, 38(3), pp. 553–568, DOI:10.1068/a37335.

Alfasi, N. and T. Fenster (2014) 'Between Socio-spatial and Urban Justice: Rawls' Principles of Justice in the 2011 Israeli Protest Movement', *Planning Theory*, 13(4), pp. 407–427, DOI:10.1177/1473095214521105.

Alterman, R. (1990) 'From Expropriations to Development Agreements: Developer Obligations for Public Services in Israel', *Israel Law Review*, 24(1), pp. 29–81, DOI: 10.1017/S002122370000978X.

Blokland, T., C. Hentschel, A. Holm, H. Lebuhn and T. Margalit (2015) 'Urban Citizenship and Right to the City: The Fragmentation of Claims', *International Journal of Urban and Regional Research*, 39(4), pp. 655–665, DOI: 10.1111/1468-2427.12259.

Bodnar, J. (2015) 'Reclaiming Public Space', *Urban Studies*, 52(12), pp. 2090–2104, DOI: 10.1177/0042098015583626.

Booth, P. (1995) 'Zoning or Discretionary Action: Certainty and Responsiveness in Implementing Planning Policy', *Journal of Planning Education and Research*, 14(2), pp. 103–112, DOI: 10.1177/0739456X9501400203.

Brenner, N., J. Peck and N. Theodore (2010) 'Variegated Neoliberalization: Geographies, Modalities, Pathways', *Global Network*, 10(2), pp. 182–222, DOI: 10.1111/j.1471-0374.2009.00277.x.

Brenner, N. and N. Theodore (2002) 'Cities and the Geographies of "Actually Existing Neoliberalism"', *Antipode*, 34(3), pp. 349–379, DOI: 10.1111/1467-8330.00246.

Burningham, K. and D. Thrush (2001) *'Rainforests are a Long Way from Here': the Environmental Concerns of Disadvantaged Groups* (York: Joseph Rowntree Foundation).

Cullingworth, B. (1993) *The Political Culture of Planning* (New York: Routledge).

Crot, L. (2006) '"Scenographic" and "Cosmetic" Planning: Globalization and Territorial Restructuring in Buenos Aires', *Journal of Urban Affairs*, 28(3), pp. 227–251, DOI: 10.1111/j.1467-9906.2006.00290.x.

Dirlik, A. (2005) 'Architectures of Global Modernity, Colonialism, and Places', *Modern Chinese Literature and Culture*, 17 (1), pp. 33–61.

Dixon, M. (2010) 'Gazprom versus the Skyline: Spatial Displacement and Social Contention in St. Petersburg', *International Journal of Urban and Regional Research*, 34(1), pp. 35–54, DOI: 10.1111/j.1468-2427.2009.00871.x.

Ellis, G. (2004) 'Discourses of Objection: towards an Understanding of Third-party Rights in Planning', *Environment and Planning A*, 36(9), pp. 1549–1570, DOI: 10.1068/a36176.

Enright, T. (2014) 'Illuminating the Path to Grand Pari(s): Architecture and Urban Transformation in an Era of Neoliberalization", *Antipode*, 46(2), pp. 382–403, DOI: 10.1111/anti.12048.

Fainstein, S. (2008) 'Mega-projects in New York, London and Amsterdam', *International Journal of Urban and Regional Research*, 32(4), pp. 768–785, DOI: 10.1111/j.1468-2427.2008.00826.x.

Fox Gotham, K. (2001) 'Urban Redevelopment, Past and Present' in K. Fox Gotham (ed.), *Critical Perspectives on Urban Redevelopment,* (Bingley: Emerald Group Publishing Limited), pp. 1–31.

Fox-Rogers, L. and E. Murphy (2015) 'From Brown Envelopes to Community Benefits: the Co-option of Planning Gain Agreements under Deepening Neoliberalism', *Geoforum*, 67, pp. 41–50, DOI:10.1016/j.geoforum.2015.09.015.

Fuller, C. (2012) 'Urban Politics and the Social Practices of Critique and Justification: Conceptual Insights from French Pragmatism', *Progress in Human Geography*, 37(5), pp. 639–657, DOI: 10.1177/0309132512469763.

Gielent, D.M. and T. Tasan-Kok (2010) 'Flexibility in Planning and the Consequences for Public-value Capturing in UK, Spain and the Netherlands', *European Planning Studies*, 18, pp. 1097–1131, DOI: 10.1080/09654311003744191.

Graham, S. and S. Marvin (2001) *Splintering Urbanism: Networked Infrastructures, Technological Mobilities and the Urban Condition* (London and New York: Routledge).

Grubbauer, M. (2014) 'Architecture, Economic Imaginaries and Urban Politics: The Office Tower as Socially Classifying Device', *International Journal of Urban and Regional Research* 38(1), pp. 336–359, DOI: 10.1111/1468-2427.12110.

Harvey, D. (2005) *A Brief History of Neoliberalism* (Oxford: Oxford University Press).

Harvey, D. (1989) 'From Managerialism to Entrepreneurialism: the Transformation of Governance in Late Capitalism', *Geografiska Annaler. Series B, Human Geography*, 71(1), pp. 3–17, DOI: 10.2307/490503.

Hatuka, T. and L. Forsyth (2005) 'Urban Design in the Context of Glocalization and Nationalism: Rothschild Boulevards, Tel Aviv', *Urban Design International*, 10(2), pp. 69–86, DOI:10.1057/palgrave.udi.9000142.

Heeg, S. and M. Rosol (2007) 'Neoliberale Stadtpolitik im globalen Kontext, Ein Überblick' *Prokla*, 149, pp. 491–510, https://www.uni-frankfurt.de/46211933/Heeg_Rosol_2007.pdf (accessed on 27 July 2016).

Keil, R. (2009) 'The Urban Politics of Roll-with-it Neoliberalization', *City*, 13(2–3), pp. 230–245, DOI: 10.1080/13604810902986848.

Kemp, A. and R. Raijman, (2004) '"Tel Aviv is not Foreign to You": Urban Incorporation Policy on Labor Migrants in Israel', *International Migration Review*, 38(1), pp. 26–51, DOI: 10.1111/j.1747-7379.2004.tb00187.x.

Künkel, J. and M. Mayer (eds) (2012) *Neoliberal Urbanism and Its Contestations: Crossing Theoretical Boundaries* (Basingstoke: Palgrave Macmillan).

Leiper, N. and S-Y. Park (2010) 'Skyscrapers' Influence on Cities' Roles as Tourist Destinations', *Current Issues in Tourism* 13(4), pp. 333–349, DOI: 10.1080/13683501003748047.

Loftman, P. and B. Nevin (1995) 'Prestige Projects and Urban Regeneration in the 1980s and 1990s: A Review of Benefits and Limitations', *Planning Practice and Research*, 10(3–4), pp. 299–316, DOI: 10.1080/02697459509696280.

Lugosi, P., D. Bell and K. Lugosi (2010) 'Hospitality, Culture and Regeneration: Urban Decay, Entrepreneurship and the "Ruin" Bars of Budapest', *Urban Studies*, 47(14), pp. 3079–3101, DOI: 10.1177/0042098009360236.

Marcuse, P. (2009) 'From Critical Urban Theory to the Right to the City', *City*, 13(2–3), pp. 185–197, DOI: 10.1080/13604810902982177.

Margalit, T. (2014) 'Multi-Spot-Zoning: a Chain of Public-private Development Ventures in Tel Aviv', *Cities*, 37(C), pp. 73–81, DOI: 10.1016/j.cities.2013.12.001.

Margalit, T. (2013) 'Land, Politics and High-Rise Planning: Ongoing Development Practices in Tel Aviv–Yafo', *Planning Perspectives*, 28(3), pp. 373–397, DOI: 10.1080/02665433.2013.737713.

Margalit, T. and A. Kemp (2015) *Justifying Planning Decisions: Institutional Response to Planning Objections in Israel*, Conference Paper (Prague: Conference AESOP), DOI: 10.13140/RG.2.1.3242.2248.

Margalit, T. and E. Vertes (2015) 'Planning Allocations and the Stubborn North–South Divide in Tel Aviv–Jaffa', *Planning Theory and Practice*, 16(2), pp. 226–247, DOI: 10.1080/14649357.2015.1026925.

Marom, N. (2014) 'Relating a City's History and Geography with Bourdieu: One Hundred Years of Spatial Distinction in Tel Aviv', *International Journal of Urban and Regional Research*, 38(4), pp. 1344–1362, DOI: 10.1111/1468-2427.12027.

Marshall, R. (2003) *Emerging Urbanity: Global Urban Projects in the Asia Pacific Rim* (New York: Spon Press).

MacLeod, G. (2002) 'From Urban Entrepreneurialism to a "Revanchist City"? On the Spatial Injustices of Glasgow's Renaissance', *Antipode*, 34(3), pp. 602–625, DOI: 10.1111/1467-8330.00256.

Mayer, M. (2013) 'First World Urban Activism', *City*, 17(1), pp. 5–19, DOI: 10.1080/13604813.2013.757417.

McNeill, D. (2002) 'The Mayor and the World City Skyline: London's Tall Buildings Debate', *International Planning Studies* 7 (4), pp. 325–334, DOI: 10.1080/1356347022000027747.

Monterescu, D. (2009) 'To Buy or Not to Be: Trespassing the Gated Community', *Public Culture*, 21(2), pp. 403–430, DOI: 10.1215/08992363-2008-034.

Nicholls, W. and F. Vermeulen (2012) 'Rights through the City: The Urban Basis of Immigrant Rights Struggles in Amsterdam and Paris', in Smith, M.P. and M. McQuarrie (eds) *Remaking Urban Citizenship: Organizations, Institutions, and the Right to the City* (New Brunswick, NJ: Transaction Publishers), pp. 10–79.

Noifeld, A. (2014a) 'A meal in Zikat Hana'a—Interview of Naama Riva, *Slow*, Tel Aviv, http://slow.org.il/2014/01/28/%D7%90%D7%A8%D7%95%D7%97%D7%94-%D7%91%D7%96%D7%99%D7%A7%D7%AA-%D7%94%D7%A0%D7%90%D7%94-2 (accessed on 28 July 2016).

Noifeld, A. (2014b) 'A picnic in the front yard of Shari Arison', *Haaretz*, 08 February, http://www.haaretz.co.il/magazine/tozeret/.premium-1.2237427 (accessed on 28 July 2016).

Peck, J., N. Theodore, and N. Brenner (2013) 'Neoliberal Urbanism Redux?' *International Journal of Urban and Regional Research*, 37(3), pp. 1091–9, DOI: 10.1111/1468-2427.12066.

Peck, J., N. Theodore and N. Brenner (2009) 'Neoliberal Urbanism: Models, Moments, Mutations', *The SAIS Review of International Affairs*, 29(1), pp. 49–66, DOI: 10.1353/sais.0.0028.

Purcell, M. (2003) 'Citizenship and the Right to the Global City: Reimagining the Capitalist World Order', *International Journal for Urban and Regional Research*, 27(3), pp. 564–591, DOI: 10.1111/1468-2427.00467.

Riba, N. (2013) 'Residents of Tel Aviv- Please do not disturb towers' residents' towers', *XNET*, 15 December, http://xnet.ynet.co.il/architecture/articles/0,14710,L-3103771,00.html (accessed on 2 December 2016).

Sagalyn, L.B. (2007) 'Public/Private Development', *Journal of the American Planning Association*, 73(1), pp 7–22, DOI: 10.1080/01944360708976133.

Sager, T. (2011) 'Neo-liberal Urban Planning Policies: A Literature Survey 1990–2010', *Progress in Planning*, 76(4), pp. 147–199, DOI: 10.1016/j.progress.2011.09.001.

Saito, A. (2003) 'Global City Formation in a Capitalism Development State: Tokyo and the Waterfront Sub-centre Project', *Urban Studies*, 40(2), pp. 283–308, DOI: 10.1080/0042098022008028l.

Scheingold, S. and A. Sarat (2004) *Something To Believe In: Politics, Professionalism and Cause Lawyering* (Stanford: Stanford University Press).

Schipffer, S. (2015) 'Urban Social Movements and the Struggle for Affordable Housing in the Globalizing City of Tel Aviv–Jaffa', *Environment and Planning A*, 47, pp. 521–536, DOI: 10.1068/a140249p.

Shiloh, S. (2011) 'Towers of Contention' *Haaretz*, Jan 31, http://www.haaretz.com/print-edition/business/towers-of-contention-1.340261 (accessed on 27 July 2016).

Sklair, L. and L. Gherardi (2012) 'Iconic Architecture as a Hegemonic Project of the Transnational Capitalist Class', *City*, 16(1–2), pp. 57–73, DOI: 10.1080/13604813.2012.662366.

Stone, C. (1993) 'Urban Regimes and the Capacity to Govern: A Political Economy Approach', *Journal of Urban Affairs*, 15(1), pp. 1–28, DOI: 10.1111/j.1467-9906.1993.tb00300.x.

Swyngedouw, E., F. Moulaert and A. Rodriguez (2002) 'Neoliberal Urbanization in Europe: Large-scale Urban Development Projects and the New Urban Policy', *Antipode*, 34(3), pp. 542–577, DOI: 10.1111/1467-8330.00254.

Tasan-Kok, T. (2008) 'Changing Interpretations of "Flexibility" in the Planning Literature: From Opportunism to Creativity?' *International Planning Studies*, 13(3), pp. 183–195, DOI: 10.1080/13563470802521382.

Tel Aviv Regional Committee (2015), Planning scheme no. 2615c, http://mavat.moin.gov.il/mavatps/forms/SV4.aspx?tid=4 (accessed on 28 July 2016).

Tel Aviv Regional Committee (2006), Planning scheme no. 2615a, http://mavat.moin.gov.il/mavatps/forms/SV4.aspx?tid=4 (accessed on 28 July 2016).

Theodore, N., J. Peck and N. Brenner (2011) 'Neoliberal Urbanism: Cities and the Rule of Markets', in G. Bridge and S. Watson (eds) *The New Blackwell Companion to the City* (Oxford: Wiley-Blackwell), pp. 15–25.

Vicario, L. and P.M.M. Monje (2003) 'Another 'Guggenheim Effect'? The Generation of a Potentially Gentrifiable Neighborhood in Bilbao', *Urban Studies*, 40, pp. 2383–400.

Weber, R. (2002) 'Extracting Value from the City: Neoliberalism and Urban Redevelopment', *Antipode*, 34(3), pp. 519–540, DOI: 10.1111/1467-8330.00253.

Willis, C. (1995) *Form Follows Finance, Skyscrapers and Skylines in Chicago and New York* (New York: Princeton Architectural Press).

Yacobi, H. (2007) 'The NGOization of Space: Dilemmas of Social Change, Planning Policy, and the Israeli Public Sphere', *Environment and Planning D*, 25(4), pp. 745–758, DOI: 10.1068/d459t.

CHAPTER 8

A 'Time' to Act: The 2015–20 Development Plan for Greater Casablanca

Nadia Hachimi Alaoui

Abstract

This chapter examines conflicts of development focusing on the 2015–20 Development Plan for Casablanca, which was the subject of a broad consultation process initiated and implemented by the Wali of Casablanca, the King of Morocco's direct representative. The study highlights the competing visions, power relationships and struggles that led to the completion of a hundred or so development projects. Unlike studies on urban development in Morocco, which mainly focus on opposition and protest against development projects, or on engendered loyalties and alliances, this chapter highlights the tactical alliances and various mediations that helped define the development plan. This encourages us to understand the state not as a 'referee' but as an 'arena'. The Casablanca development project represents a period when the balance of power and the competing forces at work in Morocco—the interconnected relations of state and society—could be brought up to date.

1 Introduction

It was a speech made by the King to Parliament in October 2013 that placed a development plan for Casablanca on the agenda. At the opening of the parliamentary session—which every year begins with a royal speech, King Mohammed VI focused on the irresponsibility of politicians in carrying out their mandate. To back up his argument, he pointed to the lack of development in Casablanca, its 'glaring' inequalities and the weakness of its public facilities. 'Mismanagement' by elected officials, said the monarch, was 'the source of problems' that had led to 'this city, one of Morocco's richest' being 'the city of the most glaring social disparities, […] the finance and business centre, but also a centre of poverty [and] unemployment'.[1] The King did not

1 Address by His Majesty the King at the opening of the first session of the third legislative session of the ninth Parliament, 11 October 2013 (MAP, 2013).

DOI 10.1163/9789004349551_009

restrict his remarks to a list of problems but also called for change: he voiced his desire for people to come up, 'as a matter of urgency, [with] a diagnosis to identify the origins of the problem and the means to remedy it.' He drew up the terms and called for the participation of all the inhabitants of Casablanca. Finally, he stated the goal of the changes: the 'transformation of Casablanca into an international financial hub.'

This disavowal of the political class was not in itself anything new under the reign of Mohammed VI. It was rooted in the crisis concerning political brokerage and the difficulties the political class was experiencing in renewing its ranks (Iraki, 2005; Zaki, 2009; Tozy, 2010). These difficulties were preventing elected officials—at both the national and the local levels—from assuming the function of 'intercession' between the monarchy and the people, a function assigned to them by the Moroccan political system (Tozy, 1991). However, the October 2013 speech was distinguished both by the explicit reference to the elected officials of Casablanca and by its development imperative. A brief summary of the place occupied by development in the modes of government employed during the reign of Mohammed VI will highlight the reasons for the King's demand for change.

The use of the vocabulary and repertoire of developmental is emblematic of the authoritative discourse with which Mohammed VI marked a break with the old order. His reign, which began in 1999, has been marked by the rise of the developmentalist agenda in the exercise of power. The monarch decided on and launched various 'programmes', 'initiatives' and 'visions' of development; these continued to punctuate the first fifteen years of his reign.[2] In the context of the state's economic and institutional transformation, the figure of the King as developer has encouraged the reconfiguration of the repertoires of state action (Catusse and Karam, 2009): the 'managerial' turn in modes of government (Jobert, 1994; Ogien, 1995; Hibou and Tozy, 2002), in line with the rising importance of donors on the public agenda, has furnished the measures necessary for this change to occur; the multidimensional nature of developmentalist action, meanwhile, has created many new areas for state intervention. As a 'Builder King with social concerns' (Catusse and Vairel, 2010), the monarch has continued to promote the technocratic and economistic concerns that have distinguished public action since independence. The social dimension

2 As a brief overview: the 'policy on major infrastructure projects' for land development, the 'slum-free city' programme and the 'major projects' policy for urban development; the national initiatives for 'Human Development' and for 'Social Development'; and sector-specific visions for economic development, such as the 'Plan Azur' for tourism, the 'Plan Maroc Vert' for agriculture and the 'Emergence' programme for new world businesses.

may indeed set Mohammed VI's developmentalist project apart from others, but it also carries over the same apolitical understanding of change. The result is that social action is 'technologised' and the political dimension of inequality remains largely ignored. Thus, efforts in the domain of public action have focused on correcting the *effects* of social and regional inequalities, not their *causes*: this 'myopia' (Bec, 2014), despite leading to significant technical and material advances,[3] has hampered action to reduce the inequalities constitutive of the social and political status of individuals. These inequalities have instead been intensified by the neo-liberal orientation of the economy and by its 'financialisation' (Bono et al., 2015). The unequal nature of the way benefits have trickled down to the population has been the subject of violent protests, but the localised nature of the demands expressed, along with their geography—confined, as they have been, to marginal regions—have limited their scope (Bennafla and Emperador, 2010), leaving largely unaffected the national consensus on the development model. In the wake of the 'Arab Spring' of 2011, the creation in Morocco of the February 20 movement, a motley coalition of Islamist sympathisers, human-rights activists and hard left parties (Smaoui and Wazif, 2013), has given a high profile to these challenges, which had previously remained scattered. During the 'sit-ins' or big marches that took place in February and March 2011, the political violence of the slogans employed admittedly spared the person of the monarch (Tourabi and Zaki, 2011), but the concentration of the demonstrations in the major cities of Casablanca, Tangier and Marrakesh, where the central government was highly active and where the new King could most effectively showcase his modernisation project, gave them a particular resonance (Hibou, 2011a). The socio-economic dimension of these demands, expressing a desire for greater equity in the distribution of the fruits of development, brought to light the limits of the model's capacity to integrate disparate groups, and thus called the consensus into question, however implicitly.

Thus, the royal speech of October 2013 seems to me to be part of the wider dispositif set up in response to the demonstrations of 2011: like the address of 9 March 2011, which called for constitutional reform and the holding of fresh legislative elections (Dupret and Ferrié, 2011), the October 2013 speech positioned the King as 'the' agent of change—in this case, both economic and social. This allowed the monarchy to maintain the initiative and to define its

3 Figures with regard to properly equipped households and home ownership have experienced marked growth over the past fifteen years, as shown by the general census of population and housing in 2014, which can be found at http://www.rgph2014.hcp.ma/Presentation-des-principaux-resultats-du-RGPH-2014_a374.html (accessed on 20 June 2016).

terms. This reading is confirmed by the launch, by the King a few weeks earlier, of a development plan for Tangier (Atlas Info, 2013; Morocco, 2014), an initiative that was repeated for Marrakesh in January 2014. In addition, the national dimension given to Casablanca by the King—whose demand for change was uttered within the very precincts of Parliament—drew on the unique symbolic position that the city occupies in the economic geography of the Kingdom and in the historical geography of Moroccan social movements, which gives any public action in the economic capital a national character. The time difference between the social unrest of 2011 and the 'economic and social' response to it explains the decision to resort to the artifice of urgency: the 'critical state' of Casablanca, as set forth in the royal speech, revives the link between, on the one hand, the desire for change on the part of social actors, and, on the other, the monarch's ability to listen and understand (*Le360*, 2013a). The sense of urgency in the royal speech—given the central role of the monarch in defining the political dimension and its lexical content[4]—imposed the need for action at a time when the discredit of local officials had disqualified their participation in advance, thus opening a 'time' for state interventionism. This took the shape of the launch of a broad consultation on the definition of a five-year development plan, initiated and implemented by the Wali of Casablanca, the King's direct representative in these territories. This process, which lasted nearly a year, bore fruit in September 2014 when around one hundred projects were placed on the agenda and EUR 3 billion mobilised through cross-financing involving the state, local authorities, public and private operators and major patrons from Casablanca.

This chapter will be devoted to a study of the consultation process, the terms of its implementation, and the conditions of the production of the measures and actions of development that have been settled on, in order to grasp what 'development' means in the Moroccan context. It thus highlights the 'battlefield'—to use the term employed by Béatrice Hibou and Irene Bono in the Introduction to this volume—in and through which the development plan has been 'shaped' (Berman and Lonsdale, 1992). This is a field in which conflict, the balance of power, and resistance are expressed in statements that mask them. This way of rendering the political dimension invisible thus places development within an area of consensus whose hidden face covers the deeply

4 The press editorials that followed the speech are enlightening: 'Gouvernance de Casablanca: incompétence sur toute la ligne' [Governance of Casablanca: incompetence all down the line], *L'Économiste* (2013); 'Discours royal: Halte à la mauvaise gouvernance [Stop bad governance]', *L'Observateur* (2013) and 'L'état critique de Casablanca au cœur du discours royal' [The critical state of Casablanca lies at the heart of the royal speech] *Le360* (2013a).

asymmetrical and inegalitarian nature of the resources mobilised by actors in the negotiations that, in Morocco, shape the actions of 'development'.

This chapter is based on research conducted as part of the preparation for my PhD thesis, which is dedicated to the figure of the *wali* and his practices of government. It is based on a combination of research tools and techniques: first, participant observation, which led me to join the focus group set up by the state's representative and participate in the work of the 'Mobility and Public Space' committee and the drafting of its proposals; an ethnographic approach, which enabled me to observe the development plan 'in the making', and involved, during the eight months over which the process was spread, many different observation sites (various working groups, public meetings and official ceremonies, meetings of the city council, etc.); I also conducted, further along in the process, a dozen interviews with community figures, administrators, and politicians so as to capture the way key players understand and intervene in the process; and, finally, I collected and analysed various kinds of data (correspondence, documentation, and grey literature) circulated in the course of the process.

2 The Wali, Actor of the Royal Demand for Change

The day after the royal speech of October 2013, the King's demand for change led to the appointment in Casablanca of a new Wali. The setting of the stage for the appointment of Khalid Safir, along with his intrinsic qualities, led—elliptically—to this regional representative of the state being positioned as the individual responsible for taking action.

As the main state authority in the region, the Wali represents both the King *and* the government in the region, a singular status that duplicates the dual nature of Moroccan power. As a devolved authority of the Ministry of the Interior, the Wali occupies a 'crucial' place in the modes of government of the region (Moujahid, 2009): his role can be considered equivalent to that of the *Préfet* (prefect) in France before the decentralisation of 1982.[5] However, unlike the functions of the Prefect (Bouabid and Jaidi, 2007), the tasks and the skills of the Wali are not explicitly recognised from the legal and institutional perspective.[6] Beyond the statement of his kingly functions, making him the

5 Until the passing of the law on regionalisation in January 2016, the Wali was the executive of the regional council and the prefectural council of the Greater Casablanca Region; until that date, these authorities' scope for intervention was limited to the conurbation of Casablanca.

6 On this subject, see Morocco, (2005).

guarantor of public order and respect for the law, the Wali has little authority of his own (Bahi, 2005); the authority he does have is limited to coordinating the state's services in the region and facilitating private investment.[7] Conversely, the activities authorised by the Ministry of the Interior (which supervises local authorities), the delegation of government power, and his formal status as representative give the Wali several different positions in the local politico-administrative field and place him at the centre of gravity of local affairs. The low degree of institutionalisation of the Wali's function (Akhmisse, 2004), however, means that the capacity for action and initiative of this representative of the state repose on essentially immaterial resources, such as the prestige accruing to him as representative of the King. The terms of appointment of Khalid Safir in Casablanca, following the royal speech, highlight this dimension. At the time of the speech, the post of Wali in Casablanca was in fact vacant: a few weeks earlier, the appointment to the Ministry of Finance of the regional representative then in the post meant that the Wali was not liable for negligence in regional governance. In addition, the King's appointment of Khalid Safir, without prior recourse to the decision of the Council of Ministers, violated the new rules established by the constitution adopted two years earlier, which made such consultation obligatory. This means of appointment thereby strengthened the perception of a direct link between the sovereign and the new representative of the state, thus symbolically conferring the power of action upon the new Wali. As a senior figure in the Infrastructure, Finance, and Interior ministries, Khalid Safir combined, at the age of 47, different registers of expertise that reinforced the impression of his ability to 'act': he had been educated at the prestigious École polytechnique, and embodied the technocratic power upon which Mohammed VI relied in order to establish his reign; in addition, as a former prefectural governor in a district in Casablanca between 2006 and 2009, he was both an expert in 'regional' affairs and in the community fabric of the city.

As an actor 'designated' from above as being responsible for implementing change, the Wali intervenes only indirectly in the definition and implementation of local public policies: he ensures the coordination of local authorities, which control institutional, legal and financial resources (there are three of these in Casablanca—namely, municipality, prefecture, and region), the central administration of the Ministry of the Interior (the supervisory authority), and various government entities. Coordinating public action is difficult in Casablanca due to the dispersed nature of the city's government: the urban fabric is institutionally fragmented and divided among a myriad of institutions and

7 The Wali is the authority in charge of regional investment centres.

authorities, competing or complementary depending on the case (*La Vie Éco*, 2003). Thus, there are '114 politico-administrative units' and '60 technical units' (Kaioua, 2015), consisting of public and private operators, active in Greater Casablanca. These structures are not fully autonomous and are functionally interdependent: they each operate as a core or as an enclave interconnected with, or in competition with, others so that they constitute a link in a chain via which localised decisions coexist with centralised decisions. The weakness of the municipal budget,[8] the subordination of local taxation to state taxation,[9] and the very low level of devolution of departmental budgets turn the central government into a key player in the definition of local public policies. This dispersal of power centres gives a significant role to mediation—and this function is specifically assumed by the Wali, whose many and varied positions at different levels of public action and the authority conferred on him by the state place him in a privileged position when it comes to holding negotiations with all decision-making centres, which is an indispensable condition for the mobilisation of resources. However, economic transformations in the state and changes affecting management (de Miras, 2005) and decentralisation (Iraki, 2010) in city government have rendered more complex the modes and working conditions of negotiation. First, the technique of five-year planning, through which resources for services and amenities were once mobilised (Zair, 2007), was finally abandoned—after a brief renaissance—in 2000; this deprived the state of a 'time' for organising a consultation by simultaneously bringing together dispersed power centres. Furthermore, planning by projects, of the sort now underway, has increasingly regionalised the planning of public action. But at the local level, the space established by the state for consultation—namely, the prefectural technical committee (which brings together around the Wali the regional administration, the external services of the state, and elected officials), has proved ineffective in the face of the many varied power centres. Indeed, the implementation, at the beginning of the new millennium, of the 'triptych of institutional decentralisation + the privatisation of public services + the participation of civil society' has ensured the rise of new actors and new dispositifs of government, and this has increased the dispersal of decision centres. Following his appointment, the first consultations undertaken by Khalid Safir with political and administrative leaders specifically highlighted this

---

8 The budget of the city of Casablanca is MAD 3 billion, of which MAD 2 billion is reserved for operating expenditure, MAD 200 million for investment, and MAD 800 million for compulsory expenditure.

9 The city of Casablanca is apportioned only 16 per cent of its tax revenues, which are accumulated centrally before being redistributed by the state.

dispersal. The consultations aimed to 'identify the projects being planned and the potentially available resources.'[10] A first list was drawn up, bringing together actions that had been scheduled, those that had been budgeted for and were awaiting additional funding and, finally, those that had been scheduled but not budgeted for; it highlighted a need for funding to the tune of MAD 13 billion. Placing these projects on the agenda required negotiation: on the one hand there was a need to hierarchise priorities and, on the other, a need to mobilise funding resources dispersed between many people and groups in the region. By drawing on the royal dimension of his appointment and the unifying nature of the concept of development, the Wali took the initiative. Two months after his inauguration, he launched extensive consultations for the scheduling of a development plan for Casablanca, which simultaneously placed an entire set of forces in a position to negotiate with the state representative, thereby giving the latter the means to act.

3 The 'Enlarged Think Tank', An Expression of Consensus with Regard to an Apolitical Vision of Development

Consultation for the definition of the development plan took shape with the forming of a focus group, the 'enlarged think tank', and in the subsequent establishment of six 'administrative commissions'. In total, between January and September 2014, the date of the presentation of the finalised development plan to the King,[11] this consultation involved nearly '800 people'[12]—community figures, private and public agents, experts, regional and central officials and local politicians. The operationalisation of the consultation process and its technical nature turned the think tank into a standardised tool whose forms of bureaucracy aided its depoliticisation and facilitated consensus with regard to its implementation, ensuring that highly fragmented social, economic, political and administrative forces formed an alliance around the development project.

The instrumentation of the consultation resulted in the deployment of a scheme designed and implemented by the state's representative, which led, firstly, to a division of labour within the focus group. Thus, the think tank was

10 Interviews, *wilaya*, city council, Casablanca, January 2015.

11 The 'Plan de développement de Casablanca 2015–2020'.

12 Figures published by the Wali. *Discours de Monsieur Khalid Safir, le Wali de la région du Grand Casablanca, Gouverneur de la Préfecture de Casablanca*, meeting to report back on the work of the think tank, 16 January 2015. The speech can be read online: http://www.casainvest.ma (accessed on 20 June 2016).

organised into eight groups defined by development themes and each group was divided into subgroups—the 'committees'.[13] From January to April 2014, these groups worked on defining proposals and on finalising a deliverable for the Wali. Subsequently, a ninth group—the 'oversight committee'—took over: this was responsible for synthesising all the proposals and linking up with the six administrative commissions set up in parallel. Placed under the responsibility of senior government officers from the Ministry of the Interior—the governors—these commissions were charged with 'structuring the proposals' of the focus group, 'retaining the "most realistic" of them' and 'studying their financing options.'[14] Secondly, working procedures were defined and a ranking of participants in the focus group carried out; this was formalised in a letter of 'general purpose'[15] addressed by Khalid Safir to the eight leaders of the think tank. Each working group would be composed of a 'chair', a 'secretariat', 'seven permanent members' and 'six or seven temporary members.' Khalid Safir co-opted the chairs of the working groups, chosen from the ranks of the elite members of the community and from the Casablancan economic milieu, and approved the appointment of members within the various working groups, leaving the flexibility for each group chair to incorporate new members—the 'temporary members'—in answer to 'specific needs'. In addition, the guidance letter 'proposed' working stages—four in total—so as to 'structure the agenda' of the groups; the letter also prescribed the 'methodology of simple consensus'—that is to say, of creating one 'deliverable per working group'. And finally, the role of chair, held 'responsible for running the working groups, the schedule and the effective participation of members', was formalised.[16] This system was completed, at the setting up of the think tank in January, by the organisation of a 'harmonisation meeting' in the *wilaya*, with all the members of the working groups present, in order to identify the working areas for the committees that comprised these groups.

The administration of the think tank was entrusted to the Regional Investment Centre (Centre Régional d'Investissement: CRI), a regional public body that depends administratively and hierarchically on the Wali. A secretariat was

---

13 *Groupes de travail dans le cadre du Think tank élargi: présentation de Monsieur le Wali du Grand Casablanca*, dinner to launch the activities of the working groups, *Wilaya* du Grand Casablanca, internal document, 9 December 2013.

14 *Discours de Monsieur Khalid Safir*, 16 January 2015.

15 *Lettre de mission générale destinée aux présidents des groupes de travail: réflexion sur la stratégie de développement du Grand Casablanca*, internal document, 2 December 2013.

16 *Lettre de mission générale destinée aux présidents des groupes de travail: réflexion sur la stratégie de développement du Grand Casablanca*, internal document, 2 December 2013.

made available to the focus group; it was responsible for running the schedule of working group meetings, organising meetings with regional officials at the request of members of the working groups, and assisting the oversight committee in the shaping of the various deliverables submitted by the eight working groups. Thereafter, this secretariat ensured coordination between the oversight committee and the administrative commissions and assisted the Wali in writing and editing the various reports published during the process. The director of the CRI liaised between the Wali and the members of the focus group; he was responsible for the formal exchanges that took place between the Wali and the participants.

While the think tank was working, the Wali intervened directly in March 2014 by organising a study day devoted to international experiences[17] in order to 'inspire the model for transforming the metropolis of Greater Casablanca'. The finalisation of the development plan was preceded by meetings in the summer of 2014 between the Wali and the chairs of the working groups.[18] The process was also punctuated by several official meetings whose ceremonial nature, protocol, and introductory addresses made by the Wali all served to underline the royal dimension of the proceedings. In this manner, the launch of the consultation with civil society was the occasion, in December 2013, of a formal dinner in the presence of the Wali and members of Casablanca's voluntary sector elite; the handing over of the deliverables created by the eight working groups were the subject of ceremonial sessions at the *wilaya* throughout the month of April, in the presence of the Wali, officials of the regional administration and local political representatives. Furthermore, the completion of the development plan was celebrated in September 2014 with a royal closing ceremony at the Palace of Casablanca during which the ten financing agreements between the local authorities, government departments, private delegates and sponsors from Casablanca, who made it possible to mobilise EUR 3 billion, were officially signed. Finally, the official dissolution of the think tank, in January 2015, one year after it had been set up, was marked by a ceremonial event at the *wilaya* at which the creation of an observatory of civil society was announced, in line with recommendations from the working groups.

The launch of the consultation on 'developing Casablanca', and its implementation, thus enabled the state's representative to act on time and space. The consultation process would indeed form a 'space-time' for the negotiations, simultaneously bringing together a set of players available to deal with

---

17 *Expériences nationales et internationales pour inspirer le modèle de transformation de la métropole du Grand Casablanca*, workshop, Club Attijariwafa Bank, 8 March 2014.

18 Interviews, Chairs of focus groups, Casablanca, July and October 2014.

the state's representative. This space-time would be divided into different negotiating venues: the groups and subgroups of the think tank and the administrative commissions would comprise formal arenas for consultation, bringing together community figures, economic operators, and administrators, with the Wali at the centre. This manufacturing of alliances makes use of the consensus as to the apolitical nature of development; in so doing, it eventually led to the exclusion of local officials from the formal consultation, moving the scene of political negotiations to the informal spaces opened up in the margins by the formal dispositif of consultation.

4 Schemes of Participation and the Establishment of Formal Arenas for Reflection

The concept of development and its multiple meanings, economic and technical, opened up room for manoeuvre for the establishment of the think tank and formal consultation arenas, which in turn helped to unite the diverse forces making up Casablancan society.

The definition of the think tank's working themes drew, first, on a plurality of imaginaries and representations of the way Casablanca could be transformed, as evidenced by the statements issued by the eight focus groups: 'Casa, a place of economic prosperity', 'Casa, a place for living', 'Casa, a city for all', 'Casa, a city of leisure, culture and history', 'Casa, a city of dreams', 'Casa, a model of devolution and decentralisation', 'Casa, a city in the vanguard' and 'Casa, a city of knowledge.' The pluralist field of development thus gave the think tank an opportunity to marry together the diversity of voluntary associations in Casablanca, allowing it, for example, to bring together the representatives of 120 Casablanca's associations. General themes were then classified into 'working areas', which in turn gave rise to subgroups (committees) which thus created more formal arenas for consultation: the group 'Casa, a place for living', for example, was divided into six committees—'Housing, urban planning, infrastructure', 'Mobility and public space', 'Security and solidarity', 'Health and emergencies', 'Environment' and 'Administrative Services'—in which participants were brought together because they belonged to the same profession or were members of the same community association.

Secondly, the economistic understanding of development established a fundamental position for representatives of the economic base and allowed experts from consulting firms, new actors on the public stage (*Leaders*, 2015), to be appointed to the working committees. In this way, senior executives of multinationals or large private companies in Morocco, senior figures in consulting firms and employees of international companies were the vital core of those co-opted members of the working groups, as was the case, for example, with the majority of the 30 participants of the group 'Casa, a place for living', of which each subgroup had 'its own' expert. The prospect of 'developing Casablanca' certainly had an impact thanks to its moral and civic character,[19] but this is insufficient to explain the attraction of the think tank; three years earlier, a similar (albeit less developed) initiative on the part of the mayor of Casablanca had left the local economic scene largely indifferent.[20] The participatory momentum generated by the Wali found its strength in the 'constellation of interests' (Hibou, 2011b, 26) through which the relationship between individual actors and the state is formed: the participants most active in the working groups were simultaneously engaged in certain economic interests and professional or social logics that made it opportune for them to be close to the government. The group 'Casa, a place for living' and two of its committees—'Mobility' and 'Security'—were an emblematic case: the experts who worked on formalising the proposals of the 'Mobility' committee won major contracts with the Ministry of the Interior, including the restructuring of the public transport bus system in Casablanca;[21] one of the most dynamic members of the 'Security and solidarity' committee (a property developer in Casablanca) and, less visibly, the chair of the group 'Casa, a place for living' (an owner of land on the outskirts of Casablanca) were both engaged in land recovery operations that put them in direct contact with the regional government, which held dispensational power with regard to urban planning.[22] Also, the quest for positions as senior civil servants was another incentive, as in the case of one of the active members of one of these two committees, whose profile (as an engineer from a major French college) fitted in with the social transformations of the state and its elite.[23] The logic of 'notables' was another of the

19 Public-spiritedness constituted, at least in the language used by members of the think tank, a form of legitimation. The text published on the Facebook account of the chair of the group 'Casa, a city for all', spoke volumes: 'When the Wali contacted me to suggest I joined the "Think Tank for Casablanca" that he was setting up [...] I admit that I did not hesitate [...] because, given my activist ethics, I do not believe that we can evade our responsibilities when our Country is appealing to us—in however modest a way.'

20 The newspaper *L'Économiste* (2010), close to Casablanca's economic circles, gave a sceptical reception to the announcement of this municipal development plan: 'Yet another development plan for Casablanca: what for?'.

21 'Analyse du contrat de gestion déléguée', *Valyans-M'dina Bus: accompagnement à la définition du plan de redressement de la société*, July 2008, Partie II. Documents confidentiels.

22 Interviews, Casablanca, 2014.

23 Interviews, Casablanca, 2014.

driving forces making the think tank so attractive, including for the chairs of certain working groups, who, faced with the prospect of the establishment of an observatory of civil society, started competing with one another for the Wali's favour. It was not that, in the decision-making process, the local level alone was decisive in strategies of self-promotion and of company growth; the royal dimension of the process too was a more general factor in the attractiveness of the think tank, and the Wali constantly reminded people of this when he was interacting with participants. This is what explains the lively participation of all those attending official meetings: their presence displayed the extent of their co-optation, and—even more so—their proximity to the state. While everyone undoubtedly attached a specific meaning to this proximity, it is certain that for many this relationship had its roots in a political economy in which positions of influence and positions of accumulation overlapped.

The establishment, in the wake of the think tank, of six administrative commissions opened up arenas for consultation, this time connecting the Wali with officials of the regional administration and external services of the state. The technical nature of development legitimised the central place of the regional administration, whose expertise had been the historic engine of its expansion in the region. The names and the working themes of these commissions this time took the administrative categories on the basis of which development issues could be discussed,[24] thus emphasising the importance of infrastructure and urban development issues. In addition, the schemes implemented when the commissions were set up allowed the Wali to involve the thirteen governors then in post in Casablanca through the principle of the co-chairmanship of committees. Indeed, given the absence of hierarchically established links between these governors and the Wali,[25] their mobilisation (which was essential both administratively and operationally), would have been made difficult or at least complicated without their presence on these committees.

In a bureaucratic environment characterised by the tendency of government bodies to split, the unifying character of development has certainly constituted a powerful resource for mobilising the regional services of the state in these commissions. But here too, the reactions triggered by the appointment of Khalid Safir following the royal speech and his proximity to the King were instrumental in mobilising local bodies; it is indeed significant that, in the

24 Thus, these commissions were constituted under the themes 'Major structural projects', 'Highways and road infrastructure', 'Housing and urban regeneration', 'Mobility and urban transport', 'Human development' and 'Governance and local public services'.

25 While the Wali coordinates and supervises the activity of governors, the relationship—in terms of authority—between the governors and the Wali is not institutionalised.

corridors of power, the Wali was given the nickname 'the post-speech man'.[26] Conversely, the involvement of regional authorities in the development plan was effectively staged, as was evident at the dozen or so public meetings that took place with members of the focus group, thus demonstrating that the state was unified behind the Wali and thus also behind the King, of whom the Wali was the envoy for the implementation of the development plan.

5 The Exclusion of Elected Officials and the Opening up of Non-Formalised Forums for Consultation

The preparation of the development plan was, however, marked by the exclusion of local elected officials from the formal consultation forums. While they did play a part before and after the process at public meetings, they were not members of the focus groups. Nor were they incorporated into the administrative committees that were drawing up the development plan. Nor were they even consulted by the think tank participants in their roles as elected politicians. When they *were* consulted, it was in an individualised manner, or was the result of formal representational protocol. This exclusion, however, did not mean that elected representatives did not play a part; simply that they were relegated to the margins of the formal process. Negotiations with city councillors actually took place outside the formal dispositif of consultation, in non-formalised places and spaces that connected the Wali, politicians, and policy makers of the central government.

The technical and apolitical nature of development made it possible to remove local representatives from the consultation process. They were initially sidelined by the 'negative' and 'accusatory' character of the King's speech, which imposed a form of silence. The interpretations of the royal address by officials of the Ministry of the Interior strengthened this silencing effect, with the announcement, the day after the speech, of the 'launching of an audit' (*Le360*, 2013b) of the accounts of the city council. The exclusion of elected representatives was also partly the result of competition between community representatives and local politicians, who, at the local level, tussle over the legitimacy of the implementation of public action (Benidir, 2010). Only in a very exceptional case did the chair of the focus group 'Casa, a place for living'—whose association had, three years earlier, been put in charge (alongside the administration) of a programme to renovate the medina of Casablanca—take the initiative to consult with a representative of the city council, unlike

26 Interviews, *wilaya* and central government, 2014, 2015.

what occurred in other groups. The dimension of 'expertise' underlying the concept of development, and the way it is interpreted apolitically, naturalised the absence of elected officials within the working groups of the think tank, especially as this very negative view of the political dimension and of politicians in Morocco is shared by social actors; it characterised many of the debates that took place within the group 'Casa, a place for living', where the management of local elites was regularly denounced and the lack of communication with local politicians was completely taken for granted. The elected officials, in their turn, interpreted this isolation in different ways, depending on their positions, their trajectories and their characters, leading some to adopt silence for fear of sanctions, and others to flaunt their non-participation, interpreting it as a badge of resistance, while yet others developed a certain indifference, so that exclusion came to be seen as a form of voluntary self-deposition of elected officials.[27]

At all events, these different logics of exclusion prevented local officials from claiming loudly and clearly any formal role in the consultation process. Instead, the situation meant that these officials were placed in a bargaining position essential for the continuation of the process. Ultimately, after all, it is the elected officials who have the legal resources necessary for the adoption of local public policies: the measures taken and announced as part of the development plan require the approval and the vote of the Municipal Assembly. And it became necessary to submit matters to the vote of councillors early in the consultation process because of the dispositifs on which the financial and institutional architecture of the development plan rested. Such was the case with mixed local development companies (LDCs), whose capital came from the city council and the state, thus necessitating the vote of the municipal assembly. It was thus to this space of negotiation that the relationship between the Wali, the regional and national governments, and the elected officials shifted.

The creation of LDCs was a result of the first consultations undertaken by the Wali after his arrival in the *wilaya*.[28] These instruments made new financial schemes possible, in particular lifting the constraints related to the underfunding of the region. A further advantage was that they circumvented the obstacle of the dispersal of power centres when projects were implemented by consolidating local and central decision-makers on their boards. The negotiations initiated by the Wali for the legal creation of these instruments and for their effective implementation opened up, in the course of the negotiation process, forums for negotiation with elected officials. In such a context, the elected officials drew firstly on the provisions relating to the holding of the municipal

27 Interviews, city council, 2014 and 2015.

28 Interviews, *wilaya*, January 2014.

assembly and, secondly, on the instability of the majority on the council, as illustrated, for example, by the municipal assembly of 27 March 2014, which was meant to vote on the creation of three new LDCs. Postponed three times for want of a quorum of councillors, the vote—during the meeting of 27 March—marked a significant move on the part of the state's representative, who used his influence and the supervisory role he exerted over the city council. Through the regional administration, the Wali intervened to support the chair of the city council in mobilising elected officials and ensuring a majority of favourable votes (*L'Économiste*, 2014). Each governor was made responsible for mobilising the chairs of each of the political groups represented on the council. The drafting of the agenda for the council session, submitted in advance to the Wali's for his approval, also made it possible to negotiate with the mayor (the chair of the council) over the order of priorities for the vote. Under pressure from the Wali, the mayor himself became very active, bringing together at his home on the day before the vote all the council's political forces so as to negotiate a majority of votes for the items on the agenda.[29] When the assembly was convened, conditions thus seemed ripe for the adoption of the LDCs listed under item 2 of the agenda: the elected officials who had been mobilised were confident and the majority had been assured. But after having ensured that the administrative point that directly concerned him had been dealt with, the mayor halted the session, on the pretext of an altercation with a member of the opposition, and postponed voting on the provisions relating to the creation of LDCs to a later meeting. The establishment of these LDCs was deferred for an entire month based on the decision of the municipal executive, which did not adopt the principle of creating new companies until 28 April (*Le Matin du Sahara*, 2014), after cancelling the meeting of the municipal assembly three times. And it was not until seven months later, during the October session, that the legal provisions for LDCs were definitively adopted, obliging people to act—while the development plan was being defined—'as though' they existed, but to manage 'without them' all the same.

In addition, the close financial supervision exercised on the city council by the General Management of Local Groups (Direction générale des collectivités locales, DGCL) opened up room for manoeuvre for the central government, which enabled it to influence, during the process, the relationship between the city council and the *wilaya* in a discreet, non-formalised manner. The financing for projects, even those approved by the city, required—if these projects were to be effective—prior negotiations with the DGCL as the DGCL administered the funds generated in the form of VAT, funds which were redistributed

29 Interviews, regional administration, city council, March 2014.

by the state to local communities. This arrangement contributes 70 per cent of the investment budget of the city council and is, for example, the main source of capital provided by the council for the creation of LDCs. LDCs were viewed with suspicion by the central government, as the strengthening of regional decision-making instruments would entail a reduction of its own influence in the region. The negotiations with the city council for the vote on LDCs thus enabled the central government to influence how they would be made up and thus negotiate its place in how they would be structured.

Political negotiation thus moved to the margins of formal spaces for reflection, shifting into individualised spaces where the administration and political representatives are brought together, which has led to the concealment of conflict, power relations, and, in short, of politics. It also explains why, faced with a process of consultation that had excluded them, elected officials often preferred to choose silence rather than protest, while exercising their power, if only to create difficulties.

6 The Concealment of the Political Dimension

The political dimension, then, is expressed at different levels in the consultation process, but the dispersed architecture of the dispositif leads to the concealment of this political dimension, hiding power struggles over the definition of development policies. The consensus around an economistic and technical vision of development upon which the consultation was built does not, in fact, remove the political dimension. It prevents neither the coexistence of divergent and conflicting visions of the choices, solutions and priorities of development, nor competition with regard to the definition of target populations and regions to be developed.

The shifting of political negotiations to the margins of the formal arenas of the dispositif of consultation is one way in which the political dimension is concealed. Using their institutional and legal prerogatives, as I have mentioned, the elected officials who were excluded came back into the fray by increasing their bargaining power vis-à-vis the regional and central administrations. This repositioning led to a placing of the political dimension within the invisible sphere of negotiation, masking its highly individualised and asymmetric character and favouring political actors able to negotiate with the state, such as those in a position to influence how elected city councillors would vote. This explains why the only occasion on which the consultation process undertaken by the Wali was the subject of public criticism from local councillors was precisely the eve of the first municipal session during which LDCs were put to the vote. By using a press conference (*Média 24*, 2014) to denounce their exclusion from the process, some thirty or so elected officials[30] marginalised by the mayor tried to join the negotiations opened with the mayor and the administration to obtain a majority in the assembly's vote by highlighting their capacity to create difficulties. The political bargaining power of local elected officials can be understood only if we remember their role in the Moroccan political system: they primarily have a function of intercession, in that they are meant to 'raise' the social demands of various segments of the population (Tozy, 1991). This function—and thus the negotiations related to it—is individual in character: negotiations materialise through officials' haggling in the electoral context and their seeking positions of power and accumulation that help strengthen their electoral base. Thus, for one influential member on the city council whom I observed during the process, what was at stake in the negotiation with regard to the vote on LDCs was a place on their boards, so as to subsequently 'have the means to influence' the implementation of projects.[31]

The central government, meanwhile, drew on its ability to mobilise—or not—financial resources in order to influence the definition of the development plan; its masterly inactivity resulted in the political dimension being concealed in a second way. The elevated rail service project is undoubtedly the most explicit example. As a technical solution advocated by the mayor, and adopted in principle by the city council a year earlier, the project was met with reluctance on the part of the central government, which preferred a less expensive, technological option—the development of a Bus Rapid Transit System (BRTS). The lack of technical and financial assistance proffered by the central government in the context of the steps taken by the mayor during the consultation process, when he approached foreign donors to finance the elevated rail service, limited his room for manoeuvre given the weakness of the municipal budget. The difficulties of reconciling the divergent views of the administration and the mayor were resolved thanks to an alliance between the Wali and the mayor when the council voted on the development plan's specific measures at the end of the process. This alliance ensured a compromise that involved, on the one hand, the extension of the tram line instead of the creation of a BRTS and, in return, on the other hand, the abandonment of the elevated rail service project.

In formal consultation forums—that is to say, the think tank's working groups—the political dimension was redeployed in the economic, technical

30 The city council has 147 councillors from 16 districts backed by the city council. In total, the city has 500 local councillors.

31 Interviews, city council, 2014.

and normative spheres, leading to a third way in which the political dimension itself was concealed. The work of the committee 'Mobility and public space', in which I took part, is particularly illuminating in this respect. The nature of the members co-opted led to urban transportation issues being addressed solely from the viewpoint of mobility. Thus, when defining working guidelines,[32] the vast majority of participants at the meeting were managers or employees of large companies, with no one representing the captive population of public transport users in Casablanca. The participants' concerns were solely focused on the proper functioning of the city's economic activities, and the international examples used as benchmarks by the experts from the consultancy Valyans, which ran the meeting, were selected in view of the economic and developmental challenges they involved.[33] Regional inequalities in access to public transport were indeed denounced, but only on the basis of the needs of new business centres and residential neighbourhoods on the outskirts of Casablanca. The needs of populations marginalised by the high cost of public transport, which largely explain the massively informal nature and the dysfunctions of this sector, went largely ignored. Thus, the consultation gave voice to an essentially economic approach to mobility and the public transport service; this is itself a highly political position, being based on social class. In addition, the meetings organised with public service operators and administrators[34] to provide material for the committee were a pretext for each to defend competing visions for the development of urban transport, but the operational and technical dimension of those involved always came first, which resulted in any controversy being confined to purely technical statements. Lastly, when finalising the proposals of the committee, consensus was built on the unquestioned authority of the experts who had drafted the final report submitted to the Wali: in the actual functioning of the committee, only two members—two employees from the private sector—took any action to identify concrete proposals. These proposals went back and forth between them and the leader of the group 'Casa, a place for living', before being submitted for discussion to all its members at the last meeting of the focus group. The proposals provoked a

32 Feedback meeting of the focus subgroup 'Mobility and public space', Regional Investment Centre, Casablanca, 29 January 2014.

33 Transport systems in the cities of Bristol, Bucharest and Kaunas were presented. The Bristol system was chosen for its organisation of freight, the Bucharest system for its fight against pollution, and the Kaunas system for its intelligent transport service.

34 I was instructed by the committee to conduct interviews with the delegate from the bus transport service, the public operator in charge of the trams, the municipal official in charge of highways, and the regional official in charge of traffic management; I was then asked to summarise the situation for all the participants.

lively debate that revealed the contradictory visions of the participants as to the 'best' transport solutions to present to the Wali. By proposing that the experts from Valyans be entrusted with drawing up the details of the final deliverable, 'in the form of a harmonious and easy-to-digest PowerPoint',[35] the chair of the working group was able to put an end to the debate and avoid arbitration, shifting that decision to the question of formatting. This, which he was in charge of, concealed the political choices that had been made, giving way, in the final document, to the options preferred by the consultants.

The avoidance of the political dimension was not just a mechanical effect related to the architecture of the process. It also resulted from the Wali's effacement in the face of the conflict, which can be understood as a fourth way in which the political dimension was made invisible. The schemes set up by the state's representative, and his whole way of acting, testify to a desire to 'defuse' the expression of the political dimension. Thus, the methodology of 'simple consensus' set out by the Wali—that is to say, the creation of one deliverable per working group, limited the controversies within the think tank. The segmentation of the feedback process for the proposals of the eight working groups also prevented any confrontation between these groups over their choices and differing proposals, even though they sometimes found themselves working on the same themes. In addition, during the process the ways in which deliverables were to be submitted to the Wali assumed a character that did not lend itself to controversy. One of the first feedback sessions of one of the eight working groups, for example, took place in the hall of the city council in the presence of its elected members. The meeting was an occasion for intense polemics, which however were aimed not at questioning the appropriateness of the proposals submitted, but at allowing each elected official to defend 'his or her' territory, or 'his or her' population.[36] This explains why subsequent meetings with the other working groups were held *in camera* in the *wilaya*, in the presence of senior officials from the Ministry of the Interior and representatives of elected bodies alone, in order of rank, giving these meetings a ceremonial and solemn nature not conducive to controversy. The study day[37] organised during the process, which brought together all the local political representatives, regional officials, and members of the think tank—that is to

35 Mustapha Mellouk, chair of the working group 'Casa, a place for living', at the meeting to finalise the deliverables of the group 'Casa, a place for living', Hôtel des Arts, Dar Bouazza, 16 March 2014.

36 Interview, think tank members, April 2014.

37 *Expériences nationales et internationales pour inspirer le modèle de transformation de la métropole du Grand Casablanca*, workshop, Club Attijariwafa Bank, 8 March 2014.

say, nearly 500 people—certainly opened a space for debate (the only one that took place during the process) even though the visibility of the focus group in the public space and the sidelining of elected officials created tensions. But the debates, dedicated to the study of models of development in other countries, focused on what was driving the transformation of *foreign* capitals,[38] thereby setting aside the issues related to the Casablanca development plan and ipso facto defusing controversy with regard to the plan's definition. Conversely, the staging of the day's events, chaired by the Wali and including all the traditional codes and symbols of the state, showed that it was under the aegis of the state, and around its emblematic figure, the Wali, that harmony and unity were established between widely dispersed forces.

If the way in which he embodies royal power gives the Wali power of action, it still weakens him: it makes any form of protest and criticism potentially destabilising since 'to challenge the approach being made and the negotiations to which it has led mean challenging royal authority' (Bono, 2010). Questioning, in any way, the preparation of the development plan thus comprises a potential threat—or at least is perceived as such by the state's representative. This aversion to the 'political' dimension thus positions the Wali not as an actor in the conflict, but as an actor situated in an 'elsewhere' of the conflict, in the space of consensus that is built in the context both of the asymmetry of power relations between actors and of the asymmetry of the resources each is able to mobilise when faced with the state.

7 The Blur of the Concept of Development—The 'Adjuster' of Conflicting Temporalities

The conflicts that arose were not only linked to negotiations over the definition of public policies, they also had a time dimension. The preparation of the development plan, indeed, involves several dispositifs for action: the state of 'urgency' that imposes the need for action, the royal order authorising the action of the state's representative, the concrete imperatives of development that require consultation and, finally, the participation that expands the circle of negotiations. Although they are all implemented in order to serve 'development', these dispositifs produce disjunctions because of their different relationships with the 'time' of public action, whether the short 'time' of urgency, the long

38 The study day was structured as six panels, each dedicated to a 'metropolitan transformation model' and including presentations from a representative of a major foreign consultancy firm and a political leader from the city in question.

'time' of development (which is the 'time' of results), the intermediate 'time' of negotiation with decision-making centres and the pre-intermediate 'time' of consultation with civil society or, finally, the uncontrollable and discontinuous time of the King, a time that cannot be discussed and is punctuated by accelerations and expectations.

Because of his central position in the process, the Wali finds himself at the intersection of these temporal requirements, whose overlap produces tensions. So the 'short time' of urgency comes into 'opposition' with the 'long time' of development (Callens et al., 2007): the language of urgency employed by the King puts the population in the position of expecting immediate solutions and forces the Wali into a position where he needs to meet this expectation. Thus one can understand how, during the consultation process, a 'Plan of priority action for the short term' was implemented, the measures of which were subsequently integrated into the development plan. Furthermore, the royal dimension of the development plan requires the state's representative to meet the expectations of the King, whose monitoring of regional public action is embodied in royal visits (Goeury, 2014): these are the object of the Wali's temporal expectations, disturbing the temporality of public action. The prevailing perspective during royal sojourns has thus resulted in moments of acceleration and intensification in the pace at which the development plan is drawn up.[39] The temporal stakes of the royal visits act both as a constraint and as a resource with regard to the actions of the state's representative. On the one hand, they strengthen the negotiating power of elected officials, who themselves are not responsible for the conduct of the process. Such was the case throughout the months of March and April, during the negotiations on the creation of LDCs; the delay in which fuelled the King's discontentment and led to the cancelling of his stay in Casablanca (*Panorapost*, 2014). On the other hand, the planning of the ceremony at which the development plan would be presented to the King accelerated negotiations with the central government.[40]

The synchronisation of the times for negotiation is, in turn, hampered by the dispersal of decision-making centres: political time (that of the city

39 The prospect of a royal visit in March 2014 first led to the hasty finalising of the proposals of the working group 'Casa, a place for living'; thereafter, the date for reporting back on the group's work was subject, throughout the month of March, to successive schedule changes: the meeting at which progress would be reported, scheduled for 20 March, was postponed to 27, then to 28 March, finally being held on 11 April, the day after the cancellation of the royal stay in Casablanca.

40 Interviews, regional and central governments, Casablanca, 2015.

council), administrative time (that of the Ministry of the Interior but also that of government entities), and the time of technical entities (the companies to which local public services are entrusted, and on which the financing of urban infrastructure mostly relies),[41] subject negotiations to many different logics. To these, the process of consultation with civil society adds a further time requirement since it presupposes the adoption of measures or projects that result from these consultations. But the simultaneity of consultation with civil society and negotiations with those centres that possess financial and legal resources means that either what is able to be approved by the central, regional and municipal administrations or what will be proposed as a result of the consultation must be anticipated. In addition, the time of consultation with civil society comes into conflict with the time of the King: the royal agenda made it necessary, in extremis, to bring forward by three weeks the official ceremony, originally scheduled for the end of October, at which the development plan would be presented, which led to the cancellation of the consultation scheduled with officials from the think tank for the 'finalisation' of the development plan, and thereby to the presentation of the plan as the result of consultation when this was not in fact the case.

The interweaving of these different times was facilitated, first, by the participatory schemes that created the think tank, the rhetoric and instruments of which were the same as those advocated by international donors: the 'strategy of extraversion' with regards to participation (Bayart, 2009, xxv) provided the means to supervise very closely the consultation with civil society, which facilitated its synchronisation with the time constraints imposed by the other political and technical dispositifs. Thus, the co-option by the Wali of the leaders of the working groups and his proximity to the vast majority of these leaders have allowed him to influence the nature of the proposals and the pace of their development. The constraints affecting the Wali's actions were, for example, fully internalised by Mustapha Mellouk, head of the working group 'Casa, a place for living', in his report to the participants: the 'urgency', 'the need to formalise proposals very quickly, to identify quick wins' and to be 'realistic' in the definition of proposals are all injunctions which use, verbatim, the guidelines and the lexicon used by Khalid Safir. Similarly, Mellouk's hesitation with regard to the issue of the elevated rail service reflect the Wali's indecision with regard to how to schedule it within the development plan, an indecision itself caused by the unfinished nature of the negotiations between the central

41 In Casablanca, at the turn of the new millennium, water management, sanitation, the supply of electricity, transport and waste collection were entrusted to private companies in the form of public–private partnerships.

government and the mayor. This also explains the choice, made by the head of the working group, not to formalise his position on the subject in his final proposals.[42] In addition, the experts involved in the think tank were—without their knowledge—important intermediaries for the Wali's actions: co-opted because of the expertise they had managed to acquire previously through their professional practice, consultants have a detailed knowledge of what is possible in terms of public policy, as I observed in the case of the 'Mobility' committee and its largely conservative proposals. The 'areas for improvement', 'target models' and 'priority projects' proposed by the committee drew on the knowledge acquired by Valyans while working alongside the central administration of the Ministry of the Interior, which had entrusted the consultancy with numerous studies on urban transport. The proposals submitted to the Wali therefore stuck to the projects being planned or studied by the Ministry of the Interior as the regulator of urban transport.[43] Finally, the combination of 'hybridisation with genuine creativity' (Bayart, 2009), upon which the schemes of participation were based, provided the instruments of persuasion that enabled the Wali to exercise his authority and ensured that he was able to influence the pace and content of the consultation; the participatory dimension was thus harmlessly combined with the repertoire of administrative authoritarianism, as evidenced by the lexical content of the 'General Letter of Mission',[44] 'proposing' the working stages and the methodology of consensus, or—indeed—the 'harmonisation meeting',[45] 'supervising' the think tank's guidelines and accompanied by the Wali's recommendation to 'work in complete freedom and think without taboos'. The dimension of participation also managed to combine with the unquestioned character of the state's authority and that of its representative, who provided the flexibility to change the agenda and the modalities of consultation and to adapt them to various time constraints.

Second, the blurring of the concept of development has opened up room for manoeuvre when it comes to adjustments imposed by the disjunctions

42 Meeting to finalise the deliverables of the group 'Casa, a place for living', Hôtel des Arts, Dar Bouazza, 16 March 2014.

43 The proposals recommended the implementation of a target model for the organisation of the transport system, the adoption of a fund for urban transport and the professionalisation of large taxis, measures that had either already been adopted or were being planned.

44 *Lettre de mission générale destinée aux présidents des groupes de travail: réflexion sur la stratégie de développement du Grand Casablanca*, internal document, 2 December 2013.

45 *Procès verbal de la réunion d'harmonisation avec le groupe Casa-Lieu de Vie*, internal document, 16 January 2014.

between the time requirements of different dispositifs for action and those related to the realisation of the development plan. The segmentation of the times of development, between short term, medium term and long term, authorised the implementation of a 'plan of priority actions for the short term', which was accompanied throughout the process by a readjustment of the lexicon surrounding consultation, now refocused on defining development actions for the 'medium term' and the 'strategic' dimension. In addition, the indeterminate nature of development provided some elasticity for the articulation of the time of negotiations for both the short times of urgency and the long times of development. Thanks to their multiple meanings, all public action measures could be described as a 'development project'. Thus, the negotiations over the priority action plan focused on 'immediately financeable actions'[46] or projects that were already planned and budgeted for, and whose implementation was hastened by the simultaneous negotiations that took place in the centres of power during the process, bogged down as they were in the tangle of channels of decision-making and funding.[47] A similar type of adjustment prevailed for the actual scheduling of the development plan: discussions focused on measures 'that were achievable'[48]—that is to say, on actions already announced and others that were scheduled and awaiting funding. The process, however, allowed for the hierarchising of priorities, the redefining of the modalities of implementation through the creation of new local development companies, and the mobilisation of financing to the tune of EUR 3 million. In addition, conflicting temporalities reinforced the strongly 'managerial' dimension of development: the central place given to the planning of infrastructure, roads and the urban fabric has removed the oppositions between the notions of urgency and development. The fact that such projects are now underway or, in some cases, the fact that work resumed and was intensified following the adoption of the priority action plan or the development plan have thus made visible the active will of the state and its power to transform the city.

Third, the material nature of the media's presentation of the development plan has opened up room for manoeuvre to cope with constraints on the visibility of the action of transformation undertaken by the state. The presentation of the development plan has assumed different shapes, has taken place under different rubrics and has been prefaced by different 'introductory

46 Interviews, regional government, Casablanca, January 2015.

47 *Programme global et actions prioritaires pour la mise à niveau de la région du Grand Casablanca*, press dossier, 10 February 2014.

48 Interviews, regional administration, Casablanca, January 2015.

paragraphs' and thematic 'statements',[49] all of which have made it possible to interweave the different times of public action with the time constraints of the requirements for 'publicising' the process. The expectations raised by the royal statement, indeed, led the Wali to increase the number of public meetings: between November 2013 and December 2014, four press conferences[50] were devoted to the action taken by the state's representative, forcing the disclosure of actions and projects as yet uncertain because of the negotiating process. The royal ceremony that was held in order to deliver the development plan to the King also marked the symbolic moment at which the negotiation process ended, making it necessary to formalise the development plan when negotiations were still incomplete for certain projects. Thus, the replacement, in the supporting materials, of the heading 'urban transport' by the much vaguer term 'urban mobility' made it possible to include urban highway projects while concealing the fact that consultation with regard to the elevated rail service project had been abandoned, though it had been announced during the first conferences.[51] Similarly, the formatting of the report presented to the King in September 2014, describing four 'development poles', made it possible to keep quiet the details of projects not yet finalised, even if the deadline imposed by the date of this royal ceremony made 'results', with regard to these projects, necessary. Such was the case with the elevated rail service, whose unfinished state was hidden by a convoluted formulation that evoked future transit lines in 'capacity mode', without specifying the nature of the 'capacity' solution decided upon. In addition, the priority actions of the 'emergency plan for the period 2014–15' were indistinguishable from those that fell within the longer term of the preparation of the development plan, but were nonetheless presented as the fruit of consultation.

---

49 *Programme global et actions prioritaires pour la mise à niveau de la région du Grand Casablanca*, press dossier, 10 February 2014; *Plan de développement 2015–2020, rapport présenté lors de la cérémonie royale*, 26 September 2014; *Plan de développement 2015–2020*, press dossier, 22 December 2014; *Discours de Monsieur Khalid Safir, le Wali de la région du Grand Casablanca, Gouverneur de la Préfecture de Casablanca*, meeting to report back on the work of the think tank, 16 January 2015.

50 The press conferences of 12 November 2013, 11 December 2013, 10 February 2014 and 22 December 2014.

51 During the press conference of 11 December 2013, the plans for an elevated rail service were announced; the conference of 10 February 2014 reported the completion of technical studies and the ongoing finalisation of the necessary financial package. Then, during the ceremony at which the development plan was presented to the King, the development of a dedicated transport system was announced, without specifying its nature.

8 Conclusion

As a manifestation of the royal speech cited at the opening of this chapter, the development plan took shape via the meanings that the various actors assigned to the royal words, based on their understanding, their position, their behaviour and the resources they could mobilise in order to participate in and to influence the process. The Casablanca Development Plan was thus achieved in and via a tangle of interests, logics, power relations and competition. The space-time opened for the process of negotiation was an arena in which, in singular forms, expression could be given to conflicts that were either directly related to the definition of the projects, or connected with competition that went well beyond that process of definition. The analysis of the process of the definition of the development plan has highlighted the conflicts that make up the plan; it has also led to progress in the understanding of the nature of those who drive development projects in Morocco. My study has thus tried to fill a gap in the major works on the development of major urban projects; works which affirm, more than they question, the royal dimension. Based on this premise, these works primarily focus attention on the objections and protests aroused by the implementation of development projects or the loyalties and alliances that form around the allocation of these projects. Such relatively Manichean readings present development as an 'instrument' outside society, placed at the service of building the consensus by which the monarchy perpetuates its hegemony. I have instead tried to show that the development plan is not so much the instrument of consensus as it is its 'object' and its 'product'. This consensus is affected by the practices and political struggles that traverse society. It is formed in the asymmetry and unequal power relations that constitute it. The process of constructing the development plan highlights the strength of the interpenetration between the state and society, and the many forms it takes, whether that be through the dependencies, the competition, the workarounds or the 'resistances'—as shown more specifically in the chapter by Adriana Kemp and Talia Margalit in this volume—that have led the players to shape it. The arrangements, alliances, and various mediations that have helped to define the development plan thus suggest that we view the state not as a 'referee' (Waterbury, 1975), but as an 'arena' (Aymes et al., 2015): the 'development' of Casablanca, marking the start of a 'time to act', thus comprised, first and foremost, a time in which the balance of power and the competing forces at work in Morocco—relations in which the state and society are interconnected—could be brought up to date.

References

Akhmisse, L. (2004) *Le Wali de Région, agent d'une 'décentration' de l'Etat au Maroc: processus complexes d'institutionnalisation dans les régions du Grand Casablanca et de* Marrakech-Tensift-Al Haouz, Mémoire de DEA en science-politique (Aix en Provence: University Sciences Po).

Atlas Info (2013) 'Lancement par le roi d'un vaste programme Tanger métropole pour le développement intégré et inclusif de la ville' [Launch by the King of a vast program for the metropolis of Tangier aimed at the integrated and inclusive development of the city], 26 September, http://www.atlasinfo.fr/Lancement-par-le-Roi-d-un-vaste-programme-Tanger-Metropole-pour-le-developpement-integree-et-inclusif-de-la-ville_a46084.html (accessed on 22 February 2017).

Aymes, M., B. Gourisse and E. Massicard (eds.) (2015) *Order and compromise: Government Practices in Turkey from the Late Ottoman Empire to the Early 21st Century* (Leiden and Boston: Brill).

Bahi, M. (2005) *Les compétences du Wali, du gouverneur et d'autres agents d'autorité* (Casablanca: Imprimerie Najah el Jadida).

Bayart, J.-F. (2009) *The State in Africa: The Politics of the Belly*, 2nd ed. (Cambridge: Polity).

Bec, C. (2014) *La Sécurité sociale. Une institution de la démocratie* (Paris: Gallimard).

Benidir, M. (2010) 'Leaders associatifs et élus locaux au Maroc: épreuves de face-à-face et controverses dans les arènes du développement', *Politique africaine*, 120(4), DOI: 10.3917/polaf.120.0087.

Bennafla, K. and M. Emperador (2010) 'Le "Maroc inutile" redécouvert par l'action publique: les cas de Sidi Ifni et Bouarfa', *Politique africaine*, 120(4), pp. 67–86, DOI: 10.3917/polaf.120.0067.

Berman, B. and J. Lonsdale (1992) *Unhappy Valley. Conflict in Kenya and Africa* (London: Eastern African Studies).

Bono, I. (2010) 'Pauvreté, exception, participation. Mobilisation et démobilisation dans le cadre de l'INDH', in Catusse, M., B. Destremau and É. Verdier (eds.) *L'Etat face aux débordements du social au Maghreb. Formation, travail et protection sociale* (Paris: Karthala), pp. 229–250.

Bono, I., B. Hibou, H. Meddeb and M. Tozy (2015) *L'État d'injustice au Maghreb. Maroc et Tunisie* (Paris: Karthala).

Bouabid, B. and L. Jaidi, (2007) *Déconcentration et gouvernance des territoires*, working document (Rabat: Fondation Ali Bouabid).

Callens, S., J. Brot and H. Gerardin (2007) 'Introduction. De l'opposition entre l'Urgence et le Développement à la prise de conscience des spécificités des problèmes de gouvernance en période d'urgence', *Mondes en développement*, pp. 7–10, DOI: 10.3917/med.137.0007.

Catusse M. and K. Karam (2009) 'Le développement contre la représentation ? La technicisation du gouvernement local au Liban et au Maroc', in Camau, M. and G. Messadier (eds.) *Démocraties et autoritarismes: fragmentation et hybridation des régimes* (Paris: Karthala), pp. 85–120.

Catusse, M. and F. Vairel (2010) 'Question sociale et développement: les territoires de l'action publique et de la contestation au Maroc', *Politique Africaine*, 120(4), DOI: 10.3917/polaf.120.0005.

de Miras, C. (ed.) (2005) *Intégration à la ville et services urbains au Maroc*, (Rabat, Paris: INAU-IRD), http://www.documentation.ird.fr/hor/fdi:010050636.

Dupret, B. and J.-N. Ferrié (2011) 'La nouvelle architecture constitutionnelle et les trois désamorçages de la vie politique marocaine', *Confluences méditerranée*, 3, pp. 25–34, DOI: 10.3917/come.078.0025.

L'Économiste (2014) 'Climat tendu au conseil de la ville' [Tense climate at city council], 24 March.

L'Économiste (2013) 'Gouvernance de Casablanca : incompétence sur toute la ligne' [Governance of Casablanca: incompetence all down the line], 15 October, http://www.leconomiste.com/article/911926-gouvernancecasablancaincomp-tence-sur-toute-la-ligne (accessed on 22 February 2017).

L'Économiste (2010) 'Un énième plan de développement pour Casablanca : pour quoi faire ? [Yet another development plan for Casablanca: what for?]', 28 September.

Goeury, D. (2014) 'La visite royale comme réponse au stress regional: les conséquences des manifestations rurales dans le Haut Atlas central et oriental marocain', *L'Espace Politique*, 24(3), http://espacepolitique.revues.org/3242 (accessed on 20 June 2016).

Hibou, B. (2011a) 'Le mouvement du 20 février, le Makhzen et l'antipolitique. L'impensé des réformes au Maroc', *Dossiers du CERI*, https://hal-sciencespo.archives-ouvertes.fr/hal-01024402 (accessed on 20 June 2016).

Hibou, B. (2011b) *Anatomie politique de la domination* (Paris: La Découverte).

Hibou, B. and M. Tozy (2002) 'De la friture sur la ligne des réformes. La libéralisation des télécommunications au Maroc', *Critique Internationale*, 14(1), pp. 91–118, DOI: 10.3917/crii.014.0091.

Iraki, A. (2010) 'Réformes institutionnelles, refonte des territoires et rapports de pouvoirs dans la ville', *Les Cahiers d'EMAM*, 19, http://emam.revues.org/116 (accessed on 20 June 2016).

Iraki, A. (2005) 'Du renouvellement des élites urbaines au Maroc. Élites urbaines, territoire et système politique local', *Annuaire de l'Afrique du Nord*, 41, pp. 81–95, http://aan.mmsh.univ-aix.fr/volumes/2003/Pages/AAN-2003-41_14.aspx (accessed on 20 June 2016).

Jobert, B. (1994) *Le tournant néo-libéral en Europe* (Paris: L'Harmattan).

Kaioua, A. (2015) 'Le Grand Casablanca-Institution et gestion urbaine', paper presented at the seminar 'Territoire et urbanisation', Institut National d'Urbanisme -École de Gouvernance, Rabat, 10 February.

Le360 (2013a) 'L'état critique de Casablanca au cœur du discours royal' [The critical state of Casablanca lies at the heart of the royal speech]', 15 October, http://fr.le360.ma/politique/letat-critique-de-casablanca-au-coeur-du-discours-royal-4623 (accessed on 22 February 2017).

Le360 (2013b) 'Casablanca : l'Intérieur reprend les choses en main [Casablanca: the Ministry of the Interior reassumes control]', 26 November, http://fr.le360.ma/politique/casablanca-linterieur-reprend-les-choses-en-main-6369 (accessed on 23 February 2017).

Leaders (2015) 'Qui élabore les stratégies au Maroc?' October, Tunis, http://www.leaders.com.tn (accessed on 23 February 2017).

MAP (Agence Marocaine de Presse) (2013) 'Texte intégrale du discours de SM le Roi Mohammed VI à l'ouverture de la première session de la troisième année législative de la 9ème législature' (Rabat : MAP), http://www.mapnews.ma/fr/discours-messages-sm-le-roi/texte-integrale-du-discours-de-sm-le-roi-mohammed-vi-louverture-de-la-pr (accessed on 16 June 2016).

Le Matin du Sahara (2014) 'Développement local. La création de sociétés approuvée à Casablanca' [Local development. Creation of societies approved in Casablanca], 28 April.

Média 24 (2014) 'À Casablanca, un groupe de conseillers dénoncent la marginalisation des élus [In Casablanca, a group of councillors criticises the marginalisation of elected representatives]', 10 February.

Morocco (Ministry of Communication) (2014) 'Sa Majesté préside la cérémonie de lancement du projet Marrakech, cité du renouveau permanent' [His Majesty chairs the launch ceremony for the project Marrakech, city of permanent renewal], 6 January, https://www.maroc.ma/fr/activites-royales/sm-le-roi-preside-la-ceremonie-de-lancement-du-projet-marrakech-cite-du-renouveau (accessed on 22 February 2017).

Morocco (Ministry of Interior) (2005) 'Réflexion sur le statut de Wali de région', Lettre des collectivités locales, April-June, p. 6, http://www.pncl.gov.ma (accessed on 23 February 2017).

Moujahid, A. (2009) 'Le Wali, pivot de la gouvernementalité?', in Miossec, J.-M. (ed.) *Terrains et échelons de la gouvernance: expériences en France et au Maghreb* (Paris: L'Harmattan), pp. 277–325.

Ogien, A. (1995) *L'Esprit gestionnaire* (Paris: Éditions de l'EHESS).

L'Observateur (2013), 'Discours royal: Halte à la mauvaise gouvernance [Stop bad governance]', L'Observateur, 15 October, http://lobservateurdumaroc.info/2013/10/12/discours-royal-halte-mauvaise-gouvernance/ (accessed on 22 February 2017).

Panorapost (2014) 'Le roi quitte Casablanca en donnant un délai supplémentaire aux responsables de la ville [The King leaves Casablanca, extending the city leaders' deadline]', 4 April.

Smaoui, S. and M. Wazif (2013) 'Étendard de lutte ou pavillon de complaisance? S'engager sous la bannière du "Mouvement du 20 février' à Casablanca", in Allal, A. and T. Pierret, *Devenir révolutionnaires. Au cœur des révoltes arabes* (Paris: Armand Colin).

Tourabi, A. and L. Zaki (2011) 'Maroc: une révolution royale?' *Mouvements*, 66, p. 98–103, DOI: 10.3917/mouv.066.0098.

Tozy, M. (2010) 'Introduction', in Tozy, M. (ed.) *Élections au Maroc, entre partis et notables (2007–2009)* (Casablanca: Publication du Centre Marocain des Sciences Sociales), pp. 11–26.

Tozy, M. (1991) 'Représentation/intercession: les enjeux de pouvoir dans les « champs politiques désamorcés » au Maroc', in Camau, M. (ed.) *Changements politiques au Maghreb* (Paris: CNRS Éditions), pp. 153–168.

La Vie Éco (2003) 'Wali, maire, président de région, qui fait quoi ?' [Wali, mayor, regional chair—who does what?], 14 November, http://lavieeco.com/news/politique/wali-maire-president-de-region-qui-fait-quoi-5290.html (accessed on 23 February 2017).

Waterbury, J. (1975) *Le commandeur des croyants* (Paris: Presse Universitaire de France).

Zaki, L. (ed.) (2009) *Terrains de campagne au Maroc. Les élections législatives de 2007* (Tunis: IRMC; Paris: Karthala).

Zair, T. (2007) *La gestion décentralisée du développement économique au Maroc* (Paris: L'Harmattan).

CHAPTER 9

The Muslim Brotherhood's 'Virtuous society' and State Developmentalism in Egypt: The Politics of 'Goodness'

Marie Vannetzel

Abstract

The rise of Islamists in Arab countries has often been explained by their capacity to offer an alternative path of development, based on a religious vision and on a parallel welfare sector, challenging post-independence developmentalist states. Taking the case of the Egyptian Muslim Brotherhood, and building on ethnographic fieldwork, this chapter aims to contribute to this debate, exploring how conflict and cooperation were deeply intertwined in the relationships between this movement and Mubarak's regime. Rather than postulating any structural polarisation, or—in contrast—any simplistic authoritarian coalition, the author argues that the vision of two models of development opposing one another unravels when we move from abstract approaches towards empirical studies. On the ground, both the Muslim Brotherhood and the former regime elites participated in what the author calls the politics of 'goodness' (*khayr*), which she defines as a conflictual consensus built on entrenched welfare networks, and on an imaginary matrix mixing various discursive repertoires of state developmentalism and religious welfare. The chapter also elaborates an interpretative framework to aid understanding of the sudden rise and fall of the Brotherhood in the post-2011 period, showing that, beyond its failure, what is at stake is the breakdown of the politics of 'goodness' altogether.

1 Introduction

Islamists' momentum in Arab countries has often been explained by their capacity to offer an alternative path of development, based on a religious vision and on a 'shadow and parallel welfare system [...] with a profound ideological impact on society' (Bibars, 2001, 107), through which they challenged post-independence developmentalist states (Sullivan and Abed-Kotob, 1999). In Egypt, which has been considered a model for both state developmentalism and Islamism, members of the Muslim Brotherhood (MB) used to be analysed

DOI 10.1163/9789004349551_010

as counter-elites, building on this parallel Islamic welfare sector to advance their own politico-religious agenda (Wickham, 2003). Their legitimacy would then derive from their ability to provide for a counter project to the state's failure in development terms, and from the mobilisation of Islamic values against the regime. Yet, in the Egyptian case as in others, a contrasting explanation holds that the MB was granted space to expand through welfare activities, in the frame of tacit cooperation with the incumbent regime in order to maintain so-called stability. Accordingly, they were therefore said to be part, though unofficially, of the authoritarian coalition leading the former regime before Mubarak's fall in 2011.

The sudden rise and fall of the Muslim Brothers in the course of the Egyptian revolution has given a new actuality to this debate. The MB's dramatic trajectory began with their victory in the parliamentary and presidential elections of 2011/2012 and, after one year in office, ended in the ousting of President Mohamed Morsi by the then General Abdel Fattah al-Sisi's military coup, following mass mobilisations in June-July 2013. This fall has been variously interpreted as the result of the structural polarisation opposing the MB to the elites of the former regime (including the military), or as the breakdown of the longstanding coalition between them.

This chapter aims to contribute to this debate, exploring the tension between the conflictual challenge and the authoritarian coproduction that the MB at once embodied under Mubarak's rule. The chapter also elaborates an interpretative framework with which to understand the MB's trajectory during the current revolutionary process. Rather than postulating any structural polarisation, or—in contrast—any simplistic coalition, I argue that conflict and cooperation were deeply intertwined in the relationships between Mubarak's regime and the MB, and that the vision of two models of development opposing one another unravels when we move from abstract approaches towards empirical studies. On the ground, both the MB and the former regime elites shared similar beliefs and practices with which to develop society. They participated in what I call the politics of 'goodness' (*khayr*), which I define as a conflictual consensus built on entrenched welfare networks, and on an imaginary matrix mixing various discursive repertoires of state developmentalism and religious welfare. The politics of goodness was therefore a competitive, yet common, ground for the MB's vision of a 'virtuous society' and for the Egyptian state's mythical representation as the main agent of social development.

First, I will show how the myth of state developmentalism has been transformed in the course of the neo-liberal period, and how it has been relocated in different welfare practices. Second, building on an ethnographic study conducted in Cairo between 2005 and 2010,[1] I will reflect on the Muslim Brothers' imaginary of 'virtuous society' and explain how it entrenched into state-promoted practices and beliefs. Finally, I will put forward an explanation of how this conflictual consensus turned to open conflict in the post-2011 period. I will show that beyond the confrontation between the MB and former incumbents, deeper changes have transformed, and challenged, the politics of goodness in the new socio-political configuration.

2 The Paradoxical Imaginary of State Developmentalism in Neo-Liberal Times

Central to Western societies, where it was born and consolidated, the belief in development has strongly shaped the political economy of Middle Eastern societies—and how they have been studied. As Myriam Catusse points out, the emergence of the 'developmentalist scheme' in the 1950s framed 'the formation of Arab states and their organisation around a model of auto-centered development, designed as a tool for decolonisation and for state (and nation) construction' (Catusse, 2006, 218, author's transl.). The state was conceived as the 'architect of structural transformation' (Richards and Waterbury, 1996, 234), whose purpose was to reshape society and fight the multiple features of 'backwardness', hence closely binding economic, social, cultural and political issues as facets of a same fundamental problem. Nasser's Egypt (1952–70) was emblematic of this state-led model of development, for the newly independent regime engaged in well-known socio-economic reforms (agrarian redistribution, import-substituting industrialisation, growth of the public sector, enlarged access to education ...). Yet, neither Sadat's *infitah* policies of economic liberalisation (1970–81), nor the neo-liberal turn witnessed during Mubarak's era (1981–2011), in the post-Washington Consensus context, came to terms with the representation of the state as being charged with the development of society—in spite of the economic shift from the public to the private sector from the 1990s onwards, cutbacks in state expenditure and declining state welfare provision (Harrigan and El Said, 2009; Abdelrahman, 2015).

The imaginary of state developmentalism, together with the ongoing perception of Arab countries through the lens of the 'developmentalist scheme' (see for example Achcar, 2013; Farah, 2009), actually survived the progressive

1 I mostly investigated the southern, working-class suburb of Helwan and the middle-class district of Madinat Nasr. Supplementary fieldwork was carried out in December 2012, December 2013-January 2014, summer 2014 and November 2015.

disappearance of Nasser's developmentalist state. Three factors account for such a discrepancy, which itself paves the way for the politics of goodness. First, institutional legacies from the state-led industrialisation of the past continued to characterise the Egyptian economy through to the first decade of the twenty-first century (Soliman, 2004; Adly, 2013): the growth pattern remained dependent on oil and natural gas exports, over which the state still held a quasi-monopoly.[2] Hence, the state kept being a main provider in the economy, drawing its own revenues from external rents, which were used to subsidise constituencies among business elites and other social groups. The second factor, related to the first, concerns the practices of patronage. On the one hand, the state nurtured a 'crony capitalism' (Sadowski, 1991) made of alliances with big capital holders (helping them to build oligopolies) and arbitrary control of business activities (Gobe, 1999; Sfakianakis, 2004). On the other hand, packages of public subsidy were made highly visible, keeping alive the image of the redistributive state personified in the presidential figure, although the actual beneficiaries lay significantly outside the advertised social targets. Energy subsidies, which amounted to about 18 per cent of total state expenditure in 2000–10, were a disguised means of rewarding big private industries as major recipients of this policy (Adly, 2013, 110). As for food subsidies, they decreased through the 1980s and 1990s, and were moreover considered to be missing many of the poorest Egyptians. However, Mubarak's regime wisely handled this policy, employing gradual contractions and allowing sudden increases when needed (as was the case a little over a decade ago, when inflation rates and international food and energy prices rose) (Adly 2013, 208). The National Housing Program (NHP) also offers a good example of these illusive social packages—especially as the building of infrastructure was long seen as the hallmark of Mubarak's regime. As researcher Yahia Shawkat shows, two ambitious, publicly subsidised housing schemes were launched as Mubarak's personal promises to Egypt's youth and the needy—*Iskan Mubarak lil-shebab* (1996–2005) and *Iskan Mubarak al-qawmi* (2005–12). But, relying 'on a legal definition of low income that completely ignored economic data', the NHP actually 'excluded all those who have informal jobs, and embedded middle-income government employees, [National Democratic Party (NDP)] parliamentarians, and governors into the allocation system—allowing these regime supporters to profiteer as middlemen between those who did not meet NHP criteria'. The policy was therefore 'deceiving the public into believing that the NHP was affordable to the poor': 'pictures of Mubarak,

2 The public Authority of Petroleum controlled around 85 per cent of total production (Springborg, 2012, 11).

governors and other officials handing over deeds to beneficiaries filled the front pages of newspapers for a few years and kept up the hopes of hundreds of thousands families for affordable housing' (Shawkat, 2014, paras. 63, 64, 67). Finally, the hope and belief in state developmentalism were maintained by the virtual upholding of a 1964 law that provides all graduates of vocational secondary and university degrees with employment in the public sector—a provision still perceived as a 'right' (Beinin and Duboc, 2014) but which had come to a complete halt by the 1990s, when most public enterprises started to be privatised.

Both factors explain why the myth of state developmentalism was still vivid in spite of the neo-liberal turn induced by twenty years of the International Monetary Fund-sponsored Structural Adjustment Program. As shown by the NHP example, a third factor must be underscored, though it is too often ignored by studies in political economy. Nasser's model of the state as an architect of development also redefined the notion of politics. In 1952, the dissolution of all political parties and voluntary associations was not only aimed at containing any kind of opposition; it also related to the vision of politics as a divisive threat to the nation, a threat that had to be replaced by the direct and fusional relationship between the leader and the nation, the corporatist and functional organisation of society, and the active role of the army in national protection and social modernisation (Waterbury, 1983; Bianchi, 1989; Fahmy, 2002). In this context, political institutions, such as the parliament, were subsumed by the developmentalist mission of the state. Former political elites, most of whom were notables and big landowners, were partly deprived of access to elected assemblies, and new strata of state bourgeoisie were promoted as Members of Parliament. Yet, rather than being political representatives of the nation—which the supreme leader alone was entitled to be—they were defined as middlemen between the state and society, their role being to redistribute public resources among local populations (Ben Néfissa and Arafat, 2005). Hence, the notion of politics was both broadened—the state and political institutions would now belong to the whole nation—and dissolved in the idea of public 'services' (*khidma pl. khadamat*).

Since then, the definition of the good representative—a member either of parliament or of the local council—as 'the one who serves people' (*elli beyekhdem al-nas*) has been strongly anchored in the political imaginary. While this can be classically described as a clientelistic pattern of political exchanges, not unique to Egypt, the public and collective dimension of these exchanges seems quite specific and compliant. MPs are expected to deliver, above all, services that will benefit a whole community, and not just individuals (building a school or dispensary, having an area connected to the electricity supply or sewage system …) and to rely on public resources rather than private wealth. Therefore, when traditional notables got back into parliament under Sadat's rule, or when wealthy businessmen showed up in politics in the first decade of the twenty-first century, they had to comply with these requirements—which Patrick Haenni rightly summed up as 'the spirit of services' (*l'esprit de service*) (Haenni, 2005a)—in order to secure legitimacy. This is how Mubarak's NDP attracted aspirant political elites, as NDP membership was a necessary condition to having access to state resources. However, with the contractions of state expenditure, even NDP elites were urged to find other sources to be redistributed, all the while sticking to the public and collective requirements of the spirit of services. This is how many became involved in various local structures of what Egyptians call 'public work' (*al-'amal al-'amm*): either state-sponsored organisations such as 'community development associations' (*gam'iyyat li-tanmiyyat al-mugtama'*), youth centres, social clubs, solidarity cooperatives in the workplace (*gam'iyyat ta'awuniyya*) and labour unions, or societal organisations such as voluntary charitable associations (*gam'iyyat khayriyya*), popular justice assemblies (*sulh*), and mosque-linked *zakat* committees (in charge of collecting Islamic alms).

Far from being a detail, this micro-level spirit of services framed, for large parts of the population, their everyday relationships with the state, which they encountered in the form of elected representatives, perceived as administration intermediaries and agents of the state's developmentalist mission. The perception of 'who serves' (*beyekhdem*) and 'who does not serve' (*mabeyekhdemsh*) stood as a determining criterion in the popular judgement of political elites. These judgments were often expressed in the moral terms of goodness (*khayr*), which the regime encouraged as it boiled down politics to public work, service, and even charity—a breeding ground for deconflictualisation and for responsibility discharge onto the local state intermediaries. The politics of goodness thus appears as the low-cost version of the developmentalist myth: keeping alive, through these local encounters, the image of a state in charge of development, while effectively 'relocating welfare' (Ismail, 2006) in charitable actions and individualised relationships.

In this process of welfare relocation, the network of Islamic social institutions largely intertwined with the regime's own networks. While the Muslim Brothers mobilised Islamic values to promote a model of 'virtuous society' through their welfare practices, this model did not stand as a counter-project of development. It was embedded in a matrix of mixed imaginaries to which the regime largely contributed.

3 The Muslim Brotherhood's 'Virtuous Society': A Pious Road *Inside* the State[3]

The entrenchment of MB and regime networks first relates to the historical conditions of the Brotherhood's re-emergence starting from the 1970s, when its leaders were gradually released from jail after Nasser's era of repression.[4] How Sadat's policies contributed to this re-emergence, incidentally or not, is well documented. While the MB never recovered its legal status as an organisation, it was informally granted margins of tolerance within which to redevelop its activities. Drawing from the register of religious legitimacy, the regime encouraged the expansion of Islamic social institutions to alleviate the effects of economic liberalisation. Egyptian entrepreneurs who had migrated and made a fortune in the Gulf, some of whom were Muslim Brothers,[5] were urged to invest in the country, especially in real estate. They were granted tax privileges provided they reserved parts of buildings they constructed for the creation of private mosques, run by charitable associations and often hosting social, health and education services. Such large 'Islamic complexes' multiplied exponentially (Ben Néfissa, 1995). MB businessmen coming back from Gulf countries relied on the support of important 'brokers'[6] inside ruling economic circles.[7] Pro-MB brokers were found, as well, inside the prestigious institution of al-Azhar, comprising the major mosque in Egypt, a large university, and several other bodies that exert authority on religious affairs. While this institution represents state Islam, some of its influential *ulama* profited from Sadat's emphasis on religion

---

3 This refers to Utvik (2006).

4 The Society of the Muslim Brotherhood was initially founded in 1928 by Hasan al-Banna as a charitable association, but it soon became a mass political movement. It supported the Free Officers Movement and coup in 1952, and briefly benefited from special treatment, escaping the dissolution that was to be the fate of all other groups, associations, and parties. However, the relationship with Nasser deteriorated quickly, and in 1954 the regime cracked down on the Brotherhood and dissolved it, arresting and sometimes condemning to death its leaders and numbers of activists.

5 Between 1954 and 1970, many members of the Brotherhood escaped repression by fleeing to the Arabian Peninsula's states. Saudi Arabia welcomed the MB refugees, with whom the Saudi royal family shared a common enemy—Nasser and pan-Arabist socialism. These favourable conditions enabled many Muslim Brothers to start what later became flourishing businesses.

6 On the notion of *passeurs de scène* or 'brokers' in the context of Islamists' relationship to the state, see Camau and Geisser (2003).

7 Examples include multimillionaire 'Uthman Ahmed 'Uthman, and the al-Sharif and Mar'i families (al-Awadi, 2004).

to become vocal and push for increased social and legal re-islamisation (Zeghal, 1996). Al-Azhar also operates a huge network of primary and secondary schools situated all over the country, which welcomed some of the now numerous MB teachers. Additionally, the regime favoured the development of 'Islamic clubs' (*gama'at islamiyya*) in universities, in order to counter leftist movements. A generation of young activists, placing reference to Islam at the core of their discourse and practices, emerged and gradually connected with the Brotherhood's released leaders. During the 1980s and 1990s, the movement recreated a broad, cross-class social base, pursuing its actions through universities and charities, but also through the professional syndicates of doctors, engineers, pharmacists, etc., which the generation of young activists came to lead. This social involvement sustained the MB's—unofficial but important—participation in legislative and local elections under Mubarak's rule. They achieved electoral gains in the 1980s and, most importantly, in 2005 when they managed to win 88 out of 444 seats in parliament—that is, around 20 per cent.

The Islamic social sector was thus anything but detached from the state: it lay at the centre of the regime's economic and political policies of welfare relocation. While the MB's implantation into this entrenched Islamic sector was effective, this does not mean that the regime's supporters were not also present there. Many pious local NDP notables founded and ran Islamic charitable associations, or ran the boards of mosques, *zakat* committees and so on. Moreover, a large number of charitable organisations or government-affiliated community development associations (CDAs), although not centred on a mosque or not claiming explicit religious motivations, would offer Islamic activities such as readings from the Koran. In fact, religious activities permeated many spaces: for example, every administrative unit or public company would have its own *zakat* committee or pilgrimage association. Conversely, my fieldwork among the lower- and middle-ranked members of the Brotherhood showed that many of them were active inside state-sponsored public work structures, such as youth centres, CDAs or solidarity cooperatives in the workplace. This was especially the case of the MB candidates in elections, in line with the spirit of services defining the role of the elected representative (Vannetzel, 2016).

During their 2005–2010 mandate, the MB Members of Parliament promoted as their motto: 'Together, we bring goodness to Egypt' (*ma'an, nahammal al-khayr li-Misr*). This encapsulated both the MB's compliance to the idea of the spirit of services defining the role of Members of Parliament, in line with the regime's strategies, and the pivotal role of religion in the politics of goodness, hence showing how the imaginary of state developmentalism was, in its turn, influenced by the MB's discursive repertoire.

This is not to say that the Muslim Brothers were spared from repression. Following their 2005 electoral success, they were subjected to a campaign of arrests, asset seizure and military trials. And this was not the first time their relationship with Mubarak's regime had significantly deteriorated. Earlier, in the 1990s, the government had intended to contain the MB's rising profile, which was at the time especially supported by the vocal professional syndicates. These syndicates were officially 'frozen' (i.e. not dissolved but internal elections and several activities were forbidden) and the regime cracked down on prominent figures of the movement who were tried in military tribunals. The regime also strengthened its control over charitable associations, dismantling some of those that appeared to be obviously affiliated to the Brotherhood. Around 1,400 assumed Brotherhood members, ranging from national leaders to local activists, were arrested during the 1995 legislative elections. From then on, illegality and semi-clandestinity increasingly shaped the complex mechanisms of the movement's social embeddedness.

Paradoxically, these constraints furthered the entrenchment of local social networks. As long as the MB's presence was not *that* visible, it was tolerated—although the margin of visibility allowed varied in time and space. MB activists would then participate as mere members with no leading responsibilities, in 'normal' associations (i.e., those not obviously affiliated to the MB), explicitly Islamic or not. In some cases, they reportedly acted as informal leaders alongside associations' official boards run by non-MB individuals who could be sympathisers, friends, relatives or simply neighbours. Boards could also include, among their 'non-MB' members, low-profile activists, not known to be Muslim Brothers by either the security services or by the people around them. Another strategy consisted in setting up charitable endeavours without a legal framework, such as 'medical caravans' (groups of physicians present in an area for a day or two and providing medical consultations for free in the rooms of a friendly association, mosque, or school …) food distribution programmes during religious festivities, the provision of clothing or school supplies, or collecting *zakat* in the neighbourhood, outside of any formal structure.

All of these activities were implemented without explicit mention of the term 'Muslim Brotherhood'. Only very rarely did activists declare that they were MB members. Usually, they were active in such structures without being *directly* identified as Muslim Brothers by the people they worked with (even if the security services knew of their affiliations, they would let them work as long as they kept a low profile). This enabled the MB to connect with many local figures who were also active in the charitable sector, including figures who might happen to be NDP members. They could then, for example, participate together, as colleagues, in the *zakat* committee or pilgrimage association of their workplace. An association could be run by local notables, more or less close to the NDP, and include among its members one or several MB activists. A businessman wishing to give alms to the poor could go to a neighbour, known for his or her involvement in charitable work—guessing or not that he or she was a member of the MB—who would play the role of intermediary, selecting needy families and transmitting to them the gifts of their generous benefactor. In fact, the pervasiveness of the Islamic social network, which permeated many spheres of life in Egypt, and the low-profile nature of 'MB identity' made connections easier between Muslim Brothers and pious individuals willing to share (for reasons of personal interest or not) in *khayr*—that is, in goodness. Most of the time, people would just identify a MB, at first, as a good person, serving people and God, doing *khayr*.

The sector of *khayr* was, then, a diffused network of blurred identities and crossed cleavages.[8] However, it was clearly not immune from conflicts, which we can analyse through two patterns: *repression by uncertainty* on the one hand, and *imputation struggles* on the other. Apart from episodes of direct violence, such as the 1992–95 and 2006–08 waves of arrests, repression was usually exerted through indirect, non-systematic and unclear means, as is often the case in authoritarian contexts (Hibou, 2006). The margin of tolerance granted to the MB was continuously renegotiated at national and local levels alike. For example, submitting associations, whether linked to the Muslim Brothers or not, to a 'pending registration' status for many years was a well-known means to prevent them from securing their activities: it gave authorities the legal right to dissolve them at any time. In spite of their legal position as elected representatives, MB deputies were themselves confronted with uncertainty on a daily basis when they organised social activities in public: 'Sometimes the state security forces come at the last minute and take away all the chairs and the material we have set up in order to prevent the event from happening', explained one member of a local team, 'then we have to quickly find another solution, like using the deputy's office, even if it is too small'.[9] Punctual detentions also constituted a permanent and arbitrary threat: I recall how the son of a deputy was arrested in the street, just in front of his father's office, for no obvious reason, while the latter was left to freely do his job—even if parliamentary immunity could easily be removed. In summer 2007, two MB deputies had their parliamentary immunity rescinded and were indicted for trying to reconstitute

8 The current difficulties that Marshal al-Sisi's regime is meeting in response to its efforts to eradicate the MB's social services is further evidence of this situation of entrenchment (Brooke, 2015).

9 Interview, July 2009, Helwan, Cairo.

the forbidden organisation of the Muslim Brothers. But the conflicts were not limited to the predatory practices of the security apparatus. *Repression by uncertainty* took place against the background of wider *imputation struggles*—that is, the competition to be perceived as 'the one who serves' and to enjoy the symbolic benefit of social actions. While the MB activists I met repeated at length that 'we have no problems if the NDP tried to imitate us and steal our ideas', they strove to distinguish themselves in the manner in which they delivered their own services. Although they could not say, for reasons of security, that they were Muslim Brothers, they deployed great efforts to let beneficiaries understand, or believe, that the aid came from the MB—even when it actually came from the budget of an association in which a Muslim Brother was only active as an individual. Reciprocally, in local associations where both MB and NDP notables were active, the latter would deny that any of the members was a Muslim Brother (Vannetzel, 2016).

Two cases illustrate perfectly the various combinatorial modalities of the conflictual consensus framing the politics of goodness. The first is the Islamic Medical Association (IMA), founded in 1977 by certain well-known Brothers, which ran 22 hospitals and several specialised medical centres, considered as *khayri* because low-cost fees or even a policy of free care were applied for low-income patients. While the association was obviously affiliated with the MB, it was spared dissolution because the government could not afford to deprive the population of such a range of medical services. However, in spite of the tolerance granted at the national level, the MB were eager, at the local level, to include many who were not MB members as members of staff or of the boards of the hospitals and health units. In al-Hadi hospital of Helwan, in a southern suburb of Cairo, only 5 per cent of the staff were Brothers, some doctors were NDP members, and the board included non-Brothers, according to its director: 'This is because the Brothers don't just want to mix with each other; on the contrary they want to cooperate with all the elements of society [...] There is nothing inside the hospital that would suggest it belongs to the Brothers. But people know this doctor or that is a leader of the Brothers, because they saw him during the elections'.[10] Hence, the IMA was both a vector of entrenchment and of gratitude imputation for the MB. The second case is that of the Sharia Association (*Gam'iyya al-Shar'iyya*, GS), one of the oldest and biggest Islamic charitable associations and active throughout Egypt. Sarah Ben Néfissa shows how, under Sadat's regime, this association had become a para-public organisation and how the regime instrumentalised it in order to implement 'the new social policy [of] charity "on behalf" of Islam' (Ben Néfissa, 2003, 222, authors'

10 Interview, August 2009, Helwan, Cairo.

transl.). The MBs were allowed to deeply integrate into the regional and local offices of the association, until 1990. In that year, their victory in the elections to the central board led to a change in the attitude of the regime towards this situation, and the board was suddenly dissolved. However, many MB activists remained active in the numerous local branches, and were often among the founders. But far from being reserved exclusively for the MB, the GS was also a place for local figures, including those close to the NDP, who sought to prove their spirit of service. It was, then, a place for interactions that cut across political identities.

The GS example is also illustrative of the second argument I would like to make here: namely, that the MB's model of 'virtuous society' is embedded in an imaginary matrix of faith-based developmentalism to which other groups and institutions, including elements of the state, contribute. The relationship between the visions of development promoted by the MB on the one hand and the regime on the other should, then, not be analysed being as extraneous, but as being 'intertextual' (Bayart, 1985, 355).

4 The Intertextuality of Faith-Based Developmentalism

One of the most famous programmes run by the GS, which accounts for much of its popularity, was established under the leadership of the Muslim Brothers: the 'Orphan project' (*Kafalat al-Yatim*). It consists in identifying people ('godfathers') who wish to sponsor one or more orphans in their neighbourhood. The 'godfather' pays a monthly sum to the GS, which passes it on to the mother or guardian of the child, who must know nothing of the sponsorship. As Ben Néfissa explains, quoting from internal documents of the association: 'This sponsorship is a form of contract between the [GS] and the godfather [...]. The aim is "to correct the relationship between the orphan and his or her entourage. Instead of having relationships with individuals who assist him, he must have a relationship with Muslim society at large, which becomes directly responsible for him". The unknown godfather is therefore a kind of "symbol" or representative of this Muslim society' (Ben Néfissa, 2003, 244, author's transl.). To complement this sponsorship, the GS also contacts members of the local community, asking craftsmen, merchants, doctors of all specialisms, pharmacists, bakers, hairdressers, butchers, etc. to provide—according to their means—food, care, medicines, school supplies, clothes, etc. to the orphans. The project's presentation document states that 'the project is in itself an act of preaching, a link between members of society, rich and poor, and a vitalisation of solidarity and mutual aid as explained by Islam [...] the project's goal is not only to support the orphan but to involve people in this support' (Ben Néfissa, 2003, 245, author's transl.).

A similar pattern was at work in other charitable projects run by the Muslim Brothers, such as 'medical caravans' or collective weddings for poor or orphaned youths who could not afford to marry. Local physicians, citizens and merchants were solicited to help with gifts and services, according to their means and to 'their conscience and conviction' (Ben Néfissa, 2003, 245, author's transl.). In these three examples, the GS and the MB sought to act as the *organisers* of local mutual aid, solidarity and individual conscious involvement, which should define—from their perspective—'virtuous Muslim society' (*al-mugtama' al-muslim al-salih*). In this model, conveyed through daily practice and talks, which I observed during my fieldwork, the individual is defined by his inner moral 'positivity' (*igabiyya*), which is latent in each person of faith. Every Muslim will possess—because of his or her faith—the seeds of positivity, which may grow. The individual is responsible for developing this latent disposition to virtue through the accomplishment of virtuous acts (*a'mal saliha*). Virtuous acts are the product of this inner strength, but it is also by engaging in virtuous acts that one manages to develop this strength. This personal striving for moral transformation is seen as the cornerstone of social reform and development. The role of the MB is therefore to detect individuals and encourage them to become positive elements in society. Programmes like the 'Orphan project', 'medical caravans' or collective weddings are not only aimed at relieving poverty, they also urge individuals to fulfil their roles as 'virtuous citizens' (*muwatinin salihin*), responsible for the social, economic and political order. This was, ultimately, the meaning of the traditional slogan of the Brotherhood, 'Islam is the solution'.

This model of 'virtuous society' is, of course, directly inspired by the MB's ideological corpus. According to Hasan al-Banna's text of reference, quoted at length by the activists and in the Brotherhood's publications even today, the 'MB method' (*al-minhag*) consists in shaping the Muslim individual, then the Muslim family, then Muslim society and finally the Islamic government, state, caliphate and nation (*umma*). This method, referred to as the 'guidance of society' (*irshad al-mugtama'*), assumes that the moral transformation of the self, thanks to faith and piety, is instrumental in building a good, sound and strong society, which, in turn, ensures the moral preservation of human souls. Hence, it is claimed to be a method for successful social development, to be applied in every domain of human life, with a focus on both individual behaviours and collective, institutional frames (Utvik, 2006).

If this model of development owes much to Hasan al-Banna's heritage, the idea of 'virtuous society' should not be isolated from other discursive repertoires to which it refers, and which add various layers of significance. We have already seen its centrality in the GS tradition. Saba Mahmood, in her ethnographic study of the mosques movement in Egypt—a movement of female preachers and pious women, which has emerged since the 1970s, with no organisational link to the Brotherhood—also showed how the notion of 'virtuous acts' was core to the conception of piety promoted by the movement (Mahmood, 2005). To these women, faith lay, first and foremost, in the daily performance of virtuous acts. They referred to the doctrine of al-Azhar *'alim*, Shaykh Sayyid Sabiq (who had been both a companion of Hasan al-Banna and a minister under Nasser) whose *Fiqh al-Sunna* stands as an authoritative *vade mecum* for virtuous actions. More generally, al-Azhar actively disseminated the conception of Islam as a virtuous behaviour that should be accomplished in all human activities. During my fieldwork, I often noticed that sympathisers of the Muslim Brothers had attended the Azhari school system, and they even used to draw an explicit link between the 'Islam they had learnt from al-Azhar' and the 'Islam promoted by the MB'. One of them expressed it in the following way:

'The Muslim Brothers seek for goodness (*khayr*) and I love *khayr*, I strive for *khayr*. They are virtuous citizens, and I hope to be a virtuous citizen as well. I am not a member of the Brotherhood, but I am just like them, I love Islam and I understand Islam like them. [...] Since primary school, I was in the Azhari system. And al-Azhar's thought is the same as the MB's thought. We have learnt the correct comprehension of Islam. Islam, religion, is a behavior (*mu'amala*).'[11]

The emphasis on virtuous behaviour has also found a new and powerful formulation since the late 1990s. Indeed, the mantra of 'Development through faith' has been praised by Egyptian preaching 'superstar' Amr Khaled,[12] and his association 'Life Makers' (*Sunna' al-Hayat*), which has dramatically spread throughout Egypt and across the MENA region. Calling on 'Muslims to become pious and entrepreneurial subjects', Khaled 'uses management science and self-help rhetoric to promote entrepreneurial activities as religious, with an emphasis on the role that voluntary work plays' (Atia, 2012, 809). Khaled's vision has built likewise on the idea of piety as a source of social positivity,

11 Interview, August 2009, Madinat Nasr, Cairo.

12 Amr Khaled is one of the 'new preachers' (*al-shuyukh al-gudad*) who have gained momentum in Egypt since the late 1990s and who have created a new form of preaching, focused on inner spirituality, self-fulfillment, individual emotions and efforts to ensure a successful life (see Haenni, 2002).

but compared to the MB's 'virtuous society' it has focused much more on the values of productivity, efficiency and economic success. As Patrick Haenni underlines, this rhetoric has resonated perfectly with the model of 'pious neo-liberalism' (Atia, 2012, 811) directly inspired by the United States' 'compassionate conservatism' and promoted by the neo-liberal 'new guard' of the NDP (Haenni, 2005b).

As such, despite its various formulations by state Islam's official institution (al-Azhar) and by the neo-liberal wing of the NDP, the discourse on 'virtuous individuals' exhibiting 'good behaviour' as a positive element for *khayr* and the development of society could be interpreted as a counter-narrative to the state developmentalist myth. However, it was actually close to a model that had been actively promoted by Mubarak's regime as part of the politics of goodness: the model of '*al-maghud al-dhati*'—literally, '*effort on oneself*'. It was propagated from the 1980s onwards, when the state began cutting social service provision. This was also the time when international development agencies were shifting their focus to poverty alleviation, which was embodied, in Egypt, by the establishment of the Social Fund for Development in 1991: the fund embraced microlending as a main strategy, behind which 'stands the supposition that devolving development down to "the people" is not only a good thing but also a moral imperative' (Elyachar, 2002). In 1988, the notion of '*al-maghud al-dhati*' was introduced into law through a reform of the state local-level administration (Law No. 145 of 1988): in order to compensate for weak local taxes and a decrease in budget allocation, the law indicates that administrative units have to appeal to the 'spontaneous' efforts of local populations in order to fund public projects, such as the building or repairing of post offices, police stations, medical centres, youth centres, public parks, and the state's local service departments, etc. (Ben Néfissa, 2009). Local communities often have no choice but to participate in such endeavours. Hence, the *maghud al-dhati* appears as a constraining 'spontaneous' effort, closely organised and controlled by the state. In fact, the Muslim Brothers directly referred to this notion as well, when they were charged with political mandates as Members of Parliament or while sitting on local councils. It was actually coupled with the notion of 'virtuous society', and reframed as a faithful endeavour in which the MB would be in charge of organising 'positive efforts', not against the state but, more often than not, in tacit cooperation with it.

In Helwan, there were many examples of cooperation between the MB Member of Parliament and local administrative units, for the funding of certain projects in the name of *al-maghud al-dhati*. These examples illustrate how imaginaries—from *al-maghud al-dhati* to virtuous participation as in the

'Orphan project'—framed both a competitive and a common ground on which actors evolved. One member the MP's staff explained:

> The officials of the Ministry of Education came to see us to ask if we would finance the furnishing of a new office space they were given. As a teacher, I know them a little so I was in charge of the case. I suggested that the deputy could make an official request to the governor, but they refused. They didn't want it to be so visible—they wanted hidden cooperation, they wanted us to find them private donors, using our network as members of the Brothers. I will help them because I can't let them sit on the floor, they don't even have chairs! We will go to see the furniture merchants we know, ask for some chairs from one, shelves from another … They will give them to me if they can, because they know I am not doing this for myself; it is voluntary work, and they may want to make a donation. Normally though, there should be a budget for this, since it is not always possible to count on the *maghud al-dhati* …

Asked why the MP's staff would cooperate with representatives of the regime, this activist answered:

> Our role is to give them ideas so they can find solutions to problems. Our goal is to cooperate in helping to reform the country, because it is our duty, according to Islam, to our morality, and to our love for the nation. […] What is important is that work be done. Maybe we, as Muslim Brothers, won't benefit from this work; but it is done and it serves people, and this is part of our religion. Serving people is like praying and loving God. Our prophet (Prayer of God be upon him and peace) said that if on the Day of the Last Judgement you find a seed, you must plant it. This is a core value of Islam.[13]

'Doing *khayr*' is supposed to be an act that one is engaged in for moral motives, for the service of the people, and for the development of the country, not for political reasons. Politics were burdened with the delegitimising picture sketched by Nasser's regime. It was considered a potential source of instability. The combination of *khayr*, development (*tanmiyya*) and stability (*istiqrar*) was central to the regime's rhetoric for limiting political opposition (Makram-Ebeid, 2012). However, it was also nurtured by the MB itself. The activists I met insisted that their aim was that, 'services be provided and good actions done,

---

13 Interview, January 2009, Helwan, Cairo.

no matter who did it'. They also refrained from engaging in open clashes with the regime, claiming that 'clashes provoke instability, which is not good for the country'. However, this was not only a strategy with which to protect themselves from repression; and nor was it obvious proof of their involvement in the authoritarian coalition. It was more deeply in line with their vision of politics as the *moral reform of behaviours*. As one member of a MP's staff, put it: 'I cannot lump together all the members of the NDP or the representatives of the regime; I don't judge the institutions, I judge each one's behaviour. I cannot say "this institution is not good", I say "this behaviour is not good".'[14]

Therefore, the politics of goodness distanced itself from clashes and favoured a steady but subtle battle to put forward one's ability to be of service and one's moral exemplarity. While political conflicts were regarded as damaging to development and stability, moral distinction was understood, by the MB and the regime alike, as a 'positive' way of achieving goodness. This euphemistic form of politics was heavily undermined during the 2011–2013 period.

5 'Goodness' in Dire Straits: The Breakdown of Local Politics and the Radicalisation of Conflicts

The politics of goodness under Mubarak's rule had, to summarise, three defining features. It was, first, a relocation of the state developmentalist myth into the micro-level of the spirit of services, placed on the shoulders of local elites. Second, it was a configuration made of overlapping networks of public work and charities, in which political identities were often blurred. Lastly, it was a conflictual consensus in which political antagonisms were understated. My argument is that the three components of this politics of goodness were challenged after Mubarak's overthrow in February 2011. Although such an argument does not account, alone, for all the dynamics of conflictual radicalisation that the period 2011–2013 witnessed, I will begin by focusing on the local level, which has been less commented upon.

The foundations of local politics were upset by the revolutionary turmoil. Parliament and local councils were dissolved, as was the NDP, following an order issued by the Supreme Administrative Court in April 2011. The reach of these dissolutions went far beyond the spectacular burning of the former governing party's headquarters in downtown Cairo. In concrete terms, it meant that tens of thousands of local elites were deprived of their positions. Many of them, fearing prosecution, also suspended their public work activities and

14 Interview, January 2009, Helwan, Cairo.

opted to adopt a low profile for several months. These local elites therefore stopped acting as the everyday interfaces of the state. The micro-level spirit of services broke down and ceased to play the role of a substitute for state intervention. This was cruelly felt by large parts of the population who suffered from growing poverty and who now even lacked informal access to patronage, adding to the fact that many state administrative units had ceased functioning. While local councils remained dissolved with no elections in sight, high expectations were placed on the parliament that was to be elected at the end of 2011. For many people, struggling on a day-to-day basis for survival, the return of parliament meant the return of a potential source of material aid, which—although seemingly negligible—did matter in this economy of survival.

It came as no surprise when the Muslim Brotherhood, followed by the Salafis, both perceived as being able to meet these expectations (Masoud, 2014), won the 2011 parliamentary elections, while those parties that embodied the spirit of the revolution did not do well. However, it seems that MB Members of Parliament turned their backs on local services and charities, and—rather—tried to dedicate themselves to legislative work: work that most of them were not used to conducting and for which they certainly lacked the requisite competences. Moreover, the chamber was caught up in an institutional battle, as the High Constitutional Court, supported by the interim military government, threatened to dissolve it—eventually succeeding. Anticipating this dissolution, MB deputies were eager to pass laws securing their presence in the Constitutive Assembly that was to be formed. They also focused on passing the Political Isolation Law, which banned officials who had served in top posts under Mubarak from running for election. Although the law was eventually suppressed when the chamber was dissolved, a related article was later included in the Constitution that Morsi introduced in late 2012.

This move from *khidma* to legislation allegedly led to much disgruntlement among voters, who deplored the MB's neglect of local demands. It also sparked anger among former NDP notables who considered the Political Isolation Law a potential threat, while many expected the MB to be as cooperative as it had showed itself to be towards the military and high-ranking businessmen of the Mubarak era. A fear of the 'Brotherhoodisation' of all institutions—whether reasonable or not—became rampant. Former NDP notables worried especially about local councils—which used to be their sanctuaries—the elections for which were constantly postponed while parliament drafted a new law with which to govern them. Many believed this to be a sign of MB manipulation, an effort to assert complete hegemony, and began mobilising against the Brotherhood (Hamdy and Vannetzel, 2014). Hence, the blurred local environment of overlapping networks and identities unravelled and gave way to sharpening cleavages. A dramatic shift in the local landscape added to this growing polarisation: while the NDP disappeared as a structured organisation, conversely, the Muslim Brothers suddenly appeared more prominently in the public sphere leaving their clandestinity behind. At this time, many people suddenly discovered who in their entourage was a member of the MB. As one inhabitant of Helwan, where the MB was deeply rooted, put it: 'Before, the Muslim Brothers were like fish under the water. And then suddenly they came to the surface. My neighbour, my relative ... We discovered that they were Brothers. They showed themselves, saying "we are here; we are strong".'[15]

The breakdown of former local politics—that is to say, the rupture of patronage and the increasing dissociation and conflictualisation of political identities and cleavages—intersected with several national and international dynamics and temporalities of radicalisation. Among them, two contributed to undermining the legitimacy both of the politics of goodness and of the Muslim Brotherhood.

First, the 2011 uprising, and before and after it the thousands of social protests that have spread throughout Egypt in the last decade or more, indicate that *khayr* is contextually not enough to sustain the paradox of 'state developmentalism without a developmentalist state'. More precisely, though these protests are not a mere consequence of a so-called lack of development, they are moments in which the politics of goodness is variously questioned, criticised, and reinterpreted, and—at least partially—rejected. Protests shed a crude light on the contradiction between the developmentalism myth and the deregulation of social protection, and have made that contradiction, in Egypt as elsewhere (Catusse et al., 2010; Allal and Bennafla, 2011), obvious and unbearable for a growing proportion of the population. The last decade, indeed, has seen the conjunction of endless protests, the wide scale privatisation of public companies, a rapid rise in the precariousness of labour (even in what remains of the public sector) (Makram-Ebeid, 2012), and the vertiginous rise of food prices due to the international financial crisis that began in 2008 (for which abovementioned state subsidies were not enough to compensate). Meanwhile, the vocal, neo-liberal wing of the NDP, gathered around Gamal Mubarak whose longing to become president has caused much resentment (Hassabo, 2012) and has given a new face to the regime; a face that clearly fails to fit the image of the protective state, and thus has unmasked the aforementioned paradox. The relocation of welfare into goodness is thus strongly put in question, in these times of rising demand for genuine social justice (*'adala igtima'iyya*) and for radical change in distributional policies.

15 Interview, June 2014, Helwan, Cairo.

Second, in this context, social expectations of protection from the state are particularly high. They are incidentally supported by a currently powerful international trend, sponsored by political and financial organisations, which reasserts the need for strong state leadership, able to prevent the collapse of institutions and to eradicate the threat of 'terrorism' (Nay, 2013) while continuing to deregulate economies. In Egypt, social aspirations of security and welfare have focused on the two major symbols of historical Egyptian state developmentalism—that is to say, the army and the president. While the image of the president as *za'im* and saviour of the nation was being revived by those expectations of state protection, Mohamed Morsi was cast in this role and did not manage to fit in it. Some judged Morsi was a 'good man, but he was a loser' (*ragil kwayyes bes fashil*): he was unable to govern 'a state that is too big for him', as a former Morsi voter told me. Beyond his lack of charisma, the absence of an economic programme, or the neo-liberal agenda, all of which have been commented on and denounced at length, I argue that this is also because *khayr*, of which the MB was the local champion, just did not meet the renewed demand for genuine state intervention. Others considered Morsi a real threat to the Egyptian state: he was quickly depicted, in the media, as the puppet of the Muslim Brotherhood's leadership office—the 'Guidance Office'—which many feared would thus take control of the state. Behind the very irreverent nickname, '*al-kharouf*' (the sheep), given to him by the press, there was more than the politicisation of a body of journalists against the MB: there was the idea that the MB was weakening the autonomy of the state, submitting it to the will of their own organisation.

6 Conclusion. Conflicts and Consensus of Development in al-Sisi's Egypt

To conclude, what is at issue in post-Mubarak Egypt goes far beyond the failure of the Muslim Brotherhood. Neither can it be defined as a clash between two opposite models of society—that is to say, the Islamist model versus the legacy of Nasser's state. The common vision of a conflict of development in which Islamists would oppose regime incumbents, and would be relegated to a separate field of religious philanthropy, has been deconstructed. State- and faith-based discourses, beliefs and practices, aimed to 'develop' society, used to be deeply entangled. The biggest contradictory tension was to be found between the survival of the imaginary of state developmentalism and the effectiveness of neo-liberalisation. In the space created by this tension, the politics of goodness was deployed, involving actors from the former regime and the

MB alike. Behind the consensus around *khayr* as an illusive avatar of state developmentalism in neo-liberal times, those actors struggled to secure positions of power on both political and moral grounds. What we are now witnessing is the crumbling of this consensus. Not only have the former micro-networks of *khayr* been dismantled with the reshaping of local political elites (in 2015, inexperienced supporters of al-Sisi supplanted former NDP members in parliament; and the MB has, so far, not been granted any margin of tolerance); but the local and national dynamics of the politics of goodness—that is to say, the relocation of welfare in the spirit of services and the survival of the developmentalist myth—have broken down.

The radicalisation of conflicts during the revolutionary period has highlighted the contradiction of neo-liberal state developmentalism and, in the course of time, altered the equation of conflict and development. In emic and academic discourses alike, open conflict has widely been seen as a hindrance to stability, and stability has consensually been linked to development. Throughout 2011–2012, recurrent street demonstrations, organised by groups of young revolutionaries, were thus harshly dismissed by the political elites—the military, the MB, and all the so-called civil political parties—by the media, and by large parts of the population tired by a lack of security (*infilat amni*) and by economic paralysis. Demonstrations, seen as chaotic expressions of conflict, were more and more seen as damaging to the 'wheels of production' (*'agalat al-intag*), a metaphor which became an overwhelming and formidable weapon that could be used to discredit anyone. Once elected, members of the MB were soon decried as the spanner in those wheels. While the struggle against incumbents to occupy positions of power intensified, they were accused of, and seen as, hurting the state itself, and consequently seen as breaking the motor of development from within. The revolt against Morsi, framed as a positive conflict with the goal of saving the state and relaunching the 'wheels of production', had the strong effect of refocusing expectations with regard to welfare on the state at the national level—away from local *khayr* practices.

The new consensus that emerged around al-Sisi was largely a consensus around this announced relocation of development to the state itself, with the army as guarantor. However, two years after Marshal al-Sisi's election as president, it is clear that the new regime has advanced neo-liberalisation further by cutting energy subsidies and has relocated the *economy*, rather than development, into the military, rather than into the public, sector. Military holding companies now monopolise the benefits of al-Sisi's policy of 'grandiose projects', causing much anger, both among private businessmen and among the working classes, who see no improvement in their conditions. Even the attempt to revive the glorious myth of state developmentalism with the pharaonic construction of the New Suez Canal, entirely overseen by the Egyptian armed forces, seems unable to cope with the asymmetries of accumulation and their conflictualisation. As a precarious worker, employed in a private textile factory in Helwan, told me angrily, addressing al-Sisi one year after having voted for him: 'The Suez Canal—you did it for you, yourself! But what have you done for us, so far?' As consensus crumbles around al-Sisi and the army alike, conflicts—on the rise—might begin to be seen as the necessary formula for development.

References

Abdelrahman, M. (2015) *Egypt's Long Revolution: Protest Movements and Uprisings* (New York: Routledge, Taylor & Francis).

Achcar, G. (2013) *The People Want. A Radical Exploration of the Arab Uprising* (Berkeley, Los Angeles: University of California Press).

Adly, A. (2013) *State Reform and Development in the Middle East. Turkey and Egypt in the Post-Liberalization Era* (London, New York: Routledge).

Allal, A. and K. Bennafla (2011) 'Les mouvements protestataires de Gafsa (Tunisie) et Sidi Ifni (Maroc) de 2005 à 2009. Des mobilisations en faveur du réengagement de l'Etat ou contre l'ordre politique ?' *Tiers Monde*, Hors-série, pp. 27–46, DOI: 10.3917/rtm.hs01.0027.

Atia, M. (2012) 'A Way to Paradise: Pious Neo-liberalism, Islam, and Faith-Based Development', *Annals of the Association of American Geographers*, 102(4), pp. 808–827, DOI: 10.1080/00045608.2011.627046.

Al-Awadi, H. (2004) *In Pursuit of Legitimacy. The Muslim Brothers and Mubarak, 1982–2000* (London: Tauris).

Bayart, J.-F. (1985) 'L'énonciation du politique', *Revue française de science politique*, 3, pp. 343–373, http://www.persee.fr/doc/rfsp_0035-2950_1985_num_35_3_411322 (accessed on 5 June 2016).

Beinin, J. and M. Duboc (2014) 'Mouvement ouvrier, luttes syndicales et processus révolutionnaire en Égypte, 2006–2013', in M. Camau and F. Vairel (eds.), *Soulèvements et recompositions politiques dans le monde arabe*, (Montréal: Presses de l'Université de Montréal), pp. 121–142.

Ben Néfissa, S. (2009) 'Cairo's City Government: the Crisis of Local Administration and the Refusal of Urban Citizenship', in D. Singerman (ed.), *Cairo Contested, Governance, Urban Space and Global Modernity* (Cairo, New York: The American University in Cairo Press), pp. 177–197.

Ben Néfissa, S. (2003) 'Citoyenneté morale en Égypte: une association entre Etat et Frères musulmans', in S. Ben Néfissa et al. (eds.) *ONG et gouvernance dans le monde arabe* (Paris, Le Caire: Karthala/CEDEJ).

Ben Néfissa, S. (1995) 'Les ligues régionales et les associations islamiques en Egypte: deux formes de regroupement à vocation sociale et caritative', *Tiers Monde*, 36(141), pp. 163–177, DOI: 10.3406/tiers.1995.4951.

Ben Néfissa, S. and A. Arafat (2005) *Vote et démocratie dans l'Égypte contemporaine* (Paris, Le Caire: Karthala/CEDEJ).

Bianchi, R. (1989) *Unruly corporatism, Egyptian associational life in the 20th century* (New York, Oxford: OUP).

Bibars, I. (2001) *Victims and Heroines: Women, Welfare and the Egyptian State* (London, New York: Zed).

Brooke, S. (2015) 'The Muslim Brotherhood's social outreach after the Egyptian coup', *Brookings Institution Working paper*, http://www.brookings.edu/~/media/Research/Files/Reports/2015/07/rethinking-political-islam/Egypt_Brooke-FINALE.pdf?la=en (accessed on 30 May 2016).

Camau, M. and V. Geisser (2003) *Le Syndrome autoritaire. Politique en Tunisie de Bourguiba à Ben Ali* (Paris: Presses de Sciences Po).

Catusse, M. (2006) 'Ordonner, classer, penser la société: Les pays arabes au prisme de l'économie politique', in E. Picard (ed.), *La Politique dans le monde arabe* (Paris: Armand Colin), pp. 215–238.

Catusse, M., B. Destremau and E. Verdier (eds.) (2010) *L'État face aux débordements du social. Formation, travail et protection sociale* (Aix, Paris: Iremam-Karthala).

Elyachar, J. (2002) 'Empowerment Money: The World Bank, Non-Governmental Organizations, and the Value of Culture in Egypt', *Public Culture*, 14(3), pp. 493–513, DOI: 10.1215/08992363-14-3-493.

Fahmy, N. (2002) *The Politics of Egypt: State-society relationship* (London, New York: Routledge).

Farah, N. (2009) *Egypt's Political Economy: Power Relations in Development* (Cairo: American University Press in Cairo).

Gobe, E. (1999) *Les hommes d'affaires égyptiens. Démocratisation et secteur privé dans l'Egypte de l'infitah* (Paris: Karthala).

Haenni, P. (2005a) *L'ordre des caïds. Conjurer la dissidence urbaine au Caire* (Paris, Le Caire: Karthala-CEDEJ).

Haenni, P. (2005b) *L'islam de marché. L'autre révolution conservatrice* (Paris: Seuil).

Haenni, P. (2002) 'Au-delà du repli identitaire ... Les nouveaux prêcheurs égyptiens et la modernisation paradoxale de l'islam', *Religioscope*, http://www.religioscope.com/pdf/precheurs.pdf (accessed on 30 May 2016).

Hamdy, M. and M. Vannetzel (2014) 'Egypte, la politique au village: le surprenant itinéraire d'un feloul', *Orient XXI*, 24 March, http://orientxxi.info/magazine/egypte-la-politique-au-village,0548 (accessed on 5 June 2016).

Harrigan, J. and H. El Said (2009) *Economic Liberalisation, Social Capital and Islamic Welfare Provision* (Hampshire, New York: Palgrave Macmillan).

Hassabo, C. (2012) *La stabilité du régime Moubarak à l'épreuve d'une "situation de succession prolongée": les limites de la consolidation autoritaire*, PhD thesis (Grenoble: Institut d'études politiques).

Hibou, B. (2006) *La force de l'obéissance. Economie politique de la répression en Tunisie*, (Paris: La Découverte).

Ismail, S. (2006) *Political Life in Cairo's New Quarters. Encountering the Everyday State* (Minneapolis, London: University of Minnesota Press).

Mahmood, S. (2005) *Politics of Piety: The Islamic Revival and the Feminist Subject* (Princeton: Princeton University Press).

Makram-Ebeid, D. (2012) *Manufacturing stability: Everyday politics of work in an industrial steel town in Helwan, Egypt*, PhD thesis (London: The London School of Economics and Political Science).

Masoud, T. (2014) *Counting Islam: Religion, Class, and Elections in Egypt* (Cambridge: Cambridge University Press).

Nay, O. (2013) 'Fragile and failed states: Critical perspectives on conceptual hybrids', *International Political Science Review*, 34 (3), pp. 326–341, DOI: 10.1177/0192512113480054.

Richards, A. and J. Waterbury (1996) (eds.) *A Political Economy of the Middle East, Boulder* (Oxford: Westview Press).

Sadowski, Y. (1991) *Political vegetables? Businessmen and bureaucrats in the development of Egyptian agriculture* (Washington: Brookings).

Sfakianakis, J. (2004) 'The Whales of the Nile: Networks, Businessmen and Bureaucrats during the Era of Privatization in Egypt' in S. Heydemann (ed.) *Networks of Privilege: Rethinking the Politics of Economic Reform in the Middle East* (New York: Palgrave Macmillan).

Shawkat, Y. (2014) 'Mubarak's Promise. Social justice and the National Housing Programme: affordable homes or political gain?' *Égypte/Monde arabe*, 3(11), http://ema.revues.org/3318 (accessed on 30 May 2016).

Soliman, S. (2004) *Argent de l'Etat et politique. La difficile sortie de l'Etat rentier en Egypte sous Hosni Moubarak*, PhD thesis (Paris: Institut d'études politiques).

Springborg, R. (2012) 'Gas and Egyptian Development', in R. Looney (ed.), *The Handbook of Oil Politics* (London, New York: Routledge).

Sullivan, D. and S. Abed-Kotob (1999) *Islam in contemporary Egypt: Civil society vs. The State* (Boulder: Lynne Rienner Publishers).

Utvik, B. (2006) *The Pious Road to Development. Islamist Economics in Egypt* (London: Hurst).

Vannetzel, M. (2016) *Les Frères musulmans égyptiens. Enquête sur un secret public* (Paris: Karthala).

Waterbury, J. (1983) *The Egypt of Nasser and Sadat: the Political Economy of Two Regimes* (Princeton: Princeton University Press).

Wickham, C. (2003) *Mobilizing Islam: Religion, Activism, and Political Change in Egypt* (New York: Columbia University Press).
Zeghal, M. (1996) *Gardiens de l'Islam: les oulémas d'Al Azhar dans l'Égypte contemporaine* (Paris, Presses de Sciences Po).

Chronology

2014 (28 May) Marshal al-Sisi elected President.

2013 (3 July) The military, headed by General Abdel Fattah al-Sisi, ousts President Morsi from power.

2013 (30 June) Massive demonstrations all over Egypt demand Morsi's departure, one year after he takes office.

2012 (17 June): Muslim Brother Mohamed Morsi wins the presidential election, while parliament is dissolved on the order of the High Constitutional Court.

2011 (December–January 2012) Parliamentary elections, the Muslim Brotherhood's Freedom and Justice Party wins around 47 per cent of seats.

2011 (March) The Supreme Council of Armed Forces, in its role at the head of the interim government, organises a referendum on constitutional amendments, with the support of the Muslim Brotherhood.

2011 (25 January) Beginning of the uprising on Tahrir Square and in other places in Egypt, leading to President Mubarak's resignation on 11 February.

2005 In the context of an increasing number of social and political protests, and international pressure, Mubarak authorises the country's first direct and multi-candidate presidential election (and in August is re-elected); the Muslim Brotherhood wins 20 per cent of seats in relatively transparent legislative elections in November.

2003 A broad programme for privatising public companies is launched.

1992 Wave of repression against the Muslim Brotherhood. Implementation of the IMF Structural Adjustment Program begins.

1981 Hosni Mubarak becomes President following Sadat's assassination by a jihadi group, tolerating the Muslim Brotherhood's participation in legislative elections.

1973 President Anwar al-Sadat allows margins of tolerance for the Muslim Brotherhood, releasing its leaders from jail. Economic liberalisation begins; a multiparty system is allowed from 1978 onwards.

1952–1970 Nasser and the Free Officers seize power from the monarchy, establish important social reforms, nationalise most of the economy, and dissolve all parties and associations. Harsh repression targets the Muslim Brotherhood from 1954 on.

PART 3

The Definition of Legitimate Conflicts

CHAPTER 10

Development and Countermovements. Reflections on the Conflicts Arising from the Commodification of Collective Land in Morocco

Yasmine Berriane

Abstract

This chapter analyses the links between development and conflict in the context of the protest movements that have arisen in response to the increasing commodification of collective land in Morocco. The transfer of this land, a transfer accompanied by a discourse linking the economic development of collective land to human and social development promoted by the state, renders visible—by exacerbating them—the inequalities inherent in the land tenure system introduced in the colonial era. Among the many forms of inequality, those relating to women's rights have become particularly important on the political scene thanks to action taken by a particular women's protest movement. This movement has managed to forge status for itself as a legitimate protest movement and is also contributing to the (re)creation of social boundaries based on the rhetoric of autochthony and on the politicisation of social inequalities based on tribal affiliation.

1 Introduction

This chapter provides an analysis of the links between development and conflict in the context of the protest movements that have arisen during the last decade in response to the growing commodification of collective land in Morocco. This land is subject to a particular form of land tenure that forms the basis of the collective property rights granted to 'tribes, fractions, villages and other ethnic groups',[1] and is governed by the 1919 *dahir*, a royal decree introduced in colonial times. Collective land extends over an estimated area of 15 million hectares and is home to 60 prefectures and provinces and

1 Excerpt from Article 1 of the 1919 *dahir* regulating collective land in Morocco.

© YASMINE BERRIANE, 2017 | DOI 10.1163/9789004349551_011

4,600 communities.[2] This is one of the main reserves of land still available in Morocco. These areas of collective land, described by the authorities as 'real levers of local and national socio-economic development', attract investors and major economic projects (Mrabi, 2014). The interest shown in these areas leads to their increasing commodification and privatisation. The national debate on collective land, held in 2014 in order to better develop such land and to launch the legal and institutional reforms necessary for this development to take place, illustrates the current craze for this category of property. However, the fact that this debate did not produce a conclusive result shows the complexity of the problem and the many issues and conflicts inherent in the land tenure institution and, in particular, its reform.[3]

Examined from the 'development' point of view, the conflicts inherent in the institution that is collective land in Morocco often appear to be an obstacle to its effective exploitation, to human development and even to the maintenance of social cohesion.[4] This approach places more particular emphasis on 'unresolved or inadequately resolved' conflicts within and between communities (El Alaoui, 2002, 61)—conflicts that are increasing, particularly due to the weakening of traditional authorities and the failure of those authorities to adapt to changes in the market and society, but also because of the overexploitation of resources, the ineffectual measures taken by the state, and the inadequacy of the legal framework. To overcome these obstacles (and thus to move away from a 'time of conflicts' and enter a 'time of development'), various options have been considered: legislative reforms, privatisation and registration of communal land, the revival of traditional authorities by their

2 These are the figures published by the Moroccan Ministry of the Interior on its web pages devoted to collective land: www.terrescollectives.ma (accessed on 31 May 2016).

3 Following five regional meetings that took place between March and May 2014, the ministry responsible announced that a conference would be organised in the summer of the same year to present the results of these deliberations and propose a reform of the *dahir* of 1919. This final conference did not take place. The debate on the legal and institutional reform of land tenure has since been revived at the Conference on State Land Policy (9 and 10 December 2015).

4 As Bouderbala notes, 'the economic critique of the status of collective land' dates back to the years 1980–90, a time of '[the] return to liberalism and [of] the implementation of structural adjustment programs' (Bouderbala 1999, 343) (our transl.). As for those prospects that present collective land 'as a dangerous obstacle to national integration', they are particularly rooted in the 'political ideal' established by national movements during the consolidation of postcolonial states, an ideal that contrasts 'state centralisation with balkanisation, national law with local custom, and written management with oral management' (Bouderbala 1999, 340) (our transl.).

'upgrading', the organising of communities into cooperatives or development associations, and the establishment of deliberative bodies likely to encourage participation.[5] All these measures have the advantage of offering solutions to a situation that is, to say the least, complex, but they rarely take into account the conflicts inherent in the 'development measures' proposed and the inequalities that the latter embody or emphasise. This chapter aims to illustrate the link between development and conflict by showing that 'development' (understood as a multidimensional process) can both be liberating and bring about inequalities and even social divisions. This two-pronged approach will also enable us to look in a somewhat different way at the contrast usually drawn between, on the one hand, culturalist representations of 'tradition' focused on local characteristics seen as a source of conflict and, on the other, a 'modernity' considered superior in terms of economic and managerial rationality, social justice and universal rights.

Property relations, the commodification of land, and the political movements related to it, lie at the crossroads of a great number of political and social issues. This area thus lends itself particularly well to an examination of the link between development and conflict. As noted by Jacob and Le Meur, the body of work on these issues has grown considerably over the past thirty years, 'in a new context characterised by a complex dialectic between tendencies towards deterritorialisation and the commodification of the world, the rise of environmental concern and a renewed affirmation of forms of belonging and identity' (2010, 5, our transl.). Of these inquiries, those conducted in Africa deal more specifically with processes that can be observed south of the Sahara, and analyse the link between ownership conflicts on the one hand and the formation of the state and political identities on the other (Lund, 1998 and 2011; Boone, 2014). These same processes are still understudied in North Africa.

Apprehended from the point of view of the transformation of the institution of collective land, the issue of 'development' has many meanings, on several levels (economic, legal, political, and social). In this chapter, 'development' refers first to the issue of the expansion of the land market in a global context marked by an increasing commodification of land. Second, the notion of development means the economic programmes implemented by states to 'make better use' of these territories and to the legal and administrative reforms that accompany, regulate, and make possible this accelerating commodification. Lastly, the issue of 'development' also refers to the protest movements that

5 Many analyses discuss collective land from the 'development' point of view and offer ideas about the solutions that need to be implemented in order to remove the obstacles observed. On this issue, see for example Mahdi (2009), El Alaoui (2002) and Bouderbala (1999).

have arisen in response to the inequalities created by the development of the land market, and that put into practice the lexicon of equality, social justice and human rights. These so-called universal reference points were given a prominent place in the Millennium Development Goals set out and promoted by major international organisations that place human development at the heart of their actions and objectives.

The work of Karl Polanyi (2001 [1957]), presented by Ayşe Buğra in this volume, encourages us to think of these different meanings of development simultaneously. In the context studied, they are constitutive of the same process, the development of a land market in a neo-liberal context marked by increased investments and land-grabbing in countries of the South (Bush et al., 2011). While the development of this economic sector appears as 'disentangled' from the political, it still remains dependent on the implementation of institutional reforms, and therefore on political interventions. Moreover, the expansion of this land market is accompanied by what Polanyi calls 'countermovements'. These stem from society and seek to regulate and limit the potentially devastating effects of this expansion. Therefore, the increasing commodification of collective land, the implementation of institutional reforms, and the emergence of protest movements will be discussed below as three intrinsically linked meanings of development that suggest an interpretation of the demonstrated interrelationship between development(s) and conflict(s) on different levels. What form does the interrelation between these processes take in the case of the current commodification of collective land in Morocco? What are the conflicts and inequalities that this commodification makes visible and/or generates? What are the countermovements that develop in this context?

To address these issues, I conducted a documentary survey (letters, reports on meetings, press articles), carried out ethnographic observations, and—finally—held unstructured interviews, between 2011 and 2015,[6] with different participants in the province of the Gharb (in Qasbat Mehdia and the environs of Kenitra) and near the cities of Meknes, Fez and Ifrane.[7] These data underscore the fact that in Morocco the transfer of collective land is accompanied

6 In 2011 and 2012, data were collected in collaboration with Fadma Ait Mous as part of the ANR ANDROMAQUE project on the anthropology of law in the Muslim world. Between 2013 and 2015, I pursued this research alone, with the support of the Centre for Modern Oriental Studies (Zentrum Moderner Orient, ZMO) in Berlin, the University Research Priority Program 'Asia & Europe' of the University of Zurich, and the Centre de Recherche Economie, Société, Culture (CRESC) of the University of Mohammed VI Polytechnic, Rabat.

7 This collective land is not far from an urban area. It differs from collective land of the pastoral type, for example land located in steppe zones. For a description of the different types of collective land see Lazarev (2014, 36–44).

by a discourse associating the economic development of this land with the human and social development promoted by the state. This rhetoric of development calls on the state to implement legal and institutional reform by presenting so-called customary regimes and the traditional representatives of communities—both of which were institutionalised in colonial times—as the main obstacles to a fair and optimised use of collective land. This discourse draws, albeit selectively, on the protest movements that have arisen due to the exacerbation of tensions and inequalities within communities and families owning collective land, tensions that exacerbated as the result of the intensification of land commodification.

By focusing my research on one of these conflicts (between women and the representatives of their community), I will show that, among the multiple forms of inequality inherent in the status of collective land, those relating to women's rights have become particularly important on the political scene. The struggle for women's rights has indeed demonstrated its capacity to advocate a vision of development that is both 'consensual' and similar to the vision currently promoted by the state. By referring to elements related to gender equality in the Constitution and the international conventions to which the country is a signatory, this movement has forged a status for itself as a 'legitimate movement' on the national public stage. However, this process of effectively including women on the lists of land beneficiaries has also strengthened social boundaries based on a rhetoric of autochthony and the politicisation of social inequalities based on tribal membership. If this process illustrates the conceptualisation of what many authors call 'local citizenship' (Jacob and Le Meur, 2010, 9–17; Lund, 2011), it also highlights the existence of many other inequalities and asymmetries that the women's movement and the demands it is voicing both conceal and (re)produce.

2 'It's all the fault of custom': Collective Land and the Rhetoric of Development

Since its creation in colonial times, the legal status of collective land was meant to allow for the necessary economic, social and political development of the country.[8] The administration of the protectorate passed the 1919 decree

8 See Bendella (2016) for a reflection on the different participants involved in the creation of the legal category of 'collective land' during the protectorate and the adaptation of this category to different configurations, as well as issues and paradigms of development ranging over time.

to oversee land that did not belong to the state or to individuals. Presented as a serious obstacle to economic development and the establishment of a modern state, the management of 'tribal areas' characterised by a 'use [of land] as required' following flexible rules was replaced by a collective mode of property based on the principle of 'permanent and exclusive occupation' under the supervision of the state (Bouderbala, 1996, 145–152, our transl.). The introduction of this new status was coupled with a process by which certain tribal entities were associated with specific territories, resulting in 'a mixing of the notions of entitlements to land and being an indigenous resident' (Aderghal and Simenel, 2012, 60, our transl.). This type of organisation was articulated in opposition to that in force in pre-colonial Morocco, a period during which 'localisations of tribal entities, including nomads' were fluctuating and 'the relative openness of lineage structures of nomadic and sedentary groups always helped to render impossible the correlation between ethnic identity and a specific space' (Aderghal and Simenel, 2012, 55, our transl.).

Moreover, the new land regime has contributed to the institutionalisation of 'custom', freezing a number of practices and power relations that had previously been flexible and based on the principle of 'group consensus' (Bouderbala, 2013, 190).[9] The 1919 decree gave 'customary law' a central role in the daily management of land use. The definition and application of these 'habits and customs' were entrusted to the 'traditional representatives'[10] of each community (*nouâbs*), whose mission was to resolve local conflicts, distribute land and provide an interface between the group (or *jmâa*) and representatives of the ministry responsible—namely, the Ministry of the Interior. Depending on the case, representatives from the communities concerned were also asked to develop new norms (Tozy and Mahdi, 1990). This form of government allowed the development of 'a free and separate area of rights where other participants [could] be freely active without challenging the state's monopoly' (our transl.), while relieving the state of the responsibility for managing conflicts within communities (Bendella, 2009, 292).

While subjecting much of the territory to a codified legal status, the institutionalisation of collective land thus strengthened the political control of the

9 This phenomenon has also been observed in other parts of Africa where the colonial administration has preserved previously flexible customs by codifying them, creating a conflict between the institution of customary law and positive law (Mamdani, 1996).

10 '*Nouâbs*' are generally described as 'traditional representatives.' The way this social institution operates today, however, has been deeply influenced and reshaped by the colonial experience.

central government over those territories now placed under the tutelage of the state and therefore weakened the sovereignty of communities over the land they used for their own needs. Moreover, the introduction of this legal status was also intended to protect collective land from a massive private colonisation by making it 'unseizable,' 'inalienable' and 'indefeasible'. The restrictions introduced by the 1919 *dahir* have actually allowed this form of property to remain to this day. But they have not slowed down the commodification and privatisation of a great deal of this land, which—in the colonial period—came under the control of settlers and of rural and urban notables (Bouderbala, 1996, 152–155), since the new tenure also fixed and codified the rules of the regulated transfer of land endowed with this legal status.

The commodification of collective land is not new, but it has been expanding since the late nineties with many new major economic projects such as the 'Plan Maroc Vert' in the field of agriculture, the 'Plan Azur' in the tourism sector, and the development of the extraction of raw materials such as phosphate (Mahdi, 2014). The land has also been used to respond to needs arising from demographic and urban growth. In the name of the economic, social and human development of Morocco, the transfer of this land to new owners (including public and private companies, both national and international) has therefore spread, in the form of long-term leases or final transfers for which the communities concerned have been variously compensated. In some cases, development or infrastructure projects have been implemented. In others, material compensation in the form of money or equipped plots of land has been distributed to persons identified by the delegates of the community as 'beneficiaries'.

In this transferral process, the Rural Affairs Department of the Ministry of the Interior plays an intermediary role. Project promoters must demonstrate how their proposal for 'upgrading' collective land will contribute to the economic and social development of the region. Their argument is all the more important as the law stipulates that the transfer of communal land is possible only if it contributes to economic development and meets a communal need. The speech by Mohammed VI on the occasion of the opening of the National Conference on State Land Policy, held on 9 and 10 December 2015 in Skhirat, was one of the most recent manifestations of this rhetoric. In his speech, the King developed the idea that institutional reform and an acceleration of the 'settling of the legal status of collective land' was required, as this would allow such land to be 'upgraded', ensuring 'that it can contribute to the development effort' and 'making it a means of integration of the beneficiaries [...] within the framework of the principles of law and social justice, apart from any outdated consideration' (our transl.).[11] The Ministry of the Interior employs similar language on the web portal that, since 2012, has been dedicated to its strategy of 'developing collective land.' The ministry's objective is to include 'communities in the process of development', both economic and human.[12]

The Ministry of the Interior's argument creates a very clear contrast between the measures implemented by the state to modernise and reform the institution of collective land and the obstacles and resistance created by customary (or 'outdated', as the King put it in his aforementioned speech) types of management methods. These obstacles are first of a human kind: the demographic growth of communities, the resistances of their representatives and the failure of their members to take out loans or to show any initiative. They also derive from the 'bad' management, the underutilisation, or the 'anarchic' use of collective land. Of the practices presented as backward and in contradiction with the development process that Morocco is currently embarked upon, the ministry particularly denounces the way local delegates have managed women's issues. The ministry regrets that local resistance opposes the efforts made by its departments to include women as beneficiaries of collective land. Yet, the advocacy of women's right on the part of the ministry arose only recently, in response to the movement of a number of women from the communities concerned; women who, since 2007, have been struggling against their exclusion from the right to enjoy this land.

3 Distributing the 'Development Rent': Collective Land and Social Inequalities

The legal status of collective land is based, as we have seen, on the principle of 'permanent and exclusive occupation' granted to communities as a right of use. Some categories of the local population are therefore excluded by definition from this form of ownership. The law provides only a loose definition of the group owning collective land (or the community) and the individuals (or 'beneficiaries') from within this group who are granted the right to use the land. The *dahir* of 1919 only mentions that the right of use is entrusted to 'heads of households', without defining the characteristics of this category. The delicate and contentious task of managing collective land—including the distribution

11 For the full text of this speech, see http://www.maroc.ma/fr/discours-royaux/sm-le-roi-mohammed-vi-adresse-un-message-aux-participants-aux-assises-nationales-d-o (accessed on 31 May 2016).

12 See www.terrescollectives.ma (accessed on 31 May 2016).

of plots of land among a community's members according to criteria defined by customary use—falls to the assembly of delegates.

Consequently, the ways of sharing out the right of use vary from community to community due to the criteria chosen by each community: birthright, the effective use of the land, notability, or marriage among others. While the criteria for determining beneficiaries vary from community to community, women are denied—totally or partially—the right to be given a plot of land in almost all communities. This practice, apparently based on practices dating from the pre-colonial period, was not questioned by the *dahir* of 1919. By making 'heads of households' the main beneficiaries of collective land, this legislation has given free rein to the dominant representations that associate this role with the figure of the man.[13]

The fact that certain categories are excluded from this right of use has undeniably led to conflicts and tensions. Disputes relating to rangeland use by livestock, the sharing of territory and the exploitation of plots of land are indeed part and parcel of the management of collective land (Bendella, 2009). They have long preserved a temporary, local character, being confined to life within communities and families. In addition, 'social pressure made it extremely rare that this type of conflict was dealt with in judicial terms' (Bendella, 2016, 276, our transl.). The situation changed with the increasing commodification of collective land, which has intensified the pressure on land and increased its value. The often definitive dimension of these transactions has also introduced the concept of a 'final deadline' (Lund, 1998, 6), defined as the date after which it is no longer possible to claim a share of the indemnities or plots of land distributed at the time of the transfer. This deadline has created a sense of urgency that has exacerbated tensions and made more visible the social inequalities inherent in the status of collective land, including cases of material compensation given to the individuals comprising the community.

As individual compensation has to be distributed according to the lists established at the time of each transfer by the community's assembly of delegates under the supervision of the ministry responsible, the criteria used to define 'beneficiaries' have become a significant issue. By legitimising their choice with reference to the customary uses mentioned above, local delegates have established these lists by applying criteria that they themselves drew up, and thus excluded certain categories of the local population. In the communities studied in the regions of the Gharb and Fez-Meknes, the excluded

13 This process is found in other contexts where the land reforms introduced during colonial times have helped strengthen the power of men over women (Englert and Dalley, 2008; Chanock, 1985).

categories were women, unmarried men, people who cannot prove a patrilineal genealogy linking them to the community, adopted persons, those whose ancestors were included at a late point in the community's existence, and—sometimes—those who have emigrated. The establishment of these lists has been the source of many local conflicts between the 'excluded' on the one hand, and delegates and representatives of the Ministry of the Interior on the other. But initially, only women from communities deprived of their right to be included on the lists of beneficiaries have managed to impose their demands on the political scene.

4 The Movement for Women's Rights to Land

Women from communities were the only ones able to impose their claims on the public stage through their movement, earning the sympathy of the national and international media as well as the support of the ministry responsible. This movement began in 2007 and is now better known as the 'Soulaliyate' movement, a reference to the *soulâlâ*, the kinship between members of the same ethnic community. This movement initially demanded women's right to receive a share equal to that of men when compensation was handed out.

The fact that women were excluded from the lists of beneficiaries exacerbated existing gender inequalities. Transfers made while the land was still being used and inhabited had dramatic consequences: Men who were compensated were able to settle in other geographical areas, but women (especially those who were widowed or single) found themselves in a very precarious situation. In other contexts, gender tensions were exacerbated by the emergence or intensification of economic and social inequalities between men and women within individual families, neighbourhoods, or villages. It is with great bitterness and anger that the women interviewed mention, for example, the substantial improvement in the economic situations of their brothers while they continue to live in very modest and even precarious conditions. The aggravation of these differences has resulted in significant conflicts within families.

Resorting to an appeal to public authorities or to justice is a long, expensive and difficult process for women who very often come from modest backgrounds and are almost illiterate. For many of them, joining the Soulaliyate movement was a way of seeking advice and support. The movement was born in 2007 with the support of a number of influential civic associations, including the Democratic Association of Women of Morocco (Association démocratique des femmes du Maroc; henceforth the ADFM) whose mission is to protect and promote the 'universally recognised human rights of women'.[14] This feminist organisation, founded in 1985, has a long history of activism and special contacts with international organisations and political representatives. It also has a good knowledge of the international instruments concerning human rights and development. The organisation became closely involved in the movement, providing it with more than just encouragement. While the Soulaliyates embodied the movement and were giving concrete expression to its demands, the ADFM undertook to provide logistical and material support to the women who mobilised locally. It gave them the benefit of its expertise in lobbying, contacted the national and international press, conducted negotiations with public authorities, and provided legal advice (Berriane, 2016).

Springing from the Gharb region where collective land is now rare and the pressure of investors particularly strong, the movement has since spread to other parts of the country. This expansion of the movement has led to a broadening of its demands, which now include the equal division of collective land in contexts where such land is not sold or leased. The movement is particularly distinguished by very high-profile actions that aim to turn the various local conflicts into a national problem. For example, the movement organised two demonstrations in front of Parliament in 2008 and 2009. In March 2009, following the second demonstration, six women resorted to the Rabat Administrative Court to lodge a case against the government, directly incriminating the Prime Minister and the Minister of the Interior in his capacity as the guardian of collective land. In the meanwhile, the movement is conducting negotiations with, and direct lobbying of, the public authorities handling the case, and of various elected officials.

5 Women's Rights and Development: What Consensus?

The women's rights movement is distinguished not only by the media exposure it has gained nationwide but also because its demands have been partially met. Between 2009 and 2012, the ministry responsible issued three circulars that gave women the right to benefit—like men—from compensation when the ownership of collective land is transferred, and a share of that land when it is divided out. The *walis*[15] and governors were invited to ensure that these

14 For a description of the aims of the ADFM, see http://www.adfm.ma (accessed on 31 May 2016).

15 The *walis* are state representatives appointed by the king at the regional and provincial levels. They hold significant power and exercise many and diverse functions, not always

new guidelines were respected, and representatives of the Department of Rural Affairs were told not to accept lists of beneficiaries that did not contain any female names (Berriane, 2015). The Ministry of the Interior has highlighted the existence of these new regulations, and the results obtained thanks to their implementation, on its electronic portal devoted to collective land, thereby emphasising the reforming role of the state.[16] According to the website, 80,000 women received material compensation between 2011 and 2013, worth USD 35.6 million in total (MAD 350 million), which represents 30 per cent of all compensation distributed. The (relatively) rapid response of the ministry in including women in the beneficiaries lists contrasts with the state's non-interventionist position in the past. In fact, until 2009, the ministry responsible did not raise any opposition to the practices of exclusion that women suffered, under the pretext that it was unable to act in the absence of any desire on the part of delegates to change customary practice.

Among the reasons that may explain the rapid reaction of the Ministry of the Interior to the Soulaliyate movement's demands is the movement's consensual approach.[17] While the movement's members claimed their right to land and criticised the practices of exclusion that then prevailed, they used a set of arguments and principles that are considered to be legitimate and therefore licit in the contemporary Moroccan context.[18] Their argument gives a central place to development, to which they refer in a manner similar to that employed by the state. The Soulaliyates' demands are based first on a critique of 'customary law', which they view as responsible for the exclusion of women. Depending on the individual case, this law is presented either as pre-Islamic—a legacy of the *jâhiliyya*, the era of 'ignorance'—and as contrary to the precepts

---

clearly defined, including reinforcing the power of the Ministry of the Interior over communities. While governors are appointed at the provincial and prefectural level, the *walis* (also known as 'super governors') are responsible for *wilayas*, which include several prefectures and provinces. The role of the *walis* in fostering development in Morocco is analysed in Nadia Hashimi Alaoui's contribution to this volume.

16 See www.terrescollectives.ma (accessed on 31 May 2016).

17 It is important to mention that this 'consensus' exists primarily at the national level. At the level of communities and families, calls for women to be included on lists of beneficiaries have met with much more resistance. Negotiations were held with communities during which other arguments were brought to the debate, such as the responsibility of men for the women in the family (Berriane, 2015). In some regions, these negotiations are still ongoing.

18 Demands relating to 'women's rights' became 'legitimate demands' following a long adversarial process in which many factors played a role, including the mobilisation of feminist organisations—such as the ADFM—over several decades.

of Islam, or as incompatible with the social and political changes occurring in Morocco today (Ait Mous and Berriane, 2016). This view is shared by the Ministry of the Interior which contrasts 'bad, backward-looking custom' with 'good, development-friendly public policy.' In distinguishing between custom and Islam, it is also possible to win the support of those participants who are critical of calls for the principle of equality between men and women to be applied, but who consider that 'customary law' is not consistent with Islamic precepts that give women the right to receive donations and legacies and to be the beneficiaries of financial transactions.

These critical voices include the women's division of the Justice and Spirituality (Al Adl Wal Ihsane, AWI) movement. As Merieme Yafout shows in this volume, AWI defends 'a vision of women's emancipation based on Islamic reference points', a vision that contrasts with those of organisations like the ADFM, which consider the rights of women to be human rights. In justifying their position by highlighting the pre-Islamic character of applied customs, AWI also promotes the inclusion of the Soulaliyates within the category of beneficiaries. According to this movement, these customs are indeed contrary to Islamic precepts that guarantee women the right of inheritance.[19] While the ADFM and AWI do not share the same vision of the role of Islam in society, the two organisations have found common ground in their condemnation of customary law and in their defence of the principle that the economic rights of women are guaranteed (in the name of Islam for AWI, in the name of human rights for the ADFM).

The arguments used by the movement gives a central place to the constitution, which guarantees equality between men and women and to the international conventions to which the country is a signatory. It thus refers to human rights, and specifically women's emancipation and their economic and social rights as formulated by international organisations like the United Nations and the World Bank. This reference to human rights is part of the broader discourse on the country's transition towards a state of law in which these rights must be respected. The reference also appears in the three circulars issued by the Ministry of the Interior. Furthermore, according to an ADFM official interviewed in Rabat in September 2011, the reference to gender equality was the strongest argument available to the movement because the 'Ministry officials could not

19 See, e.g., http://www.mouminate.net/ar/document/2652.shtml (accessed on 31 May 2016). A fatwa issued in 2010 by the Higher Council of Ulamas also puts forward a similar argument: the exclusion of women from the right to the income derived from the use of collective land is incompatible with the rights of women in Islam to benefit from financial transactions such as gifts or inheritance (Berriane, 2015, 69).

say they were against the idea of equality between men and women'. The consensual nature of this argument can be explained by the contemporary Moroccan context. Change is, indeed, on the agenda and the state primarily derives its legitimacy from its planned social and political reforms, focused on decentralisation, the establishment of the rule of law, and the fight against inequality and discrimination. The country also owes its reputation as a 'good pupil' of international development policies to the measures implemented to ensure greater gender equality and encourage the inclusion of women in decision-making bodies.

The Soulaliyate movement, however, does not question the actual foundations of the land policies pursued by the state via its sale of vast tracts of land to private investors. It differs in this respect from more recent local movements, which cast doubt on the scope of development of collective land as conceived and implemented by the public authorities and the companies to whom this land had been sold. Unlike the Soulaliyate movement, these movements were violently repressed or ignored by the authorities. In 2011, for example, the population of Khouribga staged a protest demanding the right to top-priority, unconditional recruitment to the Office Chérifien des Phosphates. Also, since 2011 the inhabitants of a village near Tinghir have organised daily sit-ins to protest against the abusive exploitation of natural resources (particularly water) by the Société Métallurgique d'Imider (SMI) and to demand a fairer distribution of the wealth generated. In 2013, the people of Taourirt protested against local officials and community representatives who appropriated profits from the transfer of the ownership of communal land. While public authorities can depoliticise the issue of gender inequality by presenting it as a 'special' issue created by the local 'resistance' of authorities that are applying the customs of another age,[20] they find it more difficult to do so when demands challenge the power relations underlying the way in which politicians, national companies and international ones are rapidly appropriating resources.

Furthermore, the demands of the Soulaliyate movement do not pose any challenge to the actual foundations of the political system. The movement even calls on the Ministry of the Interior to fulfil its supervisory role as required by law and to ensure that the egalitarian principles of the constitution and relevant international conventions are respected. The consensual nature of the movement is ultimately based on its 'disciplined' form. Drawing on over

---

20 Here we find a tendency to explain the experiences of women by what Abu-Lughod calls 'resorting to the cultural', an approach that makes it possible to ignore the historicity and the multiplicity of social and political processes at work in the production of gender inequalities (Abu-Lughod, 2002, 784).

twenty years of activism, representatives of the ADFM have resorted to now routine modes of protest perfectly well tolerated by the state, including *waqfa* (standing gatherings)—a type of demonstration akin to a sit-in (Vairel, 2005)—which the ADFM introduced into the repertoire of women in this movement. ADFM training workshops teach the foundations of this type of demonstration: apply for and obtain an authorisation, respect the start and end times of the event, do not spill over onto the highway, etc.

In a context in which the hegemonic conception of development places special emphasis on respecting women's rights, equality between the sexes thus functions as a powerful tool when the demand for new rights turns confrontational. When grounds for agreement exist, the link between development, conflict and consensus reveals and (re)produces certain inequalities, fuelling conflicts at other levels.

6 Development and Ethnic Divisions: Who are the Legitimate 'Beneficiaries'?

While a national consensus was created in the name of gender equality so that women can benefit from collective land, the same has not been true of the actual ways in which this land and its associated benefits have been shared out. Ministerial circulars specify neither the size of the share that women are supposed to receive[21] nor the selection criteria for beneficiaries. Under the regulatory regime for collective land, the members of a council of delegates decide on these issues in each community. The definition of 'beneficiary' thus remains unclear, generating conflicts and inequalities based on the exclusion of certain categories of the population. As we shall see, the Soulaliyates contribute, as do others concerned, to the reproduction of these inequalities and thus to reinforcing those social boundaries that are based on the argument of autochthony. I will illustrate this point by referring to the case of Qasbat Mehdia, a town near the Atlantic coast, which is located at the heart of the land owned by the Mehdawa community. After being repeatedly excluded from the sharing out of compensation, a group of women from the community joined the Soulaliyate movement shortly after its creation. Since, nearly 800 women from the community have received financial compensation and a plot

21 The practical arrangements for the inclusion of women are unclear, especially as regards the size of the 'share' they should be assigned. The Soulaliyate movement requests that the principle of 'equal shares' be applied, but those who are inspired by religious legislation are in favour of a 'half-share', equivalent to the right to inheritance under Islam.

of equipped land. We will now turn to an analysis of the process that allowed these women to be included on the list of beneficiaries reserved for women.

With their new visibility and support from representatives of the Ministry of the Interior and from the media, the Soulaliyates of Mehdia actively participated in drawing up this list. Their interest was focused on what they call the 'purification' (*tasfiyat*) of the list. In the person of the chairwoman of their association, a widow in her sixties, they very carefully checked the registration of the names on the list of beneficiaries reserved for women, and excluded those they considered to be 'fake Soulaliyates'. During the registration sessions, which took place on municipal premises, the main mission of the association's chairwoman and two delegates from the community was to distinguish between 'real' and 'fake' Soulaliyates, applying an analysis of the genealogy of each postulant. These three persons legitimised their role on the grounds of their age and their detailed knowledge of the different families that make up the community. Moreover, the chairwoman of the local association of Soulaliyates considered that her function as a representative conferred on her the powers necessary to carry out this task. Once the list had been drawn up, she then demanded that the local authorities strike off a number of women included on it—women she considered to be 'fake Soulaliyates'. These included women who were not related to the community by kin ties, those who had been adopted, and those residents whose ancestors had settled there well after the 'founding fathers' (believed to number ten).

The distinction between 'real' and 'fake' Soulaliyates is not specific to the establishment of lists of women beneficiaries. Genealogy occupies a central place in the land registry of collective land and, in particular, in the arrangements approved by the Ministry of the Interior when land is shared out or compensation paid. Anyone wishing to register on a list of beneficiaries must prove their membership of the community and only those related to the community by their father can be called *soulâlî* (*soulâliya* in the feminine). In the current context of land ownership transfers and the distribution of compensation, the stakes of such a reappropriation of the notions of 'tribe' and filiation assume particular importance, as access to significant material resources is conditional on the 'purity' of a patrilineal genealogy.

This change was accompanied by a reconstruction of the history and genealogy of the group.[22] The new version contrasts with the reality experienced by

22 For the *Mehdawa*, the genealogy of the community is reduced to some ten or so 'founding fathers'—soldiers from different regions who were united in the late seventeenth century by the usufruct granted by Sultan Moulay Ismail on the land surrounding the fortress of Mehdia in exchange for securing it (Ait Mous and Berriane, 2016, 130–132).

the community of Mehdawa who, over the centuries, experienced numerous processes of migration, inclusion and assimilation.[23] This rewriting of the history of the 'clan' was accompanied by the establishment of a glossary distinguishing, in order of priority, between the different categories of people living in Qasbat Mehdia. The names of these categories are not new, but they took on a new vigour when the process of land commodification intensified. The first category is that of '*soulâlî*', indigenous people possessing the right to use the land because they are linked to the community through their fathers. At Qasbat Mehdia, the members of this category can benefit from these rights, even if they do not live in the community and do not work the land. Other residents are classified as part of the non-native category of 'foreigners' (*berrânî*), those who do not enjoy this right of use because their fathers are not *soulâlî*. Some *berrâni* have grown up and lived all their lives in Qasbat Mehdia. In this case, they are called 'sons or daughters of the soil' (*weld/bent leblâd*), a term which—incidentally—is also used to refer to the '*soulâlî*'. For example, children of women who come from the community but married to a *berrâni* fall into this category. Although they are 'locals', they do not have the right to land.

For the women of Qasbat Mehdia, referring to the distinction between '*soulâlî* natives', 'non-*soulâlî* locals', and 'foreigners' has turned into a prime resource. By focusing on their own patrilineal relationship with the community, they are reclaiming the rules of belonging in order to demand their right to a share of compensation. They do more than just use this genealogical link; they are actively involved in reproducing these categories. In all interviews conducted in Qasbat Mehdia but also in other parts of the Gharb, the women involved in the establishment of lists of beneficiaries stressed the importance of their role as guarantors of the 'purity' of the lists established under their supervision, in order to distinguish themselves from men who implemented practices deemed 'corrupt' when they had a monopoly on this function. The remarks made by representatives of the Soulaliyate movement show that the exclusion of 'non-beneficiaries' has become a virtue. However, this process is giving rise to new conflicts between beneficiaries (including women) and excluded groups like the descendants of *berrâni* who have lived for generations in Qasbat Mehdia.

The *soulâla* is a commonly used term in the discourse of the women of Qasbat Mehdia, but it also finds its place in the discourse of representatives of

---

23 As in the case of Afghanistan, described by Fariba Adelkhah in her contribution to this volume, it should be recalled that in Morocco, 'tribal identity is relative and contextual' and is 'essentially a set of principles and rules according to which political statuses and roles are defined and assigned' (Rachik, 2000, 36, our transl.).

the ADFM, for whom the genealogy of women in the movement has become an argument likely to give more weight to the demands of the Soulaliyate movement they helped to create. So members of the movement request that they benefit from a share of the compensation distributed to their brothers mainly because they are the daughters of a male descendant of the community. In other words, the Soulaliyate movement is based on the concept of social equality described above and combines it with the idea of a patrilineal descent that distinguishes some women from others. Paradoxically, the principles of equality and kinship are of equal importance in this argumentation.

This observation recalls the role played by elites in the production of representations of autochthony (Bayart et al., 2001, 181). In the cases studied, these representations are gaining in strength and visibility thanks to the actions and discourse of the movement created in collaboration with the ADFM and the use of references to the constitution, which applies to all Moroccan citizens. At the intersection of these two sources of political identity (that of autochthony and that of national citizenship), the representation of a 'local citizenship' (Lund, 2011) with a plural and 'exclusivist' shape comes into being—a representation that draws both on references to so-called universal rights and on a 'constituted equality,' which refers to 'the conception of a natural and exclusive community' (Cutolo and Geschiere, 2008, 6, our transl.).

7 Conclusion

The analysis of the transformations that are accompanying the commodification of collective land in Morocco enables us to highlight the many links between development and conflict. Thus, the transfer of ownership of collective land, which is accompanied by a discourse linking the economic assessment of collective land to the furtherance of human and social development promoted by the state, has rendered visible—by exacerbating them—inequalities inherent in such a legal status. Until now, the countermovements born of this process have mainly challenged the terms upon which the profits resulting from the transfer of land ownership are shared out. In this context, the struggle for women's rights to land has been able to impose its demands on the political scene by drawing upon references considered 'legitimate' and without questioning the state's authority. Conversely, local movements that have (sometimes violently) challenged the power relations underlying the rapid appropriation of resources by politicians and national and international companies have either been suppressed or ignored by the government.

By analysing the demands being voiced ('legitimate' versus 'ignored' or repressed) and highlighting certain inequalities, my goal here has not been to question the legitimacy of the rights claimed by the women's movement, but to show that there are inequalities between movements. Individual movements' legitimacy depends largely on the historical and political conjuncture and on the opportunity offered to them to transform reference points of development—such as women's economic rights or the dichotomy between 'custom' and 'modernity'—into powerful tools of legitimation, thus reshaping power relationships. This study also invites us to consider the inequalities and hierarchies that social movements—including those of women—help to foster, even though they are fighting for an egalitarian distribution of resources and rights in society.

The consensus that was formed at the national level around the movement for women's rights is also a vector of exclusion. Processes of exclusion crystallise around the definition of the 'beneficiary'. By invoking the argument of patrilineal descent upon which the sharing out of resources generated by collective land repose, the Soulaliyate movement reproduces and strengthens social boundaries based on 'tribal identity', a process that Fariba Adelkhah discusses with regard to Afghanistan in this volume. These boundaries are the source of new conflicts, but also of new conceptions of citizenship that refer to local and national considerations. The link between development and conflict, thus, allows us to approach from a new angle the contrast usually made between, on the one hand, culturalist representations of 'tradition' focused on local particularities that are seen as causes of conflict and, on the other, a 'modernity' considered superior in the name of economic and managerial rationality, social justice and universal rights.

References

Abu-Lughod, L. (2002) 'Do Muslim women really need saving? Anthropological reflections on cultural relativism and its others', *American Anthropologist,* 104(3), pp. 783–790, DOI: 10.1525/aa.2002.104.3.783.

Aderghal, M and R. Simenel (2012) 'La construction de l'autochtonie au Maroc: des tribus indigènes aux paysans amazighs', *Espace populations sociétés,* 1, pp. 55–67, http://eps.revues.org/4847 (accessed on 30 May 2016).

Ait Mous, F. and Y. Berriane (2016) 'Femmes, droit à la terre et lutte pour l'égalité au Maroc: Le mouvement des soulaliyates', in H. Rachik (ed.), *Contester le droit. Communautés, familles et héritage au Maroc* (Casablanca: La Croisée des chemins), pp. 87–173.

Bayart, J-F., P. Geschiere and F. Nyamnjoh (2001) 'Autochtonie, démocratie et citoyenneté en Afrique', *Critique internationale*, 1(10), pp. 177–194, DOI: 10.3917/crii.010.0177.

Bendella A. (2016) 'Une catégorie juridique pour gouverner la question du social', in I. Bono and B. Hibou (eds.), *Le gouvernement du social au Maroc* (Paris: Karthala), pp. 275–320.

Bendella A. (2009) 'Les modes de régulation des conflits. Entre régulation communautaire et régulation judiciaire', in P. Bonte et al (ed.), *Développement rural, Environnement et enjeux territoriaux. Regards croisés oriental marocain et sud-est tunisien* (Tunis: Ceres Editions), pp. 291–304.

Berriane, Y. (2016) 'Bridging Social Divides: Leadership and the Making of an Alliance for Women's Land-Use Rights in Morocco', *Review of African Political Economy*, 43(149), pp. 350–364, DOI: 10.1080/03056244.2016.1214118

Berriane Y. (2015) 'Inclure les "n'ayants pas droit": Terres collectives et inégalités de genre au Maroc', *L'Année du Maghreb*, 13, pp. 61–78, DOI: 10.4000/anneemaghreb.2546.

Boone, C. (2014) *Property and Political Order in Africa. Land Rights and the Structure of Politics* (Cambridge: Cambridge University Press), DOI: 10.1017/CBO9781139629256.

Bouderbala, N. (2013) *La loi entre ciel et terre* (Rabat: Université Mohammed V).

Bouderbala, N. (1999) 'L'état et la modernisation des terres collectives', in R. Rubino and P. Morand-Fehr (eds.) *Systems of Sheep and Goat Production: Organization of Husbandry and Role of Extension Services* (Zaragoza: CIHEAM), pp. 339–344.

Bouderbala, N. (1996), 'Les terres collectives du Maroc dans la première période du protectorat (1912–1930)', *Revue du monde musulman et de la Méditerrannée*, 79–80, pp. 143–156, http://www.persee.fr/doc/remmm_0997-1327_1996_num_79_1_1741 (accessed on 30 May 2016).

Bush, R., J. Bujra and G. Littlejohn (2011) 'The accumulation of dispossession', *Review of African Political Economy*, 38(128), pp. 187–192, DOI: 10.1080/03056244.2011.582752.

Chanock, M. (1985), *Law, custom and social order: the colonial experience in Malawi and Zambia* (Cambridge: Cambridge University Press).

Cutolo, A. and P. Geschiere (2008) 'Populations, citoyennetés et territoires. Autochtonie et gouvernementalité en Afrique', *Politique africaine*, 112, pp. 5–17, DOI: 0.3917/polaf.112.0005.

El Alaoui, M. (2002) *Etude sur le statut juridique des terres collectives au Maroc et les institutions coutumières et locales dans le versant sud du Haut Atlas* (Ouarzazate: Publication du Projet Transhumance et Biodiversité), http://docplayer.fr/15308074-Www-transhumancemaroc-com.html (accessed on 30 May 2016).

Englert, B. and E. Dalley (eds.) (2008) *Women's Land Rights & Privatization in Eastern Africa*, Eastern African Series (Oxford: James Currey).

Jacob, J.-P. and P.-Y. Le Meur (2010) 'Introduction. Citoyenneté locale, foncier, appartenance et reconnaissance dans les sociétés du Sud', in J.-P. Jacob et P.-Y. Le Meur (eds.) *Politique de la terre et de l'appartenance. Droits fonciers et citoyenneté locale dans les sociétés du Sud* (Paris: Karthala), pp. 5–57.

Lazarev, G. (2014) *Les structures agraires au Maroc. Une mise en perspective historique* (Rabat: Université Mohammed V).

Lund, C. (2011) *Land Rights and Citizenship in Africa*, Discussion paper 65, (Uppsala: Nordiska Afrikainstitutet), http://www.diva-portal.org/smash/get/diva2:460067/FULLTEXT01.pdf (accessed on 31 May 2016).

Lund, C. (1998) *Law, Power and Politics in Niger. Land Struggles and the Rural Code* (Berlin: Lit Verlag).

Mahdi, M. (2014) 'Devenir du foncier au Maroc agricole au Maroc. Un cas d'accaparement des terres', *New Medit*, 13(4), pp. 2–10, http://www.iamb.it/share/img_new_medit_articoli/993_02mahdi.pdf (accessed on 30 May 2016).

Mahdi, M. (2009) 'La tribu au secours du développement pastoral', *Etudes rurales*, 2(184) pp. 133–148, https://www.cairn.info/revue-etudes-rurales-2009-2-page-133.htm (accessed on 30 May 2016).

Mamdani, M. (1996) *Citizen and Subject. Contemporary Africa and the Legacy of late Colonialism* (Princeton: Princeton University Press).

Mrabi, M.A. (2014) 'Terres collectives. Enième promesse de réforme', *L'Economiste*, 4242, 27 March.

Polanyi, K. (2001 [1957]) *The Great Transformation. The Political and Economic Origins of our Time*, (Boston: Beacon Press).

Rachik, H. (2000) 'Les usages politiques des notions de tribu et de nation au Maroc', *Identity, Culture and Politics*, 1(1), pp. 35–47.

Tozy, M. and M. Mahdi (1990) 'Aspects du droit communautaire dans l'Atlas marocain', *Droit et société*, 15, pp. 203–210, http://www.persee.fr/doc/dreso_0769-3362_1990_num_15_1_1077 (accessed on 30 May 2016).

Vairel, F. (2005) 'L'ordre disputé du sit-in au Maroc', *Genèses*, 59(2), pp.47–70, https://www.cairn.info/revue-geneses-2005-2-page-47.htm (accessed on 30 May 2016).

CHAPTER 11

Charity and Commercial Success as Vectors of Asymmetry and Inequality: The Unconceptualised Elements of Development in Islamist Sudan during the First Republic

Raphaëlle Chevrillon-Guibert

Abstract

The Sudanese Islamist experiment is far from having put an end to the conflict-ridden history of the country, despite the South achieving independence in July 2011. However, a higher degree of regional integration outside the South was one of the stated aims of the Islamists when they came to power in 1989. This chapter will investigate the apparent paradox by exploring the experiments in development undertaken by Sudanese Islamists during their first republic (1989–2011) on the basis of the study of certain social practices they actively encouraged, namely evergetism and philanthropy. It is based on an analysis of the charitable practices carried out by the main traders in the Sudanese capital's principal market during the Islamist regime. The regional—more specifically Darfurian—origin of most of these main traders makes it possible to compare what these practices produce in each different territory. The chapter shows that this encouragement, which is not part of any specific plan thought up by the Islamists, leads to different forms of development that vary depending on the local and human contexts in which the actors live, and also the way they conceive their roles within in the circles to which they belong. It then highlights how these variations produce extremely disparate and often conflict-ridden results, which ultimately pursue the asymmetric formation of the Sudanese state, prolonging a historical trajectory that has produced injustice and generated conflict (Figure 11.1).

1 Introduction

In Sudan, Islamists[1] have been in power for over twenty-five years, and have left a lasting mark on the trajectory of the Sudanese state. Before them, only

1 In this contribution, I will not go into the details of the Sudanese state apparatus; suffice to say the Sudanese regime is far from monolithic and since the early 1990's has significantly

 | DOI 10.1163/9789004349551_012

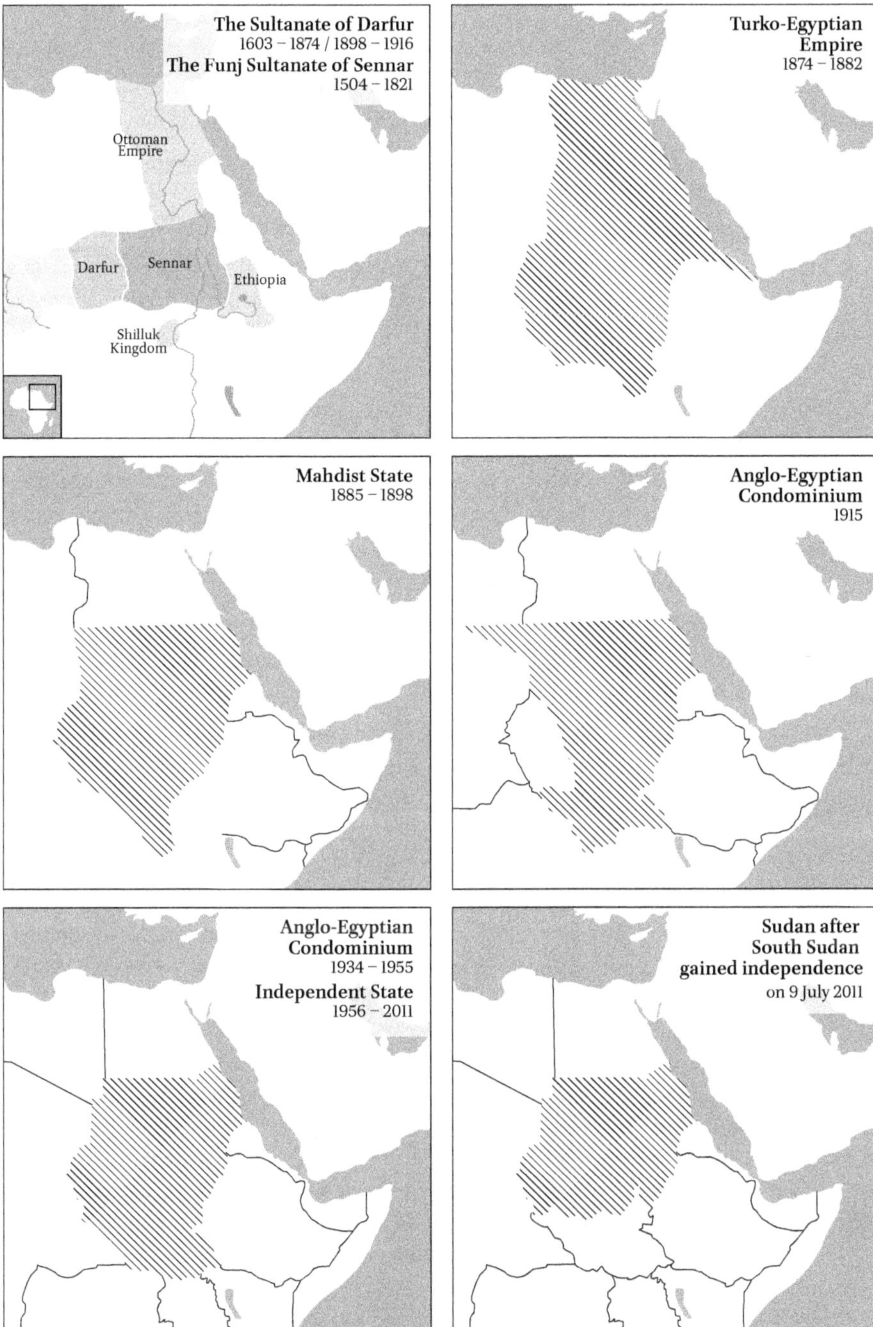

FIGURE 11.1 *Map of Sudan and the evolution of its borders*
SOURCE: ADAPTED FROM J. RYLE, J. WALLIS ET AL (EDS.) (2011), *THE SUDAN HANDBOOK*, (ROCHESTER: BOYDELL AND BREWER LTD), AND FROM A WIKIPEDIA ARTICLE *HISTORY OF SUDAN*.

General Nimeiry managed to stay in power for more than a decade (from 1969 to 1985). In addition to their longevity, and though their political orientations seem quite different (Islamic and liberal on the one hand, secular and socialist on the other), both these regimes share a number of common characteristics: the authoritarian character of their political practices, of course, but also their explicit willingness to fundamentally transform Sudanese society and state and society relationships. Both have also rejected the colonial legacy of a Sudan where political and economic resources are concentrated in the country's centre, and both have been intensely hostile to the major traditional parties and their elites, which they accuse of having maintained this heritage, and the ethnicised power relations on which it was based, during the years they ruled the country.

The pursuit of colonial development based on agricultural export located in the central regions of the country by governments from the traditional parties has been widely noted (Roden, 1974; Bernal, 1997), as have the difficulties of the socialist regime to overcome this pattern of development (Niblock, 1987). In the late 1970s a real economic crisis faced the country, and these attempts were often judged hastily. Most importantly, the resumption of war in the South in 1983 and the dreadful famine that hit western regions in 1984 and 1985 have focused the attention of analysts; few studies have explored development policies by focusing on the actors who implemented them and how they are rooted in the specific local, regional, and international contexts (oil shocks, the massive levels of emigration of qualified Sudanese citizens to the Gulf States,

evolved. I use the terms 'Islamist regime' or 'Islamists' to describe the regime that took power in Khartoum in 1989, whose main pillar is the Islamic movement, i.e. the Muslim Brotherhood in Sudan, which became, under the leadership of Hassan al-Turabi, the Islamic Charter Front, then the National Islamic Front, and is now the National Congress Party. The generic term 'Islamic movement' is that used by Hassan al-Turabi, and it seeks to encompass more than just the political party, thus including not only the institutionalised aspect of the political activities of the movement, but also the satellite organisations. The term was taken up by Ali Osman Taha to designate the branch that refused to follow Turabi, who was ousted as a result of an internal schism in the movement in the late 1990s and who then created the Popular Congress Party (PCP); relatively active in the opposition to the regime, the PCP and its leader eventually renewed close informal links with the government during the period of the 'Arab Spring', mainly because of the international prestige enjoyed by Hassan al-Turabi, but also because of the exacerbation of internal rivalries within the Islamic movement over the succession of Omar al-Bashir. Another marked feature of the second republic (which began after the South achieved independence) lies in the important debates and confrontations to which it has given rise between religious political groups on issues relating to Islamic law (which form of sharia should be applied?).

regional conflicts, and recurrent droughts in the Sahelian part of the country).[2] The literature has mainly focused on the consequences of the crisis and developed a simplistic link between climate change and societal violence masking the long-term political-economic dynamics and the Sudanese political structure underpinning the crisis.[3] Many studies have also investigated the health of the millions of Sudanese who have thronged to the suburbs of the capital to escape war or drought (Ibrahim and Ruppert, 1988); others have discussed food safety issues in rural areas (de Waal, 2005) or zones affected by conflict (Miller, 1993).

Even today, the literature on development in Sudan continues to pursue this line of analysis by exploring the problematics of the urbanisation of the capital and the modernisation of agriculture and livestock; the latter constituting the main livelihood for rural populations (Casciarri et al., 2015).[4] Special attention is also paid to the form of education that Islamists have sought to encourage (Tenret, 2016). In general, development fostered by the Islamist regime's policy choices has not been addressed in terms of its inherently conflictual nature, as were the nationalisations of the Nimeiry regime. The exploitation of oil and minerals, livestock and grain production for export to specific regions, and the construction of large infrastructural projects, such as the dams on the Nile, are not choices that are questioned by the actors concerned, or discussed in the literature;[5] rather, it is the profoundly unequal character of the regional distribution of these projects and of their principal beneficiaries that raises questions and objections. These inequalities have fomented all the opposition armed movements, whether in the South, Darfur, the East, or the regions of the Blue Nile and the Nuba Mountains. It is this aspect, too, that the literature addressing these conflicts favours; these studies detail this unequal distribution and the clientelism of the regime in developmental project selection and the allocation of public contracts. Recent studies complement these approaches by attempting to decipher what these development projects reveal about the practices of Islamist rulers and the way that the Islamist government works (Verhoeven, 2013; Beckedorf, 2012; Patey, 2014). The research on which my study is based follows the same path, shedding new light on the Islamists in

2 Apart, that is, from various studies by scholars such as R. Brown who analyzes in detail the attitude of international donors to the crisis in the Sudanese economy in the 1980s; see, especially, Brown (1989 and 1990).

3 On this issue see Verhoeven (2011) and also Brachet and Bonnecase (2013).

4 See also the work of the Feinstein International Center of Tufts University, http://fic.tufts.edu/research-item/sudan-environment-and-livelihoods/ (accessed on 29 April 2016).

5 With the notable exception of Gertel et al. (2014).

Sudan. The literature on Sudanese political Islam focuses mainly on political actors, their thinking and discourses (studies including Woodward, 2013; Ibrahim, 1999), and on their relationships within the state apparatus (e.g. Gallab, 2016; Sørbø and Ahmed, 2013; Ahmed, 2007) and with the rest of the Sudanese political arena (Warburg, 2003). By studying the experiments in government carried out by Sudanese Islamists, this research seeks to understand what the latter make of power and what power makes of them.

The present study specifically aims to explore the experiment in development conducted by the Islamists during their first republic[6] by investigating the social practices they have actively encouraged since coming to power: those of evergetism[7] and social philanthropy. In 1989, the value of the religious repertoire of redistributive generosity was systematically highlighted in the official discourse of the new regime. This was used both as a symbol of religiosity and as a tool of redistribution and development, along with its simultaneous institutionalisation, in particular through the obligatory payment of *zakat*.

By analysing how Islamists encourage redistribution practices, we can interpret their conception of development. In addition, deciphering how this appeal for generosity is variously received and translated by the governed, depending on the social roots and the sociopolitical context in which they move, should enables us to see, at least partially, how individuals and groups, each on their own scale, conceive development. How do they play a part in the production of development that varies according to groups and regions and the results of which sometimes prove paradoxical and often conflicting? How do these charitable practices combine with the development of the new entrepreneurial ethos promoted by Islamists? The answers to these questions should help us to envisage more complex configurations than expected and, in particular, show how the Islamist experience has gradually brought about a form of development that, in principle, is relatively consensual, but whose effects are widely conflicting because of the persistence of inequalities in the country's development.

To prove my point, I analyse the activities of the major markets of the Sudanese capital and the trajectories and practices of some of their actors mainly

---

6 The independence of South Sudan, which marked the beginning of the second republic, profoundly affected the regime and its economy, in particular causing the loss of most of the oil revenue that for several years had financed the regime's development projects. This led to the need for a major rethink.

7 I use the term 'evergetism' in Paul Veyne's sense: the financial investment of an individual for the public good, the gesture of 'a man who helps the community with his purse, a patron of public life' (Veyne 1976, 22); on the concept and its critics, see Andreau et al. (1978).

during the first republic (until the independence of South Sudan in 2011). This analysis is based on empirical work carried out since 2004, mainly in the Sudanese capital, during which I have conducted more than 400 interviews in English and Arabic (with a translator) with traders and businessmen as well as many observations in the markets.[8] My choice of the commercial sector is not insignificant. Although it represents only a small share of the gross domestic product (GDP), around 15 percent, this sector plays a central role in the Sudanese economic apparatus due to the low level of industrialisation of the country and the preponderance, since British colonisation, of agriculture and mining, which have become fundamental to the country's economy since the demise of the oil economy.

2 Evergetism: A Specific Tool in Islamist Development

In the very first months of their rule, the Islamists faced a severe food crisis in Darfur and Kordofan. The response to the crisis differed greatly from one region to another—in Kordofan, the governor declared a state of emergency that allowed him to obtain substantial international aid, while in Darfur, on the contrary, no state of emergency was declared and no outside help was received. This decision on the part of the governor of Darfur, a fervent Islamist, was fairly typical of the particular view that Islamists hold with regard to the role of the state and society: problems in medical care and food safety should be left to society through local NGOs (Miller, 1993). Darfuri people, especially its economic actors, were encouraged to create and finance such NGOs,[9] while the regional authority focuses primarily on security issues.[10] We must also remember that the Islamists, and especially their leader Hassan al-Turabi, view international humanitarian organisations and their political, cultural and religious roles as vectors of the acculturation of Muslim populations (Bellion-Jourdan, 2006). This highly politicised vision of aid impels Islamists to fight actively against

8 Some of these observations and interviews were conducted as part of my doctoral research conducted between 2005 and 2013, for which I analysed the Islamist experience on the basis of the development of Darfuri Zaghawa communities (Chevrillon-Guibert, 2013a).

9 Various interviews, Khartoum, 2004–2012.

10 The region has suffered violent local conflicts since the late 1970s. In the late 1980s, a precarious peace was signed between the main groups involved, but the situation remains volatile in northern Darfur (Harir and Vedt (1994) and interview with Yusif Bakhit, secretary of the governor of Darfur between 1981 and 1985, then governor himself between 1986 and 1988, in Khartoum, April 2016).

these international organisations, which they accuse of fostering a civilisation project that goes against their own, by limiting their interventions to a minimum. In 1991, Hassan al-Turabi went so far as to tell a Kuwaiti newspaper: 'Some want to use the decline in agricultural production caused by the drought to tie our hands. It is preferable for several thousand people to die rather than allow the international crusade to come to our aid. We will never proclaim that there is a famine while we are an Islamic nation (…) We will not allow international aid organisations to do what they want in our country and to oppose the plans of the Islamic Revolution in the South which, towards the end of 1991, will see the rebellion crushed.' (Sawt al-Kuwait, 25 March 1991, quoted in Bellion-Jourdan, 1997, 69).

By ascribing this role to aid organisations, Islamists were logically driven to create their own charitable organisations charged with spreading their vision of society. In 1980, even before they came to power, they set up the organisation known as Da'wa Islamiya (Islamic Call), whose initial objective was the spreading of Islam in Africa through education. The establishment of Da'wa Islamiya was supported by Mohammed al-Faisal, a director of the financial institution Dar al-Mal al-Islami and a main shareholder of the Faisal Islamic Bank created a year earlier. He was a personal friend of Turabi. The organisation also obtained the support of the Jami'at ad-da'wa al-islamiya based in Tripoli and the Muslim World League based in Jeddah. It was in 1981 that Da'wa Islamiya developed its own humanitarian arm, the Islamic African Relief Agency (IARA).[11] At that time, these associations allowed Islamists not only to gain influence among the assisted populations but also to siphon off political support beyond their traditional sphere of influence thanks to the very positive response that they met with from all actors on the northern Sudanese political scene, which was dominated by religious parties. The context was at that time marked by the resumption of war in the South and by famine in the West, which drew many international humanitarian organisations into the country. However, the proximity of these associations to the Islamic movement came to be problematic, especially for secular parties, as it was very difficult to ignore their role in the development of Islamist ideology.[12]

Once they were in power, the Islamists maintained these organisations and encouraged the establishment of new ones, in particular granting them many

11 A few years later, the IARA became autonomous and the humanitarian activities of Da'wa Islamiya were taken over by two foundations 'Health' and 'Emergency' and the African Charitable Society for Mother and Child Care (Bellion-Jourdan, 2004).

12 In the South, these associations willingly favoured Muslim populations and also proposed Islamic alternatives to other communities (El-Affendi, 1990).

tax exemptions.[13] This shows that this initial decision was not only tactical, it reinforced the idea that Islamists pay special attention to charitable practices. The emphasis on encouraging generosity in a Muslim public is not in the least specific to Islamists. Nevertheless, the way the Islamists conceive of this generosity, and the centrality they give it, shapes the roles they attribute to the state and society (Marchal, 1999).

When the Islamists came to power in 1989, they followed the Socialists twenty years before them by setting out to sustainably transform the country and its society. For the former, however, the implementation of 'good' development was not subject to a set pattern but needed to come from the 'good' actions of Islamised citizens. It was not a matter of setting up a new institutional structure or public policies designed explicitly to correct the inequities resulting from the accumulation of capital in a Sudan economically structured in favour of the central regions, but of turning each Sudanese citizen into a 'good' Muslim.[14] The Islamist project is aimed primarily at fostering a new spirit in individuals;[15] it focuses on devotion conceived both as an individual and as a social practice (Roy 1992). Therefore, the legitimacy of development implemented is linked to the legitimacy of the actors who promote it and to the legitimacy of their tools. This legitimacy should be primarily based on religion. As is clear from Turabi's aforementioned statement to the Kuwaiti newspaper, what counts is not so much the fate of potential beneficiaries as the Islamic project to which the donor contributes.[16] Thus, Islamists do not seek to transform the mode of production of material life conditions as such, but rather consider that the inherent inequalities in society will be 'naturally' corrected by the Islamisation of societies and individual practices. If they are nonetheless convinced that the entire machinery of the economy must be conquered, this is primarily to secure their position in power, which will allow them to implement their project and find positions of influence for men, whose religious

13 Interviews, Khartoum, 2011.

14 Darfur has revealed that this priority was not shared by all and that most members of the peripheral regions were probably hoping for a much more active commitment on the part of the Islamist state to transform the inegalitarian dynamics of development in the country.

15 Reversals in the economic policies of the new regime also reflect battles within the regime between advocates of a liberal approach and those favouring a more statist line. The latter lost the first battle, with the appointment in 1990 of Abdel Rahim Hamdi, who for the next two decades would be the architect of the country's economic policies.

16 The creation of a Ministry of Planning with wide prerogatives, and the various activities in every sphere of Sudanese society, illustrate the Islamists' specific social strategy aimed at renewing Sudanese society on the basis of its individuals.

faith will be the engine of change. The hesitations and debates within the Islamic movement as to the economic directions to be taken reflect this lack of a development model.[17] The choices made in this area stemmed much more from the political agenda of Islamists seeking to stabilise the North, while continuing the war in the South, than they did from an ideological imperative or any logic of expertise to implement a specific development plan (Marchal and Ahmed, 2010).[18]

Redistribution practices are a typical example of operations promoted by the Islamist project, due to their individual and social character: by acting piously, the donor earns his or her salvation while signifying his belonging to the Islamic city that he or she is building. Charity thus becomes a tool for developing Islamic society, as illustrated by the institutionalisation of several old practices of evergetism such as paying the religious tax (*zakat*),[19] which became mandatory in 1990, and whose base was also widened.

Logically, it is the generosity of those actors favoured by the regime that is primarily sought. Islamist militants donate up to 30 percent of their income to the movement.[20] Economic actors who were close to the Islamists and have directly benefited from the largesse of the new government were also eagerly asked to act on behalf of the common good,[21] as in the case of the Darfuri businessman Adam Yagoub, who—in Khartoum in the 1990s—chaired the very exclusive club that brought together the 25 most powerful Sudanese entrepreneurs.[22] Adam was particularly generous to, and especially in Darfur, his native region, where he also started his business career, but he also funded the Sudanese state while executing—for instance—certain government contracts for the Army.[23]

17 On the role played by charitable donors in social integration, see the discussion (in a different context—the end of the Roman Empire) in Brown (2002); see also Ben Néfissa et al. (2005).

18 On this aspect, see Tozy and Hibou (2015) and Singer (2008).

19 This tax was introduced at the behest of Islamists in 1984 but was at that time a purely voluntary measure, intended to be imposed only on wealthy Muslims, for an amount that generally corresponded to 2.5 percent of their annual income.

20 Interviews with former members of the movement, Khartoum, 2015.

21 Interviews, Khartoum, 2004–2012; see also the episode of a government tour of the markets of the capital, as related by Baillard and Haenni (1997).

22 I analyse his career in Chevrillon-Guibert (2013b).

23 The list of his benefactions can be found in his official biography, published by his family after his death (Adam Yagoub Haroun, 2003); interviews with one of Adam Yagoub Haroun's sons, Khartoum, 2008, 2011 and 2015.

It is easy to understand the conjunction of interests that entrepreneurs glimpse at this point, with the state appealing to their generosity in the context of practices of 'discharge' (Hibou, 1999) and their own economic interests: in exchange for their donations, these businessmen hope to obtain various benefits in return. This was particularly true in the 1990s when the government decided to privatise most large public companies; today one finds a similar dynamic in the allocation of licences for exploration and mining, an activity for which the state is responsible (Chevrillon-Guibert, 2016b). On the side of the state, one can easily imagine the mutual interest of such action as a tool to develop clientelism, and also to control prosperous individuals whose allegiance can be tested. Like the voluntary donations towards the regime's projects, the proper payment of *zakat* becomes an open sesame for developing one's business in Islamist Sudan, not only because it reflects the Islamic ethos of the entrepreneur, but also because it indicates his or her financial allegiance to the regime. And this allegiance was essential for the Islamist regime especially in the early years when it was actually fighting to survive, as its ability to provide a basic standard of living for the population was limited by an economy in crisis and the government was not yet in full control of all the machinery of state. Thus, the participation of society in public affairs did not lead to a withdrawal of the state but rather to its redeployment, since it was exercising greater control over economic actors and there was an extremely high level of permeability between society and state.

The promotion of the Islamic repertoire of values in the new form of government did not prevent a certain prevarication, in a classic pattern whereby state resources were appropriated by those actors in the system who were in positions of power (board members and administrative and/or political authorities). Soon, in addition to being the tool of generosity—as 'generous' entrepreneurs sought to win favours from the government—*zakat* also became a means of enrichment for several members of the state hierarchy who directly benefited from its funds (Muna Abdalla, 2008). Through citizen participation, development has thus become a political arena in which support is sought and also tested.

Major businessmen have never been, and are still not, the only people to be asked to contribute. All economic actors are invited to fund the civil and military operations of the state, whether this involves social philanthropy or financial tribute.[24] Thus in Khartoum, where the bulk of the country's resources

24 The distinction is made by Bellion-Jourdan (1997, 1).

are concentrated,[25] traders are encouraged to set up local charities, in the regions[26] and also in the capital, and to participate in state projects. On this last point, I should point out the long list of requests that have been and are being made to traders in the different markets of Khartoum. A letter sent, in 2002, by traders from the Libya souk, one of the largest markets in the Sudanese capital, lists the major contributions made by these traders to the community.[27] It begins by citing all the market's infrastructure (including official buildings) and then mentions SDP 50,000 (USD 38 000) donated to the Sudanese army in 1984; several donations between 1995 and 1996 for the development of Sudanese security; a billion SDD (USD 13 millions) in 1997 to support the army and SDD 500 million in 2000 (USD 1,94 million) for the development of Muslim culture:[28] to buy food for the *mujahid*—the name given to members of the Popular Defence Forces (PDF) fighting in the South in the name of jihad—and to fund mass weddings. It also mentions, without giving any amount, the financial support provided for the establishment of a camp for the PDF. This list shows that, in

25 Since independence, Khartoum has grown at a rate well above that of other Sudanese cities due to the centralisation of Sudanese politics and the unequal distribution of resources. Indeed, in 1990, the conurbation was home to 73 percent of domestic industry, 85 percent of commercial businesses in the country, 80 percent of banking services, 85 percent of bank loans to industry and 71 percent of those made with regard to real estate, 70 percent of taxpayers, and 80 percent of contributions. The decentralisation on which the Islamists embarked has not reduced the widening gap between the economy of Greater Khartoum and that of other regions, any more than has the oil economy that developed in the early years of the new millennium, even though that economy accounted for up to 7 percent of GDP and nearly 60 percent of the national government's resources in 2008. Indeed, although the oil deposits are located in the regions, most of the economic benefits are concentrated in the capital and have generated only a very small profit for the oil-producing regions. The economic recovery that began in 2012 might change this division of wealth to some slight degree by involving the regions of the north and the east, and that between the two Niles where newly promoted agricultural and mining projects are located.

26 While all of the very powerful Darfuri business figures I have met, or their entourages (Adam Yagoub, Adam Daossa, and Siddiq Wada, to mention only the most famous), have founded charities to promote the development of Darfur and their native regions in particular, the same is also true of many smaller traders, who have joined colleagues from the same village or the same community to found charities for the development of their villages or to assist members of their communities. Interviews, Khartoum, 2008 and 2011.

27 The letter can be found in the appendix of my doctoral thesis (Chevrillon-Guibert, 2013a).

28 1000 SDP (Sudanese first pound) = 100 SDD (Sudanese Dinar) = 1 SDG (Sudanese second and third pound). Historical data of exchange rates can be found on the website of the Sudanese Central Bank. Data can also be found in the Master thesis of Mussabal (2008).

addition to being encouraged to actively participate in the local development of their market by directly financing certain works, traders have also been ordered to mobilise for the nation. Just as the rest of the population was involved in the conscription of young people into the PDF, it was also expected to play an active part in the regime's war effort against the South, as it was investing in the establishment of those paramilitary forces in charge of protecting the regime. A similar pattern exists today with the Rapid Support Forces (RSF): these were created from the former Janjaweed militia and assist the PDF.

The enactment of the Popular Defence Forces Act in 1989 was part of the same context, as it established a paramilitary force whose objective was cooperation with the armed forces and the regular security services, but also the promotion, among Sudanese citizens, of a 'level of security consciousness' (Mohamed Salih, 2005, 8). The public sphere, then, was not viewed as the responsibility of a particular sector of the populace (administrators and politicians) but rather as every person in the country, combined: they were all called upon to be aware of their role. Again, the request for popular participation to establish a paramilitary security force was not specific to the Islamist regime, since the PDF were created by the Sadiq al-Mahdi government in 1986 to counter the militia of the Islamic movement, but also, and above all, to fight the Sudan People's Liberation Army in the South. However, here too the change lay in the growing importance of the PDF in the 1990s compared to that of the regular armed forces (El-Battahani, 2016a). M.A. Mohamed Salih believes that by 1996 their number exceeded that of the armed forces and in 1999 it was three times higher (80,000 regular soldiers, 3,500 Islamist militants appointed as military officers, and 150,000 PDF) (Mohamed Salih, 2005, 9). The participation of the populace was encouraged by a religious rhetoric calling upon those drafted to wage jihad in the 'godless areas' of the South. Nevertheless, we must not lose sight of the material interests also involved in this process: the PDF provided the regime with protection against any attempted coup[29] and the availability of inexpensive soldiers; for individuals who signed up, it meant an income, or at least a recognised position in society. Thus, both conviction and

29 Their effectiveness was demonstrated during the attack carried out by the Justice and Equality Movement on the capital in May 2008. It was the PDF and the national security forces (not the regular troops) that defended the city. Even now, the threat of an attack on Khartoum by the front representing the armed opposition leads the government to regularly deploy the PDF (now strengthened by rapid support forces created from the former Janjaweed militia) in all the districts and strategic locations in the city (Observations, 2013–16). This was also true during the major events of June 2012 and September 2013. The PDF took the lead in combats in which the loyalty of the military could not be counted on.

material interests dictated the actions of the different groups involved and it is still the case today with RSF (El-Battahani, 2016b).

This active participation of citizens in public affairs, which includes their charitable activities, reflects a gradual withdrawal of the state in favour of active elements working on the revolutionary project. In the episode of the famine in Darfur in 1991 and 1992, for example, one cannot say that the Darfuri state was insensitive to the tragedies afflicting its people or that it held itself aloof from development issues. Rather, it was omnipresent and omnipotent, through the mechanisms of 'discharge'. The citizens of this Islamist state were now deemed responsible and ordered to create charities and to finance the city, including its buildings in the public space (mosques, roads, special public institutions, etc.) and its services (urban roads, hospital services and security services). These practices, then, do not point to a 'failure' of the state in Sudan or its 'weakness', but reflect instead a form of government that, to some extent, strengthens the state. The high level of porosity between the state and society promoted by such a form of government is not without consequences for the forms taken by development in Sudan: the state coffers were empty in the first decade of Islamist Sudan, and so the major development projects of the 1990s were based on these redistributive practices, made possible by the direct involvement of citizens who were now the architects of development, whether this was voluntary or obligatory. The manner in which individuals participated in this redistribution thus proved central to the way development was created, and clearly shaped it in all its aspects.

3 Charity and the Creation of Asymmetry and Differentiation

On the side of the ruled, how has this summons to generosity been heard and translated into practical terms? How can we evaluate the potential transformations furthered by this form of government?

One could certainly question the nature of the generosity of the ruled, assessing the 'success' or 'failure' of the Islamist project on the basis of the stated intentions of the actors concerned. It could then be explained in one of two alternative ways: by looking at their convictions, whether religious or ethical, or at their material interests. This type of reasoning would suggest that the social philanthropy of the traders seems to be motivated more by their non-material and ideational interests (religious faith or community culture) while their evergetic practices—that is to say, their donations in favour of public life, are based on material interests (gaining a higher social status). Yet the reality is much more complex if we step back from the intentions and justifications claimed by the actors or attributed to them. We can gauge it only if we take into account the 'constellation of interests' in which their charitable practices are deployed.[30]

Take the example of the Darfuri traders from the great Libya souk; traders who flourished in the early years of Islamist domination. There was a significant demand for their support from members of their community, both those who had remained in Darfur, and were terribly impoverished by the conflicts and droughts that had lasted decades, and those who had migrated to Khartoum and needed to be taken care of, especially on arrival. The welcome offered by these wealthy individuals already settled in Khartoum was critical for Darfuris who were arriving in the capital even more impoverished than they might have been, as the roads between Khartoum and Darfur are long and expensive, making round trips between their villages and the capital few and far between.

The Libya souk, with its high level of development and preponderance of Darfuri traders from the Zaghawa communities, turned into an 'airlock' of integration for migrants from this community, who have consistently found jobs there.[31] These migrants have certainly been a burden for the traders, but they have also been a boon to them, providing a cheap and accountable workforce, in a political context where discretion and trust were the fundamental conditions for the exercise of activities that often took place outside the official channels of the economy.[32] In addition, the migrants have managed to become representatives of the traders in distributing the market's products. If we focus only on these motivations, however many and varied they may be, we will fail to take into account the actual way in which the generosity of traders is connected to the interests of power. It is precisely this connection—between an incentive to give and to act for the good of the community, the pursuit of personal goals, and the ability to respond to and to appropriate the injunctions of those in power—that generates the sometimes unconceptualised and contradictory effects of development.

30 I have been inspired by Hibou (2011) here. She draws on Weber (1978), as interpreted by Dobry (2013).

31 Interviews (2004–11) with traders who arrived in Khartoum in the 1970s, 1980s and 1990s.

32 We should bear in mind that the strategy adopted by Islamists to gain power has involved investing in the official economic sector through Islamic finance, but also more 'informal' means, using foreign exchange and money transfer services' networks. Upon their assumption of power, they implemented a witch-hunt in this parallel economy so as to ensure that the gateway to power would not be reopened by others after them.

In assessing these effects, let us look again at the traders in the Libya souk who flourished with the rise to power of the Islamists; this will help us to understand what their actual practices and their 'trajectories of accumulation' tell us about the experience of Islamist development.[33] When it came to power in the early 1990s, the Islamic movement sought to undermine the foundations of the hegemonic alliance built by the major traditional parties since the Independence of the country. In the commercial sector, this took concrete shape in the intimidation or arrest of members of these parties, but also in the systematic destruction of the established commercial bourgeoisie, even if this latter was not openly militant. In the eyes of the new regime, its dominant position in the economic field, and its sociological composition, led to suspicions that it was a potential source of support for traditional parties. The Islamists primarily targeted the major traders linked to these traditional parties, traders who had re-established their business activities during the democratic interlude that followed the fall of the Nimeiry regime. Thus, in the early years of the Islamist regime, most of them—if they were not arrested or did not lose everything due to the first economic measures taken against them—went into exile. In this sense, the Islamists had learned from the socialist experiment: a similar process had taken place at the very beginning of the Nimeiry regime under which all foreign companies had been forced to leave the country and the upper class faithful to the traditional parties had been generally repulsed (Niblock, 1987). Smaller Sudanese traders, who were not targeted by this witch-hunt, found this an excellent opportunity to engage in new business. Therefore a rather similar process took place in the early 1990s when entrepreneurs close to the major traditional parties left the country. A report by the World Bank in 2000 states that in 1994 a total of 282.6 in every 100,000 people had been imprisoned and that, for 1997 alone, 374,110 Sudanese had sought asylum abroad (*World Development Indicators*, quoted in Suleiman, 2007, 2).

The vacuum created by the expulsion of the traditional bourgeoisie did not benefit only those businessmen who were openly close to the regime. Other, less politicised entrepreneurs used their practical expertise to thrive in the space freed up by this process. In the capital, this greatly favoured the activities of the traders in the Libya souk, a popular market established in the late 1970s by Zaghawa Darfuri migrants and connected during its early years to the

33 We take this notion in the sense assigned by Geschiere and Konings (1993). It allows the authors to understand the historical variations in the possible modes of accumulation, which mean that, within the same country, there are various modes of accumulation shaping the relations between the State of Cameroon and the different regions of that country.

border trade with Libya (Chevrillon-Guibert, 2016a). This market became, at the turn of the 1990s, the major market for the import of manufactured goods such as textiles, electrical appliances and hi-fi equipment. The sociological composition of the traders in the Libya souk, who came exclusively from the regions and not the major trading families in Khartoum, explains why they were not worried by the witch-hunt that followed the coming to power of the Islamists—especially as one of them, a fervent Zaghawa Islamist (this community is very active in the market), was chosen to oversee all the popular councils[34] in Umbadda, where the Libya souk is located. His intervention has enabled the market to develop. Public investments were made in infrastructure (a road serving the market, the construction of permanent shops, sanitation, etc.) and facilities were provided to the local popular councils to fund the traders' activities thanks to their role in the distribution of products subsidised by the regime. These committees tended to favour certain market traders.

This policy has been a success: in just a few years, the Libya souk has taken over from the historic markets of the city centre. Nevertheless, one has to wonder to what extent the traders in the Libya souk, who have found themselves favoured 'by default' by the new regime because of their non-politicisation, have actually been incorporated into these new hegemonic alliance built by the Islamists. It is crucial for our argumentation to answer this question, as it is the generosity of economic actors such as those of the Libya souk that has been sought by the Islamists to develop the country. So their actions constitute the core of the regime's development model.

In Darfur, we have seen that the refusal on the part of the regional state to call on Western aid, and the decision to encourage local mutual aid mechanisms, plus the extreme intensity of the relationship between the state and society, have led the precarious populations to rely on their family, clan and village networks—which all usually overlap. This configuration has also exacerbated the competition between groups for access to the local state and its scarce resources. The generosity of this new petty bourgeoisie has thus mainly taken the form of a community-based social philanthropy; other calls on their generosity from the regime, such as participating in public welfare, have been unwelcome, as they came on top of social obligations already considered

34 Popular councils (in Arabic: al-Lijan al-Sha'biyah meaning people's committee) are a central institution in the Islamist regime. They are the ultimate level of the federal system set up by the Islamists on their coming to power. Established on the model of the socialist popular committees of the socialist regime, they mainly play an intermediary role between the population and higher institutional levels.

colossal.[35] The scale of this community-based social philanthropy was further intensified by the withdrawal of the state from certain spheres, for example in terms of aid to cover the living costs of students, who had previously been receiving large government subsidies. Many traders began funding student accommodation for members of their families or people from their villages. But this entailed changes to community bonds, because, in regions like Darfur, belonging to a family or a village largely overlaps with belonging to one's ethnic group. While, under the previous regimes, students used to be mixed together upon their arrival at the state boarding schools of main towns or the capital, they now began to live almost exclusively with people of their own ethnic community. Thus, by discharging their obligations onto various actors in society whose businesses they had favoured, the Islamists in power unwittingly fostered new forms of community even as their project proclaimed that ethnic groups would disappear because 'Muslims don't know ethnic minorities' (Lowrie, 1993).

The structure of trade in the Libya souk has also promoted the formation of these new communal bonds insofar as the souk is a wholesale market sending goods to the regions;[36] and the strengthening of links between the populations that had remained in Darfur and those who had left fostered the community spirit of the commercial networks. In Khartoum, a long-time business partner can easily be asked to host the relative of a trader who has settled in Darfur. Of course, these processes vary with the origins of the traders, because, although non-Darfuri market traders also have distribution networks in Darfur, they do not belong to the region, and thus the relationships forged in the pursuit of their economic activities do not follow community channels. Their professional relationships in Darfur are not based on the strong bonds of family or ethnic group (Granovetter, 1985). The development of their businesses in Khartoum, and their success, are part of the construction of very different trajectories from those of Darfuri traders: their paths are more independent and more in tune with the new shape taken by the old commercial bourgeoisie during the Islamist regime.

The situation of the Libya souk traders from the central regions,[37] like that of the migrants from these regions, is very different from those of the Darfuris. While, throughout the 1990s, there have been an increasing number of

35 Interviews, Khartoum, 2008.

36 Before the war, more than two-thirds of the products sold in the souk went to the markets of Darfur.

37 We define the 'central' regions as those of Khartoum, the north, the east, and the regions between the two Niles.

conflicts in Darfur that have resulted in many human tragedies, the centre of the country has grown more stable and thus more profitable economically. This improved economic situation in the central regions and their proximity to the capital has thus led to trajectories different from those of people from Darfur. For the natives of central regions, integration into the capital is easier and is certainly less dependent on the help of members of the community already settled in Khartoum. People from these central regions who decide to strike out commercially in Khartoum generally start as itinerant traders, not as employees of a major trader from their community.[38] In addition, those with the initial capital necessary to rent a shop usually have no preference with regard to the market in which they decide to settle; unlike Darfuri migrants who still systematically choose Omdurman, where members of their community live.[39] Traders from the central regions who have settled in the capital were thus called upon to provide aid by members of their native villages far less often than were Darfuri traders, and this is still true today, as the war in Darfur continues. The regime's appeal to their generosity thus finds a very different response among those from the central regions. They willingly finance the development of the market where they work, or of the locality where they live in Khartoum, and they also invest personally by becoming members of various local councils. The links they maintain with their native region also assume a different shape from those of Darfuri traders insofar as the personal needs of inhabitants from Central regions are less than those of Darfur meaning that traders from Central regions would contribute to community development of their native area rather than personal fundings. Sometimes Darfuri traders also contribute to public welfare in Khartoum or in their region, but this usually occurs at a later stage, once the needs of those around them have been satisfied, or if they have significant capital at their disposal. They are therefore less likely than traders from the central regions to practise evergetism.

So, in the end, even when what is made in the way of donations is similar, charitable practices vary from one trader to another, as do their effects. Some gifts help maintain community relations that urban life would have tended to weaken, and that the Islamists had announced they planned to fight against, while others are evidence of involvement in the development of the Islamist city.

38 Various interviews in markets in Omdurman, al-Arabi, the Shaabi souk in Omdurman and Khartoum in November 2008.

39 The city of Omdurman, which was that of the Mahdi, retains a central place in the *imaginaire* of all Darfuris. Interviews, Khartoum, 2004–12.

The war in Darfur, which broke out in 2003, reinforces this phenomenon. From the summer of 2004 onwards, many fund-raising drives have taken place in the Libya souk to assist the affected populations in the traders' native region.[40] The perpetuation of the conflict, which has now lasted for over ten years, increases even further the dependence of local populations vis-à-vis their compatriots living in other parts of the country, or abroad. In Khartoum, for example, all Darfuris are trying to help, in one way or another, the members of their community who are still in Darfur, most of whom now live in refugee camps.[41] The destruction of villages, and life in the camps, make it impossible to carry out development projects similar to those financed by traders from the central areas in their native own villages.

This differentiation is also taking shape within regions, and between social groups. In Darfur, while the prosperity of some members of the Zaghawa communities has led to a high level of redistribution and encouraged the establishment of significant links of patronage, this is not the case for communities that have few business activities, whose members can count only on themselves. Without intermediaries, they look much more directly to the state, especially as, with the arrival of oil revenues in the early years of the new millennium, the state now has substantial resources at its disposal. These differentiated expectations created by the mechanisms of 'discharge' favour a high degree of asymmetry between social groups and thus make it possible to shed light on the decision taken by various Darfuri groups at the beginning of the war to join the state militias or, conversely, to opt for neutrality.

Other government initiatives, such as the creation from scratch of a civil administration (*an-nizam al-ahli*) in Khartoum based on ethnicity, handling only people from the western and southern regions, have also favoured this differentiation. This new administration is similar to that of the traditional administration of the regions (*idarat al-ahlia*), but its members are appointed by the regime. Like the popular committees, this new institution is responsible for encouraging participation in the rallies organised by the regime but also for national security, with individual contributions this time being sought via channels of ethnicity. If the government's goal is to more effectively control the population of Khartoum, where new Darfuris and southerners are constantly arriving, this policy mainly helps to fix individuals now living in Khartoum in their ethnicity, even as urban life and the gentrification of the local

40 Observations, Libya souk, Khartoum, 2004 and 2006; interviews, 2008–14.

41 Interviews, Khartoum, France and Juba, 2006–13.

populations[42] tend to weaken this same ethnicity. In Darfur, the recreation of a traditional administration has also tended to solidify identity by ethnicising the machinery of local political power in a devastated region. This hardening of identity boundaries has also been favoured by many administrative changes (Takana, 2008), which have tended to create mono-ethnic zones in previously ethnically mixed territories, gradually attaching the authority of traditional leaders to ethnicity and not, as previously, to region (Abdul-Jalil, 2015, 223–234).

In Khartoum, the regime also created, in the case of some communities, councils (*shura*) that brought together the elites of the same ethnic group, relying on their patronage to gain the favour of their community and, through their evergetism, making it possible for them to complete various projects without engaging the state financially. For Turabi, whose thinking largely shaped the policies implemented by the Islamists in the early years of the regime, the councils are the central institutions of this new Islamic state. They comprise the democratic Islamic alternative to Western democracy (Moussalli 1994, especially 57–63).[43] *Shura* (consultation) is supposed to allow the unification (*tawhid*) of all individuals by ensuring the development of a permanent consensus among the people in the framework of God's law (*sharia*). But creating these councils on an ethnic basis that includes many major traders promotes patronage, as it gives these traders a position of power, with the regime ensuring the personal allegiance of the members of the council by granting them favours.[44] This process has given a communal flavour to the activities of this assembly, including the development projects it supervises.

Thus, the combination of different political factors and decisions (from the mechanisms of 'discharge' to the desire to control populations, from keeping Darfur in a state of underdevelopment to the increasing number of conflicts tearing the region apart), has resulted in the strengthening of ties between members of the same Darfuri ethnic, village and family communities in certain parts of the region, without this objective having been actively pursued by the authorities. This practice has, in concrete terms, brought closer together those trajectories that had tended to diverge in the 1980s, at the time of the

42 Unlike those of Darfur, the populations of Khartoum saw their living standards rise in the 1990s, and this favoured certain practices of consumption and a certain individualisation of success.

43 In this passage, Moussalli refers to Hassan Al-Turabi (1987a, 25–26; 1987b, 79–80).

44 On the way peripheral elites are used and their allegiance is negotiated in return for payment and/or positions of accumulation, see de Waal (2007). For examples of *shura*, see Abdul-Jalil (2014) and Chevrillon-Guibert (2013a, 552 ff.).

great migrations and the early years of the Islamic regime. Meanwhile, in Khartoum, it has limited the development of more horizontal links between people from different regions of Sudan—people sharing identical living conditions in markets such as the Libya souk, and has recreated a shared sense of destiny between populations that have remained in Darfur and those that have settled in the rest of the country or abroad.

Faced with the challenges that accompany the exercise of power, with the concessions and negotiations necessarily involved in day-to-day life, the construction of a new hegemonic alliance and development related to charitable practices promoted by the Islamists take unconceptualised and differentiated shapes, depending on the groups and regions involved. The difference is sharper between Darfuri traders and those from other regions because of the promotion by the Islamists of a particular entrepreneurial ethos—that of the modern, liberal entrepreneur who, while falling in with injunctions to generosity, also favours asymmetric and unequal development.

4 The Entrepreneurial Ethos as a Factor of Exclusion

During the early years of the regime, to benefit from the opening made possible by the Islamists' takeover and the 'organised bankruptcy' of the actors of the previous hegemonic alliance, new economic actors did not hesitate to move into the spheres of Islamist sociability. They did so particularly through the evergetic practices mentioned above, and, as we have seen in the Libya souk actors from the central regions have deployed more zeal in this task than their Darfuri colleagues have employed in supporting the populations of their bankrupt region. The gradual gentrification of these small-scale economic actors from the central regions reflects the gradual emergence of a new type of entrepreneur favoured by Islamists.

Before the petrodollars started coming in at the beginning of the new millennium, the launch of the 'salvation programme'—consisting of a series of reforms under the leadership of the new Minister of Finance and the Economy, Abdelrahim Hamdi—one of the founders of the Faysal Islamic Bank and a former London banker—fundamentally changed the rules of economic activity. The plan, then designed for a period of ten years, from 1992 to 2002, provided for a series of economic liberalisation measures and the privatisation of many public corporations. Such a programme would not have been unpopular with the economists of the International Monetary Fund (IMF), as the decision to reduce state spending and liberalise the economy was similar to the policies they themselves usually develop. The transition from a planned economy to a market economy in the context of a significant restriction of state budgets entailed a rearrangement of the positions of all the economic actors. Just as the seizure of power had provided the Islamists with new resources, shifted their interests, and changed their alliances, the new policies being followed again contributed to transformation.

In the trade sector, these economic developments went hand in hand with the commercial boom in Dubai, which led to a major reorganisation of the supply chain, and also of business practices. Egyptian and Libyan imports, where traders excelled, lost their competitiveness, and ease of trade with Dubai meant that the ability to endure harsh working conditions, as well as the control of several commercial channels, were no longer the great assets, in terms of achieving business success, they had once been. However, other qualities became more useful, such as having a permanent visa for Saudi Arabia or at least having contacts there; resources that individuals from the central regions of Sudan possess more frequently, since many of them have emigration experience of the Gulf.[45] The profile of the successful entrepreneur was thus transformed.

The modernisation of professional practices carried out by the Islamists also led to significant changes. Legislation now required those seeking to carry out import activities to create trading companies, and several urban projects aimed to modernise the tangible practices of traders (shop fronts, the use of new technologies, etc.). These reforms were also designed to better control the sector, by combatting the opacity of commercial networks and the illegal practices that these networks' fluidity seems to facilitate. But this modernisation and the mastering of new codes of conduct and business practices require a basic minimum of education. Now, historically, education is an important marker of the difference between the old trading families of the central markets in the capital and entrepreneurs in the Libya souk who come from the regions and lower social strata. Wealth created by wholesale and import has made it possible to finance the education of the children of traders in the central markets. The fact that they settled earlier in the capital or in the major cities where educational institutions are more numerous than in Darfur (and also more numerous than in many central regions) also favoured this higher level of schooling. The new guidelines laid down by the Islamist regime therefore allowed the least politicised traders of the old bourgeoisie to go back into business, especially as many young entrepreneurs directly favoured by the Islamists in the early years of their regime had proven to be poor businessmen.

45 On the elites that emerged from the Islamist governmental experiment, see Chevrillon-Guibert (2017).

But in the late 1990s, the Islamist movement was ready to accept businessmen who were less ideologically correct, but more successful financially, especially since the development of oil revenues provided members of the regime and their families with direct resources much more significant than those previously gained from levies on business activities. The development of trade with the Gulf also promoted this comeback of people in line with the old bourgeoisie because many young people who invested in the central souks had spent some years in the Gulf to build up their capital.

Within the Libya souk, non-Darfuri traders were (like traders from the El Arabi souk or Omdurman) better educated than their Darfuri counterparts, because although they were not from the capital they had generally been better educated in their native regions.[46] The new global configuration of trade has accentuated both this advantage and the success enjoyed by these entrepreneurs. China's rise in the 1990s as a source of cheap supplies required significant capital, and it is the biggest non-Darfuri traders who had this capital. Similarly, it is they who control the machinery needed to trade with China—such as the ability to travel in a new universe much stranger than the Arab Gulf countries, Egypt or Libya had been—and a knowledge of new technologies such as the internet. The Arabic language is no longer of any particular use, as English is becoming an indispensable asset and is conferred by a good education. The local context is also proving very unfavourable to Darfuri traders: the war in Darfur is increasing the constraints on their ability to distribute goods, and the regime's distrust of them (it suspects them of supporting armed groups) is also a hindrance to their activities.

Thus, in the Libya souk, the profile of the entrepreneurs emerging in the late 1990s is similar to that of the old bourgeoisie of the central souks: educated, coming from the central regions, and also more individualistic. With them, community ties have loosened and aspirations are becoming more individualistic. Future plans primarily concern the individual and his nuclear family (wife, children)[47] and are part of the national community. These traders, we have seen, regularly invest part of their profits in politics, or at least in the public sphere. They are also active in those organisations that manage the activities

46 These observations were made by several Darfuri entrepreneurs who had been to university and noted the discrepancy between the level of education of Darfuri traders in the souk and that of traders from other regions (Khartoum interviews, 2014). Darfur has always been the Sudanese region with the lowest level of education, though there are big differences between different regions and different populations (see in particular the report 'Literacy and Education' prepared by the Central Bureau of Statistics in Khartoum).

47 Interviews, Khartoum, June 2015.

of their market and, with age and reputation, they achieve a status that is local (on the scale of the municipality) and then national (across Khartoum State or possibly in their region of origin), in a rather traditional pattern of annexation and clientelism. The results of the 2010 general elections,[48] which were very favourable to the regime, reflected the success of this scheme of development for the central regions, which saw the virtual disappearance of the major traditional parties in favour of the ruling party, the National Congress Party.

Meanwhile, the oil economy gave the regime new ways of achieving its modernising ambitions by allowing it to invest in modern, technological infrastructure. It was, yet again, the central regions that benefited from many projects during the 'oil decade': between 2001 and 2009, several large dams were built in the north, as well as 2,800 kilometres of paved roads extending from the capital to the north, the east, and the region between the two Niles, as against barely 300 kilometres in Darfur, even though it comprised one-fifth of Sudan before the separation of the South. This new infrastructure favours the economic development of these regions—which are, as an added advantage, at peace—and thus fosters the rising standard of living of their populations. Logically, traders from these regions benefit from this economic upturn, while in Darfur the lack of infrastructure and, in particular, the war greatly hampers trade and led to the impoverishment of the part of the population that is now in refugee camps.

The processes of differentiation and, in particular, the new modes of community life for some and the increase in individualisation for others have prevented the formation of a common destiny among the traders in the Libya souk. The policies implemented have reactivated the differentiated past lives led by everyone before they arrived in the market; similarly, the maintenance or—contrariwise—the abandonment by traders of the links that existed between them and the members of their communities who had remained in the regions appear to be factors of separation rather than reconciliation. It is also these historically constructed trajectories that shape the future plans of each group and their relationship to the world, in particular to the national community. While traders from the central regions tend to lose their original regional identity, this identity remains clearly marked and manifestly organises the specific social lives of Darfuri traders.

48 In the elections of 2015, largely boycotted by the opposition, there was no real political issue at stake. This was not the case for the elections of 2010, which—admittedly—were largely rigged, but which constituted the first test of power after the South had broken away, but also after the internal split among the Islamists in the late 1990s during which the leader of the movement, Hassan al-Turabi, was ousted.

However, some features that are emerging among many Darfuri traders, particularly the Zaghawa, are not completely different from those of the new Islamist bourgeois elite. The Darfuri traders too have upgraded their professional practices and appreciate the benefits of a certain material modernity, but they are clearly very different from the bourgeois elite in the importance they place, in their social relationships, on strong bonds, often those of family. The existence of such bonds is, for many, the sine qua non of their economic success, and their relationship to the land and the state and hence to development. While the bourgeois elite strives for integration into and recognition in the national community, the framework of these much more mobile Darfuri traders is largely disconnected from the national territory. It is primarily their personal experiences and their native territory, as they imagine it through the collective memory of their ethnic community, which shape the contours of their own 'mental map' (Migdal, 2004, 9–10).

The new economic policies of the regime could further alter the situation: it is now the regime's task to remedy the loss of the oil economy, concomitant with the breakaway of the South in 2011, by encouraging investment in agriculture and mining. It is true that these new economic development policies largely reflect the framework of the old ones by fostering the modernisation of these sectors (through the promotion of industrialisation in the mining sector and the rationalisation of the commercial livestock sector), which encourages, yet again, a certain kind of entrepreneur. Similarly, the concentration of administrative procedures and business activities in Khartoum in the case of the mining sector (Chevrillon-Guibert 2016b), and in certain specific areas all located in the central regions in the case of the livestock sector,[49] reinforces a very unequal development that favours the country's capital and certain regions. However, the fact that these two sectors are largely dependent on activities in the regions, some of which are on the periphery, may alleviate this inequality, which has generated highly unbalanced regional development. The way in which activities, whether involving mineral extraction or agriculture, are conducted as well as the conflicts they generate locally promote the redeployment of regional strategies for investors who themselves usually remain in Khartoum.[50] The asymmetry that the new policies perpetuate thus leads, in parallel, to a redefinition of relations with the regions, although the profoundly unequal structure of the Islamist development experiment is not explicitly challenged by the new development projects envisaged by the government.

49 Interviews and observations carried out as part of research conducted jointly with Alice Frank, Paris 1/PRODIG, since 2014.

50 Interviews, Khartoum, June 2015 and April 2016.

5 Conclusion

The development experiment set up by the Islamists during their first decades in power does not fall into a predetermined, explicit pattern that their political opponents might have challenged before it was implemented. The specificity of their experiment does not lie, either, in the kind of neo-liberal development that they are advancing, as this neo-liberal thinking now seems widely shared by the entire political class. The tools of development count much more than its results. Thus, when it comes to development, Islamists first encourage practices they consider 'islamically' good because they are the ones which are legitimate in their eyes. The form taken by this development, and its concrete results once applied, which sometimes conflict with the political project of the Islamic movement, take second place; they count in the political agenda of power but are not part of the civilisation project in which the movement is engaged.

Charitable practices have naturally been part of the Islamic repertoire promoted by the Islamist project and, logically, it is economic actors who have mainly been asked to contribute. As no specific development blueprint has been provided for them, these actors display their charity in different ways, according to the local and human contexts in which they live, but also in accordance with the particular ways they conceive their roles in the circles to which they belong (family and ethnic, local and national communities). This participation in development, sometimes engaged in under duress, involves many changes, not only in the forms taken by development and in its scale (which is dependent on the donors' capacities) but also in the spaces concerned (regions, capital, urban and rural zones) and in the groups that benefit. Such variations necessarily produce highly disparate and often conflicting results, since—ultimately—some recipients initially targeted by the government have been excluded and the regional inequalities inherited from previous experiences are maintained and even accentuated. The same process still subsists today, yet the legitimacy of development is not really discussed because it is based on practices deemed to be legitimate. The oil economy of the early twenty-first century however, has completely reshuffled the cards, profoundly reorganising the balance of power between the state and society: during this period, the regime has not only claimed religious legitimacy, that of the Islamic revolution, but above all a modernising legitimacy, that of the developmental state (Jones et al., 2013). In the latter model, the rulers justify their position of power by their ability to transform the economy and by the material benefits that result. This transformation favours conflicts around development because it places the results, and not the tools, at the heart of the debates on its legitimacy. The glaring inequalities feed deep frustration and a sense of injustice among those excluded from development, especially since this oil wealth could have helped to proactively remedy these inequalities. The regime, however, has preferred to consolidate its base among the populations of the capital and the central regions and to ignore the inequalities at the heart of the conflicts that are now tearing the country apart, as was the case for the South. Thus, far from pursuing any original trajectory, this Islamic state seems rather to be pursuing a path of 'asymmetric formation',[51] in line with its historical trajectory—a trajectory that has produced injustice and long been a source of conflict.

References

Abdalla, Muna A. (2008) *Poverty and Inequality in Urban Sudan: Policies, Institutions and Governance*, African Studies Collection, 13 (Leiden: African Studies Center), http://hdl.handle.net/1887/13106 (accessed on 22 June 2016).

Abdul-Jalil, Musa A. (2015) 'From native administration to native system: the reproduction of a colonial model of governance in post-independence Sudan', in A.M. Assal and M.A. Abdul-Jalil (eds.) *Past, Present, and Future. Fifty Years of Anthropology in Sudan* (Bergen: Chr. Michelsen Institute).

Abdul-Jalil, Musa A. (2014) *Retribalisation of the Educated Elite in Darfur and the Phenomenon of Tribal Shura Councils; with a Special Reference to the Fur Shura Council*, CMI Sudan Working Paper SWP, 5, 22 p., http://www.cmi.no/publications/5316-re tribalisation-of-the-educated-elite-in-darfur (accessed on 20 June 2016).

Adam Yagoub Haroun (2003) *The traits of the life of a religious, Adam Yagoub Haroun* (Khartoum: private publishing house, in Arabic).

Ahmed, E. (2007) 'Political Islam in Sudan. Islamists and the Challenge of Power (1989–2004)', in B.F. Soares and R. Otayek (eds.) *Islam and Muslim Politics in Africa* (New York: Palgrave Macmillan).

Al-Turabi, Hassan (1987a), *Qadaya al-huriyya wa al-wahda wa al-shura wa al-dimucratiyya* [Issues of Freedom, Unity, Shura and Democracy] (Jeddah: Al-Dar al-Su'udiya li al-Nashr waal-Tawzi').

Al-Turabi, Hassan (1987b), *Tajdid al-fikr al-islami* [The Renewal of Islamic Thought] (Jeddah: Al-Dar al-Su'udiya li al-Nashr waal-Tawzi').

51 This analysis, based on asymmetry and differentiation, owes much to the work of Béatrice Hibou in this area, especially her chapter 'La formation asymétrique de l'État en Tunisie. Les territoires de l'injustice', in Bono et al. (2015).

Andreau, J., A. Schnapp and P. Schmitt (1978) 'Paul Veyne et l'évergétisme (note critique)', *Annales*, 33(2), pp. 307–325.

Baillard I. and P. Haenni (1997) 'Libéralité prétorienne et État minimum au Soudan', *Égypte/Monde arabe*, 32, pp. 71–96, http://ema.revues.org/1671 (accessed on 22 June 2016).

Beckedorf, A.-S. (2012) *Political waters. Governmental water management and neoliberal reforms in Khartoum/Sudan* (Berlin: Lit Verlag).

Bellion-Jourdan, J. (2006) 'Les ONG islamiques sont-elles vraiment humanitaires ? Réflexions sur une vraie fausse question', *Vacarme*, 34, http://www.vacarme.org/article558.html (consulté le 18 décembre 2015).

Bellion-Jourdan, J. (2004) 'Réseaux transnationaux de l'aide humanitaire islamique : les ONG islamiques', in S. Ben Néfissa et al (eds.), *ONG et gouvernance dans le Monde arabe* (Paris : Khartala and CEDEJ), pp. 113–142.

Bellion-Jourdan, J. (1997) 'L'humanitaire et l'islamisme soudanais—Les organisations Da'wa Islamiya et Islamic African Relief Agency', *Politique Africaine*, 66, pp. 61–73, http://www.politique-africaine.com/numeros/pdf/066061.pdf (accessed on 20 June 2016).

Ben Néfissa, S., N. Abdelfattah, C. Hanafi S. Milani, (eds.) (2005) *NGOs and governance in the Arab world* (Cairo: American University in Cairo Press).

Bernal, V. (1997) 'Colonial Moral Economy and the Discipline of Development: The Gezira Scheme and Modern Sudan', *Cultural Anthropology*, 12(4), pp. 1–33, DOI: 10.1525/can.1997.12.4.447.

Bono, I., B. Hibou, H. Meddeb and M. Tozy (2015) *L'État d'injustice au Maghreb. Maroc et Tunisie* (Paris: Karthala).

Brachet, J. and V. Bonnecase (2013) 'Les « crises sahéliennes » entre perceptions locales et gestions internationales', *Politique africaine*, 130(2), pp. 5–22, DOI : 10.3917/polaf.130.0005.

Brown, P. (2002) *Poverty and Leadership in the Later Roman Empire* (Hanover: University Press of New England).

Brown, R. (1990) *The IMF and Paris Club Debt Rescheduling: A Conflicting Role?* ISS Working Paper, 30 (The Hague: Institute of Social Studies).

Brown, R. (1989) 'The Rationale and Effects of the IMF Stabilisation Programme in Sudan', in B. Campbell (ed.), *Political Dimensions of Third World Debt* (London: Macmillan), pp. 51–91.

Casciarri, B., A.M. Assal and F. Ireton (eds.) (2015) *Multidimensional Change in Sudan 1989–2011. Reshaping livelihoods, conflicts and identities* (Oxford and New York: Berghahn).

Chevrillon-Guibert, R. (2017) 'Importing goods to Khartoum: traders between Sudan, China and Dubai', in U. Röschenthaler and A. Jedlowski (eds.) *Mobility Between*

Africa, Asia and Latin America: Economic Networks and Cultural Interactions (London: Zed Books).

Chevrillon-Guibert, R. (2016a) 'Les commerçants zaghawa du Darfour (Soudan) : des passeurs de frontières', *Territoire en Mouvement*, 29, http://tem.revues.org/3303 (accessed on 20 June 2016).

Chevrillon-Guibert, R. (2016b) 'Le Boom de l'or au Soudan', *International Development Policy* 7.2, DOI : 10.4000/poldev.2231.

Chevrillon-Guibert, R. (2013a) *Des commerçants au cœur de l'expérience islamiste au Soudan. Rapports de/au pouvoir et recompositions des communautés darfouriennes zaghawa à l'aune des alliances du mouvement islamique soudanais (1950–2011)*, PhD thesis, (Clermont-Ferrand: Université d'Auvergne), http://www.fasopo.org/sites/default/files/jr/th_chevrillon-guibert.pdf (accessed on 20 December 2015).

Chevrillon-Guibert, R. (2013b) 'La Guerre au Darfour au prisme des alliances du mouvement islamique. Retour sur quelques trajectoires d'hommes d'affaires zaghawa', *Politique africaine*, 130(2), pp. 113–136, DOI : 10.3917/polaf.130.0113.

de Waal, A. (2007) 'Sudan: What kind of state? What kind of crisis?', *CSRC Occasional Paper*, 2, LSE, April, http://www2.lse.ac.uk/internationalDevelopment/research/crisisStates/download/op/op2DeWaal.pdf (accessed on 20 June 2016).

de Waal, A. (2005) *Famine that Kills. Darfur, Sudan* (Oxford: Oxford University Press, Oxford—1st edn 1989).

Dobry, M. (2013) 'Légitimité et calcul rationnel. Remarques sur quelques complications de la sociologie de Max Weber', in P. Favre, J.E.S. Hayward and Y. Shemeil, *Être gouverné: études en l'honneur de Jean Leca* (Paris: Presses de la FNSP), pp. 127–150.

El-Affendi, Abdelwahab (1990) '"Discovering the South": Sudanese Dilemmas for Islam in Africa', *African Affairs*, 89(356), pp. 371–389, http://www.jstor.org/stable/722373.

El-Battahani, Atta (2016a) 'Civil-Military Relations in Sudan: Negotiating Political Transition in a Turbulent Economy' in E. Grawert and Zeinab Abul-Magd (eds.), *Businessmen in Arms. How the Military and Other Armed Groups Profit in the MENA Region* (Lanham: Rowman & Littlefield Publishers).

El-Battahani, Atta (2016b) *The Sudan Armed Forces and Prospects of Change*, CMI Insight vol. 4, (Bergen: Chr. Michelsen).

Gallab, Abdullahi A. (2016) *Their Second Republic: Islamism in the Sudan from Disintegration to Oblivion* (New York: Routledge).

Gertel, J., R. Rottenburg and S. Calkins (eds.) (2014) *Disrupting Territories. Land, commodification and conflict in rural Sudan* (London: James Currey).

Geschiere, P. and P. Konings (1993) *Itinéraires d'accumulation au Cameroun* (Paris: Karthala).

Granovetter, M. (1985) 'Economic Action and Social Structure: The Problem of Embeddedness', *American Journal of Sociology*, 91(3), http://www.jstor.org/stable/2780199.

Harir, Sharif and T. Vedt, (eds.) (1994) *Short-Cut to Decay* (Uppsala: Nordiska Afrikainstitutet).

Hibou, B. (2011) *Anatomie politique de la domination* (Paris: La Découverte). English translation forthcoming (2017), *The Political Anatomy of Domination* (London: Palgrave).

Hibou, B. (1999) 'La décharge, nouvel interventionnisme?', *Politique africaine*, 73(1), pp. 6–15, DOI: 10.3917/polaf.073.0006.

Ibrahim, A.A. (1999) 'A Theology of Modernity: Hassan al-Turabi and Islamic Renewal in Sudan', *Africa Today*, 46(3/4), pp. 195–222, DOI: 10.1353/at.2003.0094.

Ibrahim, F. and H. Ruppert (eds.) (1988) *Rural urban migration and identity change. Case studies from the Sudan*, Bayreuther geowissenschaftliche Arbeiten, 11 (Bayreuth: Druckhaus Bayreuth).

Jones, J., B. Soares and H. Verhoeven (2013) *Africa's illiberal state-builders*, RSC Working Paper Series 89 (Oxford: University of Oxford), https://www.rsc.ox.ac.uk/files/publications/working-paper-series/wp89-africas-illiberal-state-builders-2013.pdf (accessed on 23 June 2016).

Lowrie, A. (1993) *Islam, Democracy, the State and the West: A Round table with Dr. Hasan Turabi*, World and Islam Studies Enterprise (Florida: Tampa), pp. 35–36.

Marchal, R. (1999) 'Des contresens possibles à la globalisation. Privatisation de l'État et bienfaisance au Soudan et au Somaliland', *Politique africaine*, 73(1), pp. 68–81, DOI: 10.3917/polaf.073.0068.

Marchal, R. and Einas Ahmed (2010) 'The Multiple Uses of Neoliberalism: War, New Boundaries, and Reorganization of the Government in Sudan', in F. Guttiérrez and G. Shönwälder (eds.), *Economic Liberalization and Political Violence: utopia or dystopia?* (New York: Pluto Press).

Migdal, J.S. (2004) *Boundaries and Belonging. State and Societies in the Struggle to Shape Identities and Local Practices* (Cambridge: Cambridge University Press).

Miller, C. (1993) 'Famine, conflits et aide internationale au Darfour, 1990–1992', *Égypte/Monde arabe*, first series 15–16, http://ema.revues.org/1017 (accessed on 24 August 2015).

Mohamed Salih, M.A. (2005) *Understanding the Conflict in Darfur*, Occasional Paper from the Centre of African Studies (Copenhagen: University of Copenhagen), 29 p. http://citeseerx.ist.psu.edu/viewdoc/download?doi=10.1.1.474.3260&rep=rep1&type=pdf (accessed on 22 June 2016).

Moussalli, A.S. (1994) 'Hasan al-Turabi's Islamist Discourse on Democracy and *Shura*', *Middle Eastern Studies*, 30(1), pp. 52–63, DOI: 10.1080/00263209408700982.

Mussabal, Y.M.A. (2008) 'Export Promotion Policies in the Sudan for the period (1990–2005)', Master Thesis, University of Khartoum (mineo).

Niblock, T. (1987) *Class and Power in Sudan—the dynamics of Sudanese Politics 1898–1985* (New York: State University of New York Press).

Patey, L. (2014) *The New Kings of Crude: China, India, and the Global Struggle for Oil in Sudan and South Sudan* (London: Hurst).

Roden, D. (1974) 'Regional Inequality and Rebellion in the Sudan', *Geographical Review*, 64(4), pp. 498–516.

Roy, O. (1992) *The Failure of Political Islam*, trans. Carol Volk (Harvard, MA: Harvard University Press).

Singer, A. (ed.) (2008) *Charity in Islamic Society* (Cambridge: Cambridge University Press).

Sørbø, G. and A.G.M. Ahmed (eds.) (2013) *Sudan Divided. Continuing Conflict in a Contested State* (New York: Palgrave Macmillan).

Suleiman, Osman (2007) *Current Privatization Policy in Sudan*, Policy Brief 52 (Michigan: The William Institute, University of Michigan).

Takana, Youssef (2008) *The Politics of Local Boundaries and Conflict in Sudan. The South Darfur Case*, Sudan Working Paper 2008/2 (Bergen: Chr. Michelsen Institute).

Tenret, E. (2016) 'Exclusive Universities: Use and Misuse of Affirmative Action in Sudanese Higher Education', *Comparative Education Review*, 60(2), pp. 375–402, DOI: 10.1086/685687.

Tozy M. and B. Hibou (2015) 'L'offre islamiste de justice sociale. Politique publique ou question morale ?', in B. Hibou, I. Bono, M. Tozy and H. Meddeb, *L'État d'injustice au Maghreb. Maroc et Tunisie* (Paris: Karthala).

Verhoeven, H. (2013) 'The Rise and Fall of Sudan's Al-Ingaz Revolution: the Transition from Militarised Islamism to Economic Salvation and the Comprehensive Peace Agreement', *Civil Wars*, 15(2), pp. 118–140, DOI: 10.1080/13698249.2013.817846.

Verhoeven, H. (2011) 'Climate change, conflict and development in Sudan: global neo-Malthusian narratives and local power struggles', *Development and Change*, 42(3), pp. 679–707, DOI: 10.1111/j.1467-7660.2011.01707.x.

Veyne, P. (1976) *Le pain et le cirque. Sociologie historique d'un pluralisme politique* (Paris: Le Seuil).

Warburg, G. (2003) *Islam, Sectarianism and Politics in Sudan since the Mahdiyya* (London: Hurst).

Weber, M. (1978) *Economy and Society. An Outline of Interpretive Sociology*, (Berkeley: University of California Press).

Woodward, P. (2013) 'Hasan Al-Turabi', in J.L. Esposito and E. El-Din Shahin (eds.) *The Oxford Handbook of Islam and Politics* (Oxford: Oxford University Press).

CHAPTER 12

A Neo-liberal Exception? The Defence Industry 'Turkification' Project

Anouck Gabriela Côrte-réal Pinto

Abstract

Presented at once as an example, evidence, and even a condition of the economic, technological, political and security development of Turkey, the 'Turkification' of the defence industry lies at the heart of the government's legitimacy. Following a socio-historical approach, this chapter aims to understand how this major project, inseparable from the ongoing formation of the state and of a national bourgeoisie organically related to it, was reconfigured in the neo-liberal era not despite globalisation but based on it, particularly through the commodification of Muslim solidarity and military protection. This project appears to constitute an instrument of 'nationaliberal' extraversion that is part of an unstable quest for hegemony, riven by numerous conflicts.

1 Introduction

The coming to power in Turkey in 2002 of the Justice and Development Party (*Adalet ve Kalkinma Partisi*, AKP), an offshoot of political Islam, is generally presented as the culmination of neo-liberal reforms in Turkey. These reforms, it is said, marked the end of the military-nationalist hegemony, as evidenced both by the large number of them that furthered the demilitarisation of the political scene and by the great mass trials of Turkish officers (the *Ergenekon* and *Balyoz or* 'Sledgehammer' cases). How, then, are we to interpret the reappropriation by this same party of the major project of the 'Turkification' of the defence industry, symbol of an enlightened pro-activism and a highly illiberal interventionism? The incantatory slogan 'a national tank, a national satellite and a national airline' ('*Milli tank, milli uydu, milli uçak*'), delivered during the 2011 elections and repeated and reinforced by the '2023 Political Vision of the AKP' (*AK Parti 2023 Siyasi vizyonu*), illustrates the particular commitment of the 'moderate Islamic' party to this major military project as a legitimising tool and a form of moral armament of the population (*Sabah*, 2011; AKP, 2012). This discursive focus is also reflected in an exceptional increase in military

DOI 10.1163/9789004349551_013

expenditure since 2006, partly due to the soaring number of major national defence projects initiated by the AKP: the 'hundred percent Turkish' *Anka* drone, the 'national' *Altay* tank, the 'local' *Atak* helicopter, the *Göktürk* satellite, and the *MILGEM* warship, etc. (Yentürk, 2014). Finally, it coincides with an unprecedented internationalisation of the armament sector, marked by a diversification of partners and external suppliers and by an exceptional rise in exports.

Following a socio-historical, 'non-dependentist approach to dependence' as proposed by Jean-François Bayart (Bayart, 2006, vi), an approach itself inspired by Gramsci, this chapter aims to understand how this major project of Turkification—inseparable from the ongoing formation of the Turkish state and a national bourgeoisie organically linked to it—has continued to develop in the neo-liberal era, not *in spite of globalisation* but *based on it*. In particular, we will focus on the interrelated levels of the project's sectoral, national, and international dimensions in order to understand how this development project is a fiction with multiple power effects; how it articulates, feeds into and results from a market logic and a logic of national affirmation. By highlighting the arts of 'making do' with globalisation (Certeau, 1990), this text calls into question both the proactive vision of the political and the vision of a self-regulating market; two ahistorical theories that are largely dominant in discourses regarding development in Turkey.[1] With few exceptions, the concept of development is presented in Turkish scholarly literature either as a social engineering project (a Kemalist project or the Islamic project promoted by Necmettin Erbakan) or as an economic achievement; reflecting, respectively, a desire to break free from the past and a desire to enter into capitalist modernity (Unsaldi, 2011). By focusing on the historicity of this concept in Turkey through an analysis of the major project of the Turkification of the defence industry, we can illustrate and understand its hegemonic nature, its multiple meanings, and its concrete effects of domination.

2 An Exception to the Neo-liberal Rule? The Genesis of an 'Anachronistic' Development Project for National Emancipation

The defence industry is the alpha and omega of the project for the Turkification of the Turkish economy: the absence of an indigenous defence industry (more broadly of one employing advanced technology) is seen, first, as one of the main causes behind the Ottoman defeat against the Russian Empire in

1 Among the most fervent critics of the paradigm of development in Turkey are Fikret Baskaya (2005), Caglar Keyder (1993; 1987) and Ayşe Buğra (this volume).

the XVIIIth century and, second, as one of the conditions necessary for 'national recovery' (Inalcik, 1992; Lafi, this volume). The multiple meanings of the Turkish term *kalkınma*—which conveys both 'development' and 'healing' (of an injured national psyche)—reflects this siege mentality of development in Turkey, by which the concept is seen not just as a way of improving conditions but in itself a condition of national survival. As a proof and a gauge of national emancipation and of an ambivalent relationship with Europe, linked to a traumatic past embodied in what is referred to as 'Sèvres syndrome'[2] (Taner, 2005; Bayart, 2011; Schmidt, 2014) the project for the Turkification of the defence industry is both an affirmation and, simultaneously, a negation of imperial defeat. This ambivalence is characteristic of the Turkish collective melancholy vis-à-vis the Ottoman Empire (Celik, 2011). Development is therefore understood in terms of a double comparative process: a synchronic comparison with Turkey's Western partners and a diachronic comparison with its imperial past. The symbolic effectiveness of the idea of 'technological and civilising progress', ubiquitous in the major defence projects promoted by the AKP, is all the stronger in that it echoes national historiography (Copeaux, 1997) and the work of leading Turkish and foreign political scientists who present the Turkish army as a pioneering institution in the modernisation of the state and society, diametrically opposed to 'reactionary' Islamic forces (Ward and Rustow, 1965; Heper and Evin, 1988). This association between the army and modernisation was widespread both in the political thinking of the 1930s and among Third World thinkers from the 1950s through the 1970s. It is indicative of a 'desire for the state expressed through a generalised demand for modernity' (Hibou, 2011, 115). In an interpretation inspired by the 'educational protectionism' of Friedrich List, the formation of a national industry—especially the defence industry—is promoted as a condition of development and national security, deemed to safeguard the country from 'the fluctuations of war, foreign restrictions and commercial crises' (List, 1998, 275). Located halfway between 'high-tech Colbertism' (Cohen, 1992) and 'military Keynesianism' (Dunne, 2011; Krugman, 2011), this policy of promoting major industrial defence projects is seen as justified, on the economic level, by the promise of spillover effects in terms of jobs, improvements to the balance of trade, and technology transfer within both the defence sector and the civilian sector.

---

2 In Turkey, this expression is used to refer to the obsession with the idea of Turkey becoming encircled and the view that the state must survive: the reference is to the abortive 1920 treaty of the same name and to the draconian terms imposed on the Ottoman Empire by the victors of the First World War.

Following the passing by Parliament of Law No. 3238 in 1985, which according to its first article aims to 'make progress in the defence industry and modernise the Turkish armed forces',[3] the projected Turkification of the defence industry benefited from completely new sources of funding. The law ensured the creation of an annual fund of USD one billion and a new Secretariat of State, both dedicated to the law's stated goal. This budgetary and administrative innovation was all the more paradoxical in that it contradicted the dominant security, political and economic paradigms of the day, at both the national and the international level. How indeed should we interpret the creation of this major and extremely expensive state project in the context of Atlanticist collective defence, of a return to civilian rule after three years of military rule, and of neo-liberal reforms advocating both the withdrawal of the state from economic activity and budgetary restrictions? While in 1980 the Turkish economy, at the behest of the military junta, moved from a closed model of industrialisation through import substitution to a model open to international competition, this plan to modernise the Turkish army and defence industry thus seems to be an exception to the neo-liberal rule, challenging both structural adjustments and a belief in the superiority of market rules promoted by international financial institutions. Therefore, this major project offers a particularly interesting way of gaining an understanding of the significance of the coexistence of dirigiste interventions and neo-liberal policies advocating the withdrawal of the state from the economy (Buğra, this volume).

2.1 *Defending Turkish Society from Its Allies? A Paradoxical Developmentalist Project*

Often reduced to a simple 'exit guarantee' (Cook, 2007)—that is to say, a negotiated condition of the political withdrawal of the military in 1983 in exchange for certain material gains—the aforementioned double innovation nonetheless also marked a certain 'civilianisation'.[4] In the Turkish context, this term reflects the inclusion of the civilian Prime Minister (at that time Turgut Özal) in the decision-making processes surrounding arms purchases and the creation of a group of civilian experts within the new Secretariat of State dedicated to this major project. While reinforcing state intervention, this new law also contributed to the at least partial 'privatisation' of the related budget through the

3 Author's translation. In Turkish, the text reads, '*bu Kanunun amacı, modern savunma sanayiinin geliştirilmesi ve Türk Silahlı Kuvvetlerinin modernizasyonunun sağlanmasıdır*'; Law no. 3238, art. 1 (J.O. 7/11/85).

4 I use this term to describe the process of demilitarisation or at least the strengthening of civilian power vis-à-vis that of the army.

use of dedicated extra-budgetary funds,[5] to the benefit of the executive. These additional sources of finance ensure that parliamentary controls can be evaded de jure and contribute, in theory, to the development of a private defence sector in collaboration with, or complementary to, the public sector. Created in 1986, the private 'local' company FNSS (FMC-Nurol Savunma Sanayii A.Ş.), a major actor in this sector during the first decade of the new millennium, was thus the result of a partnership between the private Turkish holding company Nurol and the US company FMC (later bought by the British company BAE Systems). The Foundation for Strengthening the Turkish Armed Forces (*Türk Silahlı Kuvvetlerini Güçlendirme Vakfı*, TSKGV), a private foundation that in 2013 owned many companies in the defence sector, also emerged as a major player during this period.[6] In other words, in the 1980s, this area was—at least in the national imaginary—a bridge between two seemingly contradictory visions of the role of the state, the Turkish army, and armaments in the national economy: the developmentalist vision and the neo-liberal one.

2.1.1 A Traumatic Historical Trajectory

In spite of all this, it is a difficult exercise to precisely date the beginning of the project for the Turkification of the defence industry (and more widely of the economy). It began well before the 1985 law since it even preceded the creation of the Turkish state in 1923 and has continued ever since—except during the Menderes years. The transition from Empire to nation state was echoed by an interpretation that stressed security issues in the country's external financial and technological dependence, resulting in a projected Turkification of the civil and military economy initiated in the era of the Young Turks. This was illustrated by genocide, forced evictions, expropriations and the violent eradication of a cosmopolitan bourgeoisie, mostly from the ethno-religious minorities of the Empire, in favour of a nascent bourgeoisie described by Baskin Oran as '*lahasümüt*', an acronym in Turkish for 'secular, Hanafi, Sunni, Muslim and ethnically Turk': this bourgeoisie was considered more loyal to the Turkish state. This policy for the Turkification of the economy would be resumed in many different ways during the Republican period of the interwar years, particularly in the form of a wealth tax in 1942 (Bali, 2010; Buğra, 1994, 114–116), which allowed real property transfers at the expense of Turkish religious minorities,

5 Extra-budgetary resources designate state financial resources that are discretionary, flexible and partly private. They are neither included in the budget, nor subject to the normal budgetary procedures and controls.

6 The TSKGV came about due to the merger of three foundations dedicated, respectively, to each of the armed forces (land, sea, and air) and set up during the Cyprus crisis.

particularly Jews, or even anti-Greek pogroms such as the one that took place in Istanbul in 1955 (Kuyucu, 2005; Bali, 2008). Turkey was co-opted by the Western bloc as part of its containment policy and its defence against the Soviet threat, illustrated by the country's accession to the North Atlantic Treaty Organization (NATO) in 1952: this ironically marked the suspension and subsequent re-legitimisation of this project of national emancipation vis-à-vis Turkey's Western allies. For while US military aid to Turkey—estimated to have been nearly USD 400 million between 1947 and 1951—played its part in enhancing the role of the Turkish army on the international and national stage, it also reduced the legitimacy and quality of the national arms industry (Truman, 1947; Orun, 1997; Kayaoglu, 2009; SSM, 2010). So much so that a great deal of the funding, equipping and training of the Turkish army under the Menderes Administration was 'outsourced': it was no longer a matter of national priority or even one of the prerogatives of the Turkish state, but fell under NATO's collective responsibility (Ahmad, 1993, 124). This co-optation also involved the formation of a 'deep state' (*derin devlet*),[7] whose nerve centre was located in a special section of the Turkish army in direct contact with Western intelligence agencies, as part of Operation Gladio (Söyler, 2015, 101–102; Jenkins, 2009; Gingeras, 2015, 261–270). In other words, the extraversion policy of the Menderes Administration drastically reduced room for manoeuvre in the matter of armaments while contributing to the commodification of the Turkish army, to the extent that it even became one of the country's main 'export products' (*ihraç*), to cite one of the controversial expressions of George Soros (quoted in Evrensel, 2002). The military coup of 1960 and a return to protectionist practices inspired by Listian theory and Keynesian developmentalist policies did not change this situation. Only a shift in international opinion against Turkey in the 1960s and the growing self-assertion of a national bourgeoisie attested

7 'The notion of the deep state may provide an appropriate starting point for investigations of how both foreign and domestic industrial magnates, bankers, intellectuals, and social activists engage and negotiate with bureaucratic and military agents seeking to overtly and covertly suppress dissent and promote the interests of governing regimes' (Gingeras, 2015, 267). According to Élise Massicard, in Turkey the phrase *derin devlet* refers to 'a vast web of corruption linking the crime industry, the highest levels of government, and death squads from the radical right' (Massicard, 2008, 63). This term is reminiscent of the concepts developed by Peter Dale Scott (1996), who uses the term 'deep politics' or even 'parapolitics' to refer to the illegal US activities conducted in collaboration with international organised crime. For if the term 'deep state' comes from Turkey, the collusive practices that result from the criminalisation, privatisation, and internationalisation of the state are found in many other countries. The concept was taken up and used during the Arab Spring to describe the way security apparatuses resisted change (Woertz, 2014; Momani, 2013).

by the creation in 1971 of the first private employers' organisation, the Turkish Industry and Business Association (*Türk Sanayicileri ve İşadamları Derneği*, TÜSIAD), once again made the necessity and legitimacy of the Turkification of the arms industry a priority (Buğra, 1994; Billion, 2000). The withdrawal of US missiles from Turkish territory in 1963 and the international embargoes on military sales imposed on Turkey during the Cyprus crisis revealed the adverse effects of excessive external dependence while renewing a national siege mentality vis-à-vis the country's Western partners (Billion, 2000; Şahin, 2002). This particular context contributed to the development of the private defence contractor Otokar, created in 1963 and owned by the Koç holding company, and the birth of several foundations that appealed for public donations to support national armament. These foundations made the creation of several companies possible, including Aselsan, currently the country's leading defence provider.[8] However, it was not until the mid-1980s, once the emergency had passed and the economy had stabilised, that a significant public policy was implemented to carry out this major project of national development. So we are faced with a paradoxical situation: the 1960s and 1970s, usually interpreted as developmentalist, saw the privatisation of the defence industry in Turkey, while the period 1980–2010, usually seen as a neo-liberal period open to international trade and the rules of the market, was the scene of massive government intervention to foster the Turkification of this industry. This major project, the offshoot of the traumatic trajectory we have described, promoted the idea of national protection, an idea that was all the more desirable in that it coincided with a questioning of the social protection system that held sway under the yoke of the neo-liberal reforms adopted by the military junta.

2.1.2 From Collective Defence to Turkish Self-defence: A Challenge to the Atlanticist and European Alliance?

This major project, aimed at ensuring Turkey's strategic and industrial independence, also seems to reveal certain conflicts within the Western bloc, even putting certain historical caesura into perspective.

The desire to move from being a nation guaranteed by NATO (through the concept of 'collective defence' provided for in Article 5 of the North Atlantic Treaty) to being a nation also capable of self-defence recalls the prior experience of France. For this was how technological mastery of nuclear power was viewed in the 1960s by the French government and a large part of the population: not as a defence against the Soviet threat, but as a tool to free themselves from American domination following the humiliation of Suez

8 The first two letters in the name Aselsan refer to the Turkish word *asker*, meaning soldier.

(Vaïsse, 1992; Regnault, 2003). In Turkey as in France, the project of military self-empowerment—a technological, economic and industrial project—did not challenge the Atlanticist alliance. Instead, it allows the heterogeneous interests of the strategic partners to be fuelled. In the US, the Reagan Administration supported this Turkish project for commercial reasons: it would ensure the creation of a new market for US defence companies, as illustrated by two Turkish–American joint ventures—namely, FNSS (described above) and the Turkish Aerospace Industries (TAI), which is a partnership between Lockheed, General Electric and a Turkish company. TAI was created to ensure the assembly of F-16 American planes ordered by Turkey. The US government also had financial and strategic reasons for welcoming Turkey's endeavour to 'empower' itself. This was the time of the lavish Strategic Defense Initiative—nicknamed 'Star Wars'—that aimed to establish a missile defence system to protect the United States from attack by ballistic strategic nuclear weapons. The Turkish project and Turkish–American industrial alliances meant the financial burden on the US could be relieved while ensuring protection for America's Mediterranean flank. From the European standpoint, the goal of emancipating and modernising the Turkish defence industry was all the more readily accepted as European Member States had, with the exception of Germany, previously not been frequent partners in the Turkish arms market. Some member states also shared one of Turkey's aims: independence from US hegemony. Thus, French officials promoted, in the context of a 'variable geometry' European intergovernmental initiative known as 'Eureka', a 'Europe of technology' involving the development of a common European industrial research endeavour, both civilian and military, as an alternative to the 'Strategic Defence Initiative' established by the United States (Karsenty, 2006; *L'Express*, 1985).

The launch, in 1985, of this major project for the Turkification of the defence industry thus contributed to a rapprochement between Turkey and the European Economic Community (EEC). This rapprochement was ambiguous: it certainly allowed the proliferation of Turkish–European technological, industrial and military dependences in the form of various Turkish participations in European military-industrial projects (Airbus A400M) and contracts for French, English and Italian firms; but at the same time this major Turkish industrial project contributed to a real arms race with Greece, beginning at the time of the Cyprus crisis. This was coupled with a diplomatic competition between Turkey and Greece for the EEC, of which the latter had become a member in 1981 (Sezgin, 2003; Andreous and Zombanakis, 2006). Alongside this equivocal integration of Turkey in European projects, the development of the Turkish national defence industry also aimed at opening Turkey up in economic and cultural terms to (Muslim) 'brother countries'. Supported by the

United States as part of the 'green belt',[9] this policy was intended, on the international level, to better address the Soviet threat and the threat of the Iranian Islamic revolution spreading across the region. Domestically, it resulted in the establishment of a 'Turkish-Islamic synthesis' (Eligür, 2010; Copeaux, 1997), promoted as a mechanism for the depoliticisation of Turkish society. This promotion, by the military junta, of Islam as an instrument of social pacification was all the more important as the sudden opening of the Turkish economy to global competition in the early 1980s might well have led to a 'countermovement' (Polanyi, 1957), thus strengthening the Soviet Bloc. To a certain extent we find the same process at work in Egypt during the Sadat era (Vannetzel, this volume). In this regional context favourable to a cooptation of islam by military forces, the commercial diplomacy promoted by Prime Minister Özal and President Evren, himself a retired General, elected since 1984 Director of the Standing Committee for Economic and Commercial Cooperation of the Organization of the Islamic Cooperation, was meant to ensure the existence of a security rent for Turkey vis-à-vis the Gulf countries, so as to soften—in the short term—the budgetary impact of this project. In practice, however, despite numerous promises, only Libya imported arms from Turkey in the 1980s.[10]

2.2 *From the End of the Cold War to the 'War on Terror': The Twofold Turkification of Both the Threat and the Defence Industry (1990–2001)*

Neither the disappearance of the Soviet threat nor the structural adjustments put in place to deal with major economic crises (1994 and 2001) brought the project to an end. Originally scheduled to run for a period of ten years, the Turkification of the defence industry was not only extended by parliament for a period of thirty years, the annual one billion dollar revenue was increased fivefold. This increase, in apparent discord with the international context of democratisation and the reduction of military spending (what is usually called the 'peace dividend'[11]), was the result of three main interrelated factors: the drying up of the international security rent, including US military aid; the increasing militarisation of the Turkish political and economic scene, which

9 This was the term used by Zbigniew Brzeziński, adviser to President Carter in the late 1970s.

10 See SIPRI (2014, annex) (Stockholm International Peace Research Institute), http://www.sipri.org/.

11 This expression is ascribed to George Bush and Margaret Thatcher, who used it in the early 1990s to refer to the advantages of lowering defence spending as a result of the disappearance of the Soviet threat.

was accompanied by the development of the deep state; and the increasing number of criticisms and constraints to which Turkey was subjected by its European and American partners in matters of procurement and technology transfer—criticisms and constraints motivated by Turkey's multiple violations of human rights and its use of the armed forces against the Turkish civilian population of Kurdish origin.

2.2.1 The Turkification of the Threat and of the Defence Industry: The 'Low-Intensity' War on the PKK

Despite their desire to achieve, by force of arms, the independence of those parts of Turkey where Kurds were in the majority, the guerrillas of the Kurdistan Workers' Party (Partiya Karkerên Kurdistan, PKK) were viewed throughout the 1980s only as a minor threat by Turkish generals (Markus, 2007).[12] However, they gradually became one of the main political, economic and symbolic resources of the Turkish military. Described as 'terrorists' and 'separatists', they were thus officially seen as replacing the Soviets as the main threat following the disintegration of the Soviet Union. The premature death of President Özal in 1993, himself of Kurdish origin and a supporter of a political solution to the Kurdish issue, unleashed an extreme militarisation of the political sphere that benefited the deep state: this was reflected particularly in an upsurge both in political killings and the disappearance of opponents of the government. In 1994 alone, the 'low-intensity war' on the PKK resulted in over 3,700 deaths and 1,400 villages being evacuated, not counting the numerous extrajudicial executions that took place (Yerasimos, 1994). This period, which followed the fall of the Berlin Wall, also helped to boost the black market trade in weapons in the region—a trade based on secret criminal agreements between complementary enemies (Massicard, 2008). Thus, in the middle of the Gulf War, 100,000 weapons manufactured by the Turkish public company Mechanical and Chemical Industry Corporation (*Makina ve Kimya Endüstrisi Kurumu*, MKEK)—weapons that had mysteriously vanished—reappeared in the hands of Kurdish fighters from Irak (Sabah, 2010a). The extreme violence and discrimination suffered by the Kurds at that time did not prevent certain forms of state co-optation. Indeed, such co-optation was rendered essential for the maintenance of Turkish military dominance in the region. This explains, in particular, the re-institution of village guards and the signing of important military contracts benefiting Aziz Yildirim. He was a Turkish businessman of Kurdish origin active in many fields, was head of the company Maktas, official suppliers to NATO since 1973

12 The PKK, a Marxist–Leninist party formed in 1978 to oppose the Turkish central government, officially launched its struggle in August 1984 with a simultaneous attack on several military facilities, and claimed it was acting in the name of Kurdish independence.

and a partner of the company Siemens on several major projects for the Turkification of the defence industry (*Radikal*, 2011).[13]

This rise in violence in the east and the increasing number of obstacles placed in the way of arms imports from Europe[14] explain the fivefold increase, in 1995, of subsidies to the programme for the Turkification of the defence industry, despite the lack of success enjoyed by what was then a ten-year project, and also despite the 1994 slump in the country and austerity measures demanded by the International Monetary Fund (IMF). In accordance with a circular logic, the very absence of a result can always be explained by the fact that it required more time and legitimises the endless renewal of a project (Rancière, 2004, 54–59). The urgency of the need for weapons to fight the PKK simultaneously fuelled a net increase in Turkey's external dependency, helping to keep the country—until early in the new millennium—among the top four importers of weapons in the world (Hen-Tov, 2004). Qualitatively, this period marked a diversification of Turkey's suppliers, with the establishment of a Turkish–Israeli agreement on military cooperation in 1996. At the time, this agreement entailed multiple benefits and synergies: respect for US alliances in the region, relative independence from European and American suppliers, common experience of armed struggle against an 'enemy within', the mutual strengthening of projects to ensure that each country ran its own arms industry, and finally the hope of slowing the rise of political Islam in Turkey (Nachmani, 2003).

2.2.2 The 'Reactionary' Threat and the Postmodern Coup d'État in 1997: The End of Military-Islamic Co-optation

In the 1995 parliamentary elections, the historic victory of the Welfare Party (Refah Partisi), an offshoot of the Islamic movement known as National Vision (Milli Görüş)—both led by Necmettin Erbakan, marked the end of

13 Aziz Yildirim has held a large number of positions. Since 1998, he has also been chairman of the famous football club Fenerbahçe, a club that is highly popular among Turkish military officers. In 2013, he also became the owner of Dearsan, an important shipbuilding company in the military sector that was in direct competition with Koç regarding the major military project of building *MILGEM* warship (from the Turkish *Milli Gemi*, National Ship).

14 The 1999 case of the German *Leopard* tanks is a good example of the political conditionalities imposed by European governments with regard to weapons supplied to the Turkish army. The German Red–Green coalition led by Chancellor Gerhard Schröder of the Social Democratic Party (SPD) and Vice Chancellor Joschka Fischer of the Greens agreed to the delivery of German tanks to Turkey on the sole condition that they were not used for domestic repression and that Turkey would improve its record on human rights (*The Irish Times*, 1999).

the military-Islamic co-optation initiated in 1980 (Eligür, 2010; Sezgin, 2003). This reversal of alliances from Turkish-Islamic Synthesis was in some ways the paradoxical consequence of the success of the co-optation strategy and of the balance of power that favoured the Islamic party. A succession of corruption scandals (fostered by unbridled liberalisation in the absence of regulatory mechanisms), the negative social effects of the Customs Union with Europe and, finally, the 1996 Susurluk scandal—which revealed to the public, for the first time, the interdependence of elements of the security apparatus, the mafia and various co-opted Kurdish leaders—were all an implicit reinforcement of the legitimacy of Refah Partisi, which advocated the observance of Islamic morality (Massicard, 2008; Buğra and Savaşkan, 2014). The Welfare Party was a nationalist, positivist, Islamic, developmentalist and anti-capitalist project characterised in particular by a desire for reconciliation with the Kurdish population and hostility to the European project and to Turkey's membership of NATO (Yankaya, 2014). The party was hence likely to challenge the hegemony previously exercised by senior civil servants, including those in the military, a hegemony supported by part of the national bourgeoisie. This competition between hegemonic projects also had an entrepreneurial dimension: the rise of the Independent Industrialists and Businessmen Association (*Müstakil Sanayici ve İşadamları Derneği*, MÜSIAD), an employers' organisation very close to the Welfare Party, was starting to challenge TÜSIAD's monopoly of access to state-owned tangible and intangible resources, bringing together a national bourgeoisie that was urban, secular, westernised and organically linked to the state (Buğra and Savaşkan, 2012; Yankaya, 2012). The Turkish defence sector was one of the main arenas of this political struggle: as a key element in the statist and developmentalist policy promoted by Erbakan (an engineer by training), it would in theory make an international, Islamic strategic alliance possible. Due to its specificity in terms of high level of opacity and large contracts, the defence sector in Turkey has always been a field of primitive accumulation. But being part of the defence sector is also an important source of prestige for both military and industrials as it is associated with advanced technology and nationalism. Those sectoral specificities explain the interest of the rising Islamic economic elite grouped within MÜSIAD to invest and compete in this new economic field (Çerçeve Dergisi, 1997). This is probably why, in September 1996, Deputy Prime Minister Tansu Çiller, the head of the True Path Party (*Doğru Yol Partisi*, DYP), a centre-right party that had tried to remove the Welfare Party from power, signed a defence contract worth nearly USD 5.5 billion in the absence of Prime Minister Erbakan (*Hürriyet Daily News*, 1996). The latter had embarked on a series of controversial visits to 'brother countries', including

Iran and Libya, with the aim of setting up his own alternative project. Çiller's action meant that the redefinition of the project for the Turkification of the defence industry envisaged by the Prime Minister could be limited, as it was likely to endanger the material and strategic interests of the Turkish army, TÜSIAD and traditional Western partners. This competition between two competing hegemonic projects ultimately resulted in political Islam being re-evaluated as a security risk by the army. Despite the absence of direct violence, the 'reactionary' (*irtica*) threat, which echoed a traumatic historical memory, was now considered by the army to be a greater priority than the 'separatist' threat from the Kurds (Bozarslan, 2000). The memorandum of 28 February 1997, known as the 'postmodern coup', came to mark a further step in this indirect struggle with the Welfare Party and its supporters in civil society. It led, a few months later, to the resignation of the government led by Erbakan.

Many holding companies suspected of having financed the party and benefited from public contracts were later prosecuted for tax fraud and financial irregularities. Their managers were subsequently regularly ostracised at state visits and international fairs, including defence industry events in 1999 (Yankaya, 2012). The diversity of the roles played by the Turkish army on the national stage in the 1990s was nevertheless not just a matter of its own national historical trajectory; it reflected to some extent the reconfiguration of NATO's mission, as evidenced by the development in 1991 of a 'broader concept of security' including 'political, economic, social and environmental dimensions, in addition to the indispensable defence dimension' (NATO 1991, art. 25). The end of the co-optation of political Islam by the armed forces and the restoration of a pro-Western secular military hegemony at the expense of a democratically elected Islamic party could not fail to recall the cases of Algeria and Egypt in the 1990s (Vannetzel, this volume). This attempt to restore military hegemony was, however, short-lived in Turkey. The arrest and extradition of PKK leader Öcalan, the historic slump in 2000–01, the opening of negotiations with the EU and the establishment of the AKP, an offshoot of pro-European and pro-capitalist political Islam, represented a challenge to military hegemony but did not end the major project for the Turkification of the defence industry (Tuğal, 2009). Rather, a merger occurred of competing Islamic and capitalist hegemonic projects and this changed the very terms of the Turkification of the industry (Tuğal, 2009; Haenni, 2005). While the 1990s were characterised by a dual Turkification process—the Turkification of the threat and the Turkification of the industry—the following decade saw the beginning of a new period of internationalisation of the Turkish security rent. Successive AKP governments have benefited politically, strategically and financially from the 'war on terror' (Islamic terror, that is) launched by President Bush following the attacks of 11 September 2001, while legitimising it only to a certain degree.[15]

3 A Project Central to AKP's 'Nationaliberal' Hegemony

The establishment, early in the new millennium, of major structural and administrative reforms that followed the principles of 'new public management' promoted by the IMF, together with so-called democratisation reforms caught in the double stranglehold of European candidacy and the AKP, did not prevent the extension and intensification of the project for the Turkification of the defence industry. To some extent, the project weathered the historic financial crisis in Turkey in 2001 and even survived the significant budget restrictions and the widespread mistrust of the traditional economic and political elites brought about by that crisis. Similarly, the coming to power of the AKP in 2002, an event inseparable from the rise of a new Islamic bourgeoisie described by its opponents as 'green capital' (*yesil sermaye*), did not undermine the project, nor even the privileged position of the 'khaki capital'— secular bourgeoisie historically close to the military if not embedded.

3.1 *Reconfiguring Clientelist Practices*

With few exceptions, the 'green capital' so maligned by the secular elites seems to have remained secondary and marginal in the defence sector, reduced mainly to small and medium-sized enterprises (SMEs) and to subcontracting.[16] It nevertheless benefited from positive discrimination under the new forms of assessment of the Turkification of arms projects that favour Turkish SME's involvement (Akça, 2010, 20; Jane's Defence Industry, 2011).

3.1.1 Resistance of the Military-industrial Complex

The Turkish army and the traditional, pro-Western, secular national bourgeoisie, grouped within TÜSIAD, remained the main beneficiaries of the project

15 In March 2003, the Turkish parliament rejected the US military's request to use Turkish military installations as a base for its operations in Iraq.

16 Our hypothesis is based on SIPRI and Istanbul Chamber of Commerce and Industry reports. It remains, however, incomplete and disputable due to the suspension, since 2011, of the detailed annual activity reports published by the Turkish Undersecretariat for Defense Industries (*Savunma Sanayii Mustesarligi*). The undersecretariat no longer provides regular and systematic information on defence contracts (size, beneficiaries …) concluded under the auspices of the Turkification project.

for the Turkification of the defence industry: in 2013, of the top seven defence companies in the country in terms of turnover, none were created after the electoral victory of the AKP, four were controlled by the Turkish army via the 'private' foundation TSKGV and only one, MKEK, was unrelated to TÜSIAD, due to its legal status as a public company (Table 12.1). TÜSIAD also operates a working group specifically dedicated to the defence sector.

Since the coming to power of the AKP, these companies have seen their sales increase tenfold (Table 12.2).

We see the same evolution with regard to the scientific and academic institutes absorbed by the military-industrial complex, as shown by the case of the Scientific and Technological Research Council of Turkey (*Türkiye Bilimsel ve*

TABLE 12.1 *Main Turkish defence companies in 2013 (in terms of turnover)*

Rank	Name	Date of creation	Activities	Owners	Employers' affiliations
1	Aselsan	1976	Land forces equipment and electronics	Army via TSKGV (85% share).	Member of TÜSIAD.
2	Otokar	1963	Land forces equipment: tanks, armoured cars	Koç Holding.	Koç is a founder member of TÜSIAD.
3	TAI-TUSAS	1985	Aeronautics	Army via TSKGV and Lockheed until 2005. Since then, 55% TKGV/45% SID.	Member of TÜSIAD.
4	MKEK	1930	Artillery	Ministry of Defence	Public.
5	Havelsan	1989	Electronics	Army via TSKGV	Member of TÜSIAD.
6	Roketsan	1989	Missiles and rockets	Army via TSKGV (35%), MKEK (15%), Aselsan (15%), Kalekalip (10%), Others (25%).	Aselsan and Kalekalip are members of TÜSIAD.
7	FNSS	1986	Land equipment: tanks, armoured cars	Nurol Holding (59%)/BAE Systems (41%).	Nurol is a member of TÜSIAD.

SOURCES: AUTHOR'S COMPILATION OF DATA OBTAINED FROM THE RESPECTIVE WEBSITES OF THESE COMPANIES AND FROM THE 2013 RANKINGS OF THE TOP 500 INDUSTRIAL COMPANIES IN TURKEY DRAWN UP BY THE ISTANBUL CHAMBER OF COMMERCE AND INDUSTRY.

TABLE 12.2 *Exponential development of sales figures for the leading national companies in the defence industry between 2002 and 2014 (millions TRY)*

Name of company	2002	2004	2006	2008	2010	2012	2014
Aselsan	318	358	489	695	982	1,369	2,141
TAI-TUSAS	104	106	272	304	418	404	1,726
Otokar	98	282	348	485	548	894	956
MKEK	44	ND	ND	ND	ND	ND	658
Havelsan	59	ND	183	208	186	372	406
Roketsan	ND	ND	ND	138	254	414	716
FNSS	321	181	ND	ND	171	287	330
KaleKalip	ND	90	149	188	254	290	ND

Note: ND (not defined) means that the sales figures of the company are, for the year in question, lower than the sales figures recorded by any of the top 500 industrial companies in Turkey.
SOURCE: AUTHOR'S COMPILATION FROM THE ANNUAL RANKINGS OF THE TOP 500 COMPANIES IN TURKISH INDUSTRY CARRIED OUT SINCE 1997 BY THE ISTANBUL CHAMBER OF INDUSTRY.

Teknolojik Araştırma Kurumu, TÜBITAK), the Turkish equivalent of the French Centre national de la recherche scientifique, and by prestigious universities such as the Technical University of the Middle East (Orta Doğu Teknik Üniversitesi), the Technical University of Istanbul (İstanbul Teknik Üniversitesi) and Boğazici University (Boğazici Üniversitesi). These institutions are the nurseries of the elite, comprising spaces for shared socialisation between members of the military, industrial, and scientific establishment, particularly in science parks; since 2006, these institutions have seen a tripling of the contracts related to the Turkification of military scientific knowledge. Created in 2010 through the merger of the Institute of Information Technologies (*Bilişim Teknolojileri Enstitüsü*, BTE) and the National Research Institute in Electronics and Cryptology (*Ulusal Elektronik ve Kriptoloji Araştırma Enstitüsü*, UEKAE), the Informatics and Information Security Research Center (*Bilişim ve Bilgi Güvenliği İleri Teknolojiler Araştırma Merkezi*, BILGEM)—affiliated to TÜBITAK and specialising in information systems, cryptology and electronics—has benefited greatly from this financial support. BILGEM was also one of the main sources of expertise when it came to discrediting several members of the military's leadership implicated in various major scandals, including *Ergenekon* and *Balyoz* (Sledgehammer). As a result, the increased dependence of TÜBITAK on contracts promoting the Turkification of the defence sector seems to reflect at once a militarisation, a commodification and an increased politicisation of scientific knowledge in Turkey under the AKP (Table 12.3).

The Turkish military, the government and the defence companies in TÜSIAD (and, to a much lesser extent, in MÜSIAD) thus form the 'triangle of power'[17] (Wright Mills, 1956, 12), legitimised and strengthened by scientific expertise (Turse, 2009). It is still difficult to draw a distinction between these actors since the boundaries separating public from private, military from civilian, and foreign from national are porous. As the sector is characterised by many 'multipositionings' and widespread 'co-opetition'[18] that calls into question 'the theoretical contradiction between competitive relations and collaborative relationships' (Bruno, 2008, 34), the major defence companies are successively or simultaneously customers, partners, competitors and, more rarely, 'suppliers' to other defence companies, both Turkish and foreign. Cross-participation between the main 'national' defence companies in Turkey, and the Turkish–American joint ventures (FNSS, TAI) described above illustrates these complex relationships, which also to be seen in major civil infrastructure projects (Table 12.1). Similarly, although six of the seven major companies in the sector

TABLE 12.3 *The changing numbers of contracts allocated to TÜBITAK, the other great beneficiary of the Turkification of the defence industry, between 2006 and 2012 (millions TRY)*

	2006	2007	2008	2009	2010	2011	2012
TÜBITAK Sage	24.1	31.1	58.9	91.1	70.1	56.3	83.9
TÜBITAK Uzay	12.5	16.7	21.6	22.2	27.8	30.8	36.2
TÜBITAK UEKAE	72.8	90.2	99.7	125.0			
TÜBITAK BILGEM					157.8	199.6	208.4
Total	109.4	138.1	180.2	238.3	255.6	286.7	328.5

SOURCE: YENTÜRK (2014).

17 A term used by C. Wright Mills, echoing in particular the speech given by President Eisenhower at the end of his second term of office in 1961. In it, the former general highlighted the risks posed by the impact that uncontrolled strengthening of the military-industrial complex might have on American democracy.

18 'Co-opetition' is the careful mix of cooperation and competition. The term was invented by Ray Noorda based on the nascent computer networking industry in the 80's (Williamson, 2006).

are legally private and civil, this by no means implies any simple privatisation or even 'civilianisation' of the sector. The TSKGV foundation, owner of twenty companies in the defence sector, is certainly a *de jure* private entity thanks to its status as *vakif* (mortmain), but it belongs de facto to the Turkish army. It is run by army officers and finances the military effort (Akça, 2010). Free competition and the distinction between political and economic spheres are all the more illusory in this sector in that the state remains a central and multipositional player. The state is the only customer of the national market; the only investor capable of funding such expensive, long, and uncertain projects. Whether obtaining national contracts, research grants, permits required for arms exports, offsets or state export guarantees, those working in the defence industry remain structurally dependent on the government. So 'the major vested interests [the military-industrial complex] often compete less with one another in their effort to promote their several interests than they coincide on many points of interest and, indeed, come together under the umbrella of government. The units of economic and political power not only become larger and more centralized; they come to coincide in interest and to make explicit as well as tacit alliances.' (Wright Mills, 1956, 266–267).

3.1.2 Clientelist Practices and the 'Reciprocal Assimilation of Elites'

This resistance on the part of traditional military-industrial players to the AKP government is not the result of the bar being placed too high for new entrants or even of the impotence of the government in the face of the aforementioned elites. It reflects instead a 'reciprocal assimilation of elites' (Bayart, 2006), and one might even say a reciprocal and asymmetric assimilation of the AKP and the traditional members of the military-industrial complex. The holding company Nurol is a particularly good example of this convergence of interests and this shared socialisation. This company owns Nurol Teknoloji, is a co-owner of the Turkish–British defence company FNSS, a member of TÜSIAD, a pioneer in the field of Turkish defence exports in 1997, and well established in the Asian markets (Malaysia and the Philippines) and the Middle East (Saudi Arabia). Like many other 'competitors' in the Turkish defence sector, such as SFTA and Profilo, the holding company Nurol is highly active in building and public works, and also receives public contracts for construction, reconstruction and weapons, not only in Turkey but also abroad—contracts that are characterised by discretionary government interventions (Buğra, this volume). These multiple interests and reciprocal yet asymmetric dependences have led to the formation of personal connections, as evidenced in 2012 by the presence of the then Minister of the Economy and the Mayor of Ankara at the wedding of the son of the Vice President of Nurol. Another such example is the shipbuilding company Yonca-Onuk, established in 1986. Its owner personally met Erdogan to promote its products abroad; this allowed him, for example, to access the Qatari and Egyptian markets (Özdemir, 2004; SIPRI[19]). The seizure by the state of the civilian and military vehicle producer BMC, the ownership of which was later transferred to the businessman and media tycoon Ethem Sancak—an active member of the Justice and Development Party (AKP) and MÜSIAD, a former member of TÜSIAD (2007–08) and very close to Erdogan—once again proved the centrality, in the defence industry, of personal connections with the government and the multipositional nature of this sector (*Cumhuriyet*, 2015; Buğra and Savaşkan, 2014; Yankaya, 2015).

Contrary to the neo-liberal fiction that sees the international attractiveness of Turkish armaments as residing in their competitiveness alone, it is the combination of political, financial and business support provided by the state to these defence companies that ensure their success. Co-optation by the government, essential if these companies are to sell arms, works not only at home but also abroad. According to Prime Minister Erdogan, 'While people can succeed in selling refrigerators and televisions by themselves, regarding the defence industry, a state guarantee is required; that is why we support this sector' (quoted in Özdemir, 2004).[20] Bound sales, known as offsets—that is to say, the military import contracts established by the Turkish state in return for the supplier country investing in or importing products or services from Turkey that are defence-related (direct offsets) or unconnected to the defence industry (indirect offsets), follow the same logic. According to some expert estimates, in 2013 offsets constituted nearly 70 per cent of Turkish exports in the field of defence and aviation, and almost all exports to so-called Western countries (Jane's Defence Industry, 2014c; Jane's Defence Industry, 2014b). Officially set up in order to limit the negative effects of imports on the balance of payments, such practices—widespread in the international defence sector—run against the idea of free competition. Protected by a double seal of privacy (they are treated as top secret and are at the same time trade secrets), they encourage and to some extent legitimise the formation of rents for co-opted national businesses. They thus contribute to the development of clientelist practices, understood not only as 'the existence of a pragmatic exchange of goods and services in return for support and votes' but also as 'the fact that the reciprocity thus established can turn into a bond of political allegiance and the dependence thus

19 SIPRI, http://www.sipri.org/.

20 Author's translation. In the original Turkish: 'biz bu Türk savunma ürünlerini destekliyoruz, insanlar buzdolabını telvizyonu kendi başlarına satabilirler ama savunma ürünleri için devletlerin referansı gerekir o nedenle destekliyoruz'.

created can be recognised as legitimate' (Briquet 1995, 77). While it is undeniable that this policy is explained by the desire to strengthen the prestige of the state, both internationally and nationally, particularly through the increasing number of its extensions into so-called civil society, it seems legitimate to wonder about the existence of the AKP's direct financial interests in the development of this particular industry. Though they do not prove this hypothesis, the corruption cases related to the sales of Turkish arms by the company Havelsan to South Korea or the sale of German Thyssen Krupp submarines to the Turkish army, the huge amounts involved, their growing opacity, the practice of retrocession—quite common in this sector—and the recent accusations of corruption that have tainted the reputation of the AKP government appear at least to provide evidence in support of it (Bekdil, 2015, *The Korea Times*, 2015; *Cumhuriyet*, 2016).[21] The project for the Turkification of the defence industry thus involves the proliferation of asymmetrical interdependences between military, industrial, scientific and political elites underpinning the formation of a shared interest in this major project. As I was told by one of the experts in the field, 'none of the defence officials will refuse a major Turkification project. Even if they fail, or if the major project turns out to be impossible, the government will have no interest in making their failure public knowledge.'[22]

3.2 *The Major Project of Turkification: A Hegemonic Instrument of Extraversion*

This major project of Turkification and the practices of co-optation or even clientelism that underlie it have not, in the least, led to the suspension of external links. They are, rather, an expression of a strategy of extraversion based on increasing external dependences. And these dependences are the vectors of a circulation of economic, political, technological and symbolic resources, which—taken as a whole—contribute to a quest for hegemony both nationally and on the regional and international levels.

3.2.1 An Instrument of National Affirmation and International Negotiations

As an instrument for equalising power relations with its Atlanticist partners, the project enables Turkey to play with and play on diplomatic and technological dependences with Western suppliers so as to assert itself more strongly on the national level. Thus, for example, partner countries that affront Turkish national 'feelings' and official historiography have been punished

21 Concerning this growing capacity of public defence expenditure, see Footnote 15.

22 Interview with a journalist and expert on defence industry, Ankara, April 2015.

and allied countries deemed more respectful and loyal have been rewarded. French defence companies were subjected to this carrot-and-stick policy in 2001 when, following the passing of a law recognising the Armenian genocide, they experienced a freezing of military contracts with Turkey even though the Turkish army had hitherto been one of the main foreign customers of the French defence industry. This ostracism was renewed in 2006 when a bill was proposed criminalising the denial of the Armenian genocide (Jane's Defence Industry, 2012). The same applied to contracts won by Israel, which were suspended for 'technical reasons' following the resumption of the conflict in Gaza and the affair of the *Mavi Marmara* flotilla in 2010, which claimed the lives of nine Turkish civilians. South Korea and China have since taken over from the main 'Western' suppliers, while allowing Turkey to obtain significant concessions in terms of technology transfer. Thus, the recent success of a Chinese company (China Precision Machinery Import–export Corporation, CPMIEC) in the context of the Turkish call to tender for the establishment of a national air missile system to complement the protection afforded by NATO—a call estimated to be worth several billion USD—attracted significant criticism and pressure from NATO members, notably expressed through the withdrawal of Patriot missiles protecting Turkish territory (Jane's Defence Industry, 2013; Marcou, 2015). Accused of jeopardising the security and solidarity of the Atlanticist alliance through this agreement with a Chinese company subjected to sanctions by the US for its contribution to nuclear proliferation in Iran and North Korea, Turkey was strongly 'invited' to review its choice in favour of one of its Atlanticist allies Lockheed or Eurosam—American and Franco–Italian companies, respectively (Jane's Defence Industry, 2014a; Kemal, 2014). While the contract has not been finalised, Western competitors have, in the meantime, offered better conditions. The French government, indirectly competing for this contract, notably maintained a low profile during the centennial of the Armenian genocide commemorated on 24 April 2015, and thus minimised friction in Franco–Turkish trade relations (Jane's Defence Industry, 2012).[23]

In other words, this Turkification project is not only a guarantor of national honour on the international stage; it also helps to strengthen the country's ability to negotiate with the largest variety of foreign suppliers and to force them

23 The importance that the French government ascribes to its military and strategic relationship with Turkey is also reflected in the profile of the French ambassador to Ankara, in place from 2011 to 2015: a former chair of the military and civilian cabinet of the French Ministry of Defence. The same is true of the Consul General of France to Turkey, in place since 2013: she was previously the Deputy Director of French Strategic Affairs, Security and Disarmament.

to compete for contracts on the best terms. The project still does not, however, allow Turkey to emancipate itself from its Atlanticist allies: the US still largely dominates the market as the source of nearly 70 per cent of Turkish armament imports in 2014.[24] Even those weapons presented as 'one hundred per cent Turkish' by the Turkish authorities, including the *Atak* helicopter or the *Anka* drone—symbols of technological and political national independence—still rely on many different foreign licences, including American licences, which prevent their use and export without the consent of Western partners (*Sözcü*, 2015; *Timetürk*, 2012).

3.2.2 A Muslim Civilizational Development Project: High-Tech Port by MÜSIAD

The strong internationalisation of the Turkish defence industry under the AKP, evidenced by its export performance and by the creation in 2011 of the Union of Exporters of the Defence Industry and Aeronautics (*Savunma ve Havacilik Sanayi İhracatçilari Birliği*, SSI), reflects the transition from a logic of means to a logic of results, characteristic of the neo-liberal period. Since 2011, when the Turkish arms industry officially achieved 50 per cent autonomy, the issue of the origin of production and its components is no longer central in gauging the success of local development. It has been replaced by two goals: the tripling of the turnover of Turkish defence companies and the doubling of Turkish arms exports. The aim is to grow these exports from USD 1–2 billion for the period 2012–16 to USD 20 billion in 2023–the centenary of the Turkish Republic (Jane's Defence Industry, 2012). İn order to achieve this objective, the AKP government has relied on economic and cultural extraversion with regard to friendly 'brother' countries, particularly including those in the Gulf and countries that have experienced the Arab Spring (Tunisia and Egypt). It is reminiscent of the aforementioned earlier attempts to develop economic, political and strategic ties with Muslim countries conducted by premiers Turgut Özal in the early 1980s and Necmettin Erbakan in the mid-1990s, respectively.

The project 'High-Tech Port by MÜSIAD' is an example of a reciprocal assimilation of elites on the international scale, promoted by the AKP government: the main Turkish defence companies, members of TÜSIAD, have thus found themselves being co-opted by MÜSIAD, which itself promotes a transnational 'market Islam' (Haenni, 2005; Yankaya, 2015). This alliance combines the technological know-how—accumulated over several decades—of various members of TÜSIAD and market access to so-called Muslim countries thanks to MÜSIAD's international networks. All of this contributes to the influence and

24 SIPRI, http://www.sipri.org/.

prestige of the AKP nationally and internationally (Yankaya, 2015). Presented at the end of 2014 under the auspices of President Erdogan and several Turkish ministers at the 15th International Fair of MÜSIAD, High-Tech Port officially aims to place Turkish know-how at the service of 'brother countries' to ensure no 'clash of civilisations' but a Muslim 'civilisational competitiveness' vis-à-vis Western countries (*Dünya*, 2015a). This project, presented as a 'showcase' for Turkish technological excellence, was again at the heart of the meeting held in October 2015 in Qatar, in tandem with the International Business Forum, which was then devoted to 'partnerships in industry and defence between Islamic countries' (Yankaya, 2014 and 2015). A binational fair exclusively dedicated to the fostering of Qatari and Turkish companies was organised under the auspices of the Turkish President, Prime Minister and Minister of Defence and the Qatari Sheikh Bin Hamad bin Halifa es-Sani. The family links and Ottoman origins of this Qatari have also been highlighted by MÜSIAD so as to better legitimise this example of Turkish–Qatari co-optation and naturalise the military agreement established the same year (*Dünya*, 2015b). This provides for a mutual defence clause in the case of attack, which de facto means that the Turks will provide Qatar with military protection should aggression occur (Toyay, 2015; Gurcan, 2015). The political entrepreneur Ethem Sancak, who had shortly before given up a portion of his shares in the company BMC to the Industrial Committee of the Qatari Armed Forces, acted as a bridgehead for Turkish-Qatari relations, playing a significant role as an intermediary (*Star*, 2015).

However, far from signifying equality between 'brother' countries, the fact that Turkey has resorted to the argument for Muslim transnational solidarity in the defence market contributes rather to a commodification of Islam and to a 'euphemisation' or legitimisation of the inequality, conflict and competition between the countries that make up this imaginary umma. The 'civilisational competition' with Western forces is indicative of a quest for complementary status with brotherly countries. The brotherhood discourse promoted by this project is a purely superficial horizontality, and reveals an attempt to justify the international division of labour within the so-called Muslim world in favour of Turkey, involving the exclusion of Iran and its allies. High-Tech Port promotes the idea of the civilising and cultural superiority of Turkey over Arab countries; the 'big brother' among its 'brother countries' (Yankaya, 2015). This erasure of the logic of social justice and equalisation of the relationship between 'brother countries' to some extent echoes the theology of American neo-Protestant prosperity by activating an 'imaginary of social success where money becomes both the site of the great revenge and the sign of a divine election' (Haenni, 2005, 65, our transl.). Far from the heroic spirit of the 'great civilisational development' promoted by Nail Olpak, president of MÜSIAD, the policy of exporting Turkish arms to 'brother countries' reflects a certain pragmatism on the part of the government in the face of the low competitiveness of the Turkish defence industry in comparison with Western technology. It also results from a multitude of logics to be found in importing countries, inherited in part from their own historical trajectories: the shared experience of facing an embargo on their arms markets (Pakistan and Indonesia), the parallel policy of importing countries that aims to make their defence industries independent (Pakistan, Qatar and Malaysia) and the comparative historicity of bilateral ties between individual importing countries and Turkey or Iran, respectively. Finally, the attractiveness of Turkish arms for Muslim-majority countries is inseparable from the ambiguous nature of Turkey's membership of NATO, sometimes 'euphemised' and sometimes highlighted by the Turkish government in its search for international hegemony.

Thus, this project of Turkification reveals complex and organic relations with Western partners and 'brother countries'. Located at the intersection of the strategy of extraversion and that of redistribution of public resources to Turkish and foreign political entrepreneurs, the project is part of a national and international quest for hegemony. It illustrates a 'combination of globalisation and the universalisation of the nation-state' typical of the concept of 'national liberalism' (Bayart, 2012, 5).

4 2013: Year of Reaffirmation or Challenge to the Cause of Hegemony?

Internationally, the violent evolution of the Arab Spring, which turned against the new leaders who had emerged from political Islam and been co-opted by the AKP, strengthened the ties between Turkey and Qatar; witnessing in particular an exponential increase in Turkish exports to Qatar since 2012.[25] Nationally, the Gezi Park protests against the Turkish government in 2013 and the disastrous effects of the latter's neo-liberal politics in environmental, urban and social terms have considerably undermined the process of mutual assimilation of certain elites. This is the case of the most powerful holding company in the country, Koç (Cemal, 2013). As one of the main beneficiaries of the Turkification of the defence industry hitherto pursued by the AKP through its subsidiaries RMK and Otokar, the Koç family was accused of supporting the Gezi protesters. The eponymous holding company has since seen its USD 2 billion

25 SIPRI, http://www.sipri.org/.

military contract for building the 'hundred per cent Turkish' *MILGEM* warship[26] cancelled on a mere technicality while its principal operating subsidiaries in the energy sector—Tüpras, Opet and Aygaz—were subjected to a tax audit (Gursel, 2013). Similarly, TÜBITAK, a key player in this major project, suffered a veritable witch-hunt following the deterioration of relations between the Gülen community and President Erdogan, worsened by the Gezi Park movement and the revelation, on 17 December 2013, of the existence of a vast network of corruption involving key members of the government and their respective families, attributed to Gülen's followers. Formerly a key AKP ally, closely integrated into state bodies, the community is now ostracised, being considered by the government to be a terrorist 'parallel structure'. This change in alliances has resulted in the abrupt and massive dismissal of hundreds of employees of TÜBITAK suspected of sympathising with Hizmet.[27] It has simultaneously made possible a reversal of power relations through a rapprochement attempt by the AKP with some militaristic and nationalist elites who were 'victims' of the scientific expertise contributed by TÜBITAK in the *Ergenekon* and *Balyoz* (Sledgehammer) trials, formerly backed by AKP government. The vice president and director of the BILGEM laboratory, the main source of judicial expertise in both the aforementioned cases and the main beneficiary of research funds for the Turkification of the defence industry since 2010 (Table 12.3), were not only dismissed but also prosecuted for illegally bugging Erdogan's offices in 2011 (Saymaz and Çelikkan, 2015).

This breakdown of the alliance by economic means, against the new enemies within, is a counterpart to the postmodern coup of 1997 (Cemal, 2013). Gezi Park and the Arab Spring have thus, among AKP leaders, recalled traumatic memories of a military coup past and triggered fears of a new reversal, while contributing paradoxically to bolstering military legitimacy through the aforementioned changes in alliances at the expense of the Gülen movement and the halting of the embryonic peace process with the PKK. Thus, the mutual dependences, both material and immaterial, promoted by the major project of Turkification, in no way reflect the existence of harmonious relations or even any stability of interest between government, industry and the military (Wright Mills, 1969, 31). As they depend on the power relations of the moment, the conflicts that constitute this highly publicised and marketed development project may lead to reversible co-optations.

---

26 *MILGEM* comes from *Milli Gemi*, meaning 'National Ship'.

27 The word *Hizmet* means 'the service' in Turkish and is used to refer to the Gülen movement in Turkey.

5 Conclusion

The major project for the Turkification of the defence industry, promoted simultaneously as an example, a condition and evidence of national development, is thus based on a 'constitutive imagination' (Veyne, 2014); a siege mentality following a historic path structured by the trauma of the turn of the century. The multiple meanings of *kalkınma*, the Turkish term for development, reveals this very clearly. However, this project 'makes do with' dependences and external resources, be they economic, technological, political or military, and expresses a quest for a 'nationaliberal' hegemony that is unstable and reversible. Playing with and playing on relations of inequality at the international level, it helps to alter, if only in the imaginary, the ways in which Turkey is integrated into the international system, ensuring a fictitious commodification of the umma and the Turkish army in the name of the defence of Turkish society. This project thus represents an imaginary bridge not only between the logic of the market and the logic of national affirmation, but also between political Islam and the secular elite. Neither true nor false (because it is not externally verifiable), this great development project at the heart of the government's legitimacy is a real fiction with multiple domination effects, acting as a matrix for the accumulation, conversion and circulation of economic, symbolic, political and religious capital. Beyond the circle of elites belonging to the military-industrial complex, the lack of public criticism vis-à-vis this major yet extremely expensive militarist project, both uncertain and synonymous with lethal consequences for much of the Kurdish civilian population, also expresses a form of consensus, whether mandatory or not.[28] As the product of a true 'normative grammar' (Gramsci, 1977), this major project offers Turkish citizens an imaginary national protection, replacing to some extent the state-provided social protections that have been undermined by neo-liberal reforms. The project thereby contributes to a certain endorsement of state power and to the emasculation of a nascent potential 'countermovement' (Polanyi, 1957) by answering the 'citizens' desire for the state' (Hibou, 2011, 82), understood in terms of modernity, unity, prestige, sublimity and equality. For the civilian populations potentially affected by this major project, a public challenge to the last of these would constitute evidence of their betrayal of the Turkish state, as this project remains

28 'By mandatory consensus, I mean a set of opinions, judgments, and public behaviours required of citizens in connection with certain values (Kemalism and its principles), certain facts or events of the present (the war in Kurdistan, the presence of the Turkish army in Cyprus) or the past (the Armenian genocide), and certain institutions (the army, the army's control of the government)' (Copeaux, 2000).

so closely associated with the survival of the state and the nation. Thus, unlike large civil infrastructure projects, this major project is relatively free of critics because of the many forms of legitimacy it bears and the impossibility of casting doubt on the achievements claimed for it because of the double secrecy that it enjoys (it is both a trade secret and top secret). As a result, the project contributes to an unfinished depoliticisation of social inequality (Ferguson, 1994) in Turkey. Similarly, the commodification of Muslim solidarity, and the 'civilisational competition' it promotes, depoliticises inequality between so-called Muslim countries. This 'nationaliberal' consensus, located at the heart of the quest for AKP hegemony both nationally and internationally, appears nevertheless to be questioned today by the normalisation of diplomatic relations with Iran and the recent disclosure of secret Turkish arms shipments to Syria (*The Guardian*, 2016).

References

Ahmad, F. (1993) *The Making of Modern Turkey* (London; New York: Routledge).

Akça, I. (2010) 'Military Economic Structure in Turkey: Present Situation, Problems and Solutions', *TESEV Democratization Programme. Policy Report Series* (Istanbul: TESEV), http://tesev.org.tr/wp-content/uploads/2015/11/Security_Sector_Policy_Report_2_Military_Economic_Structure_In_Turkey.pdf (accessed on 23 May 2016).

AKP (*Adalet Kalkima Partisi*) (2012) *AKP Parti 2023 Siyasi Vvizyonu: Siyaset, Toplum, Dünya*, 30 September, https://www.akparti.org.tr/site/akparti/2023-siyasi-vizyon (accessed on 21 December 2015).

Andreous, A. and G. Zombanakis (2006) 'The Arms Race Between Greece and Turkey: commenting on a major unresolved issue', *Peace Economics Peace Science and Public Policy*, 12(1), DOI: 10.2202/1554-8597.1092.

Bali, R. (2010) *L'affaire impôt sur la fortune* (Istanbul: Libra Yayınevi).

Bali, R. (2008) 'The 1934 Thrace Events: Continuity and Change within Turkish State Policies Regarding non-Muslim Minorities. An Interview with Rifat Bali', *European Journal of Turkish Studies*, No. 7, http://ejts.revues.org/2903 (accessed on 23 May 2016).

Baskaya, F. (2005) *Kalkinma iktisadinin yükselisi ve dususu* (Ankara: Türkiye ve Ortadogu Forumu Vakfi).

Bayart, J.-F. (2012) *Sortir du national-libéralisme* (Paris: Karthala).

Bayart, J.-F. (2011) 'La nouvelle confiance en soi de la Turquie', *Dossiers du CERI*, pp. 1–4, https://hal-sciencespo.archives-ouvertes.fr/hal-01024169 (accessed on 23 May 2016).

Bayart, J-F. (2006), *L'Etat en Afrique. La politique du ventre* (Paris: Fayard).

Billion, D. (2000) *La politique extérieure de la Turquie: Une longue quête d'identité* (Paris: L'Harmattan).

Bekdil, B. (2015) 'Bribes paid but not taken', *Hürriyet Daily News*, 18 March, http://www.hurriyetdailynews.com/bribes-paid-but-not-taken.aspx?pageID=449&nID=79815&NewsCatID=398 (accessed on 2 June 2016).

Bozarslan, H. (2000) 'Le madhisme en Turquie: "L'incident de Menemen" en 1930', *Revue des mondes musulmans et de la Méditerranée*, 91–94, http://remmm.revues.org/261 (accessed on 23 May 2016).

Briquet, J.-L. (1995) 'Les pratiques politiques "officieuses": clientélisme et dualisme en Corse et en Italie du Sud', *Genèses*, 20, http://www.persee.fr/doc/genes_1155-3219_1995_num_20_1_1308 (accessed on 24 May 2016).

Bruno, I. (2008) 'La recherche scientifique au crible du benchmarking. Petite histoire d'une technologie de gouvernement', *Revue d'Histoire Moderne et Contemporaine*, 5(55-4bis), pp. 28–45, http://www.cairn.info/revue-d-histoire-moderne-et-contemporaine-2008-5-page-28.htm (accessed on 24 May 2016).

Buğra, A. (1994) *State and Business in Modern Turkey: A Comparative study* (New York: Suny Press).

Buğra, A. and O. Savaşkan (2014) *New Capitalism in Turkey: The Relationship Between Politics, Religion and Business* (Northampton: Edward Elgar).

Buğra, A. and O. Savaşkan (2012) 'Politics and Class: Turkish Business Environment in the Neoliberal Age', *New Perspectives on Turkey*, 46, DOI: 10.1017/S0896634600001503.

Celik, B. (2011) *Technology and National Identity in Turkey, Mobile Communications and the Evolution of Post-Ottoman Nation* (London: I.B. Tauris), pp. 17–49.

Cemal, H. (2013) 'TÜPRAŞ örneği: 28 Şubat'ın ayıpları niye tekrarlanıyor', *T24*, 31 July. http://t24.com.tr/yazarlar/hasan-cemal/tupras-ornegi-28-subatin-ayiplari-niye-tekrarlaniyor,7142 (accessed on 27 April 2016).

Çerçeve Dergisi (1997) 'Türk Savunma Sanayii Türkiye'nin Stratejik Konumu', *Müsiad*, 19.

Certeau, M. (1990) *L'invention du quotidien, 1. Arts de faire* (Paris: folio essais).

Cohen, E. (1992) *Le Colbertisme high-tech: Economie des Telecom et du Grand Projet* (Paris: Hachette).

Cook, S. (2007) *Ruling but not Governing: the Military and Political Development in Egypt, Algeria and Turkey* (Baltimore: John Hopkins University Press).

Copeaux, E. (2000) 'Le consensus obligatoire', in I. Rigoni (ed.), *Turquie: Les mille visages. Politique, religion, femmes, immigration* (Paris, Syllepse).

Copeaux, E. (1997) *Espaces et Temps de la nation turque: analyse d'une historiographie nationaliste (1931–1993)* (Paris: CNRS Editions).

Cumhuriyet (2016) 'Denizalti ihalesinde Almalardan rusvet', 16 February, http://www.cumhuriyet.com.tr/haber/diger/482393/Denizalti_ihalesinde_Almanlardan_rusvet.html (accessed on 27 April 2016).

Cumhuriyet (2015) 'Askin meyvesi', 20 May, http://www.cumhuriyet.com.tr/koseyazisi/280237/Askin_meyvesi.html (accessed on 26 April 2016).

Dale Scott, P. (1996) *Deep Politics and the Death of JFK* (Berkeley: California University Press).

Dunne, J.P. (2011) *Military Keynesianism: An Assessment*, Paper presented at the Second International Conference on Conflict Management, Peace Economics and Peace Science, November 2010, Central University of Finance and Economics, Beijing, http://carecon.org.uk/DPs/1106.pdf (accessed on 24 May 2016).

Dünya (2015a) 'Türk Savunma Sanayii Katar'dan Yogun rekabeti hazir', 2 October.

Dünya (2015b) 'Kalkinma medeniyeti projesi High Tech Port by Müsiad Qatar', 2 October.

Eligür, B. (2010) *The mobilization of Political Islam In Turkey*, (Cambridge: Cambridge University Press).

Evrensel (2002) 'Ihraç malimiz asker mi?', 20 May. http://www.evrensel.net/haber/130956/ihrac-malimiz-asker-mi (accessed on 25 April 2016).

Ferguson, J. (1994) *Anti-Political Machine: Development, Depoliticization and Bureaucratic Power in Lesotho* (Minnesota: University of Minnesota Press).

Gingeras, R. (2015) *Heroin, organized crime and the making of modern Turkey* (Oxford: Oxford University Press).

Gramsci, A. (1977) *Gramsci dans les textes. Recueil de textes réalisé sous la direction de François Ricci en collaboration avec Jean Bramant* (Paris: Editions sociales).

Gurcan, M. (2015) 'Turkey-Qatar, what are Turkish troops going to do in Qatar?', *Al Monitor*, 3 June, http://www.al-monitor.com/pulse/originals/2015/06/turkey-qatar-what-are-turkish-troops-going-to-do.html (accessed on 25 April 2016).

Gursel, K. (2013) 'Is Audit of Koç Group Erdogan's Revenge for Gezi Park?' *Al Monitor*, 29 July, http://www.al-monitor.com/pulse/originals/2013/07/koc-audit-raid-turkey-interest-rate-lobby-gezi.html (accessed on 27 April 2016).

Haenni, P. (2005) *L'islam de marché: l'autre révolution conservatrice* (Paris: Seuil).

Hen-Tov, E. (2004) 'The political economy of Turkish military modernization', *Middle East review of International Affairs*, 8(4).

Heper, M. and A. Evin (1988) *State, Democracy and the Military: Turkey in the 80's* (New York: de Gruyter).

Hibou, B. (2011) *Anatomie politique de la domination* (Paris: La Découverte).

Hürriyet Daily News (1996) 'Erbakan bypassed in Key Defense Projects Plans Revenge on Ciller', 21 October, http://www.hurriyetdailynews.com/erbakan-bypassed-in-key-defense-projects-plans-revenge-on-ciller.aspx?pageID=438&n=erbakan-bypassed-in-key-defense-projects-plans-revenge-on-ciller-1996-10-21 (accessed on 26 April 2016).

Inalcik, H. (1992) 'Some Remarks on the Ottoman Turkey's Modernization Process', in Ihnsanoglu, E. (ed.) *Transfer of Modern Science and Technology to the Muslim World* (Istanbul: Research Center for Islamic History, Art and Culture), pp. 49–59.

Jane's Defence Industry (2014a) 'Turkey Begins T-Loramids talks with Eurosam', 10 September, (London: Jane's Defence Weekly).

Jane's Defence Industry (2014b) 'Offset obligations in Turkey exceeded USD 18 billion in 2013, SSM says', 1 June, (London: Jane's Defence Weekly).

Jane's Defence Industry (2014c) 'Turkish industry announces 2013 export figures', 1 February (London: Jane's Defence Weekly).

Jane's Defence Industry (2013) 'Turkey selects Chinese HQ-9 SAM for T-Loramids', 1 October (London: Jane's Defence Weekly).

Jane's Defence Industry (2012) 'Genocide law jeopardises France's bid to supply missiles to Turkey', 1 February (London: Jane's Defence Weekly).

Jane's Defence Industry (2011) 'Turkish defence firms obliged to outsource and export under reforms', 1 September (London: Jane's Defence Weekly).

Jenkins, G.H. (2009) *Between facts and fantasy: Turkey's Ergenekon investigation*, Silk Road Paper, (Washington, D.C. and Stockholm: Central Asia Caucasus Institute Silk Road Studies program), http://www.silkroadstudies.org/publications/silkroad-papers-and-monographs/item/13091-between-fact-and-fantasy-turkeys-ergenekon-investigation.html (accessed on 24 May 2016).

Karsenty, J.-P. (2006) *Du Cesta à la création d'Eureka: Réflexions de la politique scientifique et technologique du gouvernement socialiste* (Paris: Institut François Mitterrand), 17 December, http://www.mitterrand.org/Du-CESTA-a-la-creation-d-EUREKA.html (accessed on 21 December 2015).

Kayaoglu, B. (2009) 'Strategic Imperatives, Democratic Rhetoric: The United States and Turkey, 1945–52', *Cold War History*, 9(3), DOI: 10.1080/14682740902981403.

Keyder, C. (1993) *Ulusal Kalkinmaciligin Iflasi* (Istanbul: Metis).

Keyder, C. (1987) *State and Class in Turkey: A Study in Capitalist Development* (London: Verso).

Kemal, L. (2014), 'Turkey missile maneouver', *Today's Zaman*, 3 November.

Krugman, P. (2011), 'Coalmines and Military Keynesians', *New York Times*, 28 octobre, http://krugman.blogs.nytimes.com/2011/10/28/coalmines-and-military-keynesians/?_r=0 (accessed on 23 May 2016).

Kuyucu, A.T. (2005) 'Ethno-religious "unmixing" of Turkey: 6–7 September riots as a case in Turkish nationalism', *Nations and Nationalism*, 11(3), pp. 361–380, DOI: 10.1111/j.1354-5078.2005.00209.x.

L'Express (1985) 'Les lumières d'Eurêka', 26 April, http://www.cvce.eu/obj/les_lumieres_d_eureka_dans_l_express_26_April_1985-fr-3ad525b8-57b1-4a82-bf1c-7127709ef24a.html (accessed on 26 April 2016).

List, F. (1998) *Système national d'économie politique* (Paris: Gallimard).

Marcou, J. (2015) 'L'affaire des missiles chinois', *Ovipot*, 20 February, http://ovipot.hypotheses.org/10930 (accessed on 16 April 2016).

Marcus A. (2007) *Blood and Belief: The PKK and the Kurdish Fight for Independence* (New York: New York University).

Massicard, E. (2008) 'Le politique à l'articulation entre institution de sécurité et univers criminel: les bandes en uniforme en Turquie', in Briquet, J.-L. and G. Favarel

Guarrigues (eds.) *Milieux criminels et pouvoir politique: les ressorts illicites de l'Etat* (Paris: Karthala), pp. 57–94.

Momani, B. (2013) *In Egypt, 'Deep state' vs. 'Brotherhoodization'* (Washington D.C: Brookings Institution) http://www.brookings.edu/research/opinions/2013/08/21-egypt-brotherhood-momani (accessed on 26 April 2016).

Nachmani, A. (2003) *Turkey: facing a new millennium* (Manchester: Manchester University Press).

NATO (North Atlantic Treaty Organization) (1991) *Le concept stratégique de l'Alliance*, 8 November (Brussels: NATO), http://www.nato.int/cps/fr/natohq/official_texts_23847.htm (accessed on 24 May 2016).

Orun, İ. (1997) 'TSK'nın tarihine bir bakış', *Savunma ve Havacılık*, 5(7).

Özdemir, S. (2004) 'Başbakan'a broşür verdi, Pakistan'a iki Hücumbot sattı', *Hürriyet*, 3 février, http://www.hurriyet.com.tr/basbakana-brosur-verdi-pakistana-hucumbot-satti-200088 (accessed on 24 May 2016).

Polanyi K. (1957) *The great transformation* (Boston, MA: Beacon Press).

Radikal (2011) 'Iste Isadami Aziz Yildirim', 2 September, http://www.radikal.com.tr/ekonomi/iste-isadami-aziz-yildirim-1062085/ (accessed on 2 June 2016).

Rancière, J. (2004) *Aux bords du politique*, new edition [1990] (Paris: Folio).

Regnault, J.-M. (2003) 'France's Search for Nuclear Test Sites, 1957–1963', *The Journal of Military History*, 67(4), pp. 1223–1248, DOI: 10.1353/jmh.2003.0326.

Sabah (2011) 'Parola: Büyük ekonomi', 17 April, http://www.sabah.com.tr/ekonomi/2011/04/17/parola-buyuk-ekonomi (accessed on 2 June 2016).

Sabah (2010a) 'Özal'ın adayı Bitlis Paşa'ydı', Sabah, 15 October, http://www.sabah.com.tr/gundem/2010/10/15/genelkurmay_baskani_yapmak_istiyordu (accessed on 27 April 2016).

Şahin, H. (2002) *Johnson Mektubu* (Istanbul: Gendas).

Saymaz, I. and E. Çelikkan (2015) 'Turkey's top scientific body has no digital analysts left amid "political" layoffs', *Hürriyet Daily News*, 9 March, http://www.hurriyetdailynews.com/turkeys-top-scientific-body-has-no-digital-analysts-left-amid-political-layoffs.aspx?pageID=238&nID=79394&NewsCatID=341 (accessed on 27 April 2016).

Schmidt, D. (2014) 'Turquie: le syndrôme de Sèvres ou la guerre qui n'en finit pas', *Politique étrangère*, 79(1), DOI: 10.3917/pe.141.0199.

Sezgin, S. (2003) 'A Disaggregated Analysis of Defense Expenditure and Economic growth in Turkey and Greece', in Günlük-Senesen, G. and C. Kollias (eds.) *Greece and Turkey in the 21st Century: Conflict or Cooperation a political economy perspective* (New-York: Nova Sciences).

Söyler, M. (2015) *The Turkish Deep State: State Consolidation, Civil-Military Relations and Democracy* (London, New-York: Routledge).

Sözcü (2015) 'Alman mali "yerli uçak" geliyor', 28 May, http://www.sozcu.com.tr/2015/gundem/alman-mali-yerli-ucak-geliyor-844206/ (accessed on 24 May 2015).

SSM (Savunma Sanayi Mustesarligi) (2010) *Historical Development* (Ankara: Undersecretariat for Defence Industries) http://www.ssm.gov.tr/home/tdi/Sayfalar/historical.aspx (accessed on 22 December 2015).

Star (2015) 'Savunma devlerinin Katar çikarmasina BMC damgasini', 6 October. http://haber.star.com.tr/ekonomi/savunma-devlerinin-katar-cikarmasina-bmc-damgasi/haber-1061017 (accessed on 25 April 2016).

Taner, A. (2005) *From Empire to Republic: Turkish Nationalism and the Armenian Genocide* (London: Zed Books).

The Guardian (2016) 'Turkish journalists face secret trial for revealing arms deliveries to Syria', 25 March, http://www.theguardian.com/world/2016/mar/25/turkish-journalists-can-dundar-erdem-gul-secret-trial-revealing-arms-deliveries-syria (accessed on 25 April 2016).

The Irish Times (1999) 'German cabinet faces dilemma over plan to sell tanks to Turkey', 29 October, http://www.irishtimes.com/news/german-cabinet-faces-dilemma-over-plan-to-sell-tanks-to-turkey-1.244166 (accessed on 26 April 2016).

The Korea Times (2015) 'Big-name arms broker arrested for alleged corruption', 11 March, http://www.koreatimes.co.kr/www/news/nation/2015/03/116_175076.html (accessed on 26 April 2016).

Timetürk (2012) 'Meger yüzde yüz Türk mali degilmis', 27 June.

Toyay, M. (2015) 'What does the Turkey-Qatar military deal mean for Arab conflicts?', *Al Arabiya*, 25 June, http://english.alarabiya.net/en/perspective/analysis/2015/06/25/What-does-Turkey-Qatar-military-deal-mean-for-Arab-conflicts-.html (accessed on 23 May 2016).

Truman, H. (1947) 'Special Message to the Congress on Greece and Turkey: The Truman Doctrine', *Truman Library Public Papers*, 12 March, http://www.trumanlibrary.org/publicpapers/index.php?pid=2189&st=Turkey&st1=Greece (accessed on 24 May 2016).

Tuğal, C. (2009) *Passive Revolution: Absorbing the Islamic Challenge to Capitalism* (Redwood City: Stanford University Press).

Turse, N. (2009) *The Complex: How the Military Invades Our Everyday Lives* (*American Empire Project*) (New York: Metropolitan).

Unsaldi, L. (2011) *Le développement vu de Turquie* (Paris: L'Harmattan).

Vaïsse, M. (1992) 'Le choix atomique de la France (1945–1958)', *Vingtième Siècle. Revue d'histoire*, 36, pp. 21–30, DOI: 10.3406/xxs.1992.2600.

Veyne P. (2014) *Les Grecs ont-ils cru à leurs mythes? Essai sur l'imagination constituante* (Paris: Seuil).

Ward, R. and Rustow, D. (eds.) (1965) *Political Modernization in Japan and Turkey* (Princeton: Princeton University Press).

Williamson, M. (2006) 'Ray Noorda. Pioneer of "co-opetition"', *The Independent*, 1 November., http://www.independent.co.uk/news/obituaries/ray-noorda-422415.html5 (accessed on 22 November 2016).

Woertz, E, (2014) 'Egypt: return of deep state', *Open Democracy*, 20 January, https://www.opendemocracy.net/arab-awakening/eckart-woertz/egypt-return-of-deep-state (accessed on 27 April 2016).

Wright Mills, C. (1956) *The Power Elite* (Oxford University Press).

Yankaya, D. (2015) 'Exposition industrielle, production de réseaux et construction d'imaginaires: la Foire internationale du Müsiad et les représentations de l'Etat turc', *Etudes du Ceri*, 215, pp. 1–36, http://www.sciencespo.fr/ceri/sites/sciencespo.fr.ceri/files/Etude_215.pdf (accessed on 24 May 2016).

Yankaya, D. (2014) 'International Business Forum: une tentative de régionalisation par la bourgeoisie islamique turque en "Afro-Eurasie"?', *Anatolie*, 5, CNRS Editions.

Yankaya, D. (2012) 'Sermaye, burjuvazi, tahakkum', *Birikim*, 278–279, pp. 29–37.

Yentürk, N. (2014), 'Measuring Turkish Military expenditure', *Sipri Insights on Peace and Security*, 2014(1), http://books.sipri.org/files/insight/SIPRIInsight1401.pdf (accessed on 24 May 2016).

Yerasimos, S. (1994) 'Bilan Turquie 1993: une nouvelle dimension régionale' in *L'état du monde* (Paris: La Découverte).

Index

www.ingramcontent.com/pod-product-compliance
Lightning Source LLC
Chambersburg PA
CBHW071422230926
51846CB00001B/108
* 9 7 8 9 0 0 4 3 4 9 5 2 0 *